The Capitol   *Colonial Williamsburg*

FROM THE COLLECTION OF

China's Defence Modernisation and Military Leadership

China's Defence Modernisation and Military Leadership

Ngok Lee

AUSTRALIAN NATIONAL UNIVERSITY PRESS
A division of Pergamon Press Australia
Sydney • Oxford • New York • Beijing • Frankfurt • São Paulo •
Tokyo • Toronto

Australian National University Press is a division of Pergamon Press Australia and a
member of the Pergamon Group of Companies.

AUSTRALIA	Pergamon Press (Australia) Pty Ltd, 19a Boundary Street, Rushcutters Bay, NSW 2011, Australia
UK	Pergamon Press plc, Headington Hill Hall, Oxford OX3 0BW, England
USA	Pergamon Press, Inc., Maxwell House, Fairview Park, Elmsford, New York 10523, USA
PEOPLE'S REPUBLIC OF CHINA	Pergamon Press, Room 4037, Qianmen Hotel, Beijing, People's Republic of China
FEDERAL REPUBLIC OF GERMANY	Pergamon Press GmbH, Hammerweg 6, D-6242 Kronberg, Federal Republic of Germany
BRAZIL	Pergamon Editora Ltda, Rua Eça de Queiros, 346, CEP 04011, Paraiso, São Paulo, Brazil
JAPAN	Pergamon Press, 8th Floor, Matsuoka Central Building, 1-7-1 Nishishinjuku, Shinjuku-ku, Tokyo 160, Japan
CANADA	Pergamon Press Canada Ltd, Suite 271, 253 College Street, Toronto, Ontario M5T 1R5, Canada

First Published 1989

Copyright © 1989 Ngok Lee

Cover design by Linda Gray

Typeset in Hong Kong by Graphicraft Typesetters Ltd
Printed in Singapore by Singapore National Printers

National Library of Australia Cataloguing in
Publication Data

Lee, Ngok, 1939–
    China's defence modernisation and military leadership.

    Bibliography.
    Includes index.
    ISBN 0 08 033046 0.

    1. China — Armed Forces.   2. China — Military policy.
    3. China — Defenses.   I. Title.

355'.033051

All rights reserved. No part of this publication may be
reproduced, stored in a retrieval system or transmitted in any
form or by any means, electronic, electrostatic, magnetic
tape, mechanical, photocopying, recording or otherwise,
without permission in writing from Pergamon Press
(Australia) Pty. Ltd.

Cover photo of Chinese surface-to-air missiles by courtesy of
Wide-Angle Press.

Contents

Abbreviations vii

Preface xiii

Acknowledgements xv

Introduction xviii

I **Quest for Defence Modernisation**

1 Defence Modernisation and the New Force
   Structure
   (*with B.P. Mahony*) 3

2 Improved Warfighting Capabilities
   (*with B.P. Mahony*) 42

3 The Support Base: Transport and
   Communications and the Reserve Forces 89

II **National Security and Defence Strategy**

4 China's Threat Perceptions and Major Security
   Problems 121

5 The Strategy of People's War under Modern
   Conditions 138

6 Chinese Maritime Power 175

III **Military Leadership**

7 The People's Liberation Army (PLA) and Party
   Leadership, 1979–82 201

8 The PLA and Party Leadership since the Twelfth
   Party Congress 230

Conclusion 260

Notes	273
Bibliography	345
Appendix 1	375
Appendix 2	377
Index	389

Abbreviations

A

AA	Anti-aircraft
AAA	Anti-aircraft artillery
AAM	Air-to-air missile
ABM	Anti-ballistic missile
ACV	Armoured command vehicle
ACV	Air cushioned vehicle
AD	Air defence
ADP	Automated data processing
AEW	Airborne early warning
AFV	Armoured fighting vehicle
ANZUS	Australia New Zealand United States (Treaty)
AOR	Auxiliary Oiler and Replenishment
APC	Armoured personnel vehicle
ARV	Armoured recovery vehicle
ASEAN	Association of South East Asian Nations
ASM	Air-to-surface missile
ASW	Anti-submarine warfare
ATGM	Anti-tank guided missile

B

BAM	Baikal-Amur-Magistral Railroad (mainline railway of Eastern Siberia)

C

C^2	Command and control
C^3I	Command, control, communications and intelligence
CAC	Central Advisory Committee
CAIRS	Close air support
CCP	Chinese Communist Party
CGDK	Coalition Government of Democratic Kampuchea

CGS	Chief of the General Staff
Ch	Chairman
CIWS	Close in weapon system
CLEARCERT	Clearance certificate
CMC	Central Military Commission
CODOG	Combined diesel on gas
C of S	Chief of Staff
COMD	Commander
COMINT	Communications intelligence
COMECON	Council for Mutual Economic Assistance
COMSEC	Communications Security
CPC	Communist Party of China
CPX	Command post exercise
CSM	Covert submarine minelay
CTBT	Comprehensive Test Ban Treaty
CW	Chemical warfare

D

DCdr	Deputy commander
DDG	Guided missile destroyer
Dep COM	Deputy Commander
Dep COS	Deputy Chief of Staff
DIA	Defense Intelligence Agency (US)
DIC	Discipline Inspection Committee
Dir PD	Director, Political Department
DPC	Deputy Political Commissar

E

ECCM	Electronic Counter-countermeasures
ECM	Electronic Countermeasures
EEZ	Exclusive economic zone
EFZ	Exclusive fishing zone
ELINT	Electronic intelligence
ESF	East Sea Fleet
ESM	Electronic Warfare Support Measures
EW	Electronic warfare

F

FF	Frigate
FFG	Guided missile frigate
FLOT	Forward line of own troops
FMPB	Fast missile patrol boat
FRT	Forward repair team
FTX	Field training exercise

G

Gar	Garrison
GEC	General Electric Company
GLD	General Logistics Department
GNP	Gross National Product
GPD	General Political Department
GSD	General Staff Department

H

HAAMG	Heavy anti-aircraft machine gun
HCOF	High Command of Force (Soviet)
HF	High frequency
HMLC	High mobility load carrier
HQ	Headquarters
HUDWAC	Head-up display and weapons aiming computer

I

IAEA	International Atomic Energy Agency
ICBM	Inter-continental ballistic missile
ICM	Improved conventional munition
IISS	International Institute of Strategic Studies
INF	Intermediate Nuclear Force
IOC	Initial operational capability
IR	Infra-red
IRBM	Intermediate range ballistic missile

J

JFJB	Jiefangjunbao (Liberation Army Daily)
JFJHB	Jiefangjunhuabao (PLA Pictorial)

K

K	Korean War experience
km	Kilometre
KOPP	Intergrated fire destruction of the enemy (Soviet)
KPNLF	Khmer People's National Liberation Front
kt	Kilotonne

L

L	Leftist supporter in Cultural Revolution
L (+)	Leftist turned pro-Deng
LF	Local Force
LPZU	Ground-air strike team (Soviet)
LRA	Long Range Aviation
LRINF	Longer Range Intermediate-Range Nuclear Force

LRMP		Long range maritime patrol
LRT		Long range transport
LSM		Landing ship, medium
LST		Landing ship, tank

M

MAD		Mutual assured destruction
MAL		Malaysia
MBT		Main battle tank
MCM		Mine countermeasures
MD	(1)	Military District
	(2)	Motorised division/motor rifle division
MF		Main Force
MICV		Mechanised infantry combat vehicle
MIRV		Multiple independently targeted re-entry vehicle
MM		Military modernisation record
MND		Ministry of National Defence
MR		Military Region
MRBM		Medium range ballistic missile
MRL		Multiple rocket launcher
MRT		Medium range transport
MSL		Military Service Law
MSO		Ocean minesweeper
mt		megatonne

N

NAF	Naval Air Force
NATO	North Atlantic Treaty Organisation
NBC	Nuclear, biological and chemical (warfare)
NC	North China Field Army
NCNA	New China News Agency
NCO	Non-commissioned officer
NDSTC	National Defence Science and Technology Commission
NFU	No first use
NFZ	Nuclear free zone
nm	Nautical mile
NP	Not purged
NPC	National People's Congress
NPT	Non-proliferation Treaty
NSF	North Sea Fleet
NVA	North Vietnamese Army

O

OMG	Operational Mobile Group (Soviet)

P

P	Purged
PACCOM	Pacific Command (US)
PAFD	People's Armed Forces Department
PAVN	People's Army of Vietnam
PC	Political commissar
PCMC	Party Central Military Commission (= CMC)
PHIL	Philippines
PLA	People's Liberation Army
POL	Petroleum, oils and lubricants
PRC	People's Republic of China
PTG	Guided missile patrol boat
PU	Posting unknown

R

RAM	Rapid aerial minelay
R & D	Research and development
RC	Revolutionary Committee
RD	Reserve division
RMB	Reminbi (Chinese currency)
ROC	Republic of China (Taiwan)
RPV	Remotely piloted vehicle

S

SAM	Surface-to-air missile
S & T	Science and technology
SCMC	State Central Military Council
SDI	Strategic Defence Initiative
SHF	Super High Frequency
SIGINT	Signals intelligence (includes COMINT and ELINT)
SIPRI	Stockholm International Peace Research Institute
SLAR	Sideways looking airborne radar
SLBM	Submarine-launched ballistic missile
SLCM	Submarine-launched cruise missile
SLOC	Sea lines of communication
SNI	Soviet Naval Infantry
SOVPACFLT	Soviet Pacific Fleet
SP	Self-propelled
SRINF	Shorter range intermediate range nuclear force
SRV	Socialist Republic of Vietnam

SS	Submarine (conventionally powered and armed)
SSB	Ballistic missile-armed submarine (conventionally powered)
SSBN	Nuclear powered ballistic missile submarine
SSF	South Sea Fleet
SSG	Conventionally powered submarine armed with tactical guided-missile
SSGN	Nuclear powered submarine armed with tactical guided missile
SSM	Surface-to-surface missile
SSN	Nuclear powered submarine armed with conventional weapons

T

TBO	Time between overhauls
TEWT	Tactical exercise without troops
TEZ	Total Exclusion Zone
TNW	Theatre nuclear warfare
TR	Transfer to
TSFCS	Tank simplified fire control system
TVD	Theatre of Military Operations (Soviet)

U

UHF	Ultra high frequency
ULF	Ultra low frequency
UNCLOS	United Nations Convention on the Law of the Sea
US	United States
USN	United States Navy
USSR	Union of Soviet Socialist Republics

V

VHF	Very high frequency
VLF	Very low frequency
VSTOL	Very short take-off and landing

Z

| ZOPFAN | Zone of Peace, Freedom and Neutrality |

Preface

This book is my second major work on China's defence modernisation. The first, *The Chinese People's Liberation Army 1980–82*, was published as Canberra Defence Paper No. 28 in 1983 by the Strategic and Defence Studies Centre (SDSC), the Australian National University. In 1985–87 I had the opportunity to take up a two-year appointment as Senior Research Fellow at the SDSC, where I undertook research on recent developments of the Chinese defence force. It coincided with a period which saw important changes to China's defence modernisation program, and the need for the publication of an up-to-date book became apparent.

During my stay in Canberra, I also had the opportunity to discuss these matters with my old friend Lt Col. B.P. Mahony, who, after serving many years as an Intelligence Officer in the British and Australian armed forces, is now Chief Analyst of the Intelligence and Drug Operations Division of the Australian Federal Police. These discussions culminated in collaborative work on the Chinese army's new force structure and improved warfighting capabilities which now appears as Chapters 1 and 2 in the book. Col. Mahony made major contributions to Chapter 1 and was responsible for most of Chapter 2, Appendix 1, Appendix 2 and the Abbreviations. He also gave invaluable advice on the manuscript and assisted me in writing the Conclusion.

Chapter 6 on Chinese maritime power originated as a study of China's present and future naval capabilities which I undertook in conjunction with Lt-Commander A. Hinge when he was Defence Fellow at the SDSC in 1985–86. He made a major contribution to the section on 'A Chinese Strategic Mine Offensive Against the SRV'. The three of us also presented papers on China's defence problems in the wider context of the strategic balance in the Asia-Pacific region to the Biennial Conference of the Asian Studies Association of Australia in May 1986.

Special mention must be made of the excellent collection of sources on Contemporary China in the Menzies Library at the Australian National University. Through Mr Y.S. Chan, the Division Librarian, I was able to have access to the entire collection of the Chinese Liberation Army *Daily* published in the period 1976–86, before it was made available to the public in January 1987. The latest book on the Chinese Army by Ellis Joffe, entitled *The Chinese Army After Mao* (Harvard University Press, 1987), has recently become available. Both Joffe's work and this book cover similar issues confronting the development of China's defence force, such as the strategic and economic environment since Mao, defence modernisation, 'People's War under modern conditions', and civil–military relations.

For Lt Col. Mahony and myself, the major purpose of our exhaustive inquiry is to assess the extent of China's progress in improving its warfighting capabilities and strategy. We believe that we have been particularly fortunate to have been able to concentrate on developments in the period 1984–87, which witnessed major changes to China's defence modernisation program.

Ngok Lee and B.P. Mahony
December 1987

Acknowledgements

I am grateful to the University of Hong Kong and the Australian National University for supporting my research work on China's defence modernisation. Through the Hsu Long Sing Research Fund, the former provided me with financial support in 1983–85 and the latter appointed me Senior Research Fellow at the Strategic and Defence Studies Centre for two years in 1985 and 1986. My colleagues at the Centre, especially Des Ball, Ross Babbage, Max Smart and Andy Butfoy, have been very helpful in giving their advice on regional security issues in the Asia–Pacific region. I am also indebted to Elsa Sullivan who typed the manuscript and to Jol Langtry and Billie Dalrymple who provided me with good support when I worked in the Centre. Last but not the least, I wish to thank Y.S. Chan, Head of the Asian Division of the Australian National University Libraries, who made the various collections on Contemporary China readily available to me when I was in Canberra.

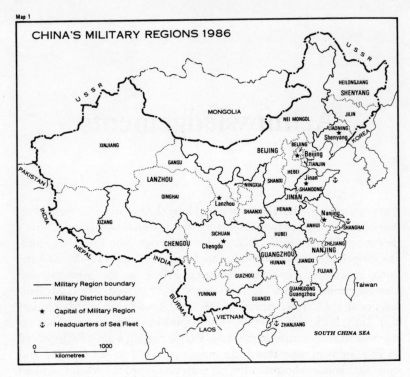

Map 1

CHINA'S MILITARY REGIONS 1986

Introduction

Deng Xiaoping has transformed China into a major power which stresses economic growth and the redistribution of material rewards in the post-Mao decade. In his successful reliance on pragmatic and shifting political alliances to modernise China, Deng Xiaoping seems to have weathered most of the opposition from diehards who have valued the traditional but unifying Marxist ideology and a Soviet-style economic infrastructure. China specialists are now assessing Chinese capabilities to launch further reforms in the series of Five-year Plans which may lead to the fulfilment of the rather ambitious economic objectives that Deng has set for China. Short of major political and economic reversals, China will play an increasingly significant role in the interplay of regional and international politics.

At the same time, both superpowers will need to give greater prominence to the China factor in managing East–West relations. Conversely, it is in China's interests to maintain an equilibrium in the global strategic balance in order to provide a stable political environment for its own economic development. Progress towards the normalisation of Sino–Soviet relations and continuing reliance on the US and the West for assistance in the 'Four Modernisations' of industry, agriculture, national defence and science and technology are features of China's 'independent foreign policy'.

It is generally acknowledged that the priority given to China's economic modernisation and expansion necessitates the relegation of defence modernisation to a secondary position. In terms of budget allocations, it is certainly true that as a percentage of national expenditure defence expenditure has gradually decreased. Nevertheless, major policy decisions on defence modernisation have set in motion a process that aims to strengthen China's military capabilities and modernise its defence forces. More importantly, a successful economic program will win China prominence in the arena of international trade, and the world economic community will need, therefore, to assess the security implications of having to protect China's economic and political interests in the context of international rivalries. These considerations point to China's need to be positive in its strategic outlook despite present constraints. In any case, the pace of defence modernisation is steering the People's Liberation Army (PLA) in the direction of revolutionary changes. The evolving rationalisation of domestic defence production with selective reliance on foreign technology may also bring about satisfactory advances in science and technology and hence lead to incremental improvements in military capabilities.

China's quest for defence modernisation, the evolution of an effective Chinese strategy as a response to major security threats, and the military leadership's contribution to a more stabilised China under Deng Xiaoping constitute the three main parts of this book, which analyses the emergence of a new defence force in China. The PLA is not only leaner and meaner in 1987, but also combat-ready. Moreover, it claims to be capable of implementing the defensive strategy of 'People's War under modern conditions'.

In Part I: Quest for Defence Modernisation, the extent of China's success in defence modernisation in the post-Mao era will be discussed. Despite budgetary constraints, well-rationalised defence modernsation programs, major retrenchment and reforms in China's force structure, and command, control, communications and intelligence (C^3I) have all contributed to the emergence of a more efficient and modernised defence force. China has striven hard to improve its military capabilities, as evidenced by the introduction of combined arms and joint operations which was supported by the modified force structure and better C^3I arrangements. In this respect, it will need to develop more effective forces and acquire better weapon systems and logistic support in sustained operations over long distances. Modest and steady progress has been made at both the strategic and tactical levels as a result of the ability to acquire western technology. Nevertheless, weaknesses at both levels still exist and the Chinese forces still lag far behind those of the USSR and the USA.

As regards incremental improvements in Chinese military capabilities, the modernisation of civil transport and communications in the 1980s and the reinvigorated efforts to mobilise China's Reserve Forces represent two significant components of the support base which provide crucial resources from the civilian sector for defence modernisation. In sum, China claims that it has introduced a new strategic outlook for defence modernisation which will best equip its defence force 'to win victory in limited war'[1] over the next two decades. More importantly, China hopes that strategic changes to defence construction will enable its capabilities to reach a level that is near to advanced world standards by the middle of the twenty-first century.[2]

The relative success of China's defence modernisation should in turn be assessed not only in the context of China's ability to narrow the strategic and technological gap with the developed nations, but also in the light of how well it supports the defensive strategy of 'People's War under modern conditions'.

In Part II: National Security and Defence Strategy, China's perceptions of its security problems will be examined. In addition, the evolution and effectiveness of the strategy of 'People's War under modern conditions' will be discussed. China's flexible foreign policy has been a contributing factor to the reduction of tension in the Asia–Pacific region. Whilst it fosters an open door policy and continues to rely on the US, Japan and the West for technological and economic needs, China regards the improvement of relations with the USSR and a solution to the Kampuchean question as crucial to its national security. There is no denying that Chinese perception of threat and its defence posture have focused on the USSR as the 'stronger' enemy. However, with a modernised defence force reinforced with new military capabilities, China believes that its chance against an invading enemy is good. Specifically, China's improved military capabilities should be able to support the strategy of active defence in positional warfare. The need to halt Soviet strategic breakthroughs has induced the Chinese to defend selected positions and integrate secondary mobile and guerrilla operations with positional warfare. Reliance on Local and Reserve Forces is another precondition for undertaking active defence.

The human factor, therefore, remains an essential ingredient in modern warefare, and gives credibility to 'People's War' in the setting of China's options for strategic defence. Emerging out of this evolution is the strategy of 'People's War under modern conditions', which is defensive in nature and dissociates China from any wider designs, characteristic of the superpowers. For as long as China pursues its present objective of economic modernisation, its security interests will best be met by confident adherence to the new strategy evolved in the post-Mao era. Naturally, China hopes that its defence posture will cater for both the 'stronger' enemy (the USSR) and other lesser ones like Vietnam.

Whilst Chinese politicians may feel that external threats are not imminent, strategic planners in the General Staff Department have increased their vigilance vis-a-vis preparations for a future war against the USSR. Naturally, the Chinese are now thoroughly familiar with Soviet doctrine and strategy. However, they are still keen on postulating scenarios for the initial stage of the war so as to ask sensibly the most important question: 'In what form will the enemy initiate a war of aggression?'[3] In 1983–84 the *Liberation Army Daily* published over 30 articles on the single theme of 'Designing the Future Battlefield'.[4] This exercise was considered a success in seeking truth through objective reality, and integrating training and the work of military academics with 'the battlefield design'. More importantly, the Chinese value the resultant 'design' as a scientific forecast of the conditions under which a future war will be fought, and as an exploration of the best methods of subduing the enemy. Postulating scenarios has continued to be a part of Chinese strategic planning as evidenced by ongoing discussions in the *Liberation Army Daily* since 1984. The Chinese hope to design a distinctly Chinese-style operational art. It is expected to match the US 'Air Land Battle' and the Soviet 'Operational Manoeuvre Group' concepts, despite the superpowers' superior technology.[5]

Over the horizon, there are prospects for China to project power through its nuclear deterrent and maritime capabilities. The 'brown water' Navy has developed some 'blue water' capabilities and has shown itself to be possessing sea denial and naval presence capabilities. It is likely that the Chinese Navy will play a much more active role in the Asia–Pacific region as China finds it necessary to protect its economic interests. In addition, political interest may provide incentives for China to use maritime power to exert influence on the region. Nonetheless, there would have to be compelling incentives, such as the preservation of vital economic or political interests, to spur China into adopting a forward defence posture. With continuing progress in the economic sphere, it would make a great deal of sense for Deng Xiaoping to designate 'People's War under modern conditions' as the strategy for strategic defence against a threat that is formidable, but no longer imminent. The more time China is given to strengthen its military capabilities, the better will be its preparation for a future war.

In Part III: Military Leadership, the contribution of the military to the building of a more stabilised political leadership in China will be examined.

Success in defence modernisation under the 'Four Modernisations' program naturally depends on whether stable conditions will persist at the end of the Deng era. A comparison of the visionary Mao Zedong and the progamatic Deng Xiaoping seems to suggest that the latter has much more to offer the Chinese people than the former. China has proceeded much further along the path of modernisation since the time that Mao claimed that political power comes from the barrel of a gun.[6] Paradoxically, it has taken Deng Xiaoping, a Long March veteran who was part of the success of the revolutionary PLA which took control of China from the Guomindang in 1949, to engineer the transformation of the PLA into an increasingly apolitical and modernised defence force. The PLA may be westernised in force structure and technological development, but it still retains a significant Chinese style in the evolution of a defence strategy that gives it confidence in its ability to win a future war. Whilst Mao's offer of a compelling ideology and an egalitarian society failed to appeal to Chinese society at large, Deng's package of a better livelihood and socialist-style prosperity in the short span of the post-Mao decade seems to have been well received by the Chinese populace. The PLA, especially the old guard, tended to be sceptical in the beginning. Nevertheless, Deng's efforts in rejuvenating the PLA and in enabling second and third echelon cadres to ascend the social ladder of success are beginning to pay off.

The continuation of a stable political structure headed by Deng, or sustained by a collective leadership after Deng, will further brighten the prospects of a Chinese leadership under the rule of a younger generation in both the Party and the PLA which will cherish the spirit of Dengism. The allegiance of the PLA to Party leadership in the future hinges in turn on the government's ability to keep up with its impressive record of economic growth. No other incentive in the course of institutionalising the PLA as the regime's willing defender could be as compelling as growing national prosperity. For the PLA, intent on achieving national security through military modernisation, would see the economic interests and preservation of the government and Party as being essential to its own success.

PART I

Quest for Defence Modernisation

1

Defence Modernisation and the New Force Structure

A NEW STRATEGIC OUTLOOK IN DEFENCE MODERNISATION

Defence spending was an easily identifiable sector of the budget in the late 1970s, which drained national resources, as China maintained an oversized and relatively obsolete defence force. Expenses incurred in the Sino–Vietnamese Border War in 1979 further accentuated the military burden on the national economy. Since the early 1980s, China has consciously aimed at balancing the budget and reducing expenses incurred in the major sectors of the 'Four Modernisations'. In the process, economic modernisation was given greater funding at the expense of defence modernisation. Nevertheless, reduction in military spending has not led to major setbacks in defence modernisation. Instead, China's decision to introduce well-rationalised defence modernisation programs and initiate retrenchments and reforms in the force structure have successfully turned its defence force into a more efficient war machine that poses a credible deterrent to attack by a stronger enemy. Thus, its decision in June 1985 to reduce the strength of the defence force by one million, its determination to strengthen wartime mobilisation by maintaining combat-ready Reserve Forces and its policy to amalgamate the principle of self-reliance and the need to incorporate foreign technology, are all major signposts of China's relative success in defence modernisation. Consequently, the Chinese Defence Force has im-

3

proved its military capabilities and endeavoured to narrow the gap between itself and the two superpowers as it acquires new but very much needed experience in conducting combined arms and joint operations.

The Chinese consider these fruits of defence modernisation as the result of China's new strategic outlook in 'national defence construction' and feel confident that they can respond well to major security threats. 'Strategic Changes to the Guiding Thoughts on National Defence Construction and Army Building' were made known to the world by the Chinese in 1985,[1] whilst evidence of reforms in force structure and retrenchment measures can be traced to the early 1980s[2] — the first strategic change in peacetime war preparation. Instead of emphasising the former policy of 'early strike, major strike and nuclear strike', the Chinese now believe that war preparation should be implemented on a step-by-step basis, and integrated with the development of the economy.[3] As they are confident that no global war will ensue for the rest of this century, the Chinese can afford to make war preparation a long-term development.[4]

The second strategic change entails the building of a crack, regular force which can deal with 'future threats to the nation'.[5] This objective is to be achieved despite constraints on defence spending. Thus the transformation of the force structure, the retrenchment policy and other reforms, the modernisation of weapons and equipment, the training program and the best use of composition and utilisation of the armed forces are all prerequisites for the new defence force.[6]

Whilst the West is pessimistic about China's progress in defence modernisation, in view of the big gap in weapons and equipment, the Chinese are in no great hurry to narrow this gap. Instead, they have set for themselves long-term and well-rationalised objectives for defence modernisation. They hope that by the middle of the twenty-first century, their defence capabilities will near the advanced world standards, and will have achieved certain breakthroughs in high technology.[7]

The Enlarged Conference of the Party Central Military Commission (PCMC) held in May–June 1985 was a landmark for the propagation of a new strategic outlook in defence modernisation.[8] The Conference, which was presided over by Deng Xiaoping, Hu Yaobang and Yang Shangkun, Permanent Deputy Chairman of the PCMC, identified the spirit of change and announced that:

> There should be a cognitive change in the basic assessment of the
> international situation for the present and the future; in accordance with

this scientific understanding and judgement, there should also be a change in policy; there should also be a change in the guiding thoughts for national defence construction.[9]

It was Deng Xiaoping who argued that a peaceful environment would persist for a long period, so that the Chinese could afford to draw up long-term strategic plans rather than believe in the imminence of war. Deng listed three factors to argue that it would be unlikely for a global war to happen in this century.[10]

In promoting the various changes in war preparation, force structure, training and retrenchment policies, the Chinese believe that a successful defence modernisation program should be based on an assessment of the needs of future wars. Defence modernisation should also be accepted as an integral part of national construction, so that the best coordination in the development of the force structure, defence technology and defence industries can be achieved and 'the solid foundation for the victory of the future war which may break out can be laid'.[11]

In concentrating on peacetime war preparation and long-term modernisation objectives, the Chinese are confident that their war-fighting capabilities will be able to cope with not only limited wars in this century, but also high-level conflicts and large-scale wars in the next century.[12] In this respect, the Enlarged Conference of the PCMC in 1985 underlined the importance of understanding the future and the world situation. Academic research was encouraged in the hope that new strategies and ways 'under modern conditions' which would defeat the better-equipped enemy (the USSR) could be found.[13]

Thus an all-army conference on 'Theories at the Campaign Level' presided over by Yang Dezhi, Chief of the General Staff, was held in September 1986.[14] Yang Dezhi underlined the PCMC's demand for research on military concepts 'in order to strengthen significantly the development strategy for national defence, and the study of the strategic changes, and to strengthen the study of army building in accordance with the new situation and new problems in the units'.[15]

The study of future wars was one of the major responsibilities of the PLA's research on military concepts. Understanding war and the conduct of war were in turn the two aspects of the study. Specifically Yang Dezhi laid down the following objectives for the study of future wars:

Based on the development of scientific technology and weaponry, research on the characteristics and laws of future wars should be conducted. This means the study of strategy in war, guidelines for campaigns and tactical problems. There should be a thorough study of the guiding philosophy, principles, types and actual methods of warfare. I wish to stress the following points. First, the problem of People's War should be creatively studied in accordance with the changes brought about by modern war conditions. Second, there should be a comprehensive study of the problem of defeating a stronger enemy on the basis of military concepts, philosophy of warfare, weapons and equipment and the art of command and control. Third, ways should be explored to perfect the composition of combat power and to achieve overall victory.[16]

To ensure that the proper leadership was provided for the study of military concepts, Yang Dezhi regarded that it was important to integrate the leadership and the masses, and research be conducted both by specialists and amateurs. In addition, the discovery and cultivation of talent should be promoted. Yang Dezhi encouraged the creation of 'a democratic and consultative mood' so that a genuinely new strategic outlook could be nurtured as a result.[17]

The following three sections examine China's painstaking efforts in bringing about strategic changes in defence modernisation as identified by leaders of the CMC. Military spending is determined by the state of the national economy and takes second place to economic modernisation. However, it cannot be assumed that defence modernisation has become stagnant. Strategic changes also reflected in China's latest reforms in war mobilisation under the general guidelines of peacetime war preparation. Similarly, revolutionary changes in the force structure have enabled the PLA to improve significantly its warfighting capabilities. The most noticeable changes which have come about with the transformation of the field armies into group armies are the PLA's initial success in combined arms joint operations and greater efficiency in C^3I.

DEFENCE MODERNISATION AND MILITARY SPENDING

The year 1981 was critical in the post-Mao decade as Deng Xiaoping was able to rectify some of the mistakes made in the Hua Guofeng interregnum when the fervour of 'Four Modernisations' culminated in excessive national spending which did not necessarily bring about expected results. This is especially obvious in defence expenditure in 1977–1980 when it constitued a range from 15.98 per cent to

17.664 per cent of national expenditure. The colossal military expenditure incurred in the Sino-Vietnamese border war in February–March 1979 is partially reflected by the figure of RMB22.27 billion which constituted 17.481 per cent of the national expenditure and exceeded defence expenditure in 1978 by 32.69 per cent.

Table 1.1:   China's defence expenditure 1977–86 (in billion RMB)

Year	National expenditure	Defence expenditure	Change in percentage in comparison with preceding year	Defence expenditure as percentage of national expenditure
1977	84.35	14.90	+10.78	17.664
1978	111.10	16.784	+12.64	15.107
1979	127.394	22.270	+33.87	17.481
1980	121.27	19.380	−14.90	15.980
1981	111.50	16.80	−13.31	15.067
1982	115.33	17.64	+ 5.00	15.295
1983	129.25	17.71	+ 0.39	13.702
1984	154.64	18.07	+ 2.03	11.685
1985	182.594	19.148	+ 5.69	10.486
1986*	214.147	20.02	+ 4.995	9.348

* = Estimates

Sources: *Chinese Statistical Yearbook 1985*, (State Statistical Bureau, People's Republic of China, 1985), pp.525–542; *FBIS-CHI* 22 April 1986, K3–14

As regards national expenditure, in 1985 China succeeded in balancing the budget after incurring a deficit of about RMB4.5 billion in 1983 and in 1984. Finance Minister, Wang Binqian, claimed that the budget for 1986 would be balanced at RMB214.147 billion.[18]

The relatively low priority given to defence modernisation is certainly reflected in the decline of defence expenditure as a percentage of national expenditure: 13.702 per cent (1983), 11.685 per cent (1984) 10.486 per cent (1985) and 9.348 per cent (1986). Nevertheless, actual defence spending since 1981 has not been reduced in real terms as it increased from RMB16.80 billion in 1981 to RMB20.02 billion in 1986 (see Table 1.2).

On the other hand, priorities in modernisation for other sections are given greater weight than defence. For instance, a greater rate of increase in capital construction expenditure is reflected in the period 1982–85:

Table 1.2:   China's national revenue and expenditure 1977–86 (in billion RMB)

Year	Total revenue	Total expenditure	Balance
1977	87.45	84.35	+ 3.10
1978	112.11	111.10	+ 0.11
1979	110.33	127.39	−17.06
1980	108.52	121.27	−12.75
1981	108.95	111.50	− 2.55
1982	112.40	115.33	− 2.93
1983	124.90	129.25	− 4.35
1984	150.186	154.64	− 4.454
1985	185.411	182.594	+ 2.817
1986*	214.147	214.147	

* = Estimates
Sources: *Chinese Statistical Yearbook 1985* (State Statistical Bureau, People's Republic of China, 1985), p.523, *FBIS-CHI* 22 April 1986, K3–14

Table 1.3:   Capital construction and defence sectors in national expenditure 1981–86 (in billion RMB)

Year	Capital Construction	Defence
1981	33.06	16.80
1982	30.92	17.64
1983	38.28	17.71
1984	47.86	18.07
1985	56.973	19.148
1986*	56.78	20.02

* = Estimates
Sources: *Chinese Statistical Yearbook 1985*, p.524; *FBS-CHI* 22 April 1986, K3–14

In any case, it would be wrong to assume that dramatic cuts and severe retrenchments were imposed on the military and that the PLA was hamstrung by serious financial difficulties. Instead, the Chinese objectives have been aimed at modernising a 'lean and mean' army which should be revolutionary, younger and better educated.[19]

With defence appropriations equivalent to six to eight per cent of GNP,[20] the Chinese are being sensible about avoiding excessive military spending at a time when China succeeds, for the first time in seven years, to balance its budget and when the major appropriation is directed towards Capital Construction in the name of economic modernisation. A comparison of estimated military expenditures in China and the USSR (six to eight per cent as opposed to twelve to fourteen per cent of the GNP)[21] reveals China's reluctance to either compete with the USSR or take on any global responsibilities which would have been reflected by a higher percentage of the GNP. The decision announced in July 1985 to streamline and restructure the PLA therefore represents the climax of China's determination to possess a modernised force which is capable of defending China against external threats in accordance with the strategy of 'People's War under modern conditions'.[22] In order to achieve this with a 'zero-growth' defence budget, defence modernisation had to be rationalised after the initial innuendoes in the post-Mao period which was often marked by a procurement policy which had not been carefully planned. In March 1983, Defence Minister Zhang Aiping reiterated in the *Red Flag* two major principles for defence modernisation.[23] The first stressed self-reliance which should take priority over the procurement of weapon systems from overseas. As an illustration of self-reliance, the second principle spelt out China's ability to develop an independent deterrent force based on its sound development of missiles and atomic energy since the 1960s. What seems apparent from Zhang's speech is China's rationale for defence modernisation based on two confirmed guidelines. First, 'man' and 'weapons' should complement each other. China's conventional force should be streamlined so that the cost of modernising it would be less. The emphasis on state-of-the-art weapon systems through self-reliance or procurement should be based on China's defence of its own territories against aggressors. In turn, the reliance on human resources and the essence of People's War are still relevant as China's potential enemy, the USSR, is *prima-facie* the stronger enemy. Emerging out of the symbiotic relationship between 'man' and 'weapon' is therefore the strategy of 'People's War under modern conditions'.[24] The second guideline refers to the development of China's deterrent force which is an amalgam of self-reliance and well-rationalised procurement policies in its acquisition of essential state-of-the-art technology and weapon systems. Thus Zhang Aiping's rhetoric on self-reliance by no means overshadows China's reliance on the procurement of foreign technology deemed critical for the development of its defence capabilities. Such arms transfers and procurements may take the form of direct acquisitions, technology transfer, Chinese production or coproduction under licence.[25] The production of near state-of-the-art weapons through 'quick-fix' methods or reverse engineering may be achieved via captured hardware items, or the acquisition of single or small quantities of specific items through overt and covert transactions.[26]

It is true that the Chinese have claimed that reliance on foreign technology either through 'quick-fix' or direct arms transfer might not be as effective as the development of indigenous weapons. Thus

Defence Minister Zhang Aiping warned that being content with copying would merely lead the PLA to fall further behind.[27] Furthermore, if China could afford foreign armaments, it would be hard to acquire really advanced weapons of military value.[28] Nevertheless, these pronouncements cannot change the fact that China needs state-of-the-art weapons in key areas of its defence. This is especially relevant to anti-air, anti-airborne and anti-armour equipment. Similarly, China badly needs computer and electronic equipment for its strategic force.

The latest agreements with the US on retrofitting the F-8 fighter aircraft with new avionic equipment would be the classic example of China's continuing reliance on foreign technology, especially in the field of aviation.[29] As regards self-reliance in defence, the Chinese are taking the longer view in improving deficient areas that still depend on foreign technology. There are indications that the Chinese are capable of improving the products of reverse engineering. Such capability speaks a great deal for the prospect of Chinese ability in producing at least some state-of-the-art weapons.[30] A good example in this regard is the export version of the A-5 FANTAN close support/ground attack aircraft. Apart from successfully producing the A-5, which is a homegrown derivative of the MiG-19, the Chinese have exported the A-5C or FANTAN-C, an upgraded version of FANTAN-A[31] with engine/avionics/weapons changes to meet Pakistan Air Force requirements. Nevertheless, it is relevant to observe that such successes very often cannot compensate for the technological gap that seems to have persisted.

In sum, China hopes that a well reasoned amalgam of self-reliance and foreign technology will not only help to reduce the colossal expenditure incurred in large bulk arms procurement, but also avoid mistakes made in the 1950s when dependence on the Soviets for major weapon systems left the Chinese in limbo in the 1960s as regards replacements, as well as research and development.

Reduced military spending: reduction in strength and structural reforms

National defence expenditure normally comprises four major components. These are:

1. pay and allowances,
2. equipment procurement,
3. operating costs, and
4. research and development (R&D).

It is generally accpeted that the pay and allowances component is not included as an item of the Chinese defence expenditure. This means that the actual savings incurred in the reduction of one million troops would apply mainly to equipment procurement, operating costs, and R&D.[32] Such savings would not only help replace dated weapons with hopefully state-of-the-art ones in critical areas, but also contribute to operating more efficiency a 'leaner' defence force.[33] Thus Yang Shangkun claims that savings from reducing the size of the PLA will mean that 'more money will be available for research and development of new weapons technology and equipment, with the result that the weapons and equipment of the entire armed forces will be gradually improved'.[34]

Apart from savings in equipment procurement and operating costs, certain shifts in defence responsibilities from the PLA to the local authorities would seem to have contributed to relieving the financial burden on the former. Thus, the People's Armed Forces Departments (PAFD), now under the control of local government at the county level, have taken over the cost of maintaining Reserve Forces which are estimated at the strength of over five million.[35]

As regards the regulars, the reduction of one million troops announced in July 1985 was undertaken in two phases. The first phase concentrated on the organisation and units under the various general departments and the Commission of Science, Technology and Industry for National Defence. By the beginning of 1986, the second phase of retrenchment was announced as the Local and Logistic forces and the military academies and other supporting units experienced similar streamlining exercises.[36] It has been a colossal task for the PLA to reach retrenchment objectives via structural reforms involving extensive areas. In Yang Shangkun's words, such reforms range from 'adjustments involving military regions, the regrouping of units, the streamlining of organs and reductions in the number of cadres, to the incorporation of the People's Armed Forces of counties and cities into the local establishment, and the transfer of frontier units to public security departments'.[37] Reduction in strength has also been achieved through the following: 'The number of levels will be fewer, organisations will be eliminated or merged, and position grade of some units will be lowered'.[38] As regards individual units, they could be abolished, merged or changed.[39] Furthermore, units will be regrouped in order that they can be prepared for combined arms operations. (See Chapter 2 for details.)

Reduction in strength was a traumatic experience for the PLA, which involved dismissals, retirements and transfers of cadres. In 1985, over 410 000 officers and men were demobilised. Great efforts were undoubtedly spent on the resettlement of demobilised soldiers.[40] These included the search for employment in the civilian sector or reallocating them to the reservist units. Evidence of opposition or reluctance to abide by party policies reveals that the magnitude of the problem is by no means negligible.[41] Nevertheless, the PLA leadership has undoubtedly devoted a great deal of time and energy to reducing the size of the problem created by demobilised soldiers in 1985–86.[42] The fact that there has not been an excessive reaction to the reduction-in-strength exercise to date, speaks for increasing party confidence in ensuring that a successful conclusion to its objectives in defence modernisation can be achieved.

All the elaborate plans for reduction-in-strength will hopefully bring about savings in equipment procurement and operating costs. Such savings would indeed contribute to the PLA's research and development as China hopes to narrow the technological gap with the superpowers. The single most important objective in streamlining and structural reform is to transform the PLA into a comparatively smaller, better educated and more revolutionary modern defence force which is capable of thwarting the 'stronger' enemy. In addition, this should be accomplished without the need for China to allocate in excess of nine to twelve per cent of its national expenditure to defence. The transformed PLA is expected to fit the image of 'crack troops, proficient in combined arms operations and war-prepared both in peacetime and wartime'.[43]

Foreign technology, arms transfer and the military-industrial complex

At the inception of the sixth Five-Year Plan, China wished to emphasise the readjustment of its economic structure and the strengthening of existing enterprises, and the technical transformation of industry. The goals that China set for itself were long-term in nature, as evidenced by Deng Xiaoping's remarks to foreigners that China would need decades to overcome its economic underdevelopment.[44] As China launches itself into the seventh Five-Year Plan, the long-term objectives of economic modernisation continue, probably at the expense of defence modernisation. This is at least apparent in the latest appropriations for the estimates of the 1986 budget.[45] Remedies to deficiencies in defence modernisation, especially regarding the military-industrial complex, could include the relatively well-established principle of integrating military and civilian industries.[46] The State believes that greater efforts can be made in making products during peacetime which can suit both civilian and military purposes. This integration of military and civilian industry represents a contribution by the defence sector to the national economy. It also promotes better research and development for both sectors. In addition, this innovative measure in some ways compensates for the financial burdens that the civilian sector has to share from time to time.[47] At the same time, the State expects that in wartime 'the industry should be able to put all its strength into guaranteeing the needs of the forces...'[48]

A more rationalised basis for the improvement of China's defence modernisation can be provided by the continuing adjustment of foreign technology and self-reliance.[49] Despite the antiquated nature of some aspects of China's military-industrial complex, its growth in the aerospace industry and the development of ICBMs and SLBMs speak a great deal for China's efforts to work toward technological independence. On the other hand, China is still striving to develop a military infrastructure that is capable of sustaining its defence program. In this connection, analysts believe that China could opt for one of two science and technology (S&T) military development courses.[50] The first model adopted by both the US and the USSR uses 'national research and development to enhance national defense....'.[51] The second option that Japan adopts, emphasises the close link between research and development on the one hand, and market forces on the other. In this model, which is dominated by economists and civilian technocrats, 'newly acquired technologies are earmarked for marketing or for long-term investment planning'.[52] China seems to have opted for the first model, although others would argue that China's policy to abolish price control and reduce economic planning by the State seems to suggest that it is veering in the direction of the second model. It is probably fair to say that China is still some way from developing the sophisticated Japanese model. Furthermore, the integration of military and civilian industries may contribute to China's adherence to the first model, as the crossover effects of similar technology and management skills in the civilian sector enhance S&T developments in the military sector.[53]

As regards China's acquisition of foreign arms and technology, certain characteristics began to develop in the first half of the post-Mao decade. First, foreign arms and technology were basically geared toward defensive weapons and equipment. Second, the Chinese were also eager to educate themselves in western doctrine and state-of-the-art weapons, for they needed to rally support for their defensive position against the Soviets. In the process, China's 'window shopping' tours often frustrated foreign arms suppliers. At the same time, the major acquisitions did not seem to have made a significant impact on the narrowing of the technological gap.[54] In the second half of the post-Mao decade, China had definitely made progress in enhancing its military capabilities through arms transfer and the acquisition of western technology.[55] In many ways, such improvements have been brought about because of changing political situations in favour of more relaxed rules regarding arms sales to China.[56] In addition, China's ability to make greater S&T advances certainly increases its domestic defence production through foreign assistance. These products are either state-of-the-art weapons or effective armament of a defensive nature. (See Appendix 1 for reference to China's Reliance on Foreign Military Technology and Equipment).

WARTIME MOBILISATION

In line with the objective of maintaining a smaller, better educated and revolutionary army, China has devised a much more efficient system of wartime mobilisation. The Military Service Law (MSL) adopted by the Second Session of the Sixth National People's Congress on 22 May 1984 is a milestone in China's mobilisation of manpower for the purpose of war-preparedness. Priorities given to economic modernisation and the objective to implement combined arms and joint operations have been criteria which in turn have urged the State and the PCMC to devise the most cost-effective way to mobilise manpower for the purpose of war.[57] The promulgation of the revised Military Service Law has been hailed as the integration of reforms introduced to active service units as well as the Reserve Forces. In the main, the new law in Yang Dezhi's words 'stipulates that China's military service system takes compulsory military services as its main body while combining with volunteers, and militia with reserves'.[58] Furthermore, the Reserve Forces have been broadened and strengthened as a result of the stipulation that the militia and the reserve service should be combined, and that the institution of reserve service for both officers and soldiers should be improved.[59] The cost-effectiveness of these reforms lies in the ability to keep a relatively smaller standing army of 3.2 million while ensuring that the Reserve Forces will provide a broad base for rapid mobilisation in the event of war. Thus Yang Dezhi believes that the objective 'will make it possible to keep fewer effectives in peace-time and accumulate sufficient reserves for war-time need'.[60] Great changes have taken place since the promulgation of the Military Service Law which denote the nation's determination to implement reforms along the lines aforementioned although the effectiveness of the wartime mobilisation process remains unclear. This is mainly because of the fact that priorities in economic construction may interfere with the building of combat-ready Reserve Forces and the effectiveness of rapid mobilisation (for details see Chapter 3).

The introduction of volunteers into the military service system which still relies heavily on conscripts is a reflection of the need to retain technical backbone personnel who are crucial to defence modernisation, especially if the CMC is serious about combined arms and joint operations.[61] Thus provisions have been made to change the service status of conscripts into volunteers (Article 19), whose active service covers a period from eight to twelve years provided that they are not older than 35 years of age. These volunteers, together with the expanded Reserve Forces, lead the way to a modified, mixed force structure which possesses distinct advantages over a force structure which relies totally on conscripts.[62] In the experience of the West, the introduction of sophisticated weapon systems in the 1960s and 1970s exposed the military inadequacies of conscripts, especially when they received limited training.[63] As China is developing more sophisticated weapon systems and tactical doctrines, it should be fully aware of the difficulty that non-regular forces would have manning complex weapon systems.[64] There is no clear indication of what percentage of technical backbone personnel apply to become volunteers each year, although it is certain that the State wishes to retain them for a long time (at least eight years). Available information suggests that the PLA allowed for extended service in the three services to be in the range of 20–25 per cent in the early 1960s.[65] Should the specialist volunteers constitute an equally substantial proportion, the PLA would indeed possess a mixed force structure congenial to defence modernisation. The three accepted universal criteria used to measure the effectiveness of a particular force structure are compulsion, cost and capabilities.[66] Whilst the PLA is mainly a 'selective service' which does incorporate the element of compulsion, China's age structure indicates a large manpower pool in the age range 18–22 from which the government selects its conscripts.[67] Furthermore, the Chinese have moved away from recruiting a peasant army to enlisting from both the urban and rural sectors in that order, with high school education as the minimum level for the recruits.[68] However, these favourable preconditions do not necessarily suggest that Chinese youths are motivated to enlist. As regards cost, China as a socialist country does not incorporate pay and allowances into military spending. In addition, the major recruiting and administrative costs (including after-service benefit package) seem to have been borne by the local governments.[69] It is in the area of capabilities that the Chinese reforms have indicated improvements, with the retention of volunteers over an extended period and the expansion of the Reserve Forces. Furthermore, the reallocation of military spending resulting from the cutting of one million troops also contributes to such improvements in capabilities.

China's claim to possess a youthful and modernised revolutionary army partly hinges on its reliance on the conscription of young people in the 18–22 age range on a three to four year cycle. For the immediate future, China is probably in a transitional period having to demobilise many more personnel every year because of its objective to reduce one million troops over a period of, say, two years from 1985. On the assumption that the strength of conscripts is at about 70–75 per cent of the entire defence force, the CMC would be demobilising from about 746 600 to 800 000 soldiers every year, should it demobilise one-third of the conscripts each year.[70] The figure at the moment is probably lower than these projected targets.

Since the promulgation of the new Military Service Law the State is in a better position to manage manpower mobilisation by standardising the registration of all eligible citizens for both active and reserve service through the PAFD network, which is now under the leadership of the local Party and government at the county level.[71] In registering all citizens eligible for conscription in the age range 18–22 by the end of each year, the State believes that 'it is not only conducive to raising the quality of new recruits, but also it [sic] helps to produce an understanding of the suitability of citizens for reserve service, thereby assisting in the strengthening of reserve forces'.[72] The registration exercise therefore provides not only the channel for the State to select conscripts who are politically motivated, physically fit and better educated, but also a manpower pool for the building of Reserve Forces which are believed to comprise at least five million reservists and some 4.3 million armed basic militia (*wuzhuang jiganminbing*).[73] The age range for each recruit intake is specified every year by the conscription order, and the 18–22 age range provides the State with some leeway to appraise the actual situation. There is reason to believe that preference is for the narrow age range of 18–20, as evidenced by the Jiangxi conscription exercise for 1985 which recruited personnel in the 18–19 age range.[74] As regards the

Table 1.4:   Populaton figures — age structure in China 1986

Age range	Total	Male	Female
15–19	129 339 341	66 558 403	62 780 938
15	27 323 306	14 071 874	13 251 432
16	26 487 340	13 614 655	12 872 685
17	28 239 541	14 522 190	13 717 351
18	24 538 257	12 638 810	11 899 447
19	22 750 897	11 710 874	11 040 023
20–24	118 236 417	59 787 314	58 449 103
20	25 686 509	13 189 846	12 496 663
21	24 417 934	12 507 810	11 910 124
22	25 131 408	12 726 845	12 404 563
23	27 379 596	13 669 206	13 710 390
24	15 620 970	7 693 607	7 927 363
25–29	77 618 231	39 960 271	35 657 960
25	10 690 834	5 320 423	5 370 411
26	14 307 196	7 337 219	6 969 977
27	14 284 240	7 396 047	6 888 193
28	19 459 780	10 132 818	9 326 962
29	18 876 181	9 773 764	9 102 417
30–34	91 038 988	46 883 945	44 156 053
30	17 932 830	9 247 831	8 684 999
31	19 662 511	10 169 169	9 493 342
32	18 604 868	9 573 341	9 031 527
33	17 487 492	8 983 153	8 505 339
34	17 351 297	8 910 451	8 440 846
35–39	68 008 390	35 528 874	32 479 516
35	14 628 858	7 545 721	7 083 137
36	15 269 938	8 007 225	7 262 713
37	13 149 025	6 881 142	6 267 883
38	12 559 119	6 585 705	5 973 414
39	12 411 450	6 590 081	5 892 369

Source: Adapted from Population Census Office (ed), *1982 Population Census of China (Results of Computer Tabulation).* (Deparment of Population Statistics, People's Republic of China, 1982), pp.272–74.

Reserve Forces, the State has a vast pool of enlisted personnel in the 18–35 age range, as Article 22 of the MSL stipulates that 'The conscript citizens who have registered for military service . . . but who have not been conscripted, should serve enlisted reserve service'.[75] In turn, the Reserve Forces are divided into two categories. The first and more significant category includes persons organised into the armed basic militia organisations and specialised technical personnel under the age of 28 registered for reserve service. The second category incorporates similar personnel in the 29–35 age range.[76] Table 1.4 illustrates that the State has a more than adequate manpower pool for wartime mobilisation and peace-time conscription. (The exact percentage of the 'pool' that the State relies on for the purpose of mobilisation requires further research.)

The MSL also makes provisions for implementing the basic principle of handling appropriately relations between the building of a standing army and that of Reserve Forces. Yang Dezhi claims that implementation can be realised by combining the militia and the reserve service. Indeed, the pivotal position of the militia and its organisations as the solid foundation for the mobilisation of Chinese troops as well as a fundamental form of organising the reserve service has been well recognised.[77] Thus the PAFD, which has experienced a long series of power transfer from the PLA to the local authorities at the county level, holds the key to the mobilisation and training of not only the armed basic militia, but also the active reservists (first category).[78] To maintain a small peacetime strength and mobilise a large force in wartime, both the General Staff Department and the General Political Department have pointed to the need to insist on the quality of the militia and reservists in regard to organisation, equipment and training. The number of militiamen should also be reduced further.[79] The question remains whether China's cost-effective way of maintaining large Reserve Forces which are expected to be combat-ready, necessarily meets the requirements for providing a modern, combined arms and joint operations capability. The most serious contradiction is that economic priorities have induced the State to curtail training time and reduce militia strength in order 'to lighten the people's burden'.[80] The obvious effect of this new policy, endorsed by both General Secretary Hu Yaobang and Permanent Vice-Chairman of the CMC, Yang Shangkun, is that the capabilities of both the armed basic militia and the active reservists may be curtailed.[81]

The major responsibility of the PAFD is to ensure that there is a smooth administrative system to effect the rapid mobilisation of the militia and the reservists. The requirements in this context include satisfactory deployment of forces to war locations, possible reorganisation or changes in C^2 arrangements for meeting a wartime situation, the deployment of fresh manpower resources for non-military work like economic construction projects, the redirection of production and resource priorities, and additional security measures for the local population such as surpervising air-raid precautions and civil defence work.[82]

In addition, the training of the Reserve Forces should enable the armed basic militia and the reservists to be combat-ready although the reduction of training time may affect the proficiency of fresh recruits in the reserve service. There are two distinct categories of active reservists. First, most provinces have established or are establishing their reserve divisions which comprise about three regiments each. They are expected to operate as a unit in combined arms and joint service operations. Many of them are a conglomeration of demobilised soldiers and armed militiamen.[83]

The second category comprises veterans, demobilised soldiers and the armed militia who can be mobilised at short notice (say, 48 hours) and assigned to all three Services for training for 7–21 days.[84] Reserve divisions and regiments have been reported to have held exercises with motorised units in preparation for positional defence, suggesting that these reserve units receive sophisticated training and possess high level combat capabilities.[85] As regards the training of individual reservist personnel, there are training centres and bases set up in the provinces which provide training on rotation for those who would normally be assigned to them over a period of 15–20 days.[86] The most rigorous type of training applies to officers of the reserve divisions or regiments who are themselves either veterans or demobilised soldiers rather than local cadres. They receive strict training in command and control, political work and logistics for an extended period.[87] At the level of the armed basic militia, training and exercises concentrate on guerrilla warfare and logistic support. Their ability to operate behind enemy lines and sabotage enemy supplies is being fully exploited. In the light of the urge to reduce training time for the sake of economic modernisation, it is highly unlikely that the State can mobilise the full strength of the Reserve Forces at the outbreak of war. One would assume that the reserve divisions and regiments would be the best equipped to engage the enemy. Should the veterans and demobilised soldiers rather than fresh recruits be relied upon, one would assume that requirements for training could be kept to the minimum. This is especially true for demobilised soldiers in the first eighteen months after demobilisation. Very much depends therefore on the 'mix'. The organisation of artillery units in the militia nation-wide as highlighted by the Chichihar Conference for artillery units in the militia in September 1983 represents the high expectations the State has for the armed basic militia at one end of the spectrum.[88] In many respects, China would be experiencing the same problems as other nations in that there are different levels of proficiency and readiness for reservists. It will be some time in the mid-1990s before China can be confident of mobilising Reserve Forces which will then be combat-ready to meet external threats.

COMBINED ARMS AND JOINT OPERATIONS

China's confidence in maintaining a cost-effective defence force is based not only on improved manpower mobilisation but also improved capabilities in combined arms operations and joint warfare. Combined arms operations is a term used by the Chinese to describe operations in which two or more combat branches of the same service coordinate their activities to fulfil a common mission, under a single operational commander. Combined arms groupings can also include logistic support elements. One such grouping in the ground forces comprised an infantry battalion, a tank company, a 122-mm howitzer company, an 82-mm recoilless rifle company, a chemical defence platoon, a flamethrower platoon, and corresponding logistic elements.[89] The Navy and Air Force also form combined arms groupings within their own services. Operations in which two or more services coordinate their activities are joint operations. In recent years the PLA has paid increasing attention to both these forms of warfare.

In the past, in contrast to developments in Western and Soviet forces, China's emphasis on guerrilla warfare and the role of the infantry contributed to a tendency within the PLA for each arm to conduct its training independently, and thus develop in relative isolation. Force structure reflected this single-arm trend, and procedures developed for coordinated action were weak. The turmoil of the Cultural Revolution caused stagnation in the development of the PLA as it did in many other areas. During this period, the major opportunity for the PLA to test its joint service capability was the capture of the Xisha (Paracel) Archipelago in January 1974. Against weak South Vietnamese opposition, the PLA conducted operations by air, ground and naval forces, but there was apparently little or no direct coordination between them.[90]

It was not until after the fall of the Gang of Four, so China claims, that Ye Jianying restored military training, and Deng Xiaoping proposed improving the PLA's joint warfare capability.[91] The catalyst for this process was probably the Sino-Vietnamese border conflict in early 1979, when weaknesses in command and control, inter-arm cooperation and other aspects became apparent under the rigorous test of battle.[92] Post-operation studies no doubt highlighted these problems for the attention of China's leadership, and in the autumn of 1979 the Minister of National Defence was sharply critical of the PLA's inability to fight a modern war and to effectively conduct combined arms operations on the battlefield. He identified a higher standard of officer training as the key to achieving success in troop training and on the battlefield.[93]

The consequent determination to improve the PLA's capabilities in combined arms operations and joint warfare has become the main thrust of military modernisation under the Four Modernisations program. It has been reflected in frequent statements on the importance of this aim, in training developments and in changes to force structure.

In November 1980, an All-Army conference considered ways to improve the PLA's training. It decided to make officer training the focus of a revised training program.[94] The General Staff Department's (GSD) Director of Training, Han Huaizhi, added a rider to this in early 1981, when he stressed the need for realistic training to culminate in combined arms exercises.[95] For the next two years or so the PLA concentrated on improving the standard of its officer and combined arms training. During this period the thrust of ground forces' combined arms training switched from infantry to tank warfare.[96] Joint warfare training was also boosted. The massive exercise at Zhangjiakou in September 1981 had joint service aspects, while NCNA claimed that China held a record number of joint service exercises in 1982.[97] An assessment of publicly revealed exercises from 1980 to 1983 and other media reports, however, suggests that during this period combined arms training received more emphasis than joint service training.[98]

A change in emphasis was heralded at an All-Army forum on training and educaton reform held in November 1983. Attended by the CGS Yang Dezhi, Deputy Chairman of the Central Military Commission Yang Shangkun, and Director of the General Political Department Yu Qiuli, the forum recognised that the logistic services had developed a capability to provide 'unified support' to combined arms forces, and agreed that joint warfare training should become the core subject in military training. It also determined that 'coordination in operations' and rapid response capabilities should be improved.[99]

The decision to make joint warfare the core of the PLA's training was intended to improve its capability to coordinate operations, particularly large-scale, 'campaign-level' operations.[100] Most of the major exercises revealed in the media since 1983 reflect 'joint service' aspects (see Table 1.5). No doubt other joint exercises have taken place, but have failed to receive public attention. Several such exercises have probably been held in the vicinity of the Sino–Vietnamese border, as alleged by the SRV.[101] A significant step in the develop-

Table 1.5: Combined arms and joint service exercises 1980–86

Date	Exercise	Combined arms	Joint service
1980	East Sea Fleet amphibious exercise. Regimental size landing force. Featured live-fire in air defence, tanks, air cushioned vehicles (ACV)[1]	?	Yes
Sept. 1981	PRC's largest scale exercises ever. Held at Zhangjiakou, about 150 km NW of Beijing. Between 150 000–200 000 troops participated, plus militia. Scenario was the defence of a mountain pass against an enemy (Soviet) attack. Bombers and ground attack aircraft also took part.[2]	Yes (major emphasis)	Yes
1981	East Sea Fleet amphibious assault exercise. Regimental-size landing force. ASW and air defence also practised.[3]	Yes	Yes
June 1982	Large exercise in Ningxia, with a border defence scenario. Featured (simulated) tactical nuclear strike.[4]	Yes	?
1982	East Sea and South Sea units concurrently conducted live-fire amphibious landing and counter landing exercises. Tested doctrine for employment of reinforced regimental-strength assault forces equipped with ACV, tanks, 'mechanised artillery', APC and chemical defence equipment.[5]	Yes	Probably
1982	East Sea Fleet landing ships conducted 26 night landings in 20 days.[6]	?	?
1982	South Sea Fleet amphibious assault exercise, with Marine Corps infantry and armoured units, to 'recapture' an island seized by the 'enemy'.[7]	Probably	No
1983 probably	An 'active defence' exercise conducted by a unit stationed on the border (probably in the northwest) against an 'enemy paratroop attack. Infantry, tanks, artillery and militia cavalry, supported by fighter aircraft, repulsed the invading paratroops.[8]	Probably	Probably
1983	PRC's largest ever airborne exercise, involving 'several thousand soldiers, hundreds of fighter planes', heavy weapons and 'ground forces'.[9]	Probably	Probably
Sept. 1983	East Sea Fleet held a complex exercise off the Zhejiang coast, involving surface warfare, ASW and minelaying operations, AAA firing. Militia (probably marine militia) also took part after concerted training beforehand.[10]	Yes	No

Date	Description		
1983	A division in Fuzhou Military Region held an exercise in anti-airborne operations. Tested procedures for rapid deployment and quick attack. Mechanised, missile, chemical defence and logistic units also participated. Unclear whether airborne forces also took part.[11]	Probably	Unclear
May 1984	Destroyers, frigates, submarines and landing ships conducted amphibious landing exercises on Hainan Island.[12]	Yes	Probably
1984	An exercise (probably an extension of one mentioned above) was held in defending the Xisha Islands against an enemy amphibious and paratroop assault. Force elements included marines, surface action groups, AD fighters, amphibious AFVs and paratroops.[13]	Probably	Yes
About July 1984	An army in Jinan Military Region conducted an anti-airborne exercise, facilitated by new, fast and secure ADP C^3 system.[14]	Probably	Probably
About Sept. 1984	East Sea Fleet, ground forces, air force and militia units participated in a large-scale maritime exercise in breaking an enemy blockade of the Changjiang (Yangtze River).[15]	?	Yes
1985	A combined arms army commanded by Xu Huizi conducted several combined arms exercises, with emphasis on command and control, and logistic and technical support. Two or three exercises were conducted with troops, others were CPX or TEWT.[16]	Yes	No
May 1986	The navy conducted its first long-range exercise in the Western Pacific, from the East China Sea to the area of Iwo Jima. Six warships participated, including a Luda guided missile destroyer, as well as several B-6 (BADGER) bombers, and possibly submarines. The exercise scenario involved assembling a task force from units based in different areas, and deploying rapidly to counter an enemy force at the earliest opportunity. Inter-branch coordination, C^3, COMSEC procedures, and most probably simulated air strikes were practised. The BADGERs were doubtless Naval Air Force aircraft, possibly the new ASW configuration or the reconnaissance version.[17]	Yes	Probably not in the strictest sense but participation of naval aircraft would involve similar planning and C^3 arrangements.
June 1986	A large-scale amphibious exercise was held, probably in the SSF area, involving 'many ship types', Naval Air Force aircraft and marines (including amphibious AFVs, engineer, chemical-defence and guided-missile elements).[18]	Yes	Yes

Table 1.5 (cont'd):

Date	Exercise	Combined arms	Joint service
Late 1986	Ground and air forces were reported to have held a large-scale joint exercise near the border with Mongolia, involving about 60 000 troops, mechanised forces and nearly 100 bombers, fighters, reconnaissance aircraft and helicopters. The scenario centred on a sudden attack by Soviet mechanised forces.[19]	Yes	Yes
Mid to late October 1986	An exercise involving the three services under unified command in Nanjing MR was announced on 1 December 1986.[20]	Yes	Yes
Mid to late October 1986	Exercises involving the deployment of group armies in FTX were held in Jinan, Shenyang and Beijing MRs.[21]	Yes	No

Notes

1 B. Hahn, 'Hai Fang', *US Naval Institute Proceedings*, March 1986, p.117
2 *SCMP*, 3 August 1983
3 B. Hahn, 'Hai Fang', p.117
4 *Ningxia Ribao*, 27 June 1983, and 28 June 1985
5 B. Hahn, 'Hai Fang', p.117
6 *Ibid.*
7 *Jiefangjun Bao*, 12 May 1982, p.1. This article described the Marines as a 'new force', responsible for seizing and securing forward bases for the Navy. In 1983, an illustrated article in the *Jiefangjun Huabao* showed photographs of a marine assault landing exercise.
8 *Jiefangjun Huabao*, 1984, No.1, pp.2–5
9 *SCMP*, 3 August 1983
10 Zhejiang Provincial Service, 1030 GMT, 13 September 1983, in *FBIS-CHI*, 19 September 1983, K19–20
11 *Ta Kung Pao*, Hong Kong, 3 November 1983, p.1
12 *FEER*, 14 June 1984, pp.46–47
13 *Ban Yue Tan*, No.24, 25 December 1984, pp.28–29; and *Ta Kung Pao*, Hong Kong, 21 December 1984
14 Xinhua, 0152GMT, 27 July 1984, in *SWB*, 3 August 1984, FE/7712/BII/7–8
15 *C³I Handbook*, EW Communications Incorporated, Palo Alto, First Edition, 1986
16 *Jing Pao*, No.2, Hong Kong, 5 February 1986
17 *Ming Pao*, Hong Kong, 3 June 1986, p.3; *Wen Hui Pao*, Hong Kong, 10 June 1986, p.2, in *FBIS-CHI*, 10 June 1986, W1
18 *JFJB*, 8 September 1986, p.1
19 *Ming Pao*, Hong Kong, 9 November 1986, p.3
20 *JFJB*, 1 December 1986, p.1
21 *Ibid.*

ment of a joint warfare capability — the formation of joint force headquarters and units — was foreshadowed in July 1985 by the Permanent Deputy Chairman of the Central Military Council, Yang Shangkun.[102] Prior to that, very few such organisations appear to have existed on a permanent basis (one example is the Beijing Garrison Command).[103]

However, reorganisation of the former field armies of the ground forces into combined arms group armies (*hecheng jituanjun*: referred to hereafter as group armies), which the Chinese claim to have 'basically achieved' in 1985, seems to address both combined arms and possibly joint service aspects, at least in some cases. Although pilot formations were tried out in 1984, and probably also in 1983, the large-scale restructuring of field armies did not begin until 1985,[104] and is presumably being achieved by incorporating elements of previously independent or mainly single arm formations into the field armies (e.g. artillery, engineers, tanks, mechanised infantry). Electronic warfare (EW) and meteorological units are included, as well as (it seems) air and naval elements 'where appropriate'.[105] This restructuring, which is being implemented at the same time as the PLA's strength is being cut by one million personnel, is aimed at producing a mix of arms and services better able to conduct combined ams operations in formations that have 'improved weapons and equipment', and a better rapid response capability.[106] These formations 'will be able to fulfil technical combat missions, and to conduct operations at the strategic level, either independently or under the command of a higher authority'. As many as 36 combined arms group armies are said to be in the process of formation, including at least a few mechanised group armies, while some 4000 units at and above regimental level are reported to have been disbanded.[107]

As can be expected, however, the Chinese have learned that re-equipment and changes to force structure must be accompanied by adjustments to tactics and command procedures. In 1984 one newly reorganised combined arms group reported on exercises that revealed breakdowns in the coordination of operations between different combat arms, and the unexpected chaos that eventuated when a reinforced motorised infantry division, obviously trying to deploy as a complete formation for the first time, found that its vehicles were so numerous that the routes selected became clogged, and the advance slowed to walking pace.[108]

In January 1986 the PLA's Deputy Chief of General Staff, He Qizong, indicated that the reorganisation had gone according to schedule, and in March 1986 the Deputy Commander of Chengdu

Military Region stated that coordination and cooperation between arms and services within the newly formed armies was working well during operations against Vietnamese forces along the Sino–Vietnamese border.[109] Media accounts, however, leave some doubts as to the degree of regrouping that has been achieved to date. It would be prudent to assume that this process has still some way to go, if only in the areas far from the high priority border regions facing the USSR and the SRV. Yet results in combat along the Sino–Vietnamese border seem to be encouraging. A major step in the development of a joint warfare and a combined arms capability was the formation in 1986 of the PLA's first joint warfare tactical training establishment in Nanjing Military Region. This establishment will conduct combat training in joint warfare involving ground and air elements, and in combined arms operations. Other training centres exist (presumably for combined arms training) but do not provide such complex battlefield conditions. The PLA intends to rotate all units in the recently formed group armies through the joint warfare establishment, which is said to be modelled in part on a similar US Army facility at Fort Irwin.[110]

To equip the PLA's officers with the necessary knowledge and skills demanded of combined arms operations and joint warfare, a new three-tiered command training system is due to be implemented.[111] Under this system, training for junior officers seems to be of a single service, probably combined arms nature, but at the intermediate level officers will be trained to become 'joint service tactical commanders' at the regimental level and staff officers in regiments and divisions.[112] Instructors in joint warfare will be trained at the All-Army Number One Education Academy.[113] Senior officers attending the Higher Command Academies will study the conduct of (joint) warfare at the campaign level.[114] In addition to this third tier of command academies, a National Defence University was established in late 1985 by the amalgamation of former military, political and logistics academies. This university will enrol up to 600 students drawn from senior commanders, leading government officials and senior academics.[115]

At unit level, the 1986 training program was designed to be centred on field operations, with emphasis on *inter alia* 'the ability to fight in coordination'.[116] In order to improve training within the group armies, special training formations have been established to train recruits, thus allowing the longer-serving personnel to move on to more complex training, unhindered by inexperienced young soldiers. This training system seems to operate on a three-year cycle, with the new troops joining the operational units in the third year, when they take part in combined arms training from section to divisional level.[117]

In sum, the PLA has taken some significant steps towards developing a combined arms capability. Although little has been revealed publicly about the tactics being developed, the PLA has studied US and Soviet doctrine, and exercises in mechanised warfare, anti-airborne operations and 'nuclear counter-attack', have been mentioned with increasing frequency. Except for amphibious operations, the PLA does not seem to have advanced very far in the field of joint warfare. Progress is limited by shortages of some resources, including modern weapon systems in critical areas. The current reorganisation probably cannot be fully implemented until strength reductions have been completed. The retraining process is only in the early stages, and joint warfare capabilities on a par with those attained by most Western and Soviet armed forces will take a long time to develop. C^3I will be the critical factor, for without commensurate improvements in that area, the combined arms and joint warfare concepts will not produce an effective counter to the Soviet threat, no matter what improvements are eventually made in the PLA's equipment and resources.

Strengthening combined arms training and raising coordinated warfighting capabilities in the arms and services

The ultimate objective in strengthening combined arms training and raising the military capabilities in the various arms and services is to best prepare China's armed forces for 'active defence in positional warfare' — the strategic guideline for the future 'anti-aggression' war as set down by the Central Military Commission.[118] In undertaking active defence in positional warfare, which should be coordinated with secondary mobile and guerrilla operations, the Chinese hope to take the initiative in the initial stage of a war. This requires the Chinese to strengthen the mobility of their forces to conduct the rapid mobilisation of Reserve Forces in order to undertake mobile operations and confront the enemy's advance (see Chapter 3 for details).[119] The Chinese have explained the basis of this defensive strategy as follows:

> Nowadays, military science and technology and weapon systems have undergone great development and changes. Military strategy and warfighting ploys have also changed continuously as a result. Modern warfare is three-dimensional war, joint warfare and total war. The

suddenness, speed and brutality of war have greatly increased. The extensive use of electronic technology and the development of electronic warfare have made command and control in war more complicated and difficult. These new conditions and new characteristics urgently necessitate our army to raise the defence capabilities under modern warfare conditions, that is, capabilities in coordination between the arms and services, rapid response, electronic warfare, logistic support and battlefield survivability — these are the 'five warfighting capabilities'.[120]

Training has been identified as the most important means of improving the 'five warfighting capabilities'. In particular, the need to increase training in joint operations is emphasised. In addition, the Chinese envisage many problems in infantry-artillery and infantry-tank cooperation, and in achieving effective chemical-defence, reconnaissance and communications capabilities.[121] In sum, the Chinese insist on three basic changes to training:

> ... [we] must thoroughly shift the emphasis in training from soldiers to cadres; for the content and methods of training, [we] should bear in mind the characteristics of the major adversary in order to study the new warfighting methods so that the lesser-equipped can overcome the better-equipped enemy. [We] must shift the emphasis in training from fighting the infantry force to fighting the enemy equipped with tanks, aircraft and airborne forces. As regards the theme and emphasis in training, [we should] concentrate on raising the comprehensive warfighting capabilities in units according to the requirements of modern warfare conditions; [we] must thoroughly shift the emphasis in training from single arms to combined arms and joint operations at the campaign and tactical levels. Only in thoroughly realising the abovementioned 'three changes' in the supervision of training can our army achieve a major breakthrough in military training so that the 'five warfighting capabilities' in the units can be significantly raised.[122]

In regard to specific training to raise the coordinated warfighting capabilities in the arms and services, by 1984 the Chinese seem to have evolved sophisticated plans:

> ... The various arms and services should excel first in basic training in tactics, second in integrated tactical training within each arm or corps, and lastly in combined arms training involving the various arms and services from bottom to top through each level. During integrated tactical training, one must follow procedures in the study of theories, of standard operating procedures, and of the enemy through map exercises, sand tables and exercises with troops... Battalions and levels below should concentrate on exercises with troops (sic. FTX), while regiments

and levels above should concentrate on tactical exercises without troops (sic. TEWT) and command post exercises (sic. CPX) for the commanding officer and headquarters with communications equipment and a small number of troops. Through training, the various problems encountered in the past years like the opening of routes, coordinated infantry/tank and land/air operations, rapid response, and communications for the arms and services, should all be overcome and practical solutions arrived at... [123]

In many ways, the above training policy resembles western methods, especially in regard to the useful interplay of field training exercise (FTX), CPX and TEWT. At first glance, this policy seems to limit the opportunity for higher level formations to prove the lessons learned in CPX and TEWT by practical application during FTX. It was probably intended, however, as an initial phase in an escalating training cycle in which the level of FTX is raised gradually until eventually all levels of command are exercised. Indeed, at least nine large-scale FTX were held during 1984–86 (see Table 1.5).

The Chinese claimed that they had achieved initial success in coordinated warfighting capabilities in late 1986 as the recently formed group armies made progress in tactical field training exercises at 'campaign-level' and in the setting of joint operations. Thus the series of exercises in August–October 1986 showed that China's modified force structure and modernised training have led to improvements in warfighting capabilities.[124] It was reported that an exercise in Nanjing MR involved the three services under unified command.[125] Other exercises witnessed the deployment of group armies in FTX in Jinan, Shenyang and Beijing MRs.[126] These reports may reflect only a small step in defence modernisation by western standards, but the Chinese would regard them as an important transformation from training in single arms to combined arms at the platoon level and to FTX in a joint operational setting.

COMMAND, CONTROL, COMMUNICATIONS AND INTELLIGENCE/ELECTRONIC WARFARE

In its efforts to acquire modern combined arms and joint operations capabilities, China has come increasingly to realise the necessity of upgrading its command and control systems (C^2). Communications, intelligence and aspects of electronic warfare[127] are now regarded as components of the wider category of C^3I.

Command and control

At national level *de facto* command and control has always been exercised by the Party's Central Military Commission, with operational control delegated to the three general departments that form the headquarters of the PLA: the General Staff Department (GSD), General Political Department (GPD) and General Logistics Department (GLD). The inclusion of several senior PLA leaders in the PCMC, and the prominent, enforcement role of the GPD with its own command structure down to unit level, have ensured close adherence to the PCMC's directives within the PLA. The Ministry of National Defence (MND) has provided mainly administrative support to the PLA.[128]

Since the State Central Military Council (SCMC) was formed under the revised State Constitution of 1982, it has assumed *de jure* C^2 of the PLA. In recent years the MND has been given added responsibilities, such as the direction of the PLA's military modernisation program. The distinction between PCMC and SCMC is somewhat blurred, but unanimity has been achieved by the concurrent appointment of leading members of the PCMC to the SCMC. Thus, for example, Deng Xiaoping is chairman of both bodies. For the time being at least, the Party remains clearly in control, but the possibility exists that in the future the composition of the State's higher command structure could differ from the Party's and thus compromise the unity of command that has usually been one of the PLA's strengths.

The establishment of the SCMC and the gradual strengthening of the MND seem to indicate an intention to concentrate national-level C^2 under these two bodies, but opposition to major reductions in the Party's role in military affairs no doubt comes from many Party members both within and outside the PLA. The dual command system that currently exists needs to be clarified and simplified for the PLA to be able to respond swiftly to developing threats, and to control effectively the deployment of strategic and joint forces.

It is possible that China will eventually consider moving in the same direction as Vietnam, which is in the process of implementing the 'one commander system' in order to maintain a modern force capable of reacting swiftly to Chinese hostilities. Under this system, the power of the political department is reduced, and the part played by political officers in PAVN's command and control system virtually eliminated. Political officers are largely confined to Party matters, maintaining morale, and organising tasks laid down by the commander, who has full authority to direct the accomplishment of military missions.[129] In China's case this would probably entail, *inter alia*, a change in the PCMC's role, if not its abolition, but the Chinese seem unable to take decisive measures in this respect at present.

Strengthening the command and control system below military commission level is also one of the goals of the military modernisation program. It is being achieved in a number of ways, including a reduction in the number of higher-level headquarters and staffs; improvements in the selection and training of officers; and the upgrading of communications links.

The Railway Engineer Corps and the Capital Construction Engineer Corps were transferred to civilian control in 1983, and the Armour, Artillery and Engineer Corps headquarters were reduced to sub-departments directly under the GSD.[130] Further plans for streamlining the chain of command were announced by Deng Xiaoping in June 1985. The number of military regions would be reduced from eleven to seven, while troop strength would be cut by one million over the next two years.[131] In July 1985 Yang Shangkun stated that the forthcoming reduction in personnel would mainly affect the GSD, GPD, GLD, NDSTC and Military Regions. The number of deputies to chiefs had already been reduced, and no more advisers (senior officers retained beyond retiring age) were being appointed. The ages of high ranking officers had been reduced (e.g. officers at divisional level were around 40 years of age), and command at all levels would become more flexible and better suited to modern warfare.[132] The subsequent drive to lower the average age for commanders at various levels may have led to problems stemming from inexperience, and a more flexible approach to age limits seems to be discernible.[133]

By 1 July 1985, the Navy had 'readjusted the leadership groups' of the three fleets.[134] Some reports also indicate a strengthening of C³I arrangements in the North Sea Fleet and East Sea Fleet areas, through the possible establishment of a new Northern Naval Region, to command both fleets.[135]

Shortcomings in the officer corps had been recognised for several years. Many lacked an educational level sufficient for them to master the more complex concepts and technical equipment introduced in recent years. In the early 1980s more stringent criteria began to be applied to the selection of potential officers in all three services, and promotion procedures were tightened. A senior middle school education became the minimum education qualification required for selection to officer training, and more tertiary level graduates were sought. Initially, in the early 1980s, somewhat piecemeal efforts were made to improve the general training of officers, including command training. Standards tended to vary, but by 1984 assistant to the CGS, Han Huaizhi, was able to state that the majority of command officers at regimental level and above had been trained in military academies and schools. He also indicated that problems in providing funds and high calibre instructors for these institutions, as well as in obtaining the release of officers from their units to attend them, were gradually being overcome. Since then the PLA has taken positive steps to standardise training and improve the quality of instruction in these institutions.[136]

By 1984 dissatisfaction with progress appeared to have prompted a thorough-going and standardised approach to training the PLA's command personnel. A Forces' Command Academy was opened in 1986.[137] This is probably identical to the 'National Defence University' first established in December 1985 to train senior commanders, instructors, leading government officials and senior academics.[138] Of potentially even greater significance, a new three-tiered system for training command officers has been in preparation since 1984. It will provide command schools at junior, intermediate and senior officer levels. As at June 1986, this system was nearing implementation point. By mid-1987 China claimed to have broadened the scope of its officer training program and to have trained 50–70 per cent of its officers in academies. Moreover 'hundreds' of foreign military experts and scholars had attended these academies as part of an 'academic exchange program'. Selected Chinese officers will also be sent to study at foreign military institutions.[139] NCO ranks are also being re-established, and schools to train these personnel should result in better leadership at the sub-unit level.[140]

However, in view of the size of the PLA (notwithstanding its planned reduction to about 3.2 million personnel), improvements to the officer corps will take a long time to become effective throughout the Armed Forces. In the meantime, in order to provide junior officers with practical command experience in combat, since about 1984 groups of probationary officers newly graduated from military colleges have been posted to units along the Sino–Vietnamese border. Many of them have distinguished themselves in battle.[141] Efficiency in major formation headquarters can be expected to improve through the appointment of staff officers with appropriate specialist experience to complement the hitherto mainly infantry-trained staff.[142] Within the higher command structure, the gradual appointment of younger senior officers with greater understanding of combined arms and joint service operations, and of the means of achieving effective training in these capabilities, should result in better direction and guidance in their development. One such officer is Xu Huizi, who was appointed Deputy Chief of General Staff in March 1986. His selection was probably influenced by the strong contribution he has made to the theoretical and practical development of tactics in nuclear, joint service, and combined arms operations.[143] Another senior officer who may play a significant role in reforming training, is Hu Changfa, the recently appointed chief of the training department.[144] Strong, clear direction from the top will be needed if the improvements sought within the PLA are to be achieved in a standardised, effective manner.

Indeed, as group armies set about conducting exercises with troops, problems began to emerge when the old system of C² was proven unsuitable for the new force structure and equipment. In one example, during a command post exercise (CPX) involving an artillery division and an anti-aircraft division, the order to attack did not reach certain units at the scheduled time. In another case, previously mentioned, the standard C² system caused great delays in an FTX involving a motorised division. In this FTX, the division, with over 1000 vehicles, was ordered to advance, but planning had not been thorough, and routes forward soon became congested. Consequently, the speed of advance was about the same as that of the foot-mobile infantry.[145]

Automation

The application of automation technology in the C³I field is receiving increasing attention. Several pilot units were selected to develop and trial such systems.[146] It is not surprising, therefore, that the PLA's first mechanised group army is claimed to use a computer system to coordinate and direct fire plans and operations.[147] According to the commander of the Air Force, Wang Hai, it too is pressing ahead with the development of an automated command and control system, but he gave no details. By early 1987 both Nanjing and Guangzhou Military Regions were reported to have developed automated C³I systems for use within their divisions. Nanjing MR had also developed the use of mini-computers for a variety of purposes, including logistic management. The Guangzhou MR system, however, was capable of interfacing with the all-army automated command and control project. The first stage of the all-army project, which by 1984 linked the 'supreme command with all major units', seems to be a computerised communications network, featuring secure radio, on-line encryption and facsimile, backed up by land-line. The second stage, which began in 1985, is intended to provide computer applications to cover 'principal combat units', including an intelligence sub-system and a management function.[148] There are few indications of the extent to which intelligence sub-systems within the various C³I systems have already been automated. The technology to achieve this, however, is obviously within the PLA's reach, despite attempts by the US and its allies to limit technology transfer in this area. The general impression is that while considerable progress has been made in applying ADP technology to the C³I field in some selected formations, force-wide development has still some way to go.[149]

Communications, intelligence and electronic warfare capabilities

The PLA's communications, intelligence and electronic warfare (EW) capabilities are probably the most difficult to assess, due to the high degree of security China maintains on these subjects.

Generalised statements have been made about the PLA's communications weaknesses during the 1979 Sino–Vietnamese border conflict. Communications equipment was reported to have been outdated.[150] The ground forces' field radios were largely blocked by the rugged hills which disrupted, *inter alia*, ground to air communications,[151] and the infantry's communications were prone to jamming by Vietnamese forces.[152]

These difficulties no doubt contributed to the 'poor coordination of units' and the failure to 'exploit initial advantages'.[153] More recently, reports indicated that the technological standards of communications now in service are uneven. The first Chinese-designed tactical HF radio (the Type 63), which uses older Soviet technology, is reported to be still widely used, although it is easily jammed.[154] Microwave links (some of which carry military traffic) suffer from poor quality control at the manufacturing stage, and most are only one-way. New digital data links are required.[155] China also admits to a ten year lag in fibre optic communications technology when compared with foreign achievements.[156] Thus Western perceptions have generally continued to hold communications and EW capabilities to be critical problems.[157]

Yet since about 1984 China has claimed to have made improvements in these areas. In mid-1984 the PLA's Deputy Chief of Staff, Zhang Zhen, stated that there had been a great improvement in

ECM capability.[158] *Xinhua* also reported that in a certain army in Fuzhou MR, secure radio telephones and rapid facsimile equipment had replaced line (telephones) and walkie-talkie radios. The C^3 system between army and front-line units provided 'fast, accurate and secure communications'.[159] Improvements on a wider scale were inferred in a *Ta Kung Pao* article in 1986, which claimed that infantry communications had been improved with equipment that was secure and 'could resist interference', while progress has been made in reducing the size of field radios and widening their compatibility.[160]

In addition, a long-distance underground communications cable network linking China's major cities and military headquarters has been announced.[161] This strategic network, which is undoubtedly backed up by other communications systems, should provide a high degree of security. China claims that this network, and ancillary systems serving the strategic missile force and strategic air and naval bases, are automated and well protected against conventional nuclear and chemical attack.[162] Another strategic communications link has reportedly been established between Headquarters Kunming MR [*sic*] and the Thai Supreme Command in Bangkok to facilitate rapid reaction by Chinese forces on the Sino–Vietnamese border whenever Bangkok reports Vietnamese attacks against Thai territory.[163]

The Chinese have also reported the operation of satellite communications, and a growing use of digital microwave and optical fibre communications. The latter development has doubtlessly been aided by recent western sales to China.[164]

The validity of these Chinese claims is difficult to judge. What does seem apparent, is the importance China has attached, over a long period, to the development of strategic-level C^3I systems. As far back as 1977, the US Joint Chiefs of Staff noted that China was moving to 'achieve a rapid, flexible, and secure C^3 capability for crisis management', suggesting that the GSD could direct operations down to local level headquarters if necessary.[165] One Chinese report stressed the need for an 'automated, computerised countdown, communications and command system', since China's ICBMs had 'only a little more than ten minutes countdown time'.[166] Actual command and control arrangements for the strategic missile forces are unclear, but it is likely that control is exercised at the highest level, possibly the PCMC, direct to the launch unit. It is possible, however, that control of the shorter-range nuclear missiles may be delegated to theatre level commanders in some circumstances during time of war. Some Western observers believe that the PCMC retains operational control in both peace and war, but that in peacetime its orders are relayed via Military Region Commanders as opposed to the direct link employed in war.[167]

The Navy's strategic communications systems are probably both extensive and secure. Its VLF transmitters at Datong, Fuzhou, Lushun, Yaxian and Zhanjiang may have supported broad ocean area (BOA) deployments to the Central Pacific as far back as 1967. They also provide some credibility for a C^3I system covering the developing SSN and SSBN force.[168]

China has undoubtedly made strenuous efforts to develop satellite communications systems, using the launch sites at Shuangchengzi and Xichang. In April 1984, it launched a communications satellite into geosynchronous orbit for the first time. Two new direct broadcast satellites are planned for development with Western participation.[169] The PLA benefits directly from these facilities. BOA deployments such as the voyages to the Antarctic in 1984 and to South Asia in 1986 have also demonstrated the effectiveness of the Navy's new satellite communications system over extended distances.[170]

The PRC has also launched six photo-reconnaissance satellites since 1975, but the resolution of imagery appears not to be as good as modern US systems. The US reportedly provides some of its satellite imagery of the USSR to China. In 1976 China's first ELINT satellite was launched.[171] In view of the part they play in China's strategic defence and response capabilities, China can be expected to place a high priority on further development of reconnaissance and communications satellites, and the sophisticated computerised processing facilities necessary to back them up.[172]

Air photo reconnaissance, however, is largely carried out by conventional, fixed-wing aircraft, although the scale of effort, and quality of imagery interpretation is probably not up to current Western and Soviet standards.[173] An indication of China's shortcomings in air reconnaissance and surveillance was contained in a 1983 Beijing article which admitted that the Naval Air Force lacked airborne early warning (AEW) and maritime patrol aircraft that could monitor ground-based, maritime and airborne targets within 'a 1000 km diameter circular region' and direct Chinese forces in engaging the enemy. China is, however, interested in developing remotely piloted vehicles (RPVs) for reconnaissance purposes.[174]

With US assistance, China has developed strategic intelligence systems which incorporate twelve sites with SIGINT facilities (see Chapter 5 for details).[175] China also operates about 1600 AD radars (copies of dated Soviet designs).[176] Modern Western radars also serve some areas, but they do not seem to provide coverage of the critical areas near the northern border where Soviet close air support and battlefield interdiction missions would be flown in the event of war.[177]

At the tactical as well as the strategic level, the PLA's capability to conduct EW intercepts and direction finding (ESM) to jam enemy electronic emissions and use electronic deception measures (ECM) have long been a subject of conjecture.[178] Chinese references to EW in the PLA have been vague. It is now apparent, however, that units dedicated to conducting EW exist. For example, the PLA's first mechanised combined arms group army has an EW unit or units that have the task of 'disrupting the enemy's radars and radios, and of destroying the enemy's command system'.[179] A rare indication of the effectiveness of the PLA's EW measures was given by the Deputy Commander of Chengdu Military Region in early 1986, when he recounted incidents from recent fighting on the Sino–Vietnamese border. In these incidents, the PLA had been able to 'read' intercepted PAVN radio transmissions, and to both isolate and jam a PAVN headquarters radio net.[180] The level of command of the PAVN units was not revealed. The lower the level of command, the more likely it would be that only low-grade cypher, or even clear speech, was used. Thus it is difficult to gauge the degree of the PLA ground force's ESM and ECM capabilities in these cases.

It is likely, however, that the ground force's mobile, tactical ESM and ECM capabilities are fairly limited,[181] and heavy reliance continues to be placed on the PLA's traditional expertise in ground reconnaissance. The Navy and Air Force's tactical EW systems are also likely to be limited. It is doubtful, for instance, that all ship classes have ESM/ECM systems. Photographs of Chinese WHISKEY and ROMEO submarines, for example, do not reveal the ESM/ECM equipment that is fitted to their Soviet counterparts, nor do all destroyers and frigates appear to have such systems.[182] While the current generation of shipboard ESM equipment is largely limited to direction-finding loops and multi-band receivers,[183] and only passive ECM systems seem to be available, China can be expected to address these weaknesses over the next few years, probably with Western assistance. Although the US may be unwilling to provide China with some countermeasures and detection equipment for tactical use, as for example in the case of the F-8 update package,[184] other nations such as France, the UK or even Israel probably would be willing. China has revealed little beyond generalities concerning its ECCM capabilities (electronic counter-countermeasures — these entail actions to ensure the effective use of one's own electromagnetic radiations, despite the enemy's use of contermeasures — ECM). The limitations on its ESM and ECM capabilities suggest, however, that in the ECCM field it has even further to go. As an example, the Navy's principal SSM, which has been developed and modified over many years to provided several different weapon systems, is still reported to be vulnerable to ECM, indicating a lack of ECCM technology.[185]

Survivability

The survivability of the C^3I system in the event of a major conflict is a matter for conjecture. Above-ground facilities such as major head-quarters, early-warning radar sites and SIGINT sites are difficult to conceal, and would be targets for early attention by an adversary such as the USSR. Those located close to the northern borders would be particularly vulnerable to both strategic and tactical assault.[186] It is probable, therefore, that some, at least, of the underground facilities that began their construction during the period of highest threat perception in the late 1960s and early 1970s, have been utilised as alternative locations for the major C^3I networks deeper in China's interior. One such hardened underground shelter for use by the central government has been reported at Huhot 260 miles west of Beijing. It is said to have complete underground control facilities, as well as an airfield.[187] The redundancy built into the PLA's major communications networks also contributes to the survivability of the C^3I system, as does the probably growing practice of providing underground communications links.

China has recognised that major changes to its command and control arrangements are necessary. It is taking steps to simplify (*yitihua*) these arrangements, particularly at the major formation level, and to upgrade its communications and strategic intelligence support. An apparently major anomaly in this process is the relationship between the PCMC and the SCMC. Its evolution has some potential for intra-elite conflict.

The emphasis the PLA is giving to the selection and training of command personnel should eventually provide the PLA with leaders who are capable of managing the highly complex business of conducting modern combined arms and joint warfare. Thus some progress is being made towards the aim of making the PLA's leadership 'more revolutionary, younger, better educated and more professionally competent'.[188] China's ability to provide its commanders with the necessary equipment in sufficient numbers remains, however, an unknown factor. Here cost and national priorities will be the main determinants. To break out of the restrained pace of indigenous R and D, foreign assistance or technology is necessary. So far China seems to have been prepared to accept foreign assistance mainly in strategic systems, such as SIGINT facilities, perhaps reflecting a deliberate choice on China's part. Despite a long-term strategic plan, automated tactical C^3I systems so far appear to be confined mainly to pilot schemes on a limited basis, using indigenous project development, and probably a minimum of direct foreign participation. Given the limited resources available for military modernisation, and the vast size of the PLA, this seems a logical choice. Buying a few thousand western radio sets, for example, would have virtually no impact.[189]

Concentration on providing the means to effectively command China's deterrent and other strategic forces, while achieving the earliest warning of developing threats from across its borders, would seem to meet China's priority defence requirements. Meanwhile, upgrading tactical C^3I and EW capabilities can proceed on a more gradual, less costly basis. It will probably be years, therefore, before China can narrow the gap with the USSR in these tactical aspects to any significant extent.

The New Force Structure

China's determined efforts to enforce retrenchment and modernise the force structure have made significant contributions to transforming the PLA into a 'smaller, better educated and more revolutionary' defence force. In turn, this achievement has made it possible for China's military spending to be kept within the range of nine to twelve per cent of the national budget. Savings in retrenchement and structural reforms have also been used to improve equipment procurement, intensify research and development of new weapons and technology and operate more efficiently a 'leaner' defence force. Whilst financial constraints have encouraged the Chinese to emphasise self-reliance in defence modernisation, it is also evident that it continues to rely on arms transfers and the acquisition of western technology to enhance its military capabilities, especially in the production of state-of-the-art weapons and of effective armament of a defensive nature.

To the Chinese, the fruits of defence modernisation are the results of their initiative in bringing about 'Strategic Changes to the Guiding

Thoughts on National Defence Construction and Army Building'. They believe that by concentrating on peacetime war preparation and long-term modernisation objectives, Chinese warfighting capabilities will be able to cope with not only limited wars in this century, but also high-level conflicts and large-scale wars in the next century. By achieving certain breakthroughs in high-technology and certain strategic weapon systems, the Chinese hope that their defence capabilities will get near to advanced world standards by the middle of the twenty-first century. To facilitate these modernisation efforts, Yang Dezhi has encouraged research on military concepts in order to understand the nature and conduct of future wars.

China's new strategic outlook in defence modernisation is especially evident in the modernisation of the force structure, the introduction of combined arms and joint warfare which has improved its warfighting capabilities and the upgrading of C^3I components.

Since the promulgation of the revised Military Service Law in May 1984, modifications to the force structure are evident. In support of a smaller standing army, the Reserve Forces have been strengthened as a result of the stipulation that the militia and the reserve service should be combined. Through the reorganised PAFD network, all citizens eligible for conscription and reserve service are required to register. The State is therefore able to build up a manpower pool which comprises at least 5 million reservists and some 4.3 million armed basic militia. Whilst the reduction of training time and militia strength in preference for economic modernisation would curtail the capabilities of the Reserve Forces, the PLA continues to demonstrate its ability to train vigorously and equip adequately some of its reserve divisions and regiments and incorporate artillery elements into some of its armed basic militia units. Nevertheless, it will be some time in the mid-1990s before China can be confident of mobilising its Reserve Forces which will then be combat-ready for external threats. As regards the military service system, which had relied heavily on conscripts, new provisions for volunteers to serve as technical backbone personnel are advantageous to defence modernisation. Should the State allow for extended service in the three services to be in the range of 20–25 per cent of the total strength of the PLA, it would enhance warfighting capabilities without sacrificing the element of compulsion essential to the effectiveness of the force structure. The strength of the Reserve Forces and the introduction of extended service suggest that the Chinese are developing a modified and mixed force structure which is more cost-effective and efficient than the previous one which relied on conscripts.

Weaknesses in C^2 and inter-arm cooperation exposed in the Sino-Vietnamese border conflict in 1979, and the lack of direct coordination between the three services revealed in the capture of the Xisha Archipelago in January 1974, have urged the PLA to improve capabilities in combined arms and joint warfare through training development and changes to the force structure. Three basic changes in training have been promoted to bring about these improvements. First, the emphasis should shift from training soldiers to training officers and from the infantry to the other arms like armour, aviation and airborne units. Second, the theme of training should concentrate on raising the comprehensive warfighting capabilities according to modern warfare conditions. Third, training should be in combined arms and joint operations at the campaign and tactical levels. Exercises conducted in 1984–86 resemble western methods in regard to the useful interplay of FTX, CPX and TEWT, and have shown that the newly formed group armies have achieved initial success in coordinated warfighting capabilities.

2

Improved
Warfighting
Capabilities

CHINA'S STRATEGIC PLANS AND
THE FORMATION OF GROUP ARMIES

Strategic changes have been brought about as China modifies its force structure and makes progress in defence modernisation by improving its war mobilisation efforts, elements of doctrine, organisation, C^3I, training and weapons and equipment. The most important impact of all these changes on the defence force is China's ability to improve warfighting capabilities. The transformation of the field armies into group armies reflects the PCMC's determination to prepare its defence force for strategic tasks in both the twentieth century as well as the first half of the twenty-first century. Initial successes by the group armies in large-scale FTX, discussed in Chapter 1, represent China's first concrete step in the direction of strategic planning.

As it considers an outbreak of global war in this century to be unlikely, China hopes to equip a crack, regular force with modernised weaponry which can be victorious in low-level conflicts and limited wars. At the same time the Chinese believe that they should 'concentrate on the developmental needs of the next century, conserve strength and fundamentally seek the best results for national defence'.[1] To achieve this, China needs to conduct research into the development of certain selected weapon systems and to improve some elements of its inventory so as to face greater strategic risks in the next century: considered to be the second and strategic stage of China's defence modernisation.[2]

Specifically, three major changes in the development of armaments are considered to be necessary:

42

1. The aim should be to strengthen overall and long-term defence capabilities rather than meet the needs of battlefields and campaigns in which the Chinese are likely to operate in the near future.

2. The development of certain strategic weapons should be preferred to that of conventional weapons, and

3. 'Content and methodology' of development should rest on solid foundations and high standards so as to achieve more advanced techniques, better quality and greater efficiency.

Research into future wars and strategic development should also be emphasised.[3]

Should these strategic targets for weapons and equipment be realised, the group armies would further improve their warfighting capabilities beyond their present scope, which seems to be limited to the divisional level.[4] Before certain strategic breakthroughs can materialise, the group armies are expected to be able to confront the enemy in limited wars during this century. Recent discussions in the *Jiefangjun Bao* (Liberation Army Daily) reflect a belief that any conflict involving China in the next two decades will be confined to such wars.[5] Strategists identify five major features of limited war based on their understanding of over ten low- to mid-level conflicts since the 1970s. First, the strategic target is limited and combat operations emphasise the need for quick decisions. The US invasion of Grenada, its air strike against Libya and the Israeli attack on Lebanon have been cited as examples. Second, high technology and low-force levels, characterised by rotary-wing aircraft, tactical guided missiles and electronic warfare, dominate the conflict. Third, such wars break out suddenly after a long period of confrontation in areas of contention. Fourth, the surface area of the battlefield is limited but the actual space in which operations are conducted is three-dimensional and extensive. Fifth, the combat troops employed are crack, highly efficient forces and the course of war is complicated and prone to change. The Chinese consider it important to train relatively compact combat units which will become the main strength of group armies operating at 'campaign-level'. In so doing, they hope to open up new battlefields and quicken the course of the war.[6]

Strategic planners considering how best to prepare the nation for future limited wars and mid-level conflicts have urged the Chinese to study the theories of conducting campaigns.[7] In turn, an identification of campaign objectives is considered crucial to the development of combined arms capabilities of the group armies, which have the task of contributing to the fulfilment of China's strategic plans. The ability to operate in great depth is recognised as the major campaign objective that will effect opportunities for seizing the initiative and blur the difference between attack and defence. An emphasis on attacking in great depth by both sides tends to lower the effectiveness of the second echelon and encourage the development of objective-oriented types of C^3 which emphasise independent but coordinated operations.[8] Chinese group armies have been urged to increase both their ability to coordinate operations and to destroy that of the enemy. In so doing they hope that the Chinese formations will learn to operate in conditions where control by higher headquarters may have been lost. By this the Chinese mean the deployment of compact, self-sufficient forces, that while operating to a plan coordinated at a higher level, can continue to function effectively if cut off from the main body. Thus the group armies can be expected to increase their adaptability and ability to respond to adverse conditions.[9]

Exercises conducted by group armies in August–October 1986, discussed in Chapter 1, reflect Chinese intentions to fulfil both strategic and campaign objectives. A great deal of emphasis has been placed on the involvement of leading cadres from the group armies headquarters in FTX during which forces may be deployed on several fronts. At the same time, training at the campaign level helps leading cadres in headquarters to shape new concepts and improve C^3 quality and work methods in accordance with the combat needs of group armies.[10] Nevertheless, Chinese emphasis on FTX at the divisional level suggests that there is currently limited opportunity for higher formations to be exercised except for the participation of leading cadres from group armies' headquarters. In effect, the concern to achieve the campaign objective of operating in great depth has urged the Chinese to concentrate on tactics for joint operations and troop exercises mainly at the divisional level. In September 1986, a motorised division of the Guangzhou MR conducted a tactical field training exercise in a joint operational setting. Two opposing forces demonstrated efficiency in coordination. The different arms participating included motorised infantry, tank and APC units, artillery, chemical-defence units, and signals and logistics units.

Three concrete successes arising from the exercise which was presided over by Yang Dezhi, were identified. First, reforms in content formulated a common training system for all arms in the ground forces. Second, a new method of training emphasised 'three completes and one small'.[11] In other words, formation headquarters and arms and services should all be represented in exercises. Participating elements should be fully manned and equipped according to their establishment. On the other hand, the actual number of elements represented should be kept to a minimum. This scaled-down approach to conducting FTX is, to the Chinese, both simple and economical. Third, C^3 procedures and equipment, and the methods of issuing operations orders have all been modernised. This indicates that the Chinese have been successful in introducing automated C^3 systems, which are replacing manual processes in headquarters, with consequent gains in efficiency.[12]

This initial success by Guangzhou MR in FTX at the divisional level may become an example for others to follow, thus providing some justification for the PLA to claim that the nature of training has changed from single arms to combined arms at platoon level and thence to FTX in a joint operational setting. On the basis of this achievement, the PLA can then tackle the training of higher formations at a later stage.

Whatever progress the Chinese can achieve in pursuing the strategic changes in defence modernisation will be facilitated by the transformation of field armies into group armies in the mid-1980s. Basically, it has been the introduction of management by objectives and control systems in the group armies, reforms in training and innovative modifications to the force structure that have been responsible for this successful transformation.[13] In efforts to improve peacetime war preparation, a certain group army in Nanjing MR introduced management by objectives and control systems.[14] Five new manuals on peacetime war-preparation were distributed to educate units in understanding fourteen concepts to improve the management of rosters, training, drills, personnel affairs, weapons and equipment and logistics. Various standard operational procedures for different situations at regiment level and above, down to platoon level were drawn up.[15] By these means, the group army from Nanjing MR was confident that it had improved its rapid response capabilities. There is no indication that all group armies have made the same progress as the aforementioned group army in Nanjing MR. Only when they have achieved this, can the Chinese justifiably claim that the group army reforms have played their full part in contributing to the strategic changes in defence modernisation.

Training and the New Force Development

In preparing group armies for training exercises in formations higher than divisional level, the PLA believes that there is a need to make military training adapt to the strategic changes in defence modernisation. Specifically, eight points have been identified as essential to this development:

1. Education and training should be recognised as strategically important in persuading units to change from their belief in the imminence of war, to pursuing peacetime war preparations.

2. The content of military training should be broadened, modernised and publicised in order to deter would-be aggressors and to encourage the exchange of ideas with foreign experts.

3. The direction of military training should be in keeping with the interests of the nation; in particular, China's role in the strategic balance should be its primary concern.

4. The mastery of technology, strategy and tactics on the one hand, and academic research and scientific and cultural pursuits on the other, should be encouraged.

5. Specialised elements should be strengthened to increase rapid response capabilities for future wars.

6. Training should focus on major issues arising from the new strategic outlook. Thus crack troops should be trained to deal with future limited wars.

7. There should be specific targets and good planning. The famous nuclear scientist, Qian Xuesen, predicted that the quality of officers by the year 2000 would reflect developments now planned for the officer corps. Thus general officers would hold doctoral degrees and field officers would have masters' degrees.

8. Military training should be seen as a means to promote professionalism in the defence force. The need to raise the standard of training vis-a-vis discipline, training objectives, careful supervision and leadership had been recognised as the means to ensure that the regular forces could improve their warfighting capabilities.[16]

As a result of the PCMC's decision to modify the force structure in 1985, the PLA has emphasised military training as the vehicle for improving the warfighting capabilities of the specialised elements (*tezhong bing* eg armour, artillery, engineers, ground force aviation). Yang Dezhi stressed the need to increase the proportion of specialised elements and to reduce the strength of the infantry in group armies after the reduction of one million troops in 1985–87. Thus military training becomes essential in order that the artillery can engage a wider variety of enemy targets rather than be confined to its traditional role of merely supporting the tank and infantry units. Similarly, engineer and chemical-defence units are expected to 'possess the means to directly annihilate the enemy'.[17] Yang Dezhi claimed that specialised elements constituted the core of the group armies. Whilst the infantry and the armour constituted the principal attack force, artillery, air defence and ground force aviation provided their main fire support. Similarly, the reconnaissance, signals, engineer, chemical-defence and electronic warfare platoons acted as combat multipliers, whilst the transport, maintenance, POL, medical, supply and ordnance platoons provided technical and logistic support. In sum, Yang Dezhi has claimed that these specialised elements have been responsible for strengthening the PLA's fire power, protection, striking power, mobility and rapid response capabilities.[18]

The introduction of training regiments and divisions (discussed in Chapter 1) was hailed by the PCMC in December 1986 as one of the major reforms in force structure which contributed to the improvement of warfighting capabilities of the recently formed group armies. Basically, these new units initiated the training of new recruits before they were posted to operational units according to the principle of training before posting (*xianxun houbu*). Two distinct advantages of this new system are that first, electronic, laser and computer technology could be introduced into the training program for suitably qualified recruits. Second, this system could facilitate the training of personnel for use by both the PLA and local government.[19] Basic formation training has also undergone revolutionary changes aimed at greater efficiency and economy. At the regimental level, training bases have been established for conducting 'uniform cyclical training'. This entails units being phased through a series of training activities designed *inter alia* to overcome the shortage of resources, accumulate more experience for later recruits, and foster better coordination amongst the five branches of formation training. (The five branches are military, political, cultural, physical education and moral education.[20]) In March 1986, a motorised regiment in Shenyang MR followed the new system which conducted training at the battalion level in two stages. The first stage, which would last for six months, concentrated on training battalions in the training base. The second stage from October would involve the whole regiment in integrated field training.[21]

To strengthen combined arms capabilities, an innovative form of training known as cross-training has been introduced in order to extend to individuals a knowledge and experience of other arms.

Thus the term *daizhi* (temporary posting to another speciality) has become popular since 1986 as the PLA had intensified its combined arms training. In a certain group army in Nanjing in 1986, a division despatched two batches of infantry company commanders to tank units to take up temporary appointments. It claimed that the quality of combined arms skills for these commanders was improved as a result. Similarly, temporary postings for the engineer, signals and chemical-defence platoons were arranged so that they could familiarise themselves with other arms.[22]

Since 1985 the formation of group armies has been well supported by improved modifications in force structure and innovative systems of military training. These strategic changes indubitably lead to improved warfighting capabilities which will better prepare China for future limited wars. Nevertheless, China's major strategic plan in war preparation has targeted the middle of the twenty-first century, which means that improvements in warfighting capabilities will need to be considered in the light of major breakthroughs in weapon and equipment design and in force development over the next six to seven decades.

PLA WARFIGHTING CAPABILITIES

When any military force introduces such radical changes to its structure and operating procedures, however, the equipment it employed up to then is often found to be inadequate for the changed circumstances. In this respect China is in no different a position than other nations have been at such a juncture. It now requires forces and weapon systems with greater mobility, increased ranges and fire power, better protection, and the logistic support to maintain these forces in sustained operations over long distances. It is against this background that the PLA's critical capabilities will now be considered.

Mobility

Despite the recent formation of group armies, a considerable proportion of the Main Forces (MF) is probably still composed largely of foot infantry (in 1984 the DIA estimated this category to cover 115 to 122 out of a total of 130 to 140 MF divisions).[23] The number of cargo and general service trucks in a standard infantry division has probably not increased much since 1976. Thus, although the relatively few mechanised group armies have quite a high degree of mobility,[24] and while some improvements have been made in recent years to the mobility of artillery and tank elements within infantry formations, most troops in the division — the infantry — still have to move on foot under normal circumstances. Making a virtue of necessity, the PLA infantry has developed a relatively good tactical mobility in terrain which is difficult for highly mechanised forces.[25]

Nevertheless, China has recognised the need to improve mobility, particularly in the ground forces, and measures are underway, on a modest scale, to meet this goal. The National Day Parade in Beijing in 1984 revealed new types of APC and SP artillery (see under Fire Support). The amphibious tracked YW534, also known as the H-1 APC, can carry more troops than the older Type 63, has eight firing ports and periscopes, and is also fitted with an NBC protective system.[26] The appearance of a 6 × 6 wheeled APC, similar in appearance to the French RV1 VAB,[27] indicates that China intends to equip the PLA with a mix of both tracked and wheeled APC. Although tracked vehicles have greater cross-country mobility, wheeled vehicles are cheaper to operate and have greater strategic mobility.

While large-scale increases to the ground forces' tracked and wheeled vehicle inventory have yet to occur, these developments and other agreements with foreign firms in recent years for the manufacture of vehicles for the PLA,[28] have probably started a trickle-flow that will pick up when the defence budget permits. It has already been possible to form mechanised infantry formations in recent years within some otherwise foot-infantry divisions, and in a few cases, largely mechanised group armies. There are few overt indications, however, that this upgrading has occurred on a significant scale. The current low levels of motorisation and mechanisation in the PLA reflect China's very limited overall vehicle production, although a major increase is planned.[29]

Increased motorisation and mechanisation will not, in themselves, solve the ground forces' strategic mobility problems. The limited road and rail networks that serve China's vast territory, and the lack of long-range transport aircraft will continue to constrain the PLA's ability to move large forces quickly over long distances.

The mobility of the Navy and Air Force also needs to be taken into account. The former is by definition a mobile force, but faces limitations due to the small number of sea-going replenishment ships (see Section B, Appendix 2). The Air Force cannot make rapid, long-range deployments of forces, but as it possesses medium range transport aircraft (including helicopters), it does have the capability for rapid, short-range deployments.[30] The Air Force practises such deployments regularly, presumably transporting the necessary administrative and logistic elements by MRT while command personnel and aircrew ferry the combat aircraft to the new base. In 1985 the Air Force's unit mobility was reported to have improved considerably.[31] Despite the lack of LRT aircraft, it is feasible that Air Force units could undertake strategic deployments by stages, although requiring more time to complete these movements than would otherwise be necessary.

Armour and Anti-Armour

If pitched against an adversary lavishly equipped with highly mobile, hard-hitting armoured forces and mechanised infantry, such as the USSR, the PLA's armour and anti-armour capabilities will be critical to its survival. In both areas the PLA has much ground to make up. Soviet AFVs are more numerous, better armed and protected than Chinese. The known ranges of anti-tank grenade and rocket launchers in Chinese infantry regiments, for example, are less than 650m, and much reliance is still placed on howitzers and anti-tank guns operated by the artillery.[32] China has claimed some improvements in range, armour-piercing ability and mobility of its tanks and guns, as well as the introduction of an 'advanced anti-tank rocket launcher with a higher penetration than the 40mm grenade launcher'.[33] The latter weapon still appears, however, to be the mainstay of the infantry's anti-armour inventory.

The eventual widespread issue of the Red Arrow (HJ-73) ATGM (Chinese SAGGER) however, should increase the anti-armour capability, particularly in terms of range (about 3000m). While the Chinese claim to have improved the missiles of this weapon system,[34] there have been persistent rumours of inadequacies, however, and even if they can be overcome, the system nevertheless belongs to the first generation of ATGM, and has been superseded long since in the Soviet armed forces. China cannot hope to close this gap in capabilities by its own R and D and reverse engineering. A limited step forward will be the purchase of eight French Gazelle helicopters fitted with HOT ATGM. These will be delivered in mid-1988.[35] Protracted negotiations have also been in hand for acquisition of another state-of-the-art system, the US TOW-II ATGM. Meanwhile, although innovative mine laying techniques offer the PLA some hope for delaying the advancing tide of Soviet armour, the absence of effective anti-armour ground attack aircraft remains a major capability gap.[36]

Up to about 1986 the PLA's armoured forces were small compared to the infantry. There were only about 11 500 tanks of various types in the ground forces,[37] including those in the Local Forces, training units and, probably to an increasing extent in recent years, the Reserve Forces.[38] Many Main Force infantry divisions were estimated to possess an organic tank regiment of about 80 tanks each, and an additional 36–45 regiments were contained in the estimated twelve to fifteen tank divisions.[39]

The formation of group armies since 1985 seems to require, however, an increase in organic AFV and APC strength. Under current economic constraints, a substantial increase in production is unlikely, and the expansion of the armoured forces reported in the Chinese media is most probably still on a modest scale. Either the new group armies will have to remain under-strength in AFVs and APCs for a considerable period, or they could be re-allocated the tank and mechanised elements (infantry, artillery, logistic etc.) from most of the tank divisions. The latter course, although entailing a reduction in the number of tank divisions, would go some way towards achieving the more balanced force structure the PLA is striving to achieve. It could also enable the release of some tanks to the Reserve Forces.[40] Whether or not this has occurred, in 1987 some tank divisions were reported to have been augmented by a tank brigade of two tank regiments. This could raise the number of tanks in a tank division to about 410, as opposed to the previous inventory of about 250,[41] thus going some way towards matching the combat power of Soviet tank divisions.

In general, however, Chinese tank units suffer from an imbalance in capabilities considered essential for success against a modern enemy. Although a range of new AFVs and equipment has appeared since 1984 in small but growing numbers, there are still insufficient supporting SP artillery and mechanised infantry units and AD systems capable of dealing with modern, high-speed, heavily armed ground attack aircraft such as the Soviet heavy strike FENCER, and the HIND armed helicopter.[42] While there have been recent improvements to protection, target acquisition, fire control and main gun systems of many Chinese MBT, it is doubtful that they could match their Soviet counterparts. Despite these weaknesses, during the 1980s the PLA's tank units, due to their growing association with other arms, have been better placed to develop a combined arms capability. They have frequently taken part in such training in recent years, as well as in other types of exercises. While weaknesses in coordination between tank units and other arms still seem to exist, considerable improvements have probably been achieved, particularly in armour-artillery-infantry cooperation. The training of tank crews has also been improved by means such as the use of simulators and instruction in computer science.[43] By 1984 the Chinese had recognised the ineffectiveness of one of their traditional practices: tanks and infantry advancing together en masse along the same axis. To enhance the use of the tanks' firepower and mobility, the tactics followed in modern armies of tanks and infantry moving on separate but coordinated axes seems likely to be followed in future. In addition, by mid-1987 the Chinese media indicated that the PLA had embarked on a large-scale revision and development of its armour doctrine and tactics.[44]

Nevertheless, for the foreseeable future, it seems inevitable that China's armour and anti-armour capabilities will lag behind those of the USSR, despite product improvements and the occasional newly-designed equipment. While a new MBT seems to be under development (one 'similar to the British Challenger' has been reported),[45] it remains to be seen whether it can match the state-of-the-art attained by modern Soviet tanks.

Fire support for the land battle — conventional artillery

Ground force formations are relatively liberally provided with a variety of artillery types, from heavy mortars to close support and heavy, long-range guns. While some systems are very effective,[46] close support artillery organic to most divisions, based mainly on the Type 54 122mm howitzer, has tended to have ranges limited to no more than 12 000m,[47] which is less than the capability of Soviet and most Western divisions. Above divisional level, artillery is both heavier in calibre and longer in range;[48] but as in the case of divisional level artillery, the bulk of Chinese non-divisional artillery is generally less mobile and less capable in terms of range and hitting power than Soviet artillery systems.[49]

Since about 1983–84, however, the development of new weapon systems and changes in organisation have laid the basis for a general upgrading of the PLA's conventional artillery capability. The formation of combined arms group armies may well have entailed the re-allocation of artillery, particularly heavy, long-range artillery, from some previously independent artillery formations to the new army-level formations, thus providing additional assets, including heavier artillery, in direct support of the commanders of major combined arms formations. At the same time, the ranges and mobility of artillery units seem to have been enhanced by limited re-equipment programs, incuding heavy towed and self-propelled (SP) systems.[50]

Current artillery organisations are unclear, but it is likely that the bulk of mobile artillery has been re-allocated to divisional-level and army-level units, with few, if any, independent main force artillery formations remaining. Such a reallocation could provide combined arms divisions with close support artillery encompassing weapon systems with ranges up to 17 200m,[51] while those possessing longer range could be allocated to army-level units. Such changes would not conflict with the PLA's practice of forming temporary tactical groups of organic and non-divisional artillery resources when required to fulfil specific tasks.[52] Some reports indicate that guided missiles as well as large calibre artillery have been issued to at least one group army, while improvements have also been made to artillery ammunition.[53]

These developments could exacerbate the PLA's artillery command and control problems by complicating the tasks of fire planning and coordination. Awareness of this is indicated by reports that PLA artillery units are developing ADP applications in these areas.[54] The PLA has long followed the principle of working out careful, detailed fire plans at the highest practical level, and then decentralising control to lower levels of command. Until recently at least, artillery communications have been described as only 'adequate', and radio links have seldom been established with the units being supported.[55] The development of ADP fire planning and control systems suggests that artillery support will become better coordinated with the operations of other units, and more responsive to quickly changing requirements during combat. Occasional reports from Chinese sources tend to support this optimistic outlook,[56] but it is not possible to estimate how far the PLA artillery has yet to go in this process. Equipment costs and the scale of provision required, however, would suggest only gradual progress is likely.

Tactical nuclear and chemical fire support

Although there is no convincing evidence that China has developed either a doctrine for the use of tactical nuclear weapons or the weapons themselves, including atomic demolition munitions, there are indications that China may develop tactical nuclear delivery systems.[57] China has successfully tested nuclear devices with yields under 20kt,[58] including those with yields suitable for tactical employment. China may consider, therefore, that its strategic nuclear deterrent force no longer provides an adequately flexible response to the growing Soviet arsenal of nuclear weapon systems, and that a complementary tactical nuclear capability is required.

Opinions on this subject appear to vary. In 1984 the US Defence Intelligence Agency assessed that while China had the capability to produce tactical nuclear weapons, it had not done so. Future Chinese tactical nuclear weapons may be developed in the form of either short-range missiles or airborne bombs. NATO experience indicates that 60 per cent of its short-range tactical nuclear weapons have a range of under 30 kilometres and most of them have a range under 15 kilometres. In the Chinese context, tactical nuclear weapons would be useful in Chinese territory against an invading enemy at or near the frontier.

The shorter range, lower-yield strategic missile systems are unlikely to be used in tactical situations. China's strategic missile force has a vital deterrent role,[59] and any diversion of part of its capability would presumably detract from its deterrent value. This view may be valid, but some authorities have suggested otherwise. In 1986 a study sponsored by the Stockholm International Peace Research Institute (SIPRI), for example, concluded that it was possible that many of China's shorter-range (nuclear ballistic missile) systems were available or intended for tactical battlefield use. Field exercises that simulated the use of tactical nuclear weapons suggested, moreover, that China had the ability to produce weapons exclusively for this purpose.[60] Support for the SIPRI suggestion concerning a tactical role for some of China's nuclear missile systems could be inferred from Chinese statements in 1984 and 1985. These statements may indicate that the DF-2 no longer has a strategic nuclear status. (This point is discussed further in the section on Strategic Nuclear Forces.) Indeed, if Soviet and US practice were to be followed, neither the DF-2 nor the DF-3 would be categorised as strategic systems. The assumption that they now have a tactical role, however, does not have a strong basis. Their estimated performance characteristics are shown in Table 2.1.

These characteristics, even if the lower figures are more accurate, seem unsuited to tactical use, where shorter ranges and smaller areas of destruction are desirable. If Soviet and US practice is a reliable guide, the DF-2 and DF-3 systems should be regarded as Longer Range Intermediate-Range Nuclear Force (LRINF) missiles, such as

Table 2.1:   Chinese longer range intermediate-range nuclear force missiles

System	Range (kilometres)	Yield
DF-2	1200–1800	15 kt
DF-3	3000–5000	1–3 mt

Sources: Yields are taken from *Handbook 1984*, p.A-44, although SIPRI shows the yield for the DF-2 as 20kt: see *SIPRI Yearbook 1986*, p.104. Ranges shown here reflect the differences between the DIA *Handbook 1984* and higher figures quoted in the official Chinese media: see *JDW*, 8 December 1984, p.1016

the Soviet SS-4 and SS-20, and the US PERSHING II and GLCM systems. LRINF systems have a theatre attack, not a tactical role.[61] Tactical nuclear missiles are more likely to have much shorter ranges and smaller yields.[62]

China's DF-2 and DF-3 missile systems thus seem unsuitable for the support of division or army level tactical operations. They are more likely to be assigned to theatre-level operations as LRINF resources to further the achievement of strategic aims. This still leaves open the question of whether China has *other* weapons that provide a tactical nuclear capability.[63] There is, in fact, an absence of sustainable references by Chinese or other sources that identify tactical nuclear weapons. On balance, therefore, it can be concluded that China does not yet have true tactical nuclear weapons, nor forces dedicated to the tactical nuclear role. Nevertheless, China has the ability to produce such weapons, and can be expected eventually to develop suitable delivery systems,[64] perhaps with some foreign assistance. For example, there have been reports of secret cooperation between the PRC and Israel, and at least one report alleging that Israel was supplying technology to help China build modern missiles and guidance systems.[65]

China is sensitive about its chemical warfare (CW) capability. The Chinese media does not mention any offensive use, but stresses defensive aspects. The PLA's CW units are termed chemical defence (*fanghua*) troops. They are organic to most formations, often down to regimental-level. Chemical defence units conduct reconnaissance of radioactive and chemically contaminated areas, and are equipped with a range of decontamination equipment, mostly of dated Soviet design.[66] They also conduct development of equipment and techniques for chemical and nuclear defence.[67]

Nevertheless, CW technology is widely available, and there is a general belief that the PLA not only has a basic offensive CW capability, but is intent on developing it in order to counter the formidable Soviet CW capability should the need arise. This process may involve discreet assistance from other nations such as Israel.[68] In 1984, the US Defence Intelligence Agency obviously believed that China had chemical munitions for use by its SSM, MRL and artillery of or above 122mm calibre, and that both persistent and non-persistent agents were available.[69]

Offensive air support

Chinese aerial platforms can support ground forces by attacking with conventional bombs, napalm, cannon, rockets or chemical warheads.[70] The PLA's capability in this area, however, has lagged behind that of Western and Soviet forces. Measures to improve it are believed to be in hand.

Although several types of aircraft are equipped for the tactical strike role, and speeds and weapon loads are reasonable,[71] due to a lack of suitable radar, Chinese pilots have had a limited ability to find their targets. They have required at least four kilometres visibility to identify ground targets visually,[72] usually on the first pass, before returning to strike. Such an attack would be extremely hazardous in the face of an enemy well equipped with modern, ground-based air defence (AD) weapon systems.[73] While air force liaison officers and forward air controllers are probably deployed with ground force divisions to coordinate air support missions, the Chinese are not believed to be able to achieve close coordination between air force and ground force units.[74] This suggests that they lack the necessary ground-to-air communications and procedures. This would preclude effective direction from the ground and thus the ability of pilots to adjust to the changing situation on the ground. Ground attack missions against targets close to the forward line of own troops (FLOT) would, therefore, probably be avoided.

The Chinese are well aware of this deficiency and are no doubt taking steps to correct it. A GEC avionics update package for the F-7 (FISHBED) fighter, including VHF/UHF communications and a head-up display and weapon aiming computer (HUDWAC), has already been acquired.[75] A similar deal for the F-8 (FINBACK) was approved by the US Congress early in 1986. These aircraft are, of course, primarily AD interceptors (the F-7 has a secondary ground attack role), and as such are classified as defensive equipments. While the US is reluctant to provide China with purely offensive weapons, such as air-to-ground guided missiles,[76] it remains to be seen what use can be derived from technology already supplied to enable China to develop a close air support (CAIRS) capability in the Western sense. Since the beginning of 1986, the Air Force has focused its tactical training on exercises involving ground forces, suggesting that battlefield interdiction and perhaps CAIRS techniques are being practised extensively. On the other hand, the Chinese may not perceive the lack of a true CAIRS capability to be a critical shortcoming. If the military theory of 1983 still reflects current thinking, the Chinese perceive the major role of offensive air support to be focused beyond the immediate battlefield. This theory recognises the advantages that modern technology has bestowed upon strike aircraft attacking ground targets: 'If (our ground forces) can hear them, then it is too late (to intercept them)'. Combat air patrols on call over the battlefield are a thing of the past. Interception must take place at the furthest possible range. The destruction of enemy theatre missile sites, logistic installations, follow-on forces and approach routes etc., and the support of guerrilla units operating in the enemy's rear areas can have a more profound effect on the outcome of the battle than the destruction of a few tanks on the battlefield. The increasing emphasis on low-level flying since 1982, and on tactical support to ground forces during 1985–86, may reflect a development of the Air Force's battlefield interdiction capability rather than its CAIRS capability.[77] China has also identified Soviet armed helicopters as a major potential threat to its ground forces. Acquisition of such helicopters would add to the PLA's own ground attack capability. China has Soviet designed and US-manufactured helicopters which are capable of being converted to this role. The recently announced intention to establish an air arm in the ground forces may encompass this role, as well as reconnassiance and battlefield mobility.[78]

In the meantime, most ground attack missions would probably be pre-planned against known, located targets, or mounted against opportunity targets well forward of the Chinese FLOT. Such battlefield interdiction missions are probably the most effective operations Chinese air forces could conduct in the offensive air support role, although their survival would be dubious when opposed by extensive modern AD systems such as those possessed by the Soviet armed forces.

Air defence (ground-based)

Until recently the bulk of the PLA's combat units have lacked a modern AD capability. They have relied mainly on the divisional and army level resources of heavy AA machine guns (HAAMG) with a tactical range of 1400m, and light AAA guns (37mm and 57mm) with tactical AA ranges from 2500 to 6000m. These weapon systems are all optically controlled, although the 57mm AA gun can be used with various forms of radar and other controls.[79] Apart from these resources, forward units have had to fall back on the use of their own small arms, and passive measures such as operating by night and emphasising concealment.

Groundforce AAA divisions, which are equipped with heavier weapons, have probably been broken up and their radar controlled resources allocated to the new group armies.[80] The protection of airfields, industrial areas and other strategic targets is the responsibility of the Air Force's fixed-site SAM and AAA units while that of naval installations is the responsibility of the Navy's AA units.[81] Major deficiencies in the PLA's ground-based AD capability need to be addressed. Of prime importance is the need for mobile SAM and AAA systems with accurate target recognition, fire control systems and sensors to provide effective protection in the very low and low altitude AD envelopes over the battlefield; and more capable SAM with an expanded AD envelope to defend strategic lines of communication, airfields etc. Available information suggests that while some indigenous developments are taking place (eg a shoulder-held SAM and heavier SAM systems — see below) they have probably not yet been deployed to operational units on a wide scale. At the same time, China's interest in acquiring the HAWK SAM from the US seems to remain in the negotiation stage, although the US has approved in principle the sale of improved HAWK SAM and AN/TPS-43 and 63 tactical and surveillance AD radars.[82]

In 1984 Yang Shangkun cited air defence as one of the four major aspects of the PLA's capabilities that needed to be improved,[83] and since about that time some measures to improve ground-based systems have been noted. A shoulder-held SAM, the HN-5, similar in appearance to the Soviet SA-7, has been offered for sale overseas, and presumably is being provided to the PLA.[84] Details of the performance and deployment of this Chinese-made weapon are unclear,[85] but it is likely that combat units in group armies are in the process of being issued with this badly needed equipment.

Other new and heavier SAM systems China is reported to have developed include the Hongqi-61 and the HQ-2J. The former is claimed to be capable of producing a 'dense network of fire', and is apparently produced in two versions: one for mobile ground operatons, and the other for fitting to warships.[86] The HQ-2J SAM is reported to have a two-stage missile, with a warhead that produces multiple fragments over a wide area, and an all-weather capability. It may not have tactical mobility, but it can also be employed to attack surface targets.[87]

While it is possible that the Hongqi-61 is being deployed with group armies, a new self-propelled AAA system, the Type 80 twin 57mm,[88] is almost certain to be. Apart from improved mobility, however, its effectiveness appears to be little better than the outdated towed systems that it will presumably replace.[89] Some 23mm AA guns, based on the Soviet ZU-23 series, are believed to exist, but little information on them has been released.[90]

Urban militia light AAA units have been in existence for many years to provide point protection for factories and key points, supplementing Air Force heavy AAA and SAM resources. Since 1984 considerable attention has been paid to forming Reserve Force AA units, including AAA divisions in the ground forces, Navy and Air Force. These seem to be composed mainly of ex-servicemen 'specialists' with probably a cadre of regular command personnel. Reports on these units also indicate an intention to integrate them with Regular PLA formations.[91] If the development of Reserve Force AD units is being counter-balanced by a corresponding reduction in Regular units, an overall decrease in effectiveness can be expected. It would be surprising, however, if such a development were to extend to first-line Main Force formations, as the Chinese consider air defence to be one of the major components of their ability to conduct combined-arms operations.[92]

In the area of static air defence, the PLA Air Force has been making considerable efforts to improve the capability of its SAM forces. The educational levels of officers and enlistees have been raised, and command and technical training improved. As a result, it has been possible to upgrade old equipments through technical modifications, and the number of units achieving A Grade status in operational capabilities has increased by 'several times'. PLA Air Force SAM units have trained an increasing number of SAM personnel for other Services, and the PLA's first SAM technical training centre has recently been established in North China under Air Force auspices. The opening of this institution is intended to lead to increased efficiency and a sharp reduction in recruit training time to seven months. By mid 1985 the Air Force's SAM units had expanded into divisional-level formations, indicating a rationalisation of command and control arrangements, or perhaps even a strengthening of existing AD networks.[93] By 1987 indigenous R & D had improved the speed and accuracy of the SAM units' target acquisition and fire control systems, which the Chinese claim has greatly raised the combat effectiveness of their SAM force.[94]

China's development of RPV also reflects efforts to improve AD capabilities. At least four models can be used as target drones or simulated targets. Their manoeuvrability and generally high speeds help increase the realism and effectiveness of ground-based AD training.[95]

The extent to which these developments can improve the PLA's ground-based AD capabilities remains to be seen. Major factors will be China's success in producing or acquiring the necessary advanced target acquisition and fire control equipment, and the ability to coordinate the various ground-based systems with aerial systems in integrated AD networks.

Combat and logistic support (ground forces)

For an account of engineer capabilities and supply, transport, ordnance, recovery, repair and medical services, see Appendix 2, Section A.

SPECIALISED OPERATIONS

In recent years the PLA has paid increasing attention to some forms of specialised warfare that complement and enhance its ability to conduct combined arms and joint operations.

Amphibious warfare

From the time of the Dachen Islands campaign in 1954–55 to the 1970s, the PLA's development of an amphibious warfare capability was greatly constrained by the low priority given to naval development generally, and by the US commitment to defend Taiwan against a Chinese invasion dating back to 1950.[96]

Nevertheless, an invigoration of the PLA's amphibious force materialised in the late 1970s with new construction programs, including new classes of LSM, LST and air-cushion landing vehicles.[97] According to a 1981 report, a new 'landing-ship brigade' had been formed in the South Sea Fleet, and it seems that most of the new vessels have been allocated to that fleet.[98] Amphibious warfare exercises conducted since 1980 reflect the growing complexity of the PLA's capability in this form of warfare (see Table 1.5). The formation in the early 1980s of the new Marine Force indicates the development of specialist amphibious warfare units equipped with artillery, ATGM, amphibious tanks and APCs, supported by paratroop, engineer and maintenance units. This development also reflects the extent of the change in China's strategic policies. In 1982 *Jiefangjun Bao* listed some of the marines' major equipment, and identified their tasks as being to:

1. Attack islands and conduct landings in conjunction with naval operations.

2. Seize and secure forward bases for the Navy.

3. Study and develop techniques, tactics and equipment for use in amphibious warfare.

Additional tasks have been revealed: countering enemy amphibious landings, and conducting deep reconnaissance and raiding missions. In its role and composition the PLA's Marine Force seems to be developing along the lines of the US Marine Corps towards becoming a self-contained fighting force.[99]

The PLA Navy is estimated to have between 505–613 amphibious warfare vessels of various types. In addition there are a number of high-speed air-cushion vehicles,[100] as well as various types of light amphibious craft operated by the ground forces. China showed keen interest in the Falklands conflict of 1982, and could be expected to follow the British example, in appropriate circumstances, of supplementing its amphibious lift with merchant shipping as well as motorised junks.

In 1984 the US Defence Intelligence Agency estimated that the PLA could conduct an amphibious operation requiring less than 30 hours transit, involving three infantry divisions, their organic armour, artillery and those personnel and equipment required during the assault phase of the operation: altogether a force of over 30 000 troops.[101] The International Institute of Strategic Studies believes that forces available to take part in amphibious operations include nine marine regiments and three ground force divisions. Parachute or helicopter-borne assaults onto or near the beachheads may also be conducted in conjunction with such operations. This tactic seems to have been practised, or at least simulated, during the amphibious exercise in the Xisha Islands in 1984 (see Table 1.5) and in other training in 1986.[102]

The Navy now has surface combatants capable of providing escorts to protect an amphibious force against enemy surface attack and to provide naval gunfire support. Weaknesses in air defence and Anti-Submarine Warfare (ASW), although gradually being addressed, would render the force vulnerable when facing a modern, well equipped adversary. Except for small-scale, surprise raids against lightly-held objectives, the PLA's lack of ship-borne combat aircraft would limit the Chinese to conducting amphibious operations within the combat radius of shore-based bombers and fighter aircraft. Thus, as the PLA currently does not possess an air-to-air refuelling capability, large-scale amphibious assaults beyond about 500nm from air bases, such as out to the Spratly Islands, are highly unlikely.[103]

The possibility of China mounting a successful invasion of Taiwan has been much debated. Major doubts centre on the PRC's ability to achieve air superiority, and on whether the size of its amphibious lift would be sufficient to land a force with the capability to seize and exploit the necessary beachheads. Most observers consider that, even if preceded by a blockade of the island, the PLA has not yet developed a force of sufficient capabilities to ensure success without suffering unacceptable high losses in personnel and equipment. (See Chapter 6 for a naval blockade scenario.)

Airborne operations

Forerunners of the PLA's Airborne Forces took part in the Korean War during the early 1950s.[104] Since that era, they expanded from regiment-size units until, by the mid-1970s, three divisions were believed to exist.[105] Stationed near Wuhan in central China, they form part of the PLA's strategic reserves. The identification of the commander of these forces (see below) suggests that they are grouped in an army-level formation, although this structure may have been modified under the reorganisatin of field armies that began in 1985. The Airborne Forces are subordinate to the Air Force, but can be expected to be allocated to ground force commanders during operations. They are capable of conducting parachute, air-transportable and helicopter-borne operations. They can be expected to be deployed against objectives such as enemy headquarters, rear area installations, and nuclear weapons launching sites; to seize key terrain, bridges etc. to facilitate the rapid movement of ground forces; to conduct sabotage missions and to support guerrillas.[106]

The Air Force's transport capability is probably insufficient to move all these forces in one lift, and could probably only support one to two regiments in combat operations. The range of action would be limited to the operating radius of the most numerous type of aircraft. This appears to be the An-26, which has an operating radius of approximately 600nm. Helicopter-borne operations are believed to be severely limited due to a shortage of helicopters. With the acquisition of Western helicopters, however, it is possible that this capability will improve. China's new Zhi-8 multi-purpose helicopter, if produced in sufficient numbers, should help in this regard.[107]

Airborne units are more lightly equipped than infantry units. They have only limited artillery, anti-tank and AA weapons, although the HJ-73 ATGM has been reported in service with some airborne units, and the HN-5 shoulder-fired SAM is also likely to be issued. While in the past heavy weapons and equipment have had to be air-landed, occasional references in recent years to 'heavy weapons' being parachute delivered may indicate the development of a heavy drop capability.[108]

Apart from taking part in internal security operations during the Cultural Revolution, the Airborne Forces' operational experience since the Korean War seems to have been very limited. During the 1980s, however, they have figured prominently in reports on training. They have participated in a number of exercises, including the huge joint exercise at Zhangjiakou in 1981, and in 1983, the largest airborne exercise China had held to date (see Table 1.5). Under the leadership of their youthful commander, Li Lianghui, training seems to have been revitalised, and improved by the adoption of new techniques, such as computer technology. The task of training has been largely removed from the shoulders of sub-unit personnel, and assumed by a group of specially qualified instructors. Unit commanders have been encouraged to contribute their ideas on the development of airborne warfare, and a Paratroop Research Institute has been founded.[109] In 1985 it was reported that as part of a Sino–Italian military cooperation agreement, Chinese airborne units might receive special training at the Italian School of Military Parachuting at Leghorn, and an exchange of military personnel might be arranged.[110]

Areas that still require improvement include airborne lift and heavy drop capabilities. In particular, Chinese airborne forces would be highly vulnerable to a well-equipped enemy without a considerable improvement in the Air Force's ability to suppress enemy ground based AD systems, and to achieve air superiority over the approach routes and drop zones.

Table 2.2: Chinese land-based nuclear missile systems

System	Type	Approx. range	Probable payload	Approx. quantity	Targetable areas
DF-2/CSS-1	MRBM	1800km	15–20kt	50	Peripheral nations; eastern USSR; some US bases in Far East.
DF-3/CSS-2	IRBM	5500km	1–3mt	60	Central and eastern Asia.
DF-4/CSS-3	ICBM	10 000km	1–3mt	4–6	Asia; parts of Middle East and European USSR; the Marianas; Álaska and northern Australia (but not the continental US).
DF-5/CSS-4	ICBM	15 000km	4–5mt	2–4	Any target in USSR, Europe, the US and Australia.

Sources: *The Military Balance 1985–86*, p.113; RMRB quoted in *JDW*, 8 December 1984, p.1016; DIA Handbook 1984, p.A-44; *FEER*, 24 April 1986, p.14; *Foreign Report*, 22 August 1985, pp 7–8; N. Lee, *The Chinese People's Liberation Army*, 1980–82, pp.14–15; R.W. Fieldhouse, 'Chinese Nuclear Weapons: an Overview', *SIPRI Yearbook 1986*, pp.106–107.

STRATEGIC NUCLEAR FORCES

China's strategic nuclear forces consist mainly of land-based ballistic missile systems, and the beginnings of a submarine-launched ballistic missile (SLBM) force. The use of aircraft to deliver strategic nuclear weapons, given the current state of Chinese technology in this field, is unlikely except against an enemy with weak air defence capabilities.

Since the first successful nuclear SSM test in 1966, China has developed four operational land-based nuclear SSM systems,[111] only two of which are classified as ICBM. The other two systems, the DF-2 (termed in the West the CSS-1) and the DF-3 (CSS-2), having much shorter ranges, are classified as MRBM and IRBM respectively. The land-based nuclear force has, for many years, been known as the Second Artillery. China claims it has steadily developed towards becoming a force self-sufficient in both offensive and defensive capabilities, in logistic support, scientific research and engineering.[112]

Estimates of the ranges and quantities of missiles shown in Table 2.2 have increased considerably over the last ten years or so, reflecting both the growth of the force and an increase in open-source information concerning it. The ranges, which represent the highest quoted by the various sources listed, may be underestimated in respect to the ICBM. The Second Artillery claims to have 'renovated' and improved its weapons, and in late 1985 it conducted a series of range extending tests. According to a senior PLA officer, one result was an increase in the range and mobility of an 'improved strategic nuclear missile'. The photograph released with this announcement in the Chinese media appeared to be of a modified DF-4/CSS-3 ICBM.[113]

In 1984 the US Defence Intelligence Agency estimated China to have between 225 and 300 nuclear warheads. These, of course, include warheads that can be delivered by all ballistic missiles, some of which are MIRV capable SLBM,[114] and by conventional bomber aircraft, as well as reserve stocks.

China's development of a ballistic missile submarine (SSBN) had its genesis in the torpedo-armed HAN nuclear attack submarine (SSN) construction program, which began in the mid- to late 1960s.[115] This provided the basis of the hull and propulsion systems required in the subsequent XIA SSBN program. Both classes are constructed at the Huludao shipyard in north China, with SLBM trials conducted at the Jinxi Missile Test and Development Range and from the North Sea Fleet base at Lushun.[116] Problems with the nuclear reactor and heat exchanger are reported to have delayed development,[117] and testing during the Cultural Revolution was disrupted due to faction fighting within the ministry responsible for missile research and development.[118] The HAN SSN reached initial operational capability (IOC) in 1974,[119] but the SLBM program, using the Golf SSB as a test bed, has dragged on, suggesting that technical problems still persist.[120] Although the first successful submarine-launched test of the SLBM was conducted in 1982, most sources believe it was conducted from the non-nuclear Golf test bed submarine.[121] The first XIA SSBN was reported to have entered service in 1985,[122] which may mean it was fully operational, complete with SLBM. By 1986, some sources believed that two XIA SSBN were operational, with possibly one or two more under construction.[123] The true capability of the XIA, however, has yet to be proved.

The probable payload of the CSS-N-3 SLBM is 500–1000 kt.[124] Most sources consider that the XIA class has twelve missile tubes, although some reports refer to fourteen or sixteen tubes, and in 1984 the US Defence Intelligence Agency stated that the boat 'can carry 16 SLBM in sea trials'.[125] The range of the missile is uncertain.

The first submarine-launched test in 1982 was not fired to the missile's full range. Estimates of its full range vary from 2000 to 2700km.[126] Such ranges would largely limit the XIA class to a regional role. Their mobility theoretically gives these SSBN the potential to deploy to distant areas of operation (AO), thus offering a wide choice of targets. In practical terms, however, their need for deep water in wartime operations, and the relatively short range of their original SLBM, would limit their usefulness (assuming the enemy to be the USSR and the SRV) to the Yellow Sea, Northwest Pacific, and the South China Sea. Moreover, the PLA Navy's current technological weaknesses in submarine warfare (see later section) and lack of experience in nuclear submarine operations would render these nuclear submarines vulnerable to modern ASW systems. It may be some time, therefore, before the XIA SSBN and the HAN SSN can be used to their full potential. In the meantime, apart from peacetime training missions, they are more likely to operate within 'bastions' such as the Bohai Gulf, protected by the Navy's extensive coastal defence forces and land-based aircraft.

A new SLBM or improved version of the CSS-N-3 seems, however, to be under development. A new type was first indicated in 1984. In late 1985 the PLA newspaper reported the successful underwater launch of an SLBM. This was followed in early 1986 by the reported successful range-extending test of an 'underwater-launched guided missile', which also increased the target areas, the number of targets it could hit, and the flexibility of the system.[127] It remains to be seen to what extent, if any, the new missile extends the AO and war fighting capability of the SLBM component, but it could be a MIRV-capable missile.

The allocation of China's current inventory of conventional bomber aircraft, such as the Il-28 BEAGLE and Tu-16 BADGER, to a nuclear delivery role seems highly unlikely. Lacking sufficient performance and ECM capabilities, they would not survive long when opposed by modern, multi-layered AD networks such as the USSR possesses. According to some reports, however, China is developing a modified BADGER with a supersonic dash capability, possibly by fitting Spey Turbofan engines.[128] If true, these reports may indicate that China intends using these aircraft in a nuclear delivery role, such as a sudden, surprise mission against targets just over its border with the Soviet Far Eastern Provinces. A stand-off nuclear weapon system would enhance the aircrafts' survivability. China has already developed a similar, non-nuclear weapon for the anti-shipping role (see section on the Navy), and the development of a nuclear cruise ASM could also be contemplated.

The survivability of the bulk of China's nuclear forces, the land-based systems, presents less of a problem. The DF-2 and DF-3 systems appear to have good off-road mobility, and practise sudden deployments to alternative launch sites, sometimes over long distances. The use of hardened underground bases or silos for ICBM systems, and concealment in rugged terrain, should encumber enemy reconnaissance and limit his ability to strike at launch sites.[129] Not satisfied with previous standards, in 1984 the Second Artillery began to implement a plan to improve its survivability and readiness under conditions of both nuclear and conventional warfare. Under this plan, camouflage, security and training in underground bases were to be improved; the rapid reaction capability of the higher command structure and the standard of command and control generally were to be raised.[130]

Until 1984 the organisation of China's strategic nuclear forces was fairly clear. The Second Artillery controlled all land-based nuclear missile systems. Its highest level of command was a directorate of the General Staff Department equal in status to the Navy and the Air Force. The SSBN had not yet achieved IOC, and its development was presumably controlled by the Navy.

In mid-1984 the picture became cloudy. The PLA's assistant Chief of Staff, Han Huaizhi, announced that the PLA had formed a strategic missile force, inferring that some change to the force composition, command structure, or both had occurred. Coupled with this announcement was a reference to the strengthening of the three Services' ability to conduct 'coordinated operations'.[131] Subsequent reports also linked the DF-4/CSS-3, DF-3/CSS-2 and possibly the DF-2/CSS-1 to the new Strategic Missile Force, which still seems to be called the Second Artillery.[132] From reports such as these it is difficult to determine what is new about the force. Based on capabilities, it is possible that the DF-2/CSS-1 component now has a non-strategic status, but corroboration for this theory is lacking. Although there is an absence of reports directly linking the Navy's SSBN component to the Strategic Missile Force, reference to the strengthening of a joint service capability in this area could indicate that the SSBN component is now controlled by the new force.

Whether or not the force composition has been changed, there remains the possibility of alterations to the command structure. Given the laudatory tenor of Chinese announcements since 1984, the status of the force could well have risen in the military hierarchy. These announcements have reflected the upgrading of the force's personnel standards, technical and war-fighting abilities, including the achievement of a second-strike capability. For example, improvements to the ranges and mobility of missiles already mentioned have been accompanied by a steady rise in the educational standards of the Force's officer corps — possibly the best qualified in the PLA — and the Chinese press has confidently claimed that the force has developed a second-strike capability.[133] An assured second-strike capability would have particularly far-reaching implications for China's strategic posture. Having been problematical in the past, it would raise the Second Artillery's role from that of minimum deterrence to what might be termed flexible deterrence.[134] The addition of an SLBM capability will add to the deterrent value. Its effect would be maximised by close coordination between the land-based, maritime and long-range aviation (if any) nuclear components. The creation of a force that encompassed all such resources could, therefore, be envisaged. The controlling element of such a joint force could be responsible directly to the Central Military Commission.

Although this scenario is speculative, it could explain the new status of the 'Strategic Nuclear Force' indicated in Chinese statements. The timing of the announcement concerning the force's existence in 1984, could have indicated those adjustments to the higher command structure necessary in anticipation of the imminent IOC of China's SLBM element.

NAVY

Force structure

By the 1980s the PLA Navy had grown into a large force, that was formidable by regional standards. Its force structure and level of technology, however, have limited its effectiveness when operating beyond China's coastal waters, or against a modern, well-equipped enemy.

The Navy's main strength lies in its diesel-powered submarine force of over 100 ROMEO and WHISKEY class boats, and about 1000 patrol craft and small, torpedo or missile-armed attack craft of various classes.[135] The force of principal surface combatants has traditionally not been so powerful, but since about the mid-1970s its numbers have increased quite significantly.[136] There are now about 15 guided missile destroyers (DDG) and nearly 31 frigates, most of which are also armed with SSM.[137]

By 1986 other force elements included a Marine Force and over 500 amphibious ships and craft (already described in the section on amphibious warfare); about five operational nuclear-powered submarines; some 80 mine warfare craft; a large number of auxiliary vessels; coastal missile and artillery units; and a naval air force of about 800 shore-based combat aircraft.[138]

Naval Headquarters in Beijing is subordinate to the GSD, and equal in status to the Air Force, the Second Artillery, and apparently the Military Regions.[139] The Navy's major operational commands are the three fleets: the North Sea Fleet (NSF) with its headquarters in Qingdao, the East Sea Fleet (ESF), headquartered near Shanghai; and the South Sea Fleet (SSF) whose headquarters is at Zhanjiang. In 1985 a re-organisation was carried out that affected the structure and strength of these fleets. The details are unclear, but personnel strengths were reported to have been reduced. Among measures taken to simplify and improve command and control, a Northern Naval Region may have been created to control the NSF and the ESF.[140]

Force development

The PLA Navy, isolated from mainstream developments in Western and Soviet navies since the 1940s and early 1960s respectively, has consequently lagged behind in some critical capabilities. These weaknesses, exacerbated by ideological opposition to naval development during the Cultural Revolution, and by budgetary restrictions since that era, are only gradually being overcome. Some trends in force development have, nevertheless, become apparent.

By making selected purchases in limited quantities from overseas manufacturers, supplemented by vigorous efforts in indigenous technical innovation, the PLA Navy is attempting to modernise in three major areas: the surface force, the submarine force, and electronic technology generally throughout the Navy.[141] These areas involve upgrading capabilities in surface warfare, anti-submarine warfare (ASW), air defence, submarine warfare and naval aviation. According to the Navy's Commander, Liu Huaqing, the Navy's modernisation will be carried out in three stages before the year 2000. Priority will be given to the development of sea combat forces, including surface combatants, submarines and aircraft.[142]

Surface warfare — current status

Numerically, China's surface forces form the largest component of the Navy. They are liberally equipped with SSM, mostly based on the elderly Soviet STYX missile, which is vulnerable to ECM. The original Chinese version has a range of 45km, but a larger version, the Hai Ying 2, with a range of 75km has been fitted to China's largest surface combatants, the Luda-class DDGs. The sheer bulk of these missiles, however, limits the number that can be carried by any ship. Most destroyers and frigates are armed with SSMs. They provide more stable weapon platforms than do the patrol craft, most of which have very limited sea-keeping qualities in bad weather, or at distance from the coast. The small missile and torpedo-armed boats would, however, pose a major threat to enemy warships entering China's coastal waters, being able to concentrate in large numbers, manoeuvre at high speed, and saturate enemy defences. Nevertheless, they would be liable to sustain heavy casualties.

The main guns fitted to Chinese destroyers (130mm) and frigates (100mm) provide a useful naval gunfire support capability for amphibious operations, but they have relatively slow rates of fire, and target acquisition and fire control equipment for these as well as other weapon systems are some years behind current Western or Soviet standards.[143] With optically sighted guns and limited C^3 capabilities, these ships would be at a disadvantage when engaging modern Soviet or Western-built equivalents.

With a limited fleet train (see Section B, Appendix 2) the endurance of about one third of China's principal surface combatants would tend to limit them to coastal defence and missions in regional waters. The most capable classes as far as extended operations are concerned are the Luda DDG, which has developed excellent sea-keeping qualities, the Jiangdong frigates (FF), and the Jianghu FFG. These classes could be employed effectively to maintain surveillance and protection of off-shore resources in the Yellow, East China and South China Seas.[144]

Chinese marine engineering capabilities seem to have been unable to develop high pressure steam turbines, resulting in reliance on diesels and geared steam turbines for the propulsion units of the Navy's principal surface combatants. In an effort to catch up with developments in other major navies, China has experimented with locally designed CODOG units (gas turbines tied with diesels for cruise propulsion) in some of the Jianghu FFG,[145] but is gradually turning to the West and Japan for assistance in acquiring modern ship propulsion systems.

The Navy's current surface warfare capability is thus characterised by outdated weapon systems, obsolete electronics, limited endurance, inadequate EW systems (see earlier section) and a shortage of ships able to operate effectively beyond coastal waters.

Surface warfare — prospects

China's efforts to upgrade its surface warfare capability currently emphasise the development of the principal combatant force. A new class of FFG has been designed, and the first of a reported six units was launched early in 1986. A new class of 4000 tonne DDG is also planned, which will have an endurance greater than that of the Luda-class. In 1985 China and the US signed a contract for the supply of GE LM2500 gas turbine engines to be fitted in a CODOG arrangement to the new DDG class, and it is possible that this propulsion system is also being fitted to the new FFG class.[146] Both classes are expected to be equipped with Creusot-Loire 100mm automatic, rapid-fire guns, and the Chinese-made C-801 sea-skimming SSM, which is believed to have a better performance than China's STYX-derived missiles.[147] The C-801 is similar in appearance to the French MM38 Exocet. Performance details have not yet been revealed, but are claimed to be superior to those of the STYX types.[148] The Chinese also claim to have equipped many of their warships with a new, improved type of STYX SSM, possibly called the Hai Ying 4, which also has an ECM capability.[149] Retrofitting of both this system and the C-801 SSM can be expected to continue throughout the surface combatant force.

The smaller surface combatant elements of the force are also receiving attention. The new Haiju-class patrol boats, successors to the Hainan-class submarine-chasers, will update the larger patrol boat element. The US-designed H3-class missile patrol boat (PTG) may soon replace the Huangfeng (Soviet OSA-1)-class PTG.[150]

Anti-missile defence systems are likely to be improved through the acquisition of weapon systems such as the US 20mm Mk15 Gatling AA gun (Phalanx).[151] These systems will help counter the threat from surface-fired, sea-skimming missiles as well as air-launched missiles, a threat that the Chinese have taken very seriously since studying the Falkland Islands conflict of 1982. To improve the Navy's training in anti-sea-skimming missile defence, China has reportedly entered into a contract with a British firm for a complete target system.[152]

ASW and air defence — current status

ASW and air defence are the two weakest aspects of the Navy's capabilities. ASW weapon systems and sensors have long been limited to 1950s vintage Soviet designs,[153] and there has been a lack of ASW torpedoes. Until recently, the Navy's only ship-borne air-craft, a handful of Super Frelon utility helicopters, were not con-figured for an ASW role, nor were other ASW aircraft available. For years the Navy lacked any operational SAM systems, having to depend on AA guns and Naval Air Force fighters. Although two Jiangdong frigates were built to carry a SAM system, development of an effective missile system was slow. The interceptors of the Naval Air Force do not have an all-weather capability, and cannot ensure the control of air space. Being shore-based, they can only support fleet units out to about 500nm. These weaknesses mean that surface units are highly vulnerable to enemy air attack when operating outside the combat range of shore-based fighters.

As with many other capability shortfalls, technological weak-nesses in such areas as underwater sensors, radars, target acquisition and fire control systems, have imposed additional limitations on the Navy's ASW and air defence capabilities.

ASW and air defence — prospects

In 1983 an authoritative Chinese journal identified the need for a strong naval aviation interceptor force with a long combat radius and look-down shoot-down capability, as well as ASW aircraft.[154]

Since than, there have been indications that the Naval Air Force will benefit from technological developments in the fields of air-to-air missiles (AAM), avionics, and ECCM capabilities.[155] These improve-ments have apparently already been applied to F-7 and A-5 aircraft,[156] both of which types are employed as interceptors in the Naval Air Force. In addition, a US update package has been approved for 50 of China's F-8 interceptors, which is due to give these aircraft an all-weather capability by the early 1990s.[157] China has assured the US that these aircraft will be deployed to deter Soviet intelligence collection overflights in north and northeast China, but a 1985 report that at least four F-8 were stationed at a naval air station in the NSF[158] suggests that some updated F-8 could be assigned to the Naval Air Force in due course to help secure control of the air space where fleet units are operating.

Several improvements in the ASW field have also been under development in recent years. A four-engined ASW flying boat, which has been under test for several years, is reported to have become operational in 1986. It is believed to resemble Japan's PS-1 ASW aircraft. The Chinese have evidently encountered a number of dif-ficulties in developing this aircraft.[159]

The US is reported to be prepared to sell China the technology for ASW sonar equipment and Mark 46 ASW torpedoes.[160] Although the Chinese have not been keen to accept the price the US has asked for the production facilities for the Mark 46 torpedo, they have maintained their interest in the prospect.[161]

The major advances in the ASW field, however, have so far centred on French ASW helicopter technology. Some of the SA 321 Super Frelon heavy helicopters have been converted to the ASW role, with the retrofitting of Western navigation, sonar, search radar and data processing equipment. Some of these aircraft may be intended for deployment on the new DDG class ships.[162] It is also possible that some of the Aerospatiale Dauphin II helicopters assembled in China since 1980 could be converted to the ASW role for service on the new DDGs, and the acquisition of Super Puma helicopters could enhance Chinese coastal ASW capabilities. The new Zhi-8 helicopter, with a maximum range of about 431nm, may also be adapted as an ASW platform.[163]

In the field of air defence, several advances are in sight. By 1986, research and development problems with the indigenous ship-borne SAM system seemed to have been overcome, with a report that some Jiangdong FF had been fitted with Hongqi-61 SAM 'similar to Sea Sparrow missiles', while the new FFG class would be equipped with a US-made 'anti-missile gun', an obvious reference to the Phalanx Close in Weapon System (CIWS).[164]

In 1984 a new planar-array radar was noted fitted to a Luda-class DDG. Its appearance suggested an air surveillance radar, to provide advance warning of air threats.[165] If successful, this equipment can be expected to be retrofitted to a growing number of combatants in the future. In addition, the Creusot-Loire 100mm rapid-fire guns to be fitted to the new FFG and DDG classes can also be used in the AA role. Further negotiations with Western suppliers for the selected purchase of other air defence systems are also likely.

China has been considering the possibilities of providing the fleet at sea with extended air cover. Since the early 1980s, reports have appeared periodically concerning plans to build aircraft carriers, and feasibility studies seem to have been conducted at a shipbuilding research institute. These reports suggest the Chinese have in mind a small carrier class of about 20 000 tonnes capable of taking around 25 ASW helicopters or VSTOL aircraft.[166] The development of a carrier-borne capability from scratch is, however, a very lengthy process, and even if pursued is unlikely to achieve an operational status before the 1990s. A more readily achievable goal would be the

Table 2.3: Combat aircraft and roles of the Naval Air Force

F-5 FRESCO, F-6 FARMER ⎫ F-7 FISHBED, A-5 FANTAN ⎭	*Air Defence*
A-5 FANTAN, B-5 BEAGLE (medium range), B-6 BADGER (intermediate range), new flying boat	*Strike*
B-6 BADGER, new flying boat	*Maritime Reconnaissance*
B-6 BADGER	*Aerial minelaying*

ability to extend the combat radius of shore-based naval aircraft through the acquisition of an in-flight refuelling capability. China has shown interest in this since the Falkland Islands conflict, and by 1985 was negotiating with Britain, France and other countries for the necessary equipment.[167]

There are prospects, therefore, for at least limited improvements in the Navy's ASW and air defence capabilities during the remainder of the present decade and into the early 1990s. Were the extension of the range of air cover to be one of these improvements, it would have considerable significance for China's regional strategic capabilities (for example *vis-a-vis* the disputed islands in the South China Sea, most of which are currently beyond the combat radius of Chinese fighter aircraft).

Naval aviation: current status

The Naval Air Force (NAF) has units assigned to all three fleets. Its main combat missions are to support the Navy's surface forces (including amphibious forces), defend naval installations and attack any enemy amphibious landing forces. The roles and types of its combat aircraft, which total about 800, are shown in Table 2.3.

The NAF's inability to provide air defence for its surface units beyond the combat radius of its land-based fighters (see under previous section on ASW and Air Defence), places considerable limitations on the Navy's ability to operate its surface forces securely beyond those ranges. Besides air defence, the NAF's principal roles are maritime reconnaissance, surface attack and ground attack.

In 1983 the Chinese acknowledged that the NAF needed maritime reconnaissance, airborne early warning (AEW) and ECM capable aircraft.[168] The B-6 has the longest combat radius of the Navy's combat aircraft (c.1650nm), and some have been employed in the maritime reconnaissance role. Its on-board sensors, however, are probably extremely limited. The NAF has no AEW aircraft, but some aircraft are probably fitted with ECM equipment. Its effectiveness is unclear.[169]

Strike aircraft have two roles to perform: surface attack against enemy shipping, and ground attack/battlefield interdiction against enemy landing forces, or in support of Chinese amphibious assaults. The aircraft employed and their performance are basically the same as the Air Force aircraft used for ground attack and battlefield interdiction, and suffer from the same limitations. (See previous section — Fire Support for the Land Battle: Offensive Air Support.)

Some of the B–6 can be fitted with an air-to-surface missile (ASM) derived from the STYX SSM and developed in the mid-1980s. This missile, the C-601, is used in the anti-shipping role, and is reported to have ECCM protective measures.[170] Assuming that it is an effective weapon system, its acquisition adds a new and potentially powerful element to the NAF's strike capability, and lifts it out of its hitherto Second World War era tactics of attacking shipping primarily with torpedoes and bombs.

Naval aviation: prospects

Future developments in the NAF are likely to include improved air defence and ASW capabilities (see earlier section), expansion of the ASM cruise missile-equipped maritime strike force, and better ground attack and maritime patrol capabilities. Regarding the latter, China's first indigenously-designed maritime patrol aircraft, a version of the Yun-8, is likely to become operational in the late 1980s.[171] Its range may not be a great improvement on the BADGER's, but its surveillance equipment is likely to be far superior. A Swedish firm was due to have provided a maritime surveillance package in late 1986, including radars, cameras and processing equipment, to which China was expected to add an infra-red scanner of its own manufacture.[172] China can also be expected to seek to fill other gaps it perceives in its reconnaissance and EW capabilities (AEW aircraft and ECM equipment) for both the Naval Air Force and the Air Force.

Submarine warfare: current status

Despite their technical obsolescence by modern Soviet or Western standards, the Navy's large force of over 100 conventional submarines[173] constitutes a powerful deterrent against a foreign navy attacking the approaches to China's coastal areas. All three fleets have conventional submarine (SS) units, and in addition the NSF and the ESF probably operate the small number of nuclear sumbarines so far in service — about two XIA SSBN and three HAN SSN.[174] Operating in strength in coastal waters, Chinese submarines would pose a potent threat to even the most modern navy, and in the South China Sea the presence of two submarine flotillas in the SSF forms the main combat power, in combination with surface units, which is able to maximise the Navy's sea denial capabilities against weaker regional navies such as the SRV's.[175]

The basic design of China's conventionally-powered submarines is at least 30 years old. This factor, coupled with China's isolation from foreign assistance since the Sino–Soviet split, led to growing technical obsolescence compared with the latest Soviet and Western designs. The WHISKEY class SS, for example, seem to lack ECM/ESM equipment found on the Soviet equivalents, and it is probable that none of these classes has the sophisticated computer fire-control systems of current Western submarines.[176] In 1985 Liu Huaqing cited other areas that needed to be improved: underwater sensors, the accuracy and hitting power of weapon systems, communications and navigation aids. He admitted that the noise level was too high, crew numbers needed to be reduced, and on-board conditions improved.[177]

Since then the combat power of the submarine force has been improved through the modification of some ROMEO class boats to take new sea-skimming SSM (possibly the C-801). The effectiveness of this conversion and the number of WUHAN class SSG (as the modified ROMEO is termed) the Navy intends to operate is unclear. Sea trials were reported to have been conducted in 1985, but in mid-1986 Chinese journalists reported seeing 'dozens of submarines armed with guided missiles' during a visit to a naval base, suggesting successful results and an extensive conversion program.[178]

Chinese ROMEO submarines can travel over 2800nm and remain at sea for 30 days. To have about ten days on-station, however, their operating radius would be about 1800nm.[179] Although the Chinese claim they can remain submerged for up to ten days,[180] they are noisy when snorkelling and running on the surface, and are thus vulnerable to modern ASW weapons.[181] China's ROMEO class, therefore, has the ability to operate in areas distant from China's coastal waters, such as the Bay of Bengal and the Behring Sea. The operating radius of China's nuclear submarines has not been revealed, but the Chinese media announced that in 1986 a nuclear submarine set new records for time submerged, speed and distance. So far, however, Chinese submarines are not believed to operate to their maximum radius[182] on a regular basis.

Submarine warfare: prospects

According to Liu Huaqing, the development of the submarine force is receiving emphasis under the Four Modernisations program. China is thus likely to seek to upgrade its large fleet of conventionally-powered submarines with indigenously produced equipment such as the C-801 SSM, as well as with whatever foreign assistance it can afford to obtain.[183]

The slow development of nuclear submarines has already been noted. Earlier engineering and water-cooled reactor problems are reportedly being overcome,[184] and at least one source has claimed that US technology is being incorporated into nuclear submarines under construction in 1986.[185] The development of the nuclear-powered component, moreover, will probably absorb a major portion of the funds available, due to its greater strategic significance. Some observers believe the costs involved will limit this component to about twelve units for the foreseeable future. The HAN SSNs, will presumably operate in support of the XIA SSBNs. Thus these two types will be needed in about equal numbers. Although the bulk of the nuclear powered component will probably continue to be based mainly in the NSF and ESF because of the presence of major strategic targets in the Soviet Far Eastern provinces for its SLBMs, it is likely that Chinese nuclear submarines will also appear in the SSF area, if only on a temporary basis, for area familiarisation and training.

Logistic and auxiliary support

For an account of Chinese efforts to improve the procedures and efficiency of naval logistic services, see Appendix 2, Section B.

Other capabilities

Mine warfare
Little emphasis seems to have been given to mine warfare since the anti-Japanese and Civil War periods. The Navy has about 30 elderly T-23 ocean mine counter-measures (MCM) vessels,[186] and some coastal minesweepers.

The T-23 are obsolete by Western standards, but the Type 312 remote-controlled minesweeper (similar to the West German Troika system), seems well suited for restricted waters such as estuaries and harbours.[187] A further area for developing China's MCM capabilities is in mine neutralisation. In 1986 it was announced that Italy would supply a Pluto mine neutralisation vehicle to China.[188] The small MCM force would, however, be inadequate to cover more than a few of China's major ports and sea lanes.

Minelaying capabilities are potentially much greater. Mines could be laid by most naval ships and by some NAF BADGER aircraft. Trawlers, junks and even merchant ships could also be used for this purpose. According to Vietnamese reports, the Chinese have recently revived the art of riverine minelaying in the Sino–Vietnamese border area, a method they used to some effect against the Japanese. Using the various resources available to them, the Chinese could effect a naval blockade of selected areas of a weaker regional neighbour's coast. The major means used would be Rapid Aerial Minelays (RAMs) and Covert Submarine Minelays (CSMs).[189]

Coastal defence

The Navy is responsible for the defence of China's coastline and straits. Its land-based defence forces are deployed to fulfil this mission. These forces include the NAF, and an extensive network of coastal radar sites for the surveillance of ships and craft offshore. These sites provide early warning for naval defensive forces such as patrol boat, coastal artillery and SSM units.[190] The Yellow Sea and the Bohai Gulf approaches are two areas of high significance in coastal defence, because of the threat of a Soviet attack (including amphibious landings) in time of war. In recent years, moreover, the Chinese have developed the concept of joint service cooperation in defence of such areas.[191] Many coastal defence positions are hardened, and fixed SSM sites have recently been supplemented by mobile SSM units.[192] The Navy also contributes to coastal fortress garrisons such as in the Zhu (Pearl) River estuary.

Naval training and operations

Since about 1980 the Navy has paid increasing attention to both individual and unit training. Efforts have been made to standardise and improve training for personnel, particularly officers. New training establishments and techniques have been introduced,[193] as well as formal mid-career training for officers and qualifying tests for commanding officers.[194] Added impetus was given to improving operating standards following a high-level naval staff conference in June 1984, which called for standardisation of command systems, tighter discipline, and improved leadership.[195]

Realistic training in submarine warfare, amphibious warfare, command and control and coordination between different types of units (maritime 'combined arms' training) has increased since about 1982, with emphasis on larger-scale operations and rapid response. By 1984, the Chinese seem to have evolved the concept of forming task forces comprising surface, sub-surface and air elements.[196] The number of combatants held at combat-readiness has risen steadily,[197] and nuclear and chemical warfare training revitalised.[198]

Training and operations at sea have also indicated the Navy's growing sense of confidence in its ability to operate at distance from Chinese shores. In the early 1980s significant events included the deployment of an eighteen-ship task force to the southwest Pacific to take part in the recovery of ICBM test launch vehicles, and the circumnavigation of the Philippines by several major combatants, during which exercises were conducted.[199] These were followed in 1983 and 1984 by training cruises for junior naval officers under instruction that involved, in one case, transiting the Nansha (Spratly Islands) in the South China Sea, the western Pacific, Osumi and Taiwan Straits; and in the other case a circumnavigation of Japan.[200] A significant development in 1984 was the SSF's show of force in the South China Sea (see Table 1.5 at Combined Arms and Joint Operations) which indicated the Navy's potential for projecting its influence in disputed waters during a time of high international tension.

The Navy's role in international relations has also come to the fore recently, with port calls being conducted by two naval auxiliaries in South America when returning from supporting the Chinese scientific base in the Antarctic in late 1984, and the first ever port calls made by a PRC warship in late 1985. This latter cruise was undertaken by a Luda DDG supported by a Fuqing class AOR, which visited Pakistan, Sri Lanka and Bangladesh.[201] The PRC Navy's relations with foreign navies has expanded considerably in recent years, due mainly to its realisation that there is much to be learned from such contacts. Australian, British, French and other European and South American warships have visited China, but in terms of strategic significance the contacts with the US Navy in 1986 are more worthy of note, underlining *inter alia* the importance China places on the US as a source of much needed technology. The PLA

Navy can be expected to make more port visits in the future. A reciprocal visit to the US is not out of the question. Lower-key visits during training cruises are also likely.[202]

In terms of the Navy's development of strategic doctrine and combat capability, however, possibly the most revealing event occurred in May 1986, when a large-scale nine-day exercise was held in an area in the East China Sea around the vicinity of Iwo Jima. According to a communist newspaper in Hong Kong, quoting the *Jiefangjun Bao*, the main aim of the exercise was to practise the rapid concentration of various units to form a task force and engage an enemy force at a distance from China's shores.[203] The emphasis was on offensive action at an early stage, the naval equivalent of active defence. At least six surface combatants, including a Luda DDG, and several B-6 aircraft took part, and possibly some submarines. The B-6 aircraft were almost certainly Naval Air Force planes, either the maritime reconnaissance version or, in view of some reports that they conducted simulated anti-shipping strikes, more likely the ASM-equipped maritime strike version. Various 'coordinated combat manoeuvres' were practised as well as communications security (COMSEC) measures.[204] Although information is scant, and the existence or composition of a 'real' opposing force is unknown, it is possible to suggest a force structure for the task force deployed: a Main Attack Task Group (surface combatants), an Air Task Group, and a Submarine Task Group. Although not mentioned in press reports, a Maritime Logistic Support Force may also have taken part (this would include replenishment ships, a submarine rescue ship (ASR) and possibly an ocean-going tug). All these elements would have been under the command of a Task Force Commander — the senior naval officer.

As the various elements of the Task Force were drawn from different commands and bases, the concentration of this force, and the coordination of its operations in a strict COMSEC environment must have constituted a searching test for the Navy's C^3I system. It suggests considerable progress in the standardisation of communications and other procedures. Whatever shortcomings there may have been, this exercise was a milestone in the Navy's process of modernisation.

Another milestone was the first patrol by surface combatants of the waters around the Spratly Islands in May–June 1987. China claims that its submarine force has also extended its operations to these waters.[205] While many limitations still remain (eg the ability to provide sustained logistic support to broad ocean area deployments), the transformation of China's Navy from a primarily coastal defence 'brown water' force to a more capable 'green water' regional navy is well and truly under way.

AIR FORCE

Force Structure

The PLA Air Force is the largest in Asia, comprising some 4500 air defence and fighter ground attack aircraft, about 620 bombers, 130 reconnaissance aircraft, over 500 fixed-wing transport aircraft and 400 helicopters.[206] It also controls an airborne army and many units of AAA and SAM systems.

The Air Force Headquarters in Beijing, directly subordinate to the General Staff Department, commands these resources through a structure of air districts (which generally cover the same areas as Military Regions), air divisions and regiments etc. Air districts facing the USSR, Vietnam and the strategic approaches to China's central coastline are provided with more combat resources than the others. The air division is the largest operational unit, and usually consists of 108–135 aircraft. Air defence zones are organised on an air district basis, and control air defence resources from all three Services stationed within its geographic boundaries.[207] In other operational situations, however, close coordination of air and ground operations has probably been limited by the stress PLA doctrine placed on independent action by air force units,[208] and the traditional tendency for ground forces to underestimate the potential contributions of other services.

Force development

The traditional single-service bias that bedevilled relationships between the PLA's three services seems, however, to be changing. Recognising the threat posed by large, hard-hitting Soviet mechanised formations, attacking with the direct-support of integral air forces and long range strategic air armies, the Chinese have begun to reorganise their field armies (see previous section on Combined Arms and Joint Operations) and Air Force formations.[209] Although these changes are aimed at the achievement of several goals, including an overall reduction in personnel strength and higher level formations,[210] it would be surprising if the Air Force's restructuring did not take into account the need to establish closer organisational links with ground and naval forces. Indeed, the organisation of the Air Force into primarily Frontal Aviation, Long Range Aviation (LRA) and Air Defence forces could be inferred by developments since 1983, with the major roles of Frontal Aviation and LRA being close air support and battlefield interdiction respectively.[211] Particular emphasis is being given to upgrading Chinese air defence fighters with the assistance of foreign technology, the development of ASM, and improvements in providing offensive air support to the ground forces.[212] Longer-range combat missions seem to be a remote possibility (see previous section on Strategic Nuclear Forces).

Efforts are also being made to improve the Air Force's command and control arrangements. Many Air units have computerised their command and control systems,[213] but progress in developing a forcewide automated system, which has been under way since at least 1984, still seems to be lagging behind.[214] Thus the Chinese are currently unable to achieve the levels of rapid response and operational flexibility they aspire to.

To assist in the guidance of force development, the Air Force Academic Research Committee was established in 1983. This body will study new developments in foreign air forces, and arrange exchanges of air power specialists. At the same time, the Air Force can be expected to rationalise its responsibilities, which have evolved over the years due to its traditional dominance in aviation matters. By handing over responsibility for air traffic control to a new civil agency, the Air Force should be able to shed a non-essential task and concentrate on military priorities.[215]

Air defence is the primary mission of the Air Force. In recent years, faced with the strengthening of Soviet and Vietnamese air power, China has directed most of its efforts in acquiring advanced aviation technology towards improving its air defence capabilities.

Air to air combat: current capability

The Air Force is generally limited to operating in a clear air mass during daylight. Until recently it had only a small number of all weather F-5 FRESCO and F-6 FARMER interceptors. The majority of its large interceptor force (over 4000 aircraft) could not operate effectively in bad weather or at night.[216] By early 1984 the PLA openly acknowledged that its air defence capability suffered from an absence of air superiority fighters and an overdependence on ground-based air defence systems. Furthermore, it had little faith in the ability of its SAM systems to operate effectively against the sophisticated ECM capability of Soviet aircraft. Only AAA was relatively unaffected by this factor, but the development of Soviet ASM-equipped aircraft with their stand-off capability was placing effective air defence beyond the PLA's reach.[217]

This realisation no doubt added impetus to efforts to improve air defence capabilities, including the essential area of air-to-air combat. Inadequate weapon systems, avionics, ECM and engine performance presented the major difficulties. In 1984 most of the PLA's fighter aircraft were probably armed with cannon only. Air-to-air missiles (AAM) were gradually being fitted to Chinese fighters, but they were mostly obsolete PL-2 infra-red (IR) homing missiles. A new radar controlled AAM was under development, as well as other IR and semi-active radar homing missiles.[218] Their performance still limited the effectiveness of the fighter force to short-range engagements, which Soviet aircraft could avoid while attacking the Chinese fighters with their longer range AAM.[219] Although the US is reported to have refused to provide China with any ASM or ECM equipment,[220] by 1986 China had developed or acquired some more effective AAM such as the PL-7.[221] China may also have some French Matra Magic AAM,[222] but the extent of the deployment of these and other improved AAM to the Air Force's operational units is unclear.

Until recently, radar equipment fitted to Chinese aircraft appeared to be based on late 1950s Soviet equipment,[223] severely limiting the ability of Chinese fighters to successfully conduct air intercepts. Since 1984, however, a gradual upgrading of some fighters has been revealed, such as the F-7M version of the FISHBED, with Western-made avionics.[224] After lengthy consideraton, the US has approved a package worth US$550 million, which will upgrade 50 of China's most recently designed F-8 (FINBACK) fighters over a six-year period. The Chinese are apparently fitting more powerful engines to this aircraft and increasing its fuel capacity, thus extending its combat radius to a claimed 800km. The result is a supersonic fighter configured for all-weather, day and night air defence missions.[225] So far, however, only a small number of upgraded F-8s may be available.

Air-to-air combat: prospects

The trend seems clear. China is gradually upgrading its more modern interceptors to form a small core force capable of all-weather operations. The majority of its air defence aircraft are, however, so outdated in basic design that the full upgrading process would probably not be cost effective. The current limited numbers of F-7s and F-8s will probably, therefore, be augmented by new production runs. If China is able to afford a continuation of the Western upgrading packages,[226] it will eventually build up a force of air defence aircraft with a combat capability which, while not matching that of the latest Soviet fighters, will at least be sufficiently effective to provide a credible deterrent to the Soviets. The numbers of such advanced aircraft will probably not be great. Some reports suggest that China is unlikely to produce more than 250 to 300 F-8s, while additional orders have been placed for kits to upgrade about 200 extra F-7s. It has been further suggested that China aims to build more advanced aircraft, including an F-10 delta-winged fighter, and an F-12 swept-wing fighter bomber. The weapon systems of air defence fighters are also likely to be upgraded with more capable AAM and cannon.[227]

Offensive air support: current capability

China's bomber force of over 600 aircraft consists of dated B-6s and B-5s. Although the B-6 has a maximum range of 4800km, the Chinese do not appear to contemplate using these aircraft as current-ly configured in either a nuclear or conventional strategic role (see previous section on Strategic Nuclear Forces).

Both types are probably still vulnerable to enemy EW.[228] They would be used mainly on pre-planned battlefield interdiction missions against such targets as theatre missile sites, follow-on forces and logistic installations (see previous section on Fire Support for the Ground Forces).

The primary ground attack aircraft is the A-5 FANTAN, of which some 600 are believed to be in service (including up to 100 in the Naval Air Force). Large numbers of F-6 FARMER and MiG 15 FAGOT can also be used in this role. The current limitations of the Air Force in its ability to conduct close air support (CAIRS) have already been described.

Offensive air support: prospects

Apart from the possibility of the development of a modified B-6 strategic bomber with a supersonic dash capability,[229] and the retirement of the elderly FAGOTs, bomber and fighter aircraft currently employed in the offensive air support role are unlikely to be replaced for some time. It seems more probable that their avionics and possibly their weapon systems will be upgraded. European firms are among the most likely sources of advanced technology.[230] The fitting of rocket pods to upgraded F-7M fighters suggests an added emphasis on its secondary role as a ground attack aircraft. New types of ground attack aircraft are not likely to be acquired from overseas, except perhaps for some modestly-priced deals. An Italo-Brazilian aircraft has been reported as a possibility.[231] Improvements to ECM equipment and ground attack techniques are doubtless among Chinese objectives, but the extent to which China will seek to develop its CAIRS capability as opposed to battlefield interdiction remains to be seen. The *Liberation Army Daily* has also predicted that the use of air-launched guided missiles could become a major form of aerial warfare. Whether this referred to tactical conventional or strategic nuclear missiles is unclear.[232]

Training

In recent years the Chinese Air Force has made considerable efforts to improve individual and unit training. Specialist training centres have been established, educational standards used in personnel selection have been raised, and training programs have been standardised. The period of training required for pilots to reach combat standard has been reduced from between four and five years to two years, and the average age of pilots has dropped from over 25 to 21–22 years.[233] A growing percentage of cadres has attended military colleges. A further measure was the establishment, in mid-1986, of training divisions for young pilots graduating from flying training schools, to prepare them for duties with operational units, rather than saddle the latter units with the task of conducting their conversion and advanced training.[234] The number of flying hours for training all pilots has been increased, including training in night flying, unit mobility, low-level flying, air-to-air and air-to-ground firing, flying in complex weather conditions and in joint exercises.[235] The first batch of young pilots trained as English linguists graduated in 1985, suggesting the Air Force intends sending selected pilots overseas to receive advanced training in future.[236]

Considerable use has been made during training of electronic, laser and computerised equipment, including ground attack tactical simulators.[237] Tactical training with ground forces, boosted since early 1986, is intended to be conducted more frequently in future.[238] The training of technical and logistic personnel, however, does not appear to have been so vigorously pursued (see Appendix 2, Section C).

The various problems that the Air Force faces should not obscure its considerable potential, and current ability to maintain a degree of deterrence that has helped China to preserve the integrity of its air space almost completely for the last decade or more. Gradual modernisation with selective acquisition of foreign technology at a pace which China can absorb, is raising this degree of deterrence. In the longer term, it should provide China the opportunity to achieve an adequate state of self-reliance in this field. Should there be a deterioration in China's strategic situation, however, requiring an accelerated infusion of foreign high technology end products, the Air Force could face serious difficulties in maintaining them, and set back the steady progress it is making towards its goal of modernisation.

WARFIGHTING CAPABILITIES: WEAKNESSES, PROGRESS AND OUTLOOK

China's current perceptions of threat underly the course of its military modernisation. While the causes of its military deficiencies can be traced back to the period of isolation arising from the Sino–Soviet split to the end of the Cultural Revolution, its current belief that global war is unlikely before the middle of the twenty-first century gives it breathing space in which to differentiate between near and long-term goals. In this context some weaknesses can be tolerated in the short-term. While some strengths can be maximised on a selective basis to meet the needs of limited wars in the near future, others can be developed for the large-scale conflict that could eventuate in the second half of the next century.

At the strategic level China is making modest but steady progress in the development of strategic nuclear missile systems supported by satellite reconnaissance, providing a shield behind which both near and long-term modernisation can take place. These systems are becoming more capable of surviving an enemy first strike and of retaliating. Ranges are gradually being extended, while the advent of SLBM systems has the potential to add new flexibility to China's nuclear deterrent once technical problems have been overcome. Strategic C^3I capabilities have made some impressive gains, which should provide immediate as well as long-term benefits. At the same time, naval aviation strike, surface warfare, submarine and amphibious warfare capabilities are being enhanced.

Assuming that China will continue to draw selectively on Western technology, these measures have the potential to develop into

F8-II (courtesy of CONMILIT)

CSS-2 Intermediate Range Ballistic Missile

New Naval Cruise Missile (right), SLBM (centre) and Hai Ying 2 SSM (left) (courtesy of CONMILIT)

LUDA Class DDG (courtesy of CONMILIT)

Jianghu Class FFG firing anti-submarine weapons (courtesy of CONMILIT)

New Anti-tank Guided Weapon (courtesy of CONMILIT)

A Combined Arms Assault during Joint Exercises at Zhangjiakou, 1981 (courtesy of CONMILIT)

Type 59 Tanks participating in an FTX (courtesy of CONMILIT)

significant improvements in China's ability to deter and counter any nuclear attack, and also to project its own power into the Western Pacific and the Southeast Asian region. Critical weaknesses in ASW and maritime air defence continue to restrict progress, but there seems a reasonable prospect of at least some improvements in these areas with Western assistance. The acquisition of an air-to-air refuelling capability, for instance, would extend air cover further out to sea and give the Navy a substantial advantage over the navies of its Southeast Asian neighbours: a prospect likely to be realised in the short as opposed to the longer-term.

Short-term benefits are also at hand due to the restructuring of the PLA. The group armies are better able to meet a modern enemy on more equal terms. Tactical weaknesses persist: for instance in armour, anti-armour, air defence and offensive air support capabilities, mobility and logistic support. These limit China's ability to realise its evolving plans for the adoption of a form of the 'Air Land Battle' concept. It will be some time before the PLA is able to meet this strategic objective.

The time factor in this case, however, is not critical from China's point of view. The form of warfare envisaged — mechanised, highly mobile, covering long distances and conducted at high intensity — is applicable to a major conflict, which China believes is unlikely to eventuate until well into the twenty-first century. The acquisition of such a capability, therefore, can proceed at a gradual pace and, initially, on a modest scale. In the meantime China can concentrate on developing capabilities in areas more essential to fighting limited wars with some of its Third World neighbours. The more likely scenarios tend to emphasise rapid response, the ability to fight in mountainous and jungle terrains, and in the shallow waters of the South China Sea. Areas of Chinese weakness such as armour, anti-armour and chemical warfare can be expected, therefore, to take second place to the development of C^3I, EW, all-weather air defence, helicopter-borne operations, fire support and logistics. On the naval side ASW becomes less critical, while offensive air support, surface, submarine and amphibious warfare assume higher prominence. The recent progress made in all these areas indicates, however, that aspects suggested as being of secondary importance in the short-term will not be neglected, but pursued at a slower pace.

With the exception of those areas already discussed, such as the strategic nuclear forces and C^3I systems, China can be expected to approach its long-term capability goals by the judicious acquisition of representative modern equipments on a small scale to enable the

PLA to keep up with state-of-the-art developments until such time as it can afford to acquire them on a force-wide basis. In the meantime, the vigorous efforts to reform training and infuse the PLA with a greater degree of professionalism are helping to build a solid foundation for future improvements in all aspects. The spirit of seeking new concepts and procedures must be sustained, as it should provide the life blood of the PLA's quest for modernisation. The despatch of selected PLA personnel to be trained at foreign military institutions can be expected, and will add impetus to this process. Force development to meet short-term objectives is likely to include an increasing emphasis on the Reserve Forces, despite current financial stringencies, while serious weaknesses in the regular forces, such as the Air Force's repair and logistic systems, will be pursued to a point deemed sufficient for a limited war scenario. The point at which the balance in China's somewhat complacent strategic development plan is tipped in favour of long-term objectives cannot be foreseen at this stage, but will provide analysts with a critical focus for examination in the years to come.

3

The Support Base: Transport and Communications and the Reserve Forces

It has been noted that China perceives defence modernisation as an integral part of its national economic development, and that military spending can only be increased when the national economy improves. Nevertheless, the preceding chapters have indicated that China has been able to make progress in defence modernisation despite the above guiding principle. It should also be noted that progress made in economic modernisation has contributed to the improvement of defence capabilities, and thus demonstrates that the resources of the civilian and defence sectors can be integrated. China's decision to resort to long-term strategic plans, which concentrates on war preparation for the next century, represents a strategic change in defence modernisation. The decision has opened up opportunities for the defence sector to take advantage of sustained contribution from the civilian sector to its warfighting capabilities. Thus improvements in the transport and communications network, and the ability to mobilise the people for reserve service provide a strong support base for defence modernisation. The goal of improvements in the transport and communications system in the seventh Five-Year Plan is to promote economic modernisation. Nevertheless, the State recognises that an improved transportation network can provide a stronger support base for the military should war break out. This support is especially relevant to the seven military regions restruc-

Map 2

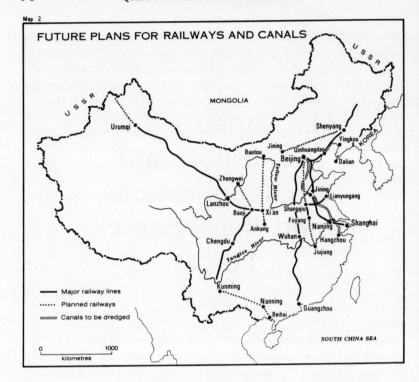

FUTURE PLANS FOR RAILWAYS AND CANALS

tured since 1985 as cost-effectiveness and self-sufficiency seem to be their major objectives. Of particular importance to the military regions is the network of railways as it provides the most efficient logistic support and facilitates quick response. As regards the mobilisation of human resources for reserve service, China realises the need to train efficient Reserve Forces in support of its regular defence force. It has to rely on a manpower pool of five million reservists in addition to the armed basic milita, which represent a critical contribution from the civilian population. Nevertheless, the task of raising the effectiveness of the combined strength of the reservists and the militia is by no means easy.

TRANSPORT AND COMMUNICATIONS IN THE MILITARY REGIONS

The major aim in building an improved transport and communications system in China in the seventh Five-Year Plan is to help promote economic modernisation. In so doing, the Chinese have identified four major tasks which are especially relevant to the railway sector. These are:[1]

1. The transport of Shanxi coal to other parts of China,
2. The strengthening of the north-south link,
3. Linking major coastal ports and cities with their hinterland,
4. Linking major economic regions.

Since the 1970s and especially in the early 1980s the transportation network has been developed mainly in the coastal areas, which is indicative of priorities given to the goal of economic efficiency rather than that of equity.[2] In other words, China is more eager to concentrate on the development of core areas than to emphasise interregional balance or the dispersion of transportation facilities. Thus of the four tasks set out in the seventh Five-Year Plan, three of them (numbers 1, 3 and 4) have distinct features of economic efficiency as their goal.

These particular economic orientations in the 1980s definitely have their impact on China's defence. Coupled with this change is the series of major PLA reforms and restructuring in 1984–85 which throws new light on China's perception of the role played by military regions in defence.[3] In the development of the transport network, concentration on the coastal areas may jeopardise border defence in the Northwest, the Northeast and the Southwest. Nevertheless, the restructuring of the military regions in 1985, which primarily increases the size and responsibilities of five out of a total of seven MRs, would suggest greater self-sufficiency in each military region, especially in the support provided by the transportation system.[4] In so doing, the State hopes tht the goal of economic efficiency does not erode greatly its efforts to build the most cost-effective way of maintaining a higher level of self-sufficiency in military regions which are expected to provide greater logistic support and quicker response to mobilisation. The transportation network and its future development are therefore essential to the seven military regions despite the overall emphasis on economic construction. The fact that transport and communications serve both economic and military goals have been well recognised by the State:[5]

> Transport and communications development is the necessary condition for guaranteeing the new construction of industrial bases . . . it is an area which is half military in nature; during wartime it should serve the military directly and is part of the defence strength . . .

What if economic goals contradict defence goals in the development of the transport network? The answer will have to be that economic goals will take priority. But the State seems to rely on the military regions to strengthen their capabilities in logistic support and mobilisation on the basis of a better developed transportation network in the seventh Five-year Plan. The very enlargement and merging of some of the military regions is one such example of the State's desire to be cost-effective and encouraging military regions to be self-sufficient as far as possible.

Out of the five major sectors in the transport and communications network of railways, roads, waterways, pipelines and airways, the first three sectors are more relevant to the strengthening of logistic support and mobilisation in the military region. In addition, the reliance on the railway for long and heavy hauls as well as for quick response dominates the need for military regions to seek State support for railway development in the seventh Five-year Plan. However, the dilemma has been one of preference for economic development. On the other hand, economic development does not necessarily contradict military requirements so that military regions do benefit from the seventh Five-Year Plan. As regards the development of roads, it would be at the Army Corps level and below that the PLA especially relies on. As a rule, road transporation tends to be short-haul and the conditions of roads will have to be improved.

(Only 78.2 per cent of China's 725 030 km of roads were surfaced in1984.)[6]

The Chinese claim that the demand from the military for railways increases with the modernisation of weaponry and equipment.[7] This is the case despite fast development in other means of transport like airways, waterways and roads. Thus the reliance on railways for the transportation of large-scale combat equipment and large bulk of war *materiel* continues and is irreplaceable. To reinforce the need to rely on railways, the Chinese have maintained that the US Airforce spent 60 per cent of its efforts to disrupt the Chinese lines of communication in the Korean War.[8] Furthermore, the Chinese and the North Koreans deployed large-scale forces with a view to protecting the 1300 km of railways inside North Korea.[9]

There is no denying nevertheless that improvements to road conditions are important as combined arms operations require greater mobility, and as the PLA becomes more motorised. The dramatic increase in the number of motor vehicles is a good indicator.[10] The waterways sector acts as a reserve militarily for railways. Despite the fact that it is a relatively slow and inefficient sector (48.1 per cent of 56 732km are under one metre in depth), its waterways have quintupled freight density in the period 1965–81.[11] Logistically, it means that waterways will become much more important and relevant in scenarios which may witness Chinese strategic retreats to the Yangtze region. In addition, waterways are less vulnerable than railways or highways. Table 3.1 illustrates the relative importance of the three sectors in providing logistic support for China's military needs.

In the context of providing logistic support for the PLA, railways easily stand out to be strategically significant as their average length of haul and freight density are far superior to those of roads. The sharp contrast in average length of haul (584 ton-km/ton) for railways as against (45 ton-km/ton) for roads in 1984 should be noted. Waterways with their much longer haul are nevertheless handicapped by their relatively lower freight density compared to that of railways.

As early as 1981, the *Economic Reporter* had criticised the Chinese road system, claiming that it was lagging far behind the demand for better quality and quantity:[12]

> ... the current mileage represents only a very small network relative to the vast territory of the country, and most of which is concentrated in south-east and coastal region. What is more, about 45 per cent of the mileage are not at par with the technical specifications laid down for the road building. First and second class roads only amount to 2 per cent of

Table 3.1: Freight performance of major modes of transport

Year	Railways		Roads		Waterways	
	Average length of haul (ton-km/ton)	Freight density in million metric ton-km/km	Average length of haul (ton-km/ton)	Freight density in million metric ton-km/km	Average length of haul (ton-km/ton)	Freight density in million metric ton-km/km
1981	530	11.378	35	0.028	1241	1.386
1982	539	12.118	38	0.033	1236	1.572
1983	559	12.879	42	0.036	1285	1.663
1984	584	14.019	45	0.038	1351	1.799

Sources: *Chinese Statistical Yearbook 1985*, (Chinese Statistical Bureau, Beijing, 1985), pp.385, 393 and 396–397.

the total mileage. One third of the roads are dirt-surfaced and hard-topped roads only amount to 17 per cent of the total.

Since 1982, China has planned to build over 10 000km of new roads in the mountainous and remote areas and upgrade several thousand kilometres of established roads. The total length of roads for 1983 and 1984 (915 079km and 926 746km respectively) seem to indicate that the Chinese are progressing well with their plan.[13]

Railways are strategically important to the PLA for logistic support and mobilisation and deserve closer examination as they serve a very useful purpose to military regions which are expected to be more self-sufficient in developing their defence capabilities. Table 3.2 illustrates this point.

Category A in Table 3.2 comprises five military regions which had direct and complete connectivity by railways. Beijing as headquarters obviously served Shenyang well for strategic and logistic support, and the transfer of the Main Forces in times of war or emergency could be done efficiently and quickly.[14] Similarly, Nanjing, Jinan and Fuzhou MRs had complete connections amongst all military districts, which guaranteed readiness for China's coastal defence as far as the PLA is concerned. Guangzhou in Category B connected directly with Hunan Military District but Guangxi Military District could only be reached indirectly; the same for Fuzhou, although it belonged to a neighbouring MR. In terms of logistic support, it does mean that Guangzhou's strategic capabilities were not as good as those MRs in Category A. Kunming, Wuhan and Lanzhou in Category C all had complete connectivity with their respective military districts but they were not in complete and direct connectivity with all neighbouring provincial capitals. Kunming and Lanzhou with border defence responsibilities were not as well supported logistically as those in Category A, but it can be assumed at the same time that Kunming for instance was fairly well supported logistically by Wuhan, the nearest industrial and militiary complex in the Sino–Vietnamese border war. Neither Chengdu nor Wulumuqi in Category D had complete connectivity with its military districts. They did not have direct connectivity with neighbouring provincial capitals either (even discarding Lhasa as an exception). Wulumuqi was connected with China's heartland by one single railway to Lanzhou. The completion of the Nanjiang railway connecting Korla and Turfan in May 1984 was an improvement.

The seven military regions reorganised since 1985 have increased their level of self-sufficiency, especially for the three MRs on the

Table 3.2:　Railway connectivity of military regions and their military districts*

Military Region	Military Districts (provincial capitals except Xinjiang)	1970 (for reference only (b)	(b1)	1985 (a)	(a1)	(b)	(b1)
(A)							
Beijing	Hebei Shanxi Nei Mongol	B		@		B	
Fuzhou	Fujian Jiangxi	B		@		B	
Jinan	Shandong	B		@		B	
Nanjing	Jiangsu Anhui	B		@		B	
Shenyang	Liaoning Jilin Heilongjiang	B		@		B	
(B)							
Guangzhou	Guangdong Guangxi Hunan Jiangxi Hainan (the exception: not accessible by rail)	‡	3/4	+	2/4	‡	3/4
(C)							
Kunming	Yunnan Guizhou	#	3/4	@		#	3/4
Lanzhou	Gansu Qinghai Ningxia Shaanxi	‡	1/6	@		#	1/6
Wuhan	Henan Hubei	‡	3/6	@		‡	2/6

Notes

* 　Chart adapted from C.K. Leung, *China: Railway Patterns and National Goals*, (Department of Geography, University of Chicago, Research Paper No.195, 1980), p.143.
(a)　Connectivity of military districts in the same military region.
(a1)　Number of military districts in the same MR represented in vertexes *not* directly connected by railway over total number of military districts in the same MR.
(b)　Connectivity with neighbouring provincial capitals (including autonomous regions).
(b1)　Number of neighbouring provincial capitals (including autonomous regions) represented in vertexes *not* directly connected by railway over a number of neighbouring provincial capitals (including autonomous regions)
@　Complete connectivity with neighbouring military districts in the same MR.
B　Complete connectivity with neighbouring provincial capitals achieved.
+　Indirect connection with all neighbouring military districts in the same MR (complete connectivity) possible; or indirect connectivity with all neighbouring capitals (complete connectivity) possible.
‡　Indirect connection with neighbouring capital achieved.
0　One military district in the same MR not connected.
#　Direct and/or indirect connection with all neighbouring capitals except Lhasa (Tibet).

Table 3.2 (cont'd):

Military Region	Military Districts (provincial capitals except Xinjiang)	1970 (for reference only) (b)	(b1)	1985 (a)	(a1)	(b)	(b1)
(D) Chengdu	Sichuan Xizang	#	4/8	0	1/2	#	4/8
Wulumuqi	Beijiang Dongjiang Nanjiang	#	2/3	0	1/3	#	2/3

northwestern, southwestern and southern frontiers; namely Lanzhou, Chengdu and Guangzhou. Whilst it is true that the transportation of Main Force units and large bulk of *materiel* will entail inter-MR links, many enlarged MRs are now better served by railways within their boundaries. This means improved efficiency in logistic support and in the mobilisation of Local Force as well as militia and reserve units. Table 3.3 helps to illustrate this point.

It should be noted that railway development in the sixth Five-Year Plan (1981–85) contributed to the improvement of connectivity both within the MR as well as in inter-MR transport. The seventh Five-Year Plan will continue to contribute to the longer average haul as well as higher freight density. This will be achieved with the targets of 58 000km combined length, 1.7 billion tons of freight volume and 1.6 billion passenger journeys (turnovers).[15] Furthermore, electrification and multiple-tracking of railways contribute to improved connectivity.[16] It is true that these develoments have been tackled mainly for economic reasons, but it should be noted that the defence capabilities of the seven MRs in varying degrees improve at the same time.

Military regions in categories A and B in Table 3.3 bear the bulk of the burden in defending China's frontiers against the 'stronger' and the 'lesser' enemies, ie the USSR and the Socialist Republic of Vietnam (SRV). Beijing and Shenyang MRs with their excellent connectivity are considered as one single theatre of war in the defence of China's North and Northeast. Their levels of self-sufficiency in logistics and firepower have been well recognised.[17] Greater improvements in connectivity in Shenyang MR will be achieved with the completion of double tracks for the Manzhouli–Haerbin–Suifen line which is 1490.9km in length.[18] Nevertheless, this line is too exposed to Soviet interdiction although it will still serve a useful logistic function in delaying Soviet advances. As for Beijing MR, the general objective to improve the transport of coal from Shanxi to the coastal ports and develop links between ports and their hinterland have strengthened the connectivity of the MR. This general improvement in fact applies to Nanjing and Jinan MRs in Category C which are well served by the railway system.[19] For instance, improvements in Jinan MR will materialise when electrification for the section between Zhengzhou and Sanmenxia on the Longhai line is complete.[20] As regards MRs in Category B, they have built up capabilities for defence in depth and increased their level of self-sufficiency. In addition, inter-MR links in this category also increase their defence capabilities against potential threats from the Northwest and the South.

In Lanzhou MR, Table 3.3 shows that connectivity within the MR has not deteriorated with the addition of Xinjiang as one of its military districts (MD). The pattern of defence in depth has been developed given that the location of Lanzhou is deep in Chinese territory and away from the Xinjiang–USSR border and that there is better connectivity between Lanzhou and Xinjiang. Thus the completion of the Lanzhou–Turfan–Korla line (470km) in May 1984 has provided good logistic support for southern Xinjiang. The completion of the northern Xinjiang line linking Wulumuqi (westward via Wusu) and the Soviet border will further strengthen Lanzhou's support for Xinjiang MD.[21] Lanzhou MR's reliance on other MRs for reinforcement in manpower and *materiel* will continue. Thus the electrification of the Lanzhou line and better access to the Yangtze valley will be crucial to Lanzhou MR's regional defence capabilities.[22]

Chengdu MR has incorporated the former Kunming MR and now comprises five MDs. Direct connectivity when compared with the pre-1985 situation has deteriorated but Chengdu now provides good conditions for defence in depth against threats from the SRV. The MR's defence capabilities have increased as a result of the electrification of the Chengdu–Chongqing and Guizhou–Kunming lines.[23] The completion of electrification for the Hunan–Guizhou line will further enhance such capabilities as will the completion of the planned Kunming–Nanning line. Chengdu MR's access to the Yangtze valley will also be enhanced with the electrification of the Xiangfan–Ankang–Chengdu and Hunan–Guizhou lines.[24] Chengdu's transport links with Tibet are still weak and reliance on road-connectivity has to take the place of railways. Guangzhou MR has

Table 3.3:   Railway connectivity of military regions and their military districts 1986

Military Region	Military Districts (provincial capitals except Xinjiang)	(a)	(a1)	(b)	(b1)
(A)					
Beijing	Hebei Shanxi Nei Monggol	@		B	
Shenyang	Liaoning Jilin Heilongjiang	@		B	
(B)					
Chengdu	Sichuan Xizang Yunnan Guizhou	0	1/4	#	4/8
Guangzhou	Guangdong Guangxi Hunan Hainan (not accessible by rail) Hubei	+	3/5	‡	3/4
Lanzhou	Gansu Qinghai Ningxia Shaanxi Xinjiang	@		‡	1/6
(C)					
Jinan	Shandong Henan	+	1/2	‡	1/3
Nanjing	Jiangsu Zhejiang Anhui Fuzhou Jiangxi	+	2/5	B	

Notes

*   Chart adapted from C.K. Leung, *China: Railway Patterns and National Goals*, (Department of Geography, University of Chicago, Research Paper No.195, 1980), p.143.
(a)   Connectivity of military districts in the same military region.
(a1)   Number of military districts in the same MR represented in vertexes *not* directly connected by railway over total number of military districts in the same MR.
(b)   Connectivity with neighbouring provincial captials (including autonomous regions).
(b1)   Number of neighbouring provincial capitals (including autonomous regions) represented in vertexes *not* directly connected by railway over a number of neigbouring provincial capitals (including autonomous regions).
@   Complete connectivity with neighbouring military districts in the same MR.
B   Complete connectivity with neigbouring provincial capitals achieved.
+   Indirect connection with all neighbouring military districts in the same MR (complete connectivity) possible; or indirect connectivity with all neighbouring capitals (complete connectivity) possible.
‡   Indirect connection with neigbouring capital achieved.
0   One military district in the same MR not connected.
Direct and/or indirect connection with all neighbouring capitals except Lhasa (Tibet).

incorporated Wuhan MD which provides the military region with crucial logistic support as Wuhan is one of the most important military-industrial complexes in China. Although direct connectivity has deteriorated as a result, the completion of double-tracking in the Hengyang–Guangzhou section of the Beijing–Guangzhou line and the completion of the Guangzhou–Zhanjiang line (hence linking Nanning with Guangzhou) will, on the other hand, improve the situation tremendously.[25] In addition to its strengthened logistic capabilities, Guangzhou MR will be of great value to Chengdu and Lanzhou MRs in providing both manpower and logistic support as railway connectivity improves in the Seventh Five-Year Plan.

THE MOBILISATION OF THE RESERVE FORCES

Since the introduction of the Military Service Law in May 1984, the task of manpower mobilisation for war and training for the Reserve Forces during peace-time lies squarely with the People's Armed Forces Department (PAFD) at the county and city levels.[26] In the setting of the military regions, the military subdistrict is the parallel organisation which participates in fulfilling objectives for mobilisation tasks.[27] In terms of leadership, there had been a series of reinvigorated efforts to transfer control of the PAFD from the dual leadership position (jointly held by the military and the local government) to the local government in 1986, and the month of June was scheduled as the completion time for the exercise.[28] The numerous tasks of the PAFD in enlisting conscripts and the Reserve Forces, and administering of militia organisations and the training of the Reserve Forces have been discussed in general terms in Chapter 1. The present discussion concentrates on the effectiveness of the combined strength of the militia and the reservists. Given the State's urge to economise and retrench the defence force (as reflected in specific policies like integrating production skills and production targets with militia training programs),[29] it would be necessary to examine first the relative strengths and weaknesses of China's cost-effective formula to mobilise the large Reserve Forces for war, and second, the effectiveness of the PAFD leadership in administering the above.

From the outset, the State's ability to keep records of personnel eligible for conscription in the 18–22 age range and for reserve service in the 18–35 age range provides the basis for manpower planning.[30] It also constitutes the basis for good civil-military inter-relations which the State relies on in order to mobilise the large supplementary force for war in a matter of 48–72 hours.[31]

The use of reservists

The Chinese are able to select from a vast manpower pool in recruiting over five million reservists and 4.3 million basic militia which support the 3.2 million strong active defence force.[32] The estimate of 5.3 million reservists necessarily comprises different levels with varying degrees of combat readiness. The reserve divisions (RD) are the most proficient and most military regions have at least one since the establishment of the first Infantry RD in Tianjin in August 1983.[33] Beijing MR established its second Infantry RD on 1 February 1985. These 'elite' forces would comprise only about 10 000 men in each RD. The fact that they have exercised with regular forces in combined arms, and the claim that most of these reservists have received rigorous training as they are veterans and demobilised soldiers speak for their capabilities as fully alert units.[34] However, it should be pointed out that training must be maintained at a level that would avoid fading reservist ability. This is the case as short-term conscripts highly trained in tactical and technical skill will lose their acquired capabilities in a civilian environment over the years. The younger the reservists are, the greater will be their chance of retaining these skills.[35] Whilst the most advanced reserve units in western countries may be able to withstand the most sophisticated of threats, it is not considered suitable for the operational commander to place them in high-risk zones.[36] Nevertheless, the Chinese RDs will incorporate the naval and air arms as well and they will be expected to be an integral part of combined arms and joint service operations. For instance, a certain reserve division in Hubei was reported for the first time in August 1984 to have successfully participated in a military exercise with a certain army in the Wuhan MR. The RD was reported to have practised mobilisation, rapid movement with motorised troops and positional defence in the tactics of attack in field operations and railway transport.[37]

Aside from the elite RD force, the major manpower pool for the Reserve Forces which can be called forward comprises 'fillers' within individual units otherwise manned by regular peronnel. The classic example of efficient mobilisation involving over 1000 men and achieving the M+2 days (combat ready in 48 hours after mobilisation) objective, were reported in June 1984 in Guangzhou as these personnel were sent to the Ground Forces, the Navy and the Air Force for the training for 7–20 days.[38] It would be unreaslistic to assume that the Guangzhou experience applies to the Reserve Forces in general. The reduction of training time and the emphasis on peacetime construction necessarily curtail the efficiency of the reservists. The Chinese are relying a great deal on the veterans and demobilised soldiers as a flow-on into the Reserve Forces. However, the fading of reservist ability can only be avoided if the Reserve Forces are kept relatively young; and in any case it should not exceed the maximum age of 28 specified for the first category of active reservists.[39] Switzerland has been cited as an example illustrating the principle of 'every man constitutes a soldier in the nation'.[40] The commonality being drawn is that citizens can be mobilised without further training. In the Swiss case, military personnel have 'a relatively short overall period of service to perform, but that service is spread over a great many years'.[41] The Chinese can see the advantage of the Swiss system as it minimises the fading of reservist ability.

Leadership in the Reserve Forces is provided by the reserve officers who should be recruited from the pool of demobilised officers first and foremost. The sources for recruitment in the descending order after that are (a) demobilised soldiers, (2) eligible graduates from tertiary institutions, (3) militia and PAFD cadres and (4) non-military and specialised technical cadres. In order to increase the pool of manpower for leadership in the Reserve Forces, reserve officers should serve specific terms and then retire. They are also required to leave their production work every year to a specified period so as to concentrate on training. This is regarded as essential in order to improve their war-preparedness.[42]

To gauge the efficiency and capabilities of reservists, western experience addresses four major questions and issues which are all applicable to the Chinese case.[43]

1. Have the reservists received recent military training?
2. Are their mobilisation procedures prepared and practised?
3. Has the training been within the type of unit in which they would be mobilised?
4. Would the reservists be in a position by M+3 (the third day after mobilisation)?

The answer to question 1 in the Chinese experience is that priorities in economic construction require the Chinese to reduce training time and rely on the flow of veterans and demobilised soldiers into the reservist pool. The Guangzhou mobilisation experience in June 1984 represents the ideal answer to questions 3 and 4. The leadership of the PAFD which provides an answer to question 2 will be examined presently.

The militia: leadership, training and capabilities

Militia organisations under the leadership of the PAFD are responsible not only for the mobilisation of the reservists but also for training and preparing the huge militia force both for production and for war. Since the declaration of the MSL in 1984, China has shifted its emphasis from a reliance on the vast manpower pool of the common militia, to a serious upgrading of the armed basic militia, to an acceptable level in the Reserve Forces. The common militia, which have been known to be paper organisations, were estimated at 44–250 million. They are no longer considered significant although those supplementary and loose organisations may remain a labour force which would prove to be handy to the State in emergency situations. It is the armed basic militia, estimated to be 4.3 million, that the PAFDs concentrate on integrating with the five million reservists in accordance with the 1984 MSL which stresses the need to combine the two in order to provide the numerical strength in wartime:[44]

> In the event of war, the state will be able to use the PLA as the backbone and the militia and the reserves as the broad base for forming new troops and expanding existing units at the highest possible speed, and mobilise the whole nation for a people's war under modern conditions, so as to drown the invading enemy in the vast ocean of people's war.

Apart from logistic support the militia can render, the armed basic militia has been providing a supportive role in border defence, in which local knowledge of the terrain and linguistic skill have made it unique in the history of Sino–Vietnamese border clashes since 1979 (details to be discussed later).

Dual leadership

In the pre-Cultural Revolution period, Mao Zedong saw the militia as part and parcel of the doctrine of People's War, in which every man can be transformed into a soldier (*quanmin jiebing*). Nevertheless, the grim reality of politics since the Cultural Revolution provided a rather different picture.

When Jiang Qing and Zhang Chunqiao called upon the masses to 'learn from Shanghai in Militia Building', central control of militia organisations began to appear and it persisted all the way into October 1976. This came in the establishment of Municipal Militia General Headquarters which existed in the cities of Shanghai and

Canton, and which served to bolster the positions of the Revolutionary Left who expected support at the local levels.[45] Harlan Jencks
claims that regional PLA commanders only paid lip service to 'learning from Shanghai', and that they continued to maintain control over
militia affairs through 1974–76.[46] It is generally true to say that the
Gang of Four failed to enlist significant support from the local
commanders and that their attempt to establish an alternative armed
force via the Shanghai militia also failed. However, it has to be said
at the same time that (irrespective of Jencks' claim) the Party's thorny
problems regarding 'three supports and two militaries', especially in
early 1980, bear witness to the influence the Gang of Four must have
had in some military regions, especially over management of the
militia: Shanghai and Guangzhou are the case in point.

In any case, the need to defuse the Leftist influence of the PLA in
militia leadership must have been realised as Deng Xiaoping took
over leadership. In the first place, the PLA is structurally tied to the
militia in that the former at the various levels supervises the work of
the armed units, with the People's Armed Forces Department providing the administrative base. Further, the effective functioning of the
three major duties of combat, albeit in a supportive role, production
(with the necessary contradictions between the two functions) and
political work have traditionally been closely guided by the PLA at
the relevant levels. When the Party moved to exercise firmer control,
contradictions emerged.[47]

As new militia regulations were promulgated in 1978, the Party's
closer supervision of the militia became evident. In 1979 it decreed
that all Party secretaries should hold the concurrent post of political
commissar of the PAFD at the different levels.[48]

As regards the PLA, its strong ties with the militia have been
reflected in professional supervision and training of militia units. It
also participated in the selection of full-time and part-time military
cadres who were very often demobilised soldiers and specialised
technical personnel. Thus a system of dual leadership had become
prevalent as Deng Xiaoping took over the helm. The system guaranteed PLA commanders authority to assist the work of the PAFDs,
especially in the area of military training. At the same time, the
political commissar structure guaranteed the Party secretary's position in leadership. In the Tianjin Garrison Command in September
1979, the nature of dual leadership in militia work is well
illustrated:[49]

At the conference a responsible comrade of Tianjin Garrison announced
the order issued by the Beijing PLA units in regard to appointing

secretaries of various district and county CCP committees to be concurrently the first political commissars of the people's armed forces departments in their own localities... (He) urged comrades of the various district and county CCP committees to adhere to the dual leadership of local party committee and military department, to give the full role of the military departments to local party committees, to be active good staff officers of the local party committees, and to advance practical proposals for militia work in a timely manner; on the basis of the central task in achieving the four modernisations so as to raise the militia building of our municipality to a new level.

A good illustration of the close ties PLA cadres had with the PAFDs can be drawn from the Guangdong Provincial People's Armed Forces Committee in August 1979, which confirmed that militia commanders of the people's communes, state farms, forest plantations, etc. should be of the same rank as Party committee members:[50]

Besides doing their best to select full time armed cadres from among the existing state cadres and soldiers who became cadres, they will also choose full time armed cadres from among the demobilised soldiers who have returned to the rural areas and those outstanding militia cadres who are not divorced from production. The required labor quota is arranged according to the overall planning of the departments of each area and prefecture (city).... The militia commanders of the people's communes, state farms, forest plantations, factories and mines, and of the streets should be of the same rank as party committee members. Party committees at various levels should strengthen their training.

Under dual leadership the militia experienced reforms ranging from more discriminatory recruitment criteria for full-time cadres, clearer classification of cadres. Greater material incentive for full-time/part-time militia work, more assured links with the masses at the grassroots level to better organised training programmes and logistic support.[51] In the first place, the size of such leadership provided by these full-time cadres must not be misunderstood. For instance, two specific missions undertaken by military sub-districts (parallel to county level) in 1978 involved only 89 and 250 cadres respectively who had to cover work in all the relevant communes and brigades. In the latter case (the Anyang Military Sub-district of Henan), the team had to supervise 246 000 militia men in a fight against drought.[52]

Second, the nature of dual leadership is also amply reflected in the two major classifications of the political and military or armed cadres.[53] The political cadre had to be a senior member of the Party whilst the military cadre should be a demobilised soldier. In fact, the ruling that military cadres should be demobilised soldiers does provide a critically important channel for veterans to seek alternative employment after demobilisation, but the alarming projected figure of one million ex-soldiers would only add problems to the militia system which would not be able to absorb such vast numbers. Besides, there was also a tendency for some military regions to prefer the employment of full-time armed cadres from amongst the existing militia cadres who might be regarded as knowing the local scene and thus better suited, than specially assigned demobilised soldiers who were sometimes estranged by the local environment, and who probably would be older, as indicated by the move in May 1977 that the age limit of demobilised soldiers serving in the militia be extended.[54] Indeed, an article in October 1980 in *Dazhong Ribao* (The Masses Daily) in Jinan makes no secret of its preference for local personnel whose youthfulness in its opinion will effect the rejuvenation of the cadres of the PAFD:[55]

> According to the traditional method of selection full-time armed cadres, first, they can be selected from among specialised, demobilised army-men and, second, they can also be selected from among outstanding militia cadres and others who are suitable for this type of work. At present every year a group of specialised demobilised army-men come to the localities, and there are also many outstanding militia cadres who have both ability and political integrity. For one county, there are many persons who are suitable for and ready to do militia work. It will not be difficult to select several tens of young cadres if we carry our work into the family household.
>
> From the long-term point of view, we ought to set up a necessary system for maintaining the youthfulness of fulltime armed cadres. Departments concerned can, according to actual conditions, make rules that separately require youthfulness for secretaries in charge of people's armed forces and for people's armed forces and department heads, thereby systematically ensuring the youthfulness of people's armed forces cadres. To set up a fixed system that puts an age limit on cadres engaged in people's armed forces work will also be of benefit in making satisfactory arrangements for full-time people's armed forces cadres.

Another changing emphasis on militia work was greater recognition for full-time and sometimes part-time work in the militia, on condition that such incentives extended to individual cadres do not affect the total income of the militia forces. The exact detail of how this can be worked out with no detriment to interested parties is not known, but some PAFDs made allowance for material incentives to be extended both to armed cadres and militiamen for specific purposes. The Guangdong People's Armed Force Committee under the chairmanship of Yang Shangkun, for instance, resolved in August 1979 that full-time militia cadres should be given a lesser workload although this would obviously work against the well-nigh obsessed policy for production.[56] Militia battalion commanders were to be remunerated via either a fixed subsidy or a method of subsidising for missing work. To facilitate this, the same commanders were to become the principal leading cadres of production brigades and members of the Party branches. As for the militia, when assigned to special duties or attending training sessions, the recording of work points and the issuance of wages should continue.[57]

The third thrust concentrated on establishing a better grassroots link with the masses, with the expectation that the militia in its various functions could serve as a genuine link between the PAFDs on the one hand and the masses on the other. Basically, this entails the shifting of the major operating level of militia work from the county to the commune. Individual PAFD claimed that the armed cadres would be able to conduct militia training in person at the commune level whilst previous operations at the county level would only involve the same individuals in a supervisory role and from a distance. Undoubtedly, this move consolidated the position of the armed basis militia as the important link between the PLA and the masses as it received much closer attention from armed cadres. In addition, it was claimed that operations at the commune level could economise on expenditure.[58]

People's armed forces department under party leadership

Since the beginning of 1984, the Party had launched campaigns to transfer the control of the PAFDs from military departments to local governments. The declaration of the MSL in May 1984 revealed the rationale for Party control over the PAFD, as it intended to effect swift mobilisation of the combined strength of the militia and the reservists. Nevertheless, such transfer of power to the Party committees had taken a long time. It was in the first half of 1986 that the Party reinvigorated the transfer and set the end of June deadline. The relatively long history of this power transfer reveals problems the Party had with the military departments, who found it difficult to adjust to the new policies. There are about 2000 PAFDs at county level throughout the country which are being transferred to the local authorities.[59] As late as May 1986, the Party was reporting on experiments involving only 60 PAFDs in the transfer of command.[60]

The national forum of advanced cadres of county PAFDs in March 1986 recognised the transfer of command to be 'a glorious yet arduous task'.[61] It also pointed out the need to ensure that 'all the barracks of the PAFDs are in good condition and that all public property and funds do not fall short'.[62] An examination of difficulties confronting the provinces in the transfer of PAFD command reveals the reluctance on the part of military departments to give up power. Nevertheless, it seems that the Party is determined to maintain control. In Heilongjiang, guarantees were given to the military that they could have access to training bases and facilities and that their rights to the use and management of equipment and *materiel* could be retained.[63] In Zhejiang, re-eduction was emphasised to ensure 'a smooth channel of communications'.[64] In Jiangxi and Hebei the problems were more serious as they involved specific issues as well as fraud. In Jiangxi, specific problems touched on included housing, jobs for dependants and children's education,[65] whilst the Hebei provincial conference on PAFD transfer of command held at the provincial Military District in early April 1986 warned against fraudulent practices like the transfer of funds and the private disposal of equipment and *materiel*.[66] In Shandong and Henan, the problem was over the settling of surplus cadres.[67]

Integrating economic construction and militia training

The Party's urge to ensure that the 2000 odd PAFDs throughout the country complete the transfer of command has been spurred on by the enforcement of new directions in militia work. Increasing emphasis on economic construction and the need to integrate production skills with the militia program have induced PAFDs to reduce training tasks. The *Liberation Army Daily* gave prominence to Yang Shangkun's article on the new directions which appeared on 22 Feburary 1985:[68]

> Efforts must be made to organise militia-men to work hard in order to become well-to-do, and to maintain the militia forces by organising them to do manual labour. By doing so, we shall be able to lighten the people's burden and help support local construction at the same time. This is a new and fine path.

In some provinces, militia training has been made part of the responsibility system so that training and production can become an integral part of the livelihood of production teams. In Shanxi, the secretary of the Provincial Party Committee announced in January

1986 that 'the past state of combat or semi-combat readiness in Militia and Reserve Service work should be switched to peaceful construction'.[69]

It seems that the present preference for economic production at the expense of militia training will affect the level of readiness of the armed basic militia. In wealthy provinces, the responsibility system and economic organisations can ensure that adequate militia training is provided for by subsidies. Nevertheless militia training in the relatively poor provinces suffers as economic production becomes a necessity. In well-to-do provinces like Jiangsu, militia activitives are becoming more self-sufficient under the scheme of 'support military training with production labour'. Thus 400 townships, or 19 per cent of the province's total, were capable of financing their own militia activities in January 1986.[70] The incentive to militia work has been based mainly on prosperity resulting from the activities of economic organisations which succeeded in responding to the State's call to 'making the militia rich'.[71] Thus 1000 economic organisations in 800 townships and towns made a profit of over RMB14 million in 1985–86 out of an output value of RMB100 million. The actual expenditure involved in militia work was only RMB2.8 million.[72] The prosperous situation can be explained by the successes Jiangsu PAFDs had in engaging militiamen in commodity production when over 200 000 militiamen were mobilised to run factories. The resultant profit would then be subsidising the militia training program under various arrangements, including the responsibility system.[73] In less fortunate provinces, militia training suffered as a result of reduction in time allocated, and when local governments could not afford to subsidise training.

Thus Gansu Military District (obviously the transfer of power in the PAFD had not happened) found it necessary in May 1985 to reduce militia training tasks by 34 per cent in order to serve the overall interest in economic construction.[74] The picture was especially grim in Gansu as it had to solve problems of people's livelihood in proverty stricken areas. Thus targets to lighten the masses' burdens were set on a five-year basis in 1983. Worst still, 'the target of stopping sabotage' was also set at the same time.[75] In Guangxi, it was specified that militia training in poor counties and townships could be reduced, eased or waived.[76]

One glaring exception to the trend to reduce militia training came from Hunan in January 1986, when Mao Zhiyong, Party Secretary and First Political Commissar of the Hunan MD, 'pointed out emphatically that militia and reserve service work can be neither weakened or cancelled, but must be strengthened vigorously'.[77] He added that even with economic construction, militia work involving 1.8 million militiamen (including common militia) must not be weakened.[78] Mao's statements suggest that he is at odds with the central directives and that the Hunan PAFDs will find it more difficult to reduce militia training tasks and to make way for economic production.

The Hunan case reflects the worries of the militiary as they fear that the capabilities of China's Reserve Forces will suffer in the long run. The most innovative way of avoiding this seems to be the integration of production incentive with militia training as illustrated by the Jiangsu example. (One does realise that poverty-stricken areas will find it impossible to follow the Jiangsu experience.) Since 1985, the State has unashamedly called upon provinces to devise ways and means to help militiamen get rich on the basis of integrating productive labour with militia duties. In the wake of Hu Yaobang's visit, Yunnan MD worked out measures to reduce militia training whilst upgrading its quality and imparting 'knowledge about getting rich and introducing professional skills...'.[79] Very often, militiamen devoted one-third of their time to acquiring production skills and actual production. This explains why there is general enthusiasm in militia work in those provinces which can afford to implement the integrative measures.[80]

Militia training and the responsibility system

Since the inception of the responsibility system in the late 1970s, problems were created for the regulars and the militia alike because able-bodied men spent their time serving or being involved in militia training rather than contributing to production in the agricultural and urban sectors. Nevertheless, policy-makers had, since 1981, devised ways and means to incorporate militia duties into the responsibility system whilst providing economic incentive and recognition for services rendered. Bascially, the State had given the local governments the task of financing the cost incurred in militia training. Thus the responsibility system is extended not only to production but also to the financing of essentials at the local level. Instead of the central government bearing the cost, local governments are now charged with the financial responsibility of supporting militia development. The ideal situation is illustrated by Jiangsu's successes as economic benefits emerging from the responsibility system are such that local governments are more than happy to cover the cost of militia training.

Pioneering PAFDs at the county level in the enterprising provinces of Jiangsu, Anhui and Shandong have begun to incorporate elements of the responsibility system into the militia system. By 1982–1983, the term *shuangbao* (double-contract) was used to denote the new venture whilst *sibao* (quadruple-contract) indicated the vertical chain of command operating from the county PAFD downwards to the commune PAFD, the militia companies and the militia households.[81] Each of the commune PAFD would work out an efficient accounting system so that the cost of militia training and administration could be precisely computed and borne by the commune and its members as part of the producton contract.[82]

From available information, militia work in the responsibility system seems to have three major objectives. First, individual county PAFDs are expected to look into ways of minimising the cost of militia training by deploying armed militia cadres to take up concurrent positions of responsibility in order to compensate for their absence, albeit for good reasons, from production. At the same time, investigations are conducted to ensure that militia training is done during the off-peak agricultural seasons in the rural areas. Second, elaborate systems of accounting at the county PAFD level and below have been instituted to ensure a fair sharing of the cost of militia training. Third, preferential treatment is extended to the households of armed militia cadres, who because of their militia duties cannot contribute to production.[83]

The first objective of minimising cost and in providing efficiency in militia training was practised in Shandong where militiary cadres of the PAFD were encouraged to take concurrent posts at lower levels. Thus military cadres could hold concurrent posts as militia platoon or company commanders in order to mix well with militiamen.[84] These arrangements not only served the purpose of reducing the cost of militia training but also became a common practice as the Party wished to supervise county PAFDs. Nevertheless, this new development was not without problems. In Liaoning in 1982–83 for instance, many militia company commanders found it difficult to handle meetings and concentrate on militia work when their concurrent posts proved too heavy and when there was no standardisation in workload.[85]

As regards the second objective of sharing the cost of militia training, an elaborate accounting system divided cost into training (including sentry duties), education, control of firearms, security duties and administration. In the past, militiamen were given work points for taking part in training. One way of calculating the work load in the new responsibility system was the allocation of points to production as well as to the different activities in militia building.[86]

The new system claimed that three major advantages had been achieved. First, the masses were enthusiastic and closely linked to the militia leadership. Second, there was good guarantee that the personnel in charge of training were up to standard. Third, political work in the militia was guaranteed. Other ways of sharing the cost of militia training included:

1. The commune requiring brigades to share the cost of militia training.

2. The commune setting aside profits from certain enterprises under its sponsorship to cover the cost.

3. The commune subcontracting the responsibility of militia training to a specialist team in the armed basic militia team (*wuzhuang jigan minbing zhuanye dui*) at the company level.

The first method was adopted by Wendeng County, Shandong, in 1981 as an experiment in which remuneration for workload in militia training was borne systematically by the commune, with production brigades under it sharing the cost equally. Production teams in turn contributed their share of the work load, and any inadequacies or insufficiencies would be borne by the production brigade above them.[87] Emerging from the pioneering experiment in Shandong, and probably other advanced areas in 1981, is the well-popularised militia system in Shandong instituted in May 1983, that is 'quadruple-contract'.

The second method of financing militia activities was relatively simple and did not involve subcontracting militia duties. In 1983 in Gu'an County, Hebei, certain percentages of profit accrued from enterprises were set aside as remuneration for militia activities. Militia training was centralised with the establishment of bases so that significant savings could be made. It was reported that RMB 27 000 and 1200 sq.metres of land were saved in 1984 by the county which took over the supervision of firearms for the militia.[88]

The third method involved the commune subcontracting militia training to a specialist team in the militia company. In 1981 in Shandong, the militia company in the Zifu production brigade of Douyu Commune in Fushan County organised specialist teams comprising 30 men each. Led by the militia company commander, each team supervised 50 *mu* of orchards and the maintenance of roads and public works. On top of these duties, the team was able to participate in fifteen days of scheduled militia training and four extra days of shooting and tactical training. In addition, it normalised political education and confirmed the practice of controlling firearms. These good results were claimed to be due to the close link between militia activities and labour. In addition, the team did not have to claim remuneration from the production brigade.[89]

It does seem apparent that the second and third methods in conducting militia activities were relatively simple and easy to administer in meeting the demands from county PAFDs. On the other hand, 'quadruple-contract' seems to be the most prevalent.

The third objective in incorporating militia work in the responsibility system was to extend preferential treatment to the households of the armed militia cadres. Such measures seemed to have reactivated mutual aid teams of the Yan'an days when the principle of *laowu hezuo* (cooperation between labour and military) was applied to the Communist anti-Japanese resistance bases where both agricultural production and self-defence capabilities were essential for survival. In Liaoning and Jiangsu in 1983 there were reports of how these teams operated. Basically these were task forces within the militia companies who were assigned the duty of tending to the so-called 'responsibility fields' (*zeren tian*) which were allocated to militia households, but which the militiamen had to leave because of training duties. Major work would include insecticiding, manuring and irrigation work.[90] In Suzhou Military Subdistrict, the militia did work on 23 000 *mu* for military families and harvested another 12 000 *mu* for them in 1983.[91]

Militia capabilities in the 1980s

It remains to be seen whether China is jeopardising militia capabilities as a result of its pronounced emphasis on economic construction. Nevertheless, in so far as the militia's supportive role in combat and logistics is concerned, significant changes have been brought about in the 1980s.

The introduction of the revised 'Regulations on Militia Work' in August 1978 following the all-China Militia Work Conference did bring about a better focus in militia training in the 1980s.[92] In the first place, a clear distinction is being drawn between the training of the urban and the rural militia because they sometimes have different

objectives. In the cities, for instance, the urban militia would naturally be concerned primarily with city defence construction, including
the servicing of air defence, or in specific terms, the mastering of
anti-aircraft exercises. Wang Enmao, as Chairman of the Jilin Provincial Revolutionary Committee, thus emphasised in a symposium on
defence of cities in March 1980 that city defence construction
depended a great deal on cooperation between the various military
and people's air defence departments and the local departments
concerned.[93] Similarly, the Guangzhou Urban Militia Conference
held on 2–4 April 1980 distinctly aimed at improving the training of
the urban armed militia cadres to a sophisticated level when it
resolved to strengthen the training of the commanders of the artillery
battalions and regiments within the armed militia force. This provided the opportunities for them to participate in joint operations,
especially in strategic urban areas like the various border provinces
where specialised exercises such as anti-air defence, anti-tank and
anti-airborne manoeuvres are regarded as essential.[94]

Militia capabilities in guerrilla warfare were reported in Ningxia
in June 1982 when a militia exercise under modern conditions
'carried out in the light of the peculiarities of future wars to oppose
aggression, the tasks of the people's militia and their present
facilities'.[95] Prominence was given in the report to the role of the
militia in sabotaging the enemy's petroleum pipelines (POL). PAFD
cadres took part in the exercise in the Shizuishan District and leading
commanders and party membrs of Lanzhou MR were spectators in
the exercise.[96]

Similar exercises can be undertaken by the rural armed militia.
But training in the rural sector would also incorporate what Wang
Enmao summarised as 'building three networks — forest work, road
network and ditch network',[97] which seems to cover an even greater
area of work than the urban counterpart in a more massive and
supportive role *vis-a-vis* the PLA.

Both the urban and rural militia seem to be better armed than
the common militia which is only armed with old-style and light
weapons. The basic militia is armed with light and heavy weapons as
well as communication facilities. At the senior level, ie battalion and
regiment, artillery commanders are deliberately trained together with
the regulars. At the same time, the 1978 'Regulations on Militia
Work' emphasise the maintenance and safekeeping of weapons and
equipment.[98] Moreover, the PAFDs at the various levels control all
weapons and conscious efforts are being made to train a greater
number of ordnance cadres to handle the situation.

The training of ordnance and armed cadres reveal the highest calibre of militia work and their responsibilities are crucial to the defence of the region. A report from Shandong Military District speaks for the importance of ordnance work at the local level:[99]

> The Shandong Military District has recently put into operation an ordnance cadre training unit [dui] to train some 130 ordnance cadres from the military subdistricts and county-level people's armed forces departments. The training is to improve ordnance management work and the cadres' professional level in view of the characteristics of militia ordnance work under the new historical conditions and on the basis of existing weapons and equipment, which will speed up the building of the rank and file of ordnance cadres and strengthen logistics work to meet the needs of modern warfare. In order to effectively run the training unit, the Shandong Military District made special efforts to establish a teaching office and to transfer cadres with professional know-how, practical experiences and teaching abilities to assume teaching positions.

Similarly, the amazing leadership calibre of the militia cadres is revealed in a report from Hunan MD in March 1985 where about 130 cadres undertook to supervise construction projects which involved 600 000 militiamen in the beginning of 1985.[100]

The militia's combat and logistic capabilities were put to test in the Sino–Vietnamese border war in 1979. The result was by no means satisfactory but great improvements have been made since, so that the militia's role in border defence has been strengthened. In the border war, it was reported that the Yunnan and Guangxi armed militia units had actually slowed down the PLA's advance and limited the capacity of the supply line. They therefore proved to be ill-suited to warfare beyond the border despite the fact that they were mobilised in large numbers for logistic purposes.[101] Immediately after the war, decision-makers wasted no time in applying such lessons learned to future training. The exercise started by about May 1979 and covered not only Yunnan and Guangzhou MRs but also as far as Hebei, and apparently other areas. It is not exactly clear whether militia units which participated in the war were actually sent to the north as models for training or whether it was merely a case of drawing a lesson from the war as far as the other MRs are concerned. What is certain nevertheless is that training sessions in this category concentrate on the work of the armed basic militia, reflecting first the level of militia participation in the war and second, the dual leadership's policy to intensify the training of the militia for war-preparedness. It was thus reported in May 1979 in *Beijing Ribao*:[102]

The People's Armed Unit of Yan Qing County held special training classes for members of guerrilla detachments and key members of the militia, basing on the experiences of the Sino–Vietnam War; the classes dealt with intelligence gathering skills, individual skills, mines, submachine guns and anti-tank skills.

The Vietnam experience no doubt would enrich the training sessions, in which the PAFDs saw the company as the basic and organic unit, as a higher level is seen as uneconomical. There were also two types of training sessions, namely those centralised and those locally supervised. Centralised training sessions were reserved for more sophisticated units such as the armed basic militia, but rotational training applied to both and serves as one of the means to fulfil training requirements laid down while not jeopardising production targets.[103]

In Hebei, militia training has been revitalised since 1983 as the decentralised system with commune/township as the basis changed to a centralised system based on the county or city. Under this system, which followed the instructions of the State Council and the Central Military Commission, Hebei Province had established 39 militia training centres by 1984–85. The advantages of the new system include the concentration of resources, better standardisation and quality of training, the saving of manpower and financial resources, the development of agricultural and sideline production and better availability of local resources to assist in broadening militiamen's knowledge of agriculture, and science and technology.[104]

China's recent experience in border defence is reflected in its clashes and skirmishes with the SRV which continued after the 1979 War. In turn, the militia has served a useful function in respect of the mastery of local knowledge, terrain and linguistic skills. In many ways, these militia capabilities can serve as a model for border defence in general. SRV information in the period 1980–85 reveals that the Chinese militia plays a not insignificant role in causing economic and political disruption to the Vietnamese on the border. In the first place, the SRV recognises China's ability to launch psychological and spy warfare when scouts, commandos and spies are used to capture cadres for information, and when bandits are encouraged to disrupt law and order.[105] The SRV reported that the Chinese had organised special guerrilla units comprising Hoa and Vietnamese for sabotage work. It was claimed that there were seven centres established in 1980 in Yunnan and Guangzhou for the purpose of political, military and spy training. In all these activities, it can safely be assumed that the Chinese armed militia with special local knowledge played an active part. They also prove to be indispensable in their ability to communicate with Vietnamese residents across the border as they share common local dialects.[106] This facilitated disruptive activities in 1985 when it was reported that the PRC distributed rifles to Vietnamese residents in the border area in exchange for rewards to the distributors who would often be the armed militia.[107] Disruption to the SRV also applies to maritime skirmishes in the disputed waters of the Spratley Islands. In 1980, the Vietnamese complained of attacks launched by 'over 1000 armed craft' (probably armed fishing boats crewed by the armed militia) on Vietnamese-held islands.[108] Another unique role played by the armed militia in the border area is its ability to create a sense of permanency by disrupting the enemy's confidence. In 1980 the SRV claimed that the Chinese conducted 750 incursions, seized 34 heights and 27 points and 'cultivated them'.[109] It is most likely that 'Chinese troops' described by the SRV were Chinese peasants in the armed militia who were not only carrying out military duties, but were probably more than happy to increase their own cultivatable areas for a profit.

The support base

China's warfighting capabilities have been enhanced by improvements made to the various sectors of the support base. The seven Military Regions have benefited from both the modernised transport and communications systems and the strengthened Reserve Forces. In providing logistic support for the PLA, railways, roads and waterways share the burden, but railways are strategically significant in average length of haul and freight density. Continuing improvements in railway communication designed for economic development in the seventh Five-Year Plan will also benefit the defence sectors. Thus electrification and multiple-tracking continue to improve capabilities in defence in depth and inter-MR connectivity, providing a better support base for the modernised PLA which now demands high logistic performance if it were to challenge the 'stronger' enemy.

As regards the mobilisation of the Reserve Forces, the introduction of the revised Military Service Law and the transfer of PAFD leadership to local governments have brought about reinvigoration in the work of the reservists and the militia. The mobilisation of the reservists in Guangzhou in June 1984 acts as a model for the ideal situation. The Chinese hope that their Reserve Forces can be mobilised in 48 hours, and trained to support all three services of the armed forces. Their reliance on veterans and demobilised and younger soldiers, and on the younger, active reservists to minimise the fading of reservists' ability suggests their intention to learn from Western models.

Nevertheless, priorities given to economic modernisation have imposed constraints on the training of the Reserve Forces. Such priorities are also reflected in the major task of the PAFD under the leadership of the local governments to integrate militia work and economic construction. In many ways, the PAFD have striven to integrate militia work into the responsibility system with promising results in the wealthier provinces like Jiangsu and Liaoning. However, the poorer provinces will continue to attend to urgent economic objectives at the expense of militia work. Despite these constraints, significant changes have been brought about in the 1980s regarding the militia's combat and logistic role in the support base. In support of 'People's War under modern conditions', both the urban and rural militia units are better trained and are expected to coordinate with Local and Main forces in joint operations. Their greatest assets are the knowledge of the local terrain and their numerical strength as the Chinese attempt to halt enemy strategic breakthroughs by undertaking active defence in positional warfare.

PART II

National Security and Defence Strategy

4

China's Threat Perceptions and Major Security Problems

The extent of China's success in defence modernisation should be measured not only in terms of how it attempts to narrow the strategic and technological gap, but also in the context of how it strengthens China's defence posture. In the first place, progress made in defence modernisation provides good support for the implementation of China's defensive strategy against an invading enemy.

Nevertheless, China no longer believes that war is imminent. Its reliance on peacetime war preparation and long-term strategic planning, discussed in Chapters 1 and 2, indicates that China takes a more optimistic view toward probable threats to national security. Deng Xiaoping's arguments that a peaceful environment would exist for a long period, and that it is unlikely that global war will break out in this century, further reinforce China's new threat perceptions.

No matter what span of time they may schedule for war preparation, the Chinese would need to assess the major sources of threats to national security and respond positively by improving their warfighting capabilities and evolving the most effective defence strategy against an enemy that will possibly invade Chinese territory. Furthermore, there is no denying that Chinese strategic planners have identified the USSR as the 'stronger enemy' who poses the greatest, though not imminent, threat to the nation. Disputes with their neighbours have also brought about low to mid-level conflicts which the Chinese would also consider to be threats to regional security. Conflicts with the SRV since 1979 fall into this category. It is therefore in the interest of national security that China has found it significant to play a positive role in the global strategic balance, so that it can rely on international interdependence and mutual deterrence as ways to strengthen its defence posture.

CHINA AND THE STRATEGIC BALANCE

Despite violence and tension, East–West relations over the past 42 years can be described as relatively stable and characterised by the avoidance of direct hostilities between the two superpowers. To the optimists, such a phenomenon has been attributed to prudent crisis management in a situation of alliance stability and mutual deterrence.[1] It remains true that the US and the USSR as central balance powers have managed to survive major crisis. Moreover, nations with nuclear strike capabilities have been confined to the US and the USSR and, on a smaller scale, China, Britain and France.

Although the two superpowers still hold the key to global balance, the growth of political and economic influence in the Asia–Pacific and other regions suggests that the world is no longer bi-polar pure and simple.[2] China's emergence as a nuclear power with limited second-strike capabilities, and Japan's growing economic power are the two relatively new forces in the international system.

China's role in the strategic balance is first and foremost guided by the way it conducts itself in international relations. China claims that it pursues an independent, self-reliant foreign policy which 'determines its policy independently on the merits of each case proceeding as we do from the fundamental interests of the Chinese people and the people of the world. That's what we mean by an independent foreign policy'.[3] To the Chinese, this position should not be confused with an equidistant policy towards the superpowers which would entail the sacrifice of the Five Principles of Coexistence.[4] In addition, China demonstrates its determination to distance itself from alliances that may cause shifts in the global strategic balance, as a US–China *entente* indeed would. Further, China seems to be keen to utilise international interdependence in the 1980s as a means of maintaining the regional strategic balance, as illustrated by its support for the position of the Association of Southeast Asian Nations (ASEAN) in the search for a solution to the Kampuchean question.[5] At the same time, its foreign policy has enough flexibility to accommodate the 'fundamental interests of the Chinese people'. Thus China justifies its open door policy and its reliance on the US and the West for its technological and economic needs on the grounds that they serve the fundamental interests of the people. Likewise the US regards China as a 'friendly non-aligned nation', highlighting its closer relations with China with the beginnings of nuclear cooperation and technological transfers like the latest US$550 million sale of avionic retrofits to upgrade the F-8 aircraft.[6]

On the other hand, China wishes to improve relations with the USSR. *Rapprochement* with the Soviets is probable although China specifies three obstacles to normalisation which remain significant barriers. The three obstacles are Soviet military build-up on the Sino–Soviet border, Soviet support for Vietnam's invasion of Kampuchea and Soviet invasion of Afghanistan.[7]

At first glance, the Sino–Soviet conflict involves higher risk and poses greater danger to the global strategic balance, while the Kampuchean question is confined more to the regional level though the superpowers are all involved. Nevertheless, it can be argued that China, in developing a more independent foreign policy which seeks to secure political equilibrium in the Pacific, wishes to reach certain understandings over the Kampuchean question. This urge has in turn taken priority over considerations for the longer conflict with the USSR. In addition, China may be hoping that improvements in regional security would contribute to stabilising the global balance should it succeed in distancing the Soviets from the Vietnamese as well as securing afterwards certain agreements with the Soviets over the border conflict.

SINO–SOVIET CONFLICT AND REGIONAL SECURITY ISSUES

To the Chinese, the three obstacles to the normalisation of Sino–Soviet relations had been regarded as equally durable. Whilst China denounces the Soviet invasion of Afghanistan, it also objects to the American invasion of Grenada. Both are considered to be hegemonic acts. In reply to the Chinese, the Soviet-backed Afghan regime attacks China for supplying arms to the rebels via Pakistan.[8] The Afghan situation can be considered a medium-level regional conflict, with China being involved on the side. As far as Chinese strategic interest is concerned it cannot be argued that Soviet presence in Afghanistan directly challenges China's security. Soviet-controlled Afghanistan poses a direct threat to Pakistan and the Persian Gulf states, not China.

As regards Soviet military build-up on the Sino–Soviet border, and Soviet support for Vietnam's invasion of Kampuchea, China has shown its willingness to reach certain understandings with the USSR. In the process, it demonstrates its skill in playing a 'semi-America card' and a 'semi-Soviet card'. American treatment of China as a 'friendly non-aligned nation', the beginnings of Sino–American nuclear cooperation, and increased American fulfilment of China's technological and economic needs (including defence hardware) in the modernisation program are adequate evidence of China's tilt towards the US. Having reached this stage in the international strategic balance, China may now try to appease the USSR without being too mindful of American wrath. Despite American displeasure with Soviet overtures resultant from Arkhipov's nine-day visit to Beijing in December 1984, it may be argued also that the US cannot afford to distance itself too much from its newly-found friend.[9] Thus China hopes to reach a certain position over Kampuchea–Vietnam which is to defuse tension in Southeast Asia, and the most significant ingredients for such moves are 'flirtation' with the USSR and greater success with international interdependence in the Pacific. Surprisingly, 'flirtation' has come from the Soviets as highlighted by Gorbachev's Vladivostok speech on 28 July 1986.[10]

As early as July 1984 Chinese Vice-Minister Zhu Qizhen identified the global implications of the Sino–Soviet border conflict when he maintained that the deployment of large numbers of Soviet SS–20 missiles in the Far East was mainly directed against the US and Japan although it also posed a threat to China's security.[11] Thus a major conflict on the Sino–Soviet border would probably also involve the Americans. It is true that there is no Sino–American alliance treaty, but mutual deterrence may now be called into play as the Americans are well aware of the threat of Soviet missiles in the Far East. At the same time, China's anti-Soviet defence posture is ample warning to the USSR of the high-risk involved in the event of confrontation.

There is no secret that 'People's War under modern conditions' which advocates active defence (jiji fangyu) in the face of an invading enemy aims at the USSR. The original doctrine of 'People's War' is still partially relevant. Although the Chinese Main Forces will be deployed in the second line of defence, the militia and the reservists will be mobilised to 'drown the enemy'.[12] With renewed defence modernisation, and the introduction of combined arms and joint operations for active defence in positional warfare, China hopes to be able to withstand Soviet conventional and nuclear attacks.[13] (See Chapter 5 for details.) However, turning the Chinese Northeast into an Afghanistan may invoke too great a risk as it might induce the

Chinese to deploy their limited strategic weapon systems and might force China to enter into a military alliance with the US.

From the perspective of the Chinese leaders, they would want to avoid confrontation with the Soviets by keeping the channels for negotiations open. The half-yearly talks established since 1982 have thus opened the avenues for *detente*. After eight rounds of talks, the two countries have not resolved anything on the three obstacles, but they have established better economic, cultural and trade ties.[14] Without doubt, China's determination to maintain its status as an independent power and achieve its long term goal of economic modernisation has urged it to develop *detente* with the USSR. The failure to remove the three obstacles has not deterred the development of better relations between the two countries. Arkhipov's visit to China in December 1984 prepared the way for the signing of the important, long-term trade agreement which involved US$14 billion. The agreement, signed in July 1985, involves Soviet supplies to the Chinese items like machinery, chemicals, cars and trucks, building materials and unspecified materials. Chinese exports include consumer goods, agricultural commodities and raw materials. In addition to the barter arrangements, the Soviets will help modernise seventeen industrial installations constructed by the Soviets in the 1950s.[15] Whilst the trade arrangement marks an important development in Sino–Soviet relations, its economic significance remains modest in comparison with China's strengthened trade ties with the US and Japan.

As if to remind itself that these moves towards *detente* would betray China's primary objective to oppose 'hegemonism', the Chinese snubbed the Soviets in January 1986. In the wake of Soviet Deputy Foreign Minister Mikhail Kapitsa's visit to Beijing, his counter-part, Qian Qichen, made it clear in no uncertain terms that the Soviets must not take improvements in ties for granted, and that they had to be reminded of the underlying realities of the three obstacles to normalisation. Qian reiterated that '... the Soviet side has a misconception that it can get round these obstacles, or that the obstacles will vanish by themselves. This calculation of the Soviets is unrealistic and unwise'.[16]

Nevertheless, Sino–Soviet relations did not take a turn for the worse. The eighth round of talks took place in Moscow in April 1986 with none other than Qian Qichen continuing to represent Beijing.[17] In addition, the two foreign ministers are expected to be exchanging visits sometime in the near future. These meetings are generally regarded as an important landmark for the future *detente*. There seems to be great expectations that the two foreign ministers will be able to seek certain conciliations or understandings over the three obstacles.[18] Signals of conciliation were evident in April 1985 when Deng Xiaoping claimed that the USSR could still retain bases in Vietnam and maintain its relations with the SRV as long as the Soviets urged the latter to withdraw from Kampuchea.[19] Even in the thorny question of party-to-party relations, there are encouraging signs. These include the restoration of Sino–Soviet trade unions relations in April 1985, and the exchange of visits of delegates from the Chinese National People's Congress and the Supreme Soviet.[20]

The most recent breakthrough in Sino–Soviet relations has been initiated by Gorbachev's speech at Vladivostok on 28 July 1986 when he proposed an Asia–Pacific disarmament conference to reduce naval forces, remove foreign bases and control nuclear weapons in Asia. Such a Helsinki-style Asian forum would undoubtedly win recognition for the USSR as a full partner in the region. Specifically, Gorbachev offered China the following positive proposals:[21]

1. That the official Sino–Soviet border on the Amur could pass along the main channel (rather than follow the south bank, to China's disadvantage).

2. That the Soviet Union was examining the question of withdrawing 'a considerable number of Soviet troops from Mongolia' in consultation with the leadership of that country.

3. That the Soviet Union would withdraw six regiments, their weapons and equipment from Afghanistan by the end of this year.

4. That the USSR was prepared to discuss with China specific steps aimed at a balanced reduction of land forces on the Sino–Soviet border.

As regards the Kampuchean question, Gorbachev made it clear that the normalisation of Sino–Vietnamese relations held the key to a possible solution.[22]

China's response to the Gorbachev's peace overtures was cautious but positive as evidenced by Deng Xiaoping's remarks on 2 September 1986:[23]

> There is something new in Gorbachev's Vladivostok speech. This is why we have expressed a cautious welcome to what is new and positive therein. However, Gorbachev's remarks also show that he has not taken a big step. . . . The Soviet Union can play its part in urging Vietnam to withdraw all its troops from Cambodia. . . . Gorbachev evaded this question in his Vladivostok speech.

Although Deng Xiaoping seized upon the opportunity to criticise Gorbachev for not being positive on the Kampuchean question, he must have been quietly welcoming the offer to ease tension on the Sino–Soviet border. The less imminent the Soviet threat is, the longer time the Chinese strategic planners will have in modernising China's defence force to face future aggression. In this respect, the USSR is offering the Chinese concrete concessions. In the wake of replacing the entrenched Y. Tsedeubal with a flexible Jambyn Batmonh in Mongolia,[24] Gorbachev announced at Vladivostok the withdrawal of 75 000 Soviet troops stationed in Mongolia.[25] Further evidence of progress made in this respect came from Deputy Foreign Minister Rogachev when he called the decision to reopen border talks in the ninth round of talks with his counterpart Qian Qichen in October 1986 'one of the most significant results'.[26] A joint communique at the end of the ninth round revealed that 'border discussions would be held at the deputy ministerial level'.[27] Without doubt, Gorbachev's Vladivostok speech will have long-term effects on Sino–Soviet relations. China's cautious but positive attitude is a reflection of its continuing effort to play a pivotal role in the strategic balance.

As if to put the US at ease, China announced on 9 October 1986 that three naval vessels would pay a 'friendly, courtesy call to Qingdao from 5 to 11 November',[28] although the Chinese official statement did stipulate that 'China's consistent policy is not to allow foreign warships carrying nuclear weapons to make port calls to China'.[29] An amicable understanding must have been arrived at by the two sides as the US practice of neither confirming nor denying that their warships are nuclear-powered or nuclear-armed while visiting friendly ports is at variance with the official Chinese policy. As a prelude to this historic visit, US Defence Secretary Weinberger's tour of China in early October further confirmed the increased military ties between the two countries.[30] Short of a formal alliance, China continues to benefit from US military technology essential to its defence modernisation program. In sum, China continues to play its 'semi-Soviet' and 'semi-US' cards. It seems to be playing them rather well.

THE KAMPUCHEAN QUESTION

China regards the Kampuchean question as one of its major security problems. Many believe that the normalisation of Sino–Soviet relations holds the key to its solution. In other words, it takes the great powers to resolve a long-term regional conflict. Soviet commitments to Vietnam are well known. The Treaty of Friendship and Cooperation in November 1978, Vietnam's membership of COMECON (Council for Mutual Economic Assistance) in June 1978 and an increase in Soviet strategic and naval capabilities in Cam Ranh Bay and Da Nang, all secure a firm foothold for the USSR in the Pacific.[31] Nevertheless, the cost involved is high. At the same time, Vietnam can hardly be considered a core member of the Eastern Bloc, nor would it wish to be seen as one.

It is not certain whether the USSR approves all of Vietnam's quests for expansionist and territorial control in Indochina, as these moves lead to increased international tension.[32] For instance, it is believed that Vietnamese domination of Kampuchea might lead to a Sino–Soviet confrontation. Further, it could lead to disruption in the Strategic Arms Limitation Talks with the US. The *fait accompli* in Kampuchea is one thing, a major attack across the Thai border, which may set the scene for the 'fall of the dominoes', is another. Similarly, it is highly unlikely that the Soviets would avail the Vietnamese of many strategic weapons which have nuclear capabilities for fear of a possible Sino–Vietnamese confrontation. Thus the likelihood of Soviet permission to supply the Vietnamese Navy with SS-21 Frog and SS-23 Scud missiles which can be armed with nuclear warheads is extremely unlikely.[33] In fact, it may be argued that over the next decade the USSR will be satisfied with its increased distant-area capabilities for the Navy, and its enhanced global capability by acquiring Cam Ranh Bay, and would not wish the new strategic balance in the Pacific to be destabilised by rash Vietnamese moves in Indochina. This is especially so considering not only the diplomatic front put up by China and ASEAN against Vietnamese presence in Kampuchea, but also China's likely intervention under certain circumstances. For instance, a major Vietnamese attack against Thailand, the front-line state across the Kampuchean border, or a likely obliteration of the Khmer Rouge could easily provoke the Chinese.

China's position is clear. There is no way that China will abandon the Khmer Rouge whose military strength persists despite earlier setbacks. Furthermore, there is no common ground between the SRV's strategic advantage in Kampuchea on the one hand and the determination of ASEAN and China to champion the sovereign rights of Kampuchea on the other. Any serious worsening of the present situation will provoke the Chinese whose geo-strategic position demands the scaling down of Vietnamese expansionist activities in Indochina. There is indeed some sense in considering Vietnam as China's Cuba. Surely the Soviets would wish to prevent any serious military confrontation in this region, having recently secured strategic advantages in the Pacific. It is true that the initial risk involved in a Chinese 'second lesson' may be low but the probability of escalation also exists. Should the Chinese attack again, the Soviets would then be in an unenviable position of having to decide whether or not to commit themselves heavily in Indochina. What the USSR does not want is to repeat the American mistake in Vietnam. Whether the Soviets might be bogged down in Indochina, in turn, largely depends on China's military capabilities and initiatives.

From the Chinese strategic planners' point of view, China is in a position to give Vietnam either the carrot or the stick in the sense that it will confront Vietnam if pushed. On the other hand, it looks as if the Kampuchean question will be a stalemate for some years.[34] Vietnam's isolation in Southeast Asia has not been broken except for certain links with the Indonesian military. Vietnam's military offensive in late 1984 and early 1985 did not succeed in eliminating the Khmer Rouge nor did it manage to talk Sihanouk into deserting the Coalition Government of Democratic Kampuchea (CGDK).[35] At the same time, ASEAN's peace proposals, supported by both the US and China, which demand Vietnamese troop withdrawal and the establishment of a genuinely independent Kampuchea, have floundered, mainly because of Vietnam's reluctance to give up advantages already gained.[36] No doubt, many moral issues and technicalities in negotiations all blur the picture.[37] Short of a major and perhaps disastrous confrontation with Vietnam as the last option, China's stick does not seem to be effective.

Conversely, there is a great deal of attraction in offering the carrot, not so much to Vietnam as to the USSR. K.K. Nair suggested that there can be only one factor that would have a profound effect upon the stalemate in Kampuchea. This would be the result of the ongoing negotiations between Moscow and Beijing for the normalisation of relations between the two major powers.[38]

In addition, it would seem logical for the Chinese to secure certain Soviet guarantees in Indochina as part of the conditions in the bilateral talks aimed at normalisation. Thus, it has been suggested that the first round of talks in Beijing in October 1982 witnessed a possible Chinese request for a Soviet halt in its assistance to Vietnam in Kampuchea, and for Soviet persuasion to effect a Vietnamese withdrawal of troops from Kampuchea.[39] Short of troop withdrawal from Kampuchea, even a Sino–Soviet understanding over Indochina will secure better stability for Southeast Asia. At the same time, the interested parties do not have any confidence in the SRV's announcement to withdraw troops by 1990.[40] A genuine Soviet attempt to eradicate this particular obstacle (Vietnamese consent is by no means guaranteed) will contribute a great deal to Asian security in general.

The USSR had made it clear that it would not wish to have to choose between the SRV and China over regional conflicts in Indochina. In other words, the interest of the SRV would not be sacrificed for the sake of the normalisation of Sino–Soviet relations.[41] In June 1985, SRV Party Secretary Le Duan secured Soviet support for SRV occupation of Kampuchea. Nevertheless, in the same joint declaration, it was stated that 'normalisation of relations of the Soviet Union and the SRV with the PRC contributes to the aims of strengthening peace in Asia and international security'.[42] This statement is a departure from the standard disclaimer in the past which stipulated that the same normalisation should not be at the expense of third countries. The Soviets' unusually ambivalent position should be encouraging to the Chinese.[43] Thus Gorbachev's recent proposal for an All-Asia Forum also has the effect of de-emphasising Soviet containment of China.[44] Deng Xiaoping's response to Gorbachev's peace initiatives on 2 September 1986 pinpointed the need for the Soviets to persuade the SRV to withdraw troops from Cambodia.[45]

> The main obstacle in Sino-Soviet relations is Vietnamese aggression against Cambodia. Vietnamese troops stationed in Cambodia constitute a problem which has actually placed Sino–Soviet relations in a hot spot. Once this problem is resolved, I am willing to meet Gorbachev.

Deng Xiaoping has therefore highlighted for the first time the Kampuchean question as the most knotty of the three obstacles, and forced the hands of the Soviets despite Gorbachev's stand that 'problems in Southeast Asia depends on normalisation of Chinese-Vietnamese relations'.[46] Gorbachev was merely repeating the standard disclaimer that the normalisation of Sino–Soviet relations should not be at the expense of a third country (ie the SRV). However, signs of progress have continued to emerge. Probably for the first time, Cambodia was on the agenda in the ninth round of Sino–Soviet talks on normalising relations. It was reported that Qian Qichen emphasised that Vietnam's troop pullout from Kampuchea was the key to improving Sino–Soviet relations.[47] Although

Rogachev repeated the official Soviet position in order to urge the Chinese to hold direct negotiations with the SRV, it is a good sign that the two big powers have begun to address the problem seriously (this is the case despite Qian Qichen's comment that there was no major change on Cambodia during the talks in October).[48]

The Kampuchean question itself has been regarded as so knotty that the stalemate seems to have given Vietnam the ticket to justify its presence in Kampuchea. In other words, Vietnam's presence is justified by the continuing insurrection in Kampuchea; from that point of view it would not be in Vietnam's interests to wipe out the Khmer Rouge even if Hanoi could achieve it.[49] In view of Gorbachev's peace initiative, there is pressure on the SRV to ease tension in Indochina. To Moscow, conflict in Cambodia has outlived its usefulness, as Soviet economic and political interests in the Asia–Pacific region urge it to seek acceptance by China, ASEAN states, Japan and other indigenous nations. Weighted against this primary objective is the need for the Soviets to preserve basing rights at Cam Ranh Bay and investments in general in the SRV which requires Moscow to honour its backing for Hanoi over the Kampuchean question. In addition, it can be argued that the SRV would choose to remain adamant and uncompromising. Nevertheless, the wind of change seems to have moved Moscow and Beijing closer toward normalisation. It would therefore be more sensible for the SRV to be more responsive to proposals from the relevant quarters on a possible solution in order not to be left out in the interplay of big power politics. Should China prove itself successful in negotiating with the USSR and the SRV for a settlement in Cambodia, it would enhance its prestige in the Asia–Pacific region as a central balance power which is adept in crisis-avoidance.

CHINA'S RESPONSE TO SECURITY THREATS: THE NUCLEAR DIMENSIONS

In the unlikely event of conflict with the USSR over the Sino–Soviet border dispute or the Kampuchean question, China will need to consider the probability of a general nuclear war. In addition, a global confrontation of the two superpowers may voluntarily or involuntarily involve China after it begins. China's defence posture in this respect has been one of adherence to the principle of no-first-use (NFU), reliance on retaliatory second-strike capability and the ability to survive major nuclear attacks.

In the first place, China 'has long declared on its own initiative and unilaterally that at no time and under no circumstances will China be the first to use nuclear weapons, and that it undertakes unconditionally not to use or threaten to use nuclear weapons against non-nuclear countries and nuclear-free zones'.[50] It follows that the NFU principle would rule out a Chinese first-strike against the USSR, especially given the fact that there is no assured destruction effect on the USSR whatsoever as its number of warheads is limited.[51] The USSR will also have to consider the cost of Chinese retaliatory second-strike capability which will improve as time goes by. It has been estimated that 100 Chinese missiles carrying 50–kilotonne warheads would be able to destroy about half the industrial capacity in seventeen major Soviet cities, and kill fifteen million people in a successful second-strike scenario. In addition, as if to counter the weaknesses inherent in minimum deterrence, the Chinese wish to convince the enemy of the colossal cost involved in attempting to occupy China's vast territory with its relatively dispersed population.[52] In addition, it emphasises its ability to survive major nuclear attacks, the consequence of which is that the Chinese can continue to conduct a protracted war under nuclear conditions without yielding to the enemy. This is the chance the enemy will have to take.

Despite the cost incurred, it might still be probable for the USSR to launch a nuclear attack on China. It is pertinent here to examine the probability of an escalation of a conventional war. Should the Soviets attempt to occupy China's Northeast in an Afghanistan-style *Blitzkrieg* end up in a stalemate, the Soviets might have to use tactical nuclear weapons to launch a large-scale nuclear attack.[53] In addition to deploying the SS–20 missiles, the Soviets can target most of China from a safe distance with their long-range missiles (5000–6000km). Targeting Chinese military installations has also been facilitated by improved accuracy in the development of the MIRV war-heads.[54] In any case, the Soviets would need to have an extremely good reason to provoke the Chinese whose nuclear forces are capable of deterrence. Moreover, the political costs of such action in Asia, that is a first use of nuclear weapons, would be excessive for the Soviets. Nevertheless, Treverton believes that an improved Chinese nuclear force will cause Moscow to have nightmares, especially if China is driven towards alignment with the West as a result of more strength the Soviet Union will have built against China.[55] Should this happen, Treverton believes that the Soviets will build an anti-Chinese ABM system, and 'Moscow might be tempted to make such a strike [sic pre-emptive strike] even against a much larger future Chinese force. That would confront the United States with some unpleasant choices'.[56] China's development of improved nuclear capabilities, including limited second-strike capabilities, reinforces its independent role in deterrence which inevitably has a significant impact on the superpowers. China's nuclear posture has been understood as one of deterrence by denial, which is necessarily a part of its strategy of 'People's War under modern conditions' (see Chapter 5 for details). In turn, deterrence by denial adds to the credibility of China's strategy of active defence in its hope to contain enemy attacks as it confines itself to strategic defence in the initial stage of the war. It therefore adds to the cost of the enemy as it contemplates an attack on China.[57]

It has been suggested that China relies on minimum deterrence, and that it does not emphasise large numbers in each category. At the same time, China sees the importance of maintaining an adequate range in the arsenal to ensure strategic deterrence capabilities. The development of the SLBMs is a case in point. On the other hand, the limitations of minimum deterrence are also obvious. In the first place, it is uncertain what role China can play in a general nuclear war, as the two superpowers involve themselves in scenarios of mutual assured destruction (MAD). Possessing only minimum deterrence capabilities is certainly no immunity from becoming major nuclear targets.[58] Furthermore, China needs to assume that future nuclear wars launched against it can either be limited in scope or large in scale. In the case of the former, its specific nuclear arsenal is more capable of deterring the enemy. In this respect, China's intention to develop greater capabilities in tactical nuclear weapons represents the same reasoning (see Chapter 2). In the case of a large-scale nuclear attack, the Chinese response to Soviet pre-emptive strikes must rely on the successful execution of the strategy of 'People's War under modern conditions' which incorporates nuclear deterrence with strong mass support.[59]

The biggest question that still remains in regard to the drawbacks of China's deterrence posture is its predicament in the event of a general nuclear war. Irrespective of Chinese rhetoric dealing with 'anti-hegemonism' and independence in its conduct of international relations, Chinese strategists are hoping for improvements on the bleak situation.[60]

In the event of a major nuclear war between the two superpowers, China's probable role should also be examined. An optimistic scenario, which is also consistent with China's independent foreign policy, would be for China to stay out of the conflict. This of course may not be possible if the consequence of the conflict would mean mutually assured destruction. However, this optimistic scenario is based on the rationale that China believes in the NFU principle, and that the Soviets would not wish to launch pre-emptive strikes against China.[61] Favourable conditions for the Soviets would also include the absence of any alignments between China and the West, and of any major political conflict between China and the USSR. Arguments against the above hinge on the 'two-front' problem Moscow faces as it would need 'to retain a reserve of nuclear warheads for use against China'.[62] Treverton claims that any slow moving crisis (or major war in Europe) would present the Soviet Union with the continuing possibility of a war with China and the accompanying nuclear threat'.[63] The pessimistic scenario is therefore that China would be attacked by the Soviets with a large nuclear force.

From the perspective of the US and the West, China does come into the equation in a major global nuclear confrontation, albeit on the periphery. In the first place, it is believed that most of the Soviet IRBM and MRBM effort is directed at China. This means that the number of missiles directed at the US and Europe is proportionally less.[64] Second, the fact that the Soviets might be deterred by some limited Chinese second-strike capability goes in favour of the US in the USSR–US nuclear balance. For instance, the Soviet deployment of some of their ICBMs and SLBMs, and to a lesser extent the SS–20s in Asia, has the US as the target. However, the Soviets feel that these missiles are vulnerable to Chinese attacks and they feel obliged to make due allowances in order to secure the survival of their nuclear force.[65] In the absence of an alliance with China, the US will need to devise measures, and reach a certain understanding with China in order to take advantage of the above favourable strategic positions.

As regards the role in arms control, China takes a hard line in insisting that both superpowers should reduce their conventional and nuclear arsenals by 50 per cent before it would contemplate proportionate cuts.[66] Whilst China has good reasons as an independent nuclear power to be aloof, such a stand has especially been considered unstable for the world.[67] However, major issues in superpower arms race and arms control do affect China, forcing it to take stands in order to preserve its security interests. Thus China maintained that the removal of SS–20 missiles from Europe, proposed in the intermediate Nuclear Forces (INF) talks, should not harm third-party interests, for fear that they might be redeployed on the Sino–Soviet border.[68] This position remains unchanged in 1987 as a US–Soviet outline agreement to abolish medium-range nuclear missiles becomes a reality, and as China welcomes the superpower arms pact. A more serious challenge to China's deterrent capability is Reagan's Strategic Defence Initiative (SDI). Should the US make significant progress in developing SDI, it may not feel as keen to come to China's rescue should the Chinese face Soviet nuclear attacks. In addition, the successful establishment of a Soviet defensive shield would reduce the effectiveness of China's deterrent capabilities.[69] Thus 'China openly opposed any plan leading to a space arms race',[70] but it seems that the extension of the arms race to outer space is an issue over which China has no real control.

In view of the effect of superpower arms race on China's security, the Chinese have taken a more positive attitude in multilateral forums and have relied more on interdependence as the means to maintain their prestige in opposing superpower dominance in the arms race. Thus in January 1984 China joined the International Atomic Energy Agency (IAEA) in order to secure greater international cooperation in its development of nuclear energy.[71] Nevertheless, China stopped short of becoming a signatory to the Non-Proliferation Treaty (NPT) or the Comprehensive Test Ban Treaty (CTBT).[72] Premier Zhao Ziyang's offer to cease conducting nuclear tests in the atmosphere merely confirmed China's acquisition of better technology for testing.[73] In the final analysis, China should realise that despite its low opinion of superpower competition in the arms race, a positive posture in arms control can only encourage *detente* and therefore contribute to the well-being of China's national security.

Threat perceptions and security problems

China's threat perceptions have undergone changes as its strategic outlook emphasises peacetime war preparation and long-term strategic planning. As a result, it takes a more optimistic view toward probable threats to national security and follows new directions in foreign policy in the 1980s. Thus China plays a particular role in the strategic balance which is guided by what it defines as 'an independent, self-reliant foreign policy'. On this basis, it feels justified to adopt an open door policy and rely on the US and the West for technological and economic needs on the one hand, and favour an improvement in Sino–Soviet relations, especially since Gorbachev's Vladivostok speech in July 1986, on the other.

Despite general optimism that there is time for long-term

peacetime war preparation, China continues to rely on international interdependence and mutual deterrence in the face of major security threats. The two obstacles to normalisation of Sino–Soviet relations, namely, Soviet military build-up on the Sino–Soviet border and Soviet support for Vietnam's invasion of Kampuchea, are the major threats to its national security which force China to play a particular role in both the global and regional balance. Thus Deng Xiaoping responded positively to Gorbachev's peace overtures in September 1986 with a view to improving Sino–Soviet relations. Similarly, China realises that the normalisation of Sino–Soviet relations holds the key to breaking the stalemate in Indochina. In the wake of Gorbachev's peace initiative for the Asia–Pacific region, there is pressure on the SRV to ease tension in Indochina. A general improvement in Sino–Soviet relations will hopefully reduce the level of conflict, but the stalemate in Kampuchea will probably persist in the near future. Indeed, the Kampuchean question has been regarded as so knotty that the stalemate seems to have given the SRV the ticket to justify its presence in Kampuchea as continuing insurrections persist.

China's nuclear capabilities support its role in the strategic balance in that mutual deterrence has become a relevant factor as China prepares for a positive response to a probable nuclear attack from the Soviets. Although its position is limited by its adherence to the NFU principle, China's retaliatory second-strike capability and self-proclaimed ability to survive major nuclear strikes denote a nuclear posture which has been understood as deterrence by denial. Such capabilities do not rely on large numbers but emphasise the importance of maintaining an adequate range in order to secure strategic deterrence. In the face of large-scale nuclear attacks from the Soviets, the Chinese will need to rely on 'People's War under modern conditions' which incorporates deterrence capabilities with the strategy of active defence. Should a general war between the superpowers break out, the Soviets may attack China if the crisis is slow moving or if it begins with a major war in Europe in order that they can avoid the 'two-front' problem. An optimistic assessment of this situation suggests that the US and the West will need to count China into the equation in a nuclear confrontation because Soviet IRBM and MRBM effort directed at China will proportionally lessen the number of missiles directed at the US and Europe. Furthermore, Chinese second-strike capabilities favour the US in the nuclear balance as the Soviets need to make due allowances to ensure the survival of their nuclear force. Finally, China's realisation that the superpower arms race will seriously affect its national security has caused it to respond more positively to arms control, which in turn encourages *detente* and interdependence as the means to oppose superpower dominance in the arms race.

5

The Strategy of People's War under Modern Conditions

China's new strategic outlook in defence modernisation has influenced its responses to major threats, which are now based on the well-rationalised perception that takes into full account the particular role China plays in the strategic balance and its improved warfighting and deterrence capabilities. The clearly identified threat from the USSR has become China's main concern and has prompted the Chinese to actively seek an effective way to evolve a formula that can incorporate the fruits of modernisation with the strategy of active defence. The traditional doctrine of People's War, which emphasises the politicisation and mobilisation of the entire populace against the invading enemy, would seem irrelevant to the situation in the late 1980s as China no longer believes in the imminence of war. Nevertheless, strategic planning for war, which has targeted the mid-twenty-first century, cannot discard the importance of the human factor as expounded in the doctrine of People's War. For as long as it remains significantly behind the superpowers in the development of technology and strategic weapons, China will find it necessary to rely on its populace to defend its home territory against the invading enemy. At the same time, Chinese strategic planners no longer subscribe to the Maoist concept that it is solely people and not guns which constitutes the decisive factor in winning a war.

It is now opportune to examine the transformation of the traditional concept of People's War into a pragmatic doctrine and strategy, which has been known as 'People's War under modern conditions' since the early 1980s. The newly evolved strategy has taken full advantage of modernisation in the force structure, improvements in warfighting capabilities, and advances made in weapons and equipment. It emphasises the need for strategic defence in the initial stage of the war and relies on active defence in home territory to inflict maximum attrition on the enemy. Greater attention is now being paid to defence in depth in a theatre of war and the concept of a three-dimensional defence system of great depth. In addition, the strategy incorporates well-planned operational principles which are supported by improved Chinese fire power so that the newly formed group armies will have a better chance against superior Soviet capabilities and fire power.

PEOPLE'S WAR AND CHINA'S DEFENCE POLICY: FORMATIVE YEARS OF THE POST-MAO DECADE

The Sixth Plenum of the Central Committee of the Eleventh Party Congress, convened in late June 1981, can be regarded as a triumph of pragmatism not only for the Party's implementation of new policies *vis-a-vis* China's economic modernisation, but also for Deng Xiaoping who was more confident of his leadership in the People's Liberation Army. Thus it was Deng who became the Chairman of the Party's Central Military Commission (PCMC) in the Sixth Plenum, and not Hu Yaobang, the Party Chairman.[1] This seemingly 'unconstitutional' measure had obviously been undertaken out of necessity, as the emerging pragmatists Hu, Zhao Ziyang and others were neither military men nor senior enough in the eyes of leading commanders to command the respect of the PLA. But such a measure does provide the first glimpse of how the mastermind of pragmatism realised that the PLA's support for the Party's new policies would require not only such 'unconstitutional' reshuffles, but also painstaking efforts to direct the PLA, as well as its central and regional commanders, toward accepting the new leadership with its pragmatic policies toward modernisation. Given its complex structure and long historical tradition, the PLA was by no means a homogenous body; thus its support at the various levels for the Party was bound to vary. However, one common front the PLA had, despite its diverse and factional interest, was a desire to mount and reinforce an effective defence system for China against external threats, a system which in turn conformed to the nation's ideological beliefs and foreign policy. Political and economic developments since the fall of the Gang of Four had steered the PLA to accept as its common front 'People's War under modern conditions' which should represent the essence of China's defence policy, incorporating both

'Red' and 'Expert' and minimising the old conflicts between the principles of professionalisation and politicisation.[2]

Since its inception in 1965, People's War as a doctrine had gone through a metamorphosis in the light of turbulent political development since the Cultural Revolution, but it had by no means been forgotten. On the contrary, it was still very relevant and considered by the Party to be crucial to China's defence provided that the necessary conditions were observed to make it workable.

According to the Defence Intelligence Agency (DIA) *Handbook on the Chinese Armed Forces*, the definition of People's War is:[3]

> ... a doctrine for the defense of China against various types of war ranging from a surprise long-range nuclear strike combined with a massive ground invasion to a conventional ground attack with limited objectives. It is premised on participation of the whole populace and mobilization of all the country's resources for as long as it takes to defeat any invader. The doctrine of people's war is meant to assure both the Chinese people and any potential invader that in case of war there will be no surrender, no collaboration, and that even if China's conventional forces are defeated, widespread and unremitting resistance will continue until the invader withdraws. Ideally, China's main forces, using conventional tactics, would carry out a strategic withdrawal supported by guerrilla operations until the invading forces were overextended and dispersed. When this occurred Chinese forces would be concentrated to annihilate the enemy. . . . In part, people's war is meant to deter potential enemies by making it clear that any invasion of China would be a very expensive proposition and one with no chance of a satisfactory resolution. Seen this way, there is no contradiction between people's war and conventional war, or between the doctrine of people's war and the establishment of modernized conventional military forces.

As Lin Biao was the original author of 'Long Live the Victory of the People's War' in 1965, it would have been unscrupulous for China to maintain the same militant stand in the early 1980s that it had taken in 1965 when 'anti-hegemonism' and 'anti-imperialism' were the order of the day. As China's foreign policy had changed significantly over the last fifteen years, so had its national defence priorities in the light of changing global strategies. A closer relationship with the West in general, and the continued rift with the Soviet Union had combined to induce the post-Mao pragmatic leadership to reset their national priorities for defence. Friendship with the West and the eagerness of the latter, especially the United States, to sell arms and consider the prospect of military alliance definitely provided China with the incentive to modernise its defence capabilities. On the other hand, there was little possibility of China's defence capabilities catching up with the Soviet Union during this decade (nor would this be China's intention for a long time).[4] Furthermore, China faced serious constraints, namely, cuts in the national defence budget imposed as a necessity in the name of economic development, the heartfelt fear of a Soviet invasion and the well-nigh unmanageable and extensive border China has with its neighbours.

People's War in this new setting was thus a most relevant and necessary doctrine in order that Deng's leadership could proceed with his national priorities, and at the same time re-orientate the PLA towards a well specified and stable direction. When the Gang of Four fell in October 1976 and Deng re-emerged in the summer of 1977, and when de-Maoisation seemed to be the order of the day, it would have been assumed that People's War with its originally politicised doctrine would not have been welcome by the pragmatists in power. There was nevertheless no denunciation of the doctrine from the new Party leaders despite its 'Mao-Lin' connotation. On the other hand there was a firm message from certain senior commanders who cherished political work in the PLA and regarded People's War as the representing the greatness of the Party-army tradition. This they called the 'great democratic tradition' of the PLA which was attributed to Mao and what he stood for in Chinese military thought. Although their views could not have represented the consensus within the PLA, their stand was glaringly inconsistent with the criticism of Mao's mistakes in the Great Leap Forward and the Cultural Revolution.

Huang Kecheng, a veteran general disgraced in the Mao-Peng Dehuai feud during the Great Leap Forward, summed up the situation extremely well in his article in the *People's Daily* in April 1982 where he underlined Mao's political and economic mistakes from the past, but paid tribute to the man for his contribution to the greatness of the tradition of the PLA.[5] The article throws light on Party-Army relations since late 1976 in that the Party finally confirmed Mao's well-earned reputation in the military realm. Worries and uncertainties expressed by many senior commanders, especially in 1977–79, that the 'great democratic tradition' of the PLA attributed to Mao and incorporating the doctrine of People's War might be jeopardised, seemed to have died down in the wake of assurances from the Party that 'Red' and 'Expert' work together, and that 'People's War under modern conditions' was most relevant to China's present national defence policy. This shift in the party attitude, which was well publicised amongst PLA and militia units, is worth a closer examination.

Since the death of Mao in 1976, there seemed to have been a growing tendency for the military to realise that modernisation did not necessarily clash with the ideals of People's War as long as professionalisation and stress on weaponry were not overemphasised. It took the military two to three years to reach this more conciliatory position. In August 1977, Su Yu, in his capacity as a member of the reconstituted CMC, spoke on the foundations of People's War. The principle that revolutionary war must involve the masses was stressed by Su, who also noted that the strategy of the Sino–Japanese War would serve as a model guideline. Such war should involve the proletariat as well as all revolutionary peoples to resist the two superpowers (ie the Soviet Union and the United States, as Mao asserted).[6] To Su Yu, Mao's military line and military thought, which embraced the above strategy, provided the most powerful ideological weapon for the Chinese military to defend China against imperialism and nuclear attacks. The military, after a period of silence, began in 1977 to reassert Mao's unconventional and politicised slogans: 'Be prepared against war, be prepared against natural disasters and do everything for the people. Dig tunnels deep, store grain everywhere, and never seek hegemony'.[7]

Xiao Hua, holding the concurrent posts of First Political Commissar of Lanzhou Military Region and member of the CMC since September 1979, also emphasised that 'a correct party line guarantees everything, so that a lack of manpower could be turned into abundance, and a lack of guns likewise turned into abundance'.[8] Mao's assertion of 'whether the ideological and political line is correct determines all'[9] was also quoted by Xiao.

Observers may not be aware of the fact that in the early stage of the Four Modernisations in 1977, there appeared to be a polemical dispute between the pragmatic school for military modernisation and the 'conscience' of the PLA who favoured People's War. It was not until 1979 and 1980 that a clear pattern began to emerge when signs of resurgence in the ideological and political arena appeared. There was increased use of phrases like 'People's War', 'Red and Expert', 'Political Consciousness', 'Organisational Discipline', 'Political Education', 'Party and Army', 'Ideological Guidance', etc.

In October 1979, during the celebration of the 30th anniversary of the founding of the PRC, Xu Xiangqian, then Minister of Defence, wrote: 'the future war against aggression will be a People's War on an unprecedented scale in human history'. He further stated in the same article:[10]

To master advanced modern military thinking we must combine
Marxism-Leninism-Mao Zedong Thought with the practice of modern
warfare and realistically solve problems regarding the theory and
practice of building a people's army and launching a people's war under
modern conditions.

Xu saw the modernisation of the PLA and the adaptation of new
ideas to the concept of People's War as complementary rather than
to the detriment of national defence. He also advocated the balance
of 'Red and Expert' as he said:[11]

To modernise our national defence, we need not only modern weapons
but also people, especially cadres, who are devoted to the socialist cause
and are versed in modern weapons and operational methods.

In August 1979 Xiao Ke, as Head and First Political Commissar
of the Military Academy, also identified the importance of political
work in the Four Modernisations, stressing the need to change the
'unrealistic formalism' of the past, and strengthen the 'relevant
opportune and combat' nature of political work.[12] Xiao's statement
marked a softening of at least some senior commanders' attitudes
towards modernisation. Thus political work was seen by Xiao Ke as
thorough and in-depth work reaching the grassroots level, in line
with the Gutian spirit and the PLA's 'great democratic tradition'
rather than with Lin Biao's model of launching flamboyant political
campaigns which Xiao condemned as superficial. Political work was
not seen as conflicting with the Four Modernisations. Xiao asserted
thus:[13]

We must develop the wartime and magnetic nature of the glorious
tradition, and let political work filter into the various practical missions
with the programme of Four Modernisations.

Xiao Ke's statement clarifies any doubts China scholars might have
in identifying the intentions and objectives of the commissars and
politically conscious commanders, who constitute an important
balancing force in the central military elite where the pro-Deng
elements were dominant but not overwhelmingly in command. The
ideal of 'man' over 'weapons' was by no means refuted as situations
might still arise in which mass-line strategy will apply. Nevertheless,
commissars who in the past seemed to be particularly concerned with
the preservation of the PLA's democratic tradition and of the Gutian
spirit which represents the very essence of political work, were now
in a position to realise that the modernisation of the PLA as an

urgent task did not necessarily jeopardise the PLA's chance to strengthen political work.

This same emphasis on political awareness was magnified in the New Year's editorial appearing in the *Liberation Army Daily* in 1980. It stated:[14]

> Reorganisation of the army mainly means reorganising the ideological style of leading bodies and the troops, raising political consciousness, strengthening organisational discipline, and restoring and developing the honorable traditions of our army.... It should still be emphasised that politics takes command and ideology leads the way, because to do anything always requires a correct political viewpoint and always requires correct ideological guidance.

This political orientation was the essence of People's War: a soldier who was politically conscious, ideologically disciplined, selflessly dedicated with a willingness to sacrifice for the glorification of the State.[15]

THE EVALUATION OF THE STRATEGY OF 'PEOPLE'S WAR UNDER MODERN CONDITIONS'

The doctrine of People's War for the 1980s

If People's War seemed to be acceptable to the Party as the PLA's doctrine, crystallising the essence of what Mao and the PLA stood for in Chinese Communist history, one would still need to discern the metamorphosis in its 22 years of existence, and to identify how such modifications are central to China's defence policy as it consistently emphasised 'People's War under modern conditions'.

Because of the dramatic cut to the military funds in the 1981 budget, Yang Dezhi as Chief of the General Staff had the good sense to submit to the Party's modernisation priorities. Against this financial constraint was the cost of force modernisation which would reveal the impossible task China faced if the 250 combat divisions and 2800 independent regiments in the Main and Local Forces were to be modernised to the minimum level of adequacy, requiring at least two to three times the full complement of the active US Army.

A Pentagon study indicated that modernisation of the PLA would call for:[16]

3000 to 8600 improved tanks

8888 to 10 000 armoured personnel carriers

16 000 to 24 000 heavy-duty trucks

6000 air-to-air missiles

200 air-superiority aircraft

240 fighters and or fighter bombers

In the same study, it was estimated that it would cost China about $US41 billion to buy US arms and equipment to upgrade its forces to a minimum level of adequacy. This equalled roughly about three and a half times the total Chinese defence budget for 1979 of $US12.9 billion.[17] Economically, for China to sustain this immense cost of modernisation it had to have a very strong, stable and resourceful economy; possibly with large quantities or the availability of foreign exchange, and a favourable trade position or high potential export markets for its locally produced goods. It should also be a reliable credit risk, enabling China to plan its industrial capacity to satisfy its civilian and military needs.

This euphoric condition, however, could not be met due to a disastrous RMB17 billion deficit in the State budget in 1979, especially when military spending was cut by almost $US2 billion in the 1980 budget.[18]

Accordingly, People's War offered China a way out of the above dilemma as its doctrine relied a great deal on the masses to oppose an invading enemy. It would therefore cost China much less, although present policy is to proceed simultaneously with force modernisation at a pace in line with the latest economic thinking. The associated financial constraints might have been accepted by Yang Dezhi and others in the central military elite, but there had been indeed murmurs that individual commanders were not at all happy with the latest defence budget cuts. 'People's War under modern conditions' was thus preached as a doctrine of necessity although it might not have been welcome by the modernisation-minded commanders. However, those politically minded commanders who had earlier in 1977–79 been agitating for the preservation of the 'great democratic tradition' of the PLA, would presumably have supported the doctrine.

Threat perceptions and defence posture

In the history of the People's Republic of China, 'anti-hegemonism' as defined by China has been governed by the way that it has perceived threats to the state. Thus the single concern for threats from 'American Imperialism' in the 1950s developed into strong opposition to both the 'Soviet Social-Imperialists' and the 'American Imperialists' in the 1960s and early 1970s. Whilst it has dropped its strong anti-American stand after normalisation, China has continued to denounce Soviet expansionism in Afghanistan, Indochina and Northeast Asia (see Chapter 4 for details).

Chinese threat perceptions in the 1980s have had the USSR as the major aggressor and the Chinese have responded to Soviet threats by adapting their strategic doctrine, emerging with the doctrine of 'People's War under modern conditions'. China's anti-Soviet perception in defence will persist for a long time and its inclinations towards the West will also persist unless the the Chinese strategic doctrine continues to take on an anti-Soviet stand, although the option of Sino–Soviet *rapprochement* has a cushioning effect. In the unlikely event of China taking an anti-American stand in the distant future, the Chinese would have to modify their doctrine accordingly. Nevertheless, such a doctrine incorporates indispensable elements which enable it to respond to different threat situations and scenarios. As such, it is a long-term doctrine and strategy and should not be regarded as an interim or transitional one as some would have us believe.[19] To be sure, the perfection of the doctrine necessitates the fulfilment of a number of preconditions, namely a supportive party leadership, a prospering economy and a successful military modernisation program. The doctrine itself may change in name, but the essence remains.

A successful military modernisation program entails long-term plans which also take into consideration budgetary constraints and the nation's top priority being given to economic modernisation. Nevertheless, the Chinese have set their targets to bring about, first, advances in weapon systems which require 'rapid advances' in scientific and technological establishments, and second, basic reforms in force structure and the command and control system. China's advancement in developing its strategic deterrent weapons is well known as it possesses ICBMs and SLBMs. It will also increase its second-strike capabilities by increasing its number of nuclear-powered submarines and by developing more capable long-range bombers and more sophisticated missile launch sites. While such strategic capabilities will assure China's continuing independence as a nuclear power, it should be noted that it has no intention to compete with the two superpowers.

Analysts have asked fundamental questions of the strengths and weaknesses of China's defence system. Inquiries of China's threat perception naturally lead to an investigation of the possible evolution of a new military doctrine. Similarly, an examination of force structure and the command and control system within the PLA (see Chapter 1) and of China's efforts in international interdependence (see Chapter 4) will contribute to a better understanding of the complexities and the degree of coherence in China's defence postures.

The strategy of 'People's War under modern conditions' not only aspires to improve China's own preparedness *vis-a-vis* the obvious enemy, the USSR, but also provides the vehicle to improve on China's defence capabilities against lesser enemies on its borders. Thus military modernisation in the form of the procurement and development of a better weapons system will help strengthen China's position in future Sino–Vietnamese conflicts. Similarly, the present reforms in force structure and C³I should have a general impact on China's capabilities in dealing with its lesser enemies, be they actual or potential. Nevertheless, it should be borne in mind that the demands on China's war-preparedness *vis-a-vis* its greater as opposed to lesser enemies is to say the least not identical. Thus China's war plans drawn up to handle conflicts with the USSR and the Socialist Republic of Vietnam (SRV) are necessarily different.

'People's War under modern conditions': Interim doctrine?

It has been claimed that the doctrine of People's War incorporates the central elements of mobilisation, the use of protraction and a decidedly defensive flavour.[20] By the beginning of the 1980s, the Chinese still maintained that the human factor was paramount, especially in the crucial first stage of the war which was characterised by strategic defence.[21] Nevertheless, changes in modern conditions require Chinese strategists to defend positions such as cities and industrial centres, as well as operating under desert and steppe conditions.[22] The 'weapons' factor has featured much more significantly as China's military modernisation improves the capabilities of China's conventional and nuclear forces, reinforcing Chinese war preparedness as they 'lure the enemy in deep'. Whilst the Chinese are clear about what the strategy represents, analysts differ in their interpretations as to whether the strategy is or is not capable of doing what the Chinese claim that it could.

In the first place, there are some who believe that the strategy has been rejected by the Chinese. For instance, Godwin believes that '. . . there is now sufficient evidence that the current military elite seeks to reject people's war, however, modified, as an approach to strategy and force structure requirements. While the label of "People's War" may well be retained, the content of Chinese strategy is likely to be very different from what has gone before'.[23] For those who believe that 'People's War under modern conditions' remains a workable strategy, the following two questions are often asked. Can the strategy work effectively against full-scale Soviet conventional and nuclear attacks? Does the strategy represent Chinese measures to improvise before a grand strategy emerges when China becomes more successful with its modernisation programs? The following will attempt to answer these two questions.

It has been accepted by many that 'People's War under modern conditions' is not a rigid doctrine. It retains the basic nature of People's War while allowing for natural changes in its more operational sub-principles.[24]

To understand the totality of 'People's War under modern conditions' one must first appreciate Chinese strategists' development of conventional and nuclear deterrence capabilities in the setting of Soviet attacks and Chinese responses. Second, defence modernisation incorporating the development of the industrial base, the force structure and the command and control systems must be regarded as part and parcel of China's defence strategy. Third, no Western analyst should overexaggerate China's reliance on its diplomatic position as a means to make up for military weakness.

On the first and the most important point, it must be understood that the Chinese would not exclude nuclear options from any formula when they draw up war plans against Soviet attacks. Thus a scenario of Soviet attack on China's territory, eg, the Northeast, should include an examination of the effect of a Soviet nuclear attack on the Chinese.[25] Furthermore, it would be important to examine in this context China's nuclear capabilities. From the outset, China is determined to develop and procure appropriate weapon systems and to improve C^3I in order to deny Soviet forces the chance of gaining quick victories in Chinese territory. China's recent incentives to develop combined arms operations is one significant step forward toward modernising theatre command,[26] although it is still doubtful whether Chinese C^3I could effectively handle land-sea-air operations in a theatre war comprising several group army formations.[27]

China also hopes to increase its conventional and nuclear deterrence capabilities by relying on its limited second-strike arsenal.[28] In addition, it aims at increasing the survivability of the nuclear force. In the long run, China's nuclear force must aim at the creation of a credible independent general deterrent.[29] In this context, China's policy of no-first-use (NFU) should be put under the microscope. Would it be advisable for the Chinese to adhere to the NFU principle should a major conventional attack threaten the survival of Chinese Main Forces at a critical stage in an important theatre of war?

Despite advantages that the NFU principles may have in promoting China's image, Chinese strategists should face the reality that the NFU principle would disadvantage the Chinese because it minimises the effectiveness of Flexible Response. This is the reason why the NFU principle does not apply to NATO deterrence. For as long as the NFU principle is relevant to the Chinese theatre of war, the Chinese will be able to maximise their deterrence by nuclear punishment and will have to be happy with mainly conventional deterrence by denial.[30] Other questions relevant to nuclear deterrence are as follows:[31]

1. Given China's main concern for limited nuclear war and deterrence by denial, what threshold can China identify before the USSR would consider a preemptive nuclear strike?

2. Is China going to move from minimum to massive deterrence?

3. If the answer to (2) is yes, where would China stand in relation to the Soviet–American arms race?

4. How should one assess China's development as an independent nuclear power?

All these questions deserve analysts' further attention.

STRATEGIC DEFENCE: THE STRATEGY OF ACTIVE DEFENCE

Discussions in the authoritative *Liberation Army Daily* make no pretence about the source of threat to China's security system. The Soviet Union has been closely identified as the 'stronger' enemy in the future 'anti-aggression war'.[32] 'People's War under modern conditions' constitutes the rallying point for strategic defence at the crucial first stage of the war.[33] Chinese strategists believe that there should be an effective combination of active defence (*jiji fangyu*), also known as resolute defence (*jianshou fangyu*), and guerrilla warfare. This is crucial to the success of strategic defence in the first stage of the 'anti-aggression war'[34]

> To put into effect the combination of resolute defence and guerrilla warfare would not only facilitate a full play of the merits of People's War, but also constitute a new demand on defence tactics under modern conditions. We are aware of the favourable conditions of resolute defence. First, it can take advantage of the favourable terrain and it has solid and well established positions to rely on. Second, it can prepare the battleground in anticipation of the enemy.

The US DIA's *Handbook of the Chinese Armed Forces* classifies forms of Chinese defence into positional defence and mobile defence, likening the former to the US concept of area defence and the latter to a 'hit-and-run' type of defence.[35] Active defence in combination with guerrilla warfare, as defined by the Chinese would seem to fit into the pattern of positional defence or area defence except that guerrilla warfare adds extra weight to the mobility of such defence. The Maoist concept of 'luring the enemy in deep', an integral part of People's War, is still relevant in that the Chinese choose their home territory to be the battleground in strategic defence. Nevertheless, modern conditions have induced Chinese strategists to abandon excessive 'hit-and-run' tactics, and defending positions is now considered to be significant, although such positions are normally far away from the front line. In fact, the defence of cities and industrial centres is regarded as essential, although the human factor remains relevant and indispensable. Thus guerrilla and militia units continue to contribute to the strength of human resources, but they are not likely to be deployed to surround the cities from the countryside. Indeed, they are expected to defend cities and operate under desert and steppe conditions.[36]

In sum, the Chinese put a great deal of emphasis on strategic defence in the initial stage of the war, hoping that active defence which relies on positional warfare supplemented by mobile and guerrilla warfare can provide themselves with the opportunity to reverse the fortune of war:[37]

> Without doubt, defensive war is not capable of developing initiatives in the way that an offensive war can, but acquires the contents of initiatives from the form of being passive. It can move from the stage of being passive in form to that of taking initiatives both in form and content. When we say that defence is the means to assist or prepare attack to

move into (sic. the stage of) attack, we are in general talking about the entire process and not about attack being the major form of war in the entire process. Quite the opposite, in the major defence directions, the initial stage of the war can only rely on active defence as the major form of combat in order that we can defend our vital strategic and battle zones. In so doing (sic. we can) shatter the enemy's strategic strikes and stop the enemy's direct entry into our open territories, so that our nation can be shielded as it assumes a wartime structure. Without defensive operations based mainly on active defence in the initial stage of the war, there cannot be the strategic counter-offensive and the strategic offensive stages which are based on attack as their major form of combat. It is therefore obvious that defensive operations at the initial stage of the war are not only not passive, but that it is the major strategic means to win initiatives.

In many ways, the above arguments justifying strategic defence are likened to Mao's first stage of the Protracted War which specified the need to be on the defence strategically against a stronger enemy.[38] Nevertheless, active defence which stresses positional warfare stands out in sharp contrast to the anti-Japanese experience which emphasised mobile and guerrilla warfare at the initial stage of the War.[39] To emphasise the point on how strategic defence can change the fortune of war, the Chinese claim that they were able to inflict heavy casualties on the enemy (equivalent to 54.4 per cent of casualties in the whole war in 25 months) as a result of the adoption of strategic defence in the Korean War.[40]

The major weakness of active defence is inadequate mobility. To remedy the situation, since 1983 the Chinese have started to preach the need to integrate positional, mobile and guerrilla warfare (*sanzhan jiehe*),[41] labelling the exercise as the development of 'cross-breed' tactics.[42] Thus Su Yu (First Party Secretary of the Academy of Military Sciences) proposes that mobile warfare should be conducted within the main defensive position and in adjacent areas. In doing so, Su claims that mobile warfare can increase the mobility of positional defence.[43] Mobile warfare based on positional defence can therefore be undertaken in the form of deep attack in accordance with the slogan of 'when the enemy advance, we advance' (*dijin wojin*).[44] Chinese initiatives to 'cross-breed' tactics have also led to the emergence of positional guerrilla warfare (*zhendi yujizhan*), which claims to coordinate directly with the main strength and take full advantage of the terrain.[45] Apart from the general objective of operating on the exterior lines and in the enemy's rear, guerrilla warfare can now take the initiative in active defence in combination with mobile warfare to annihilate either enemy air-borne troops or the enemy who have just achieved a breakthrough.[46] In sum, the Chinese hope that guerrilla warfare will add greater mobility to positional defence in the face of a Soviet *blitzkrieg*.[47]

> ... if we can fully make use of unfortifiable areas and vast deserts, steppes, mountainous and forest terrain situated in front of the zone for resolute defence, and if we can undertake widespread guerrilla warfare to harass the enemy, cause attrition, delay the enemy's advance and disperse enemy concentration, it would cause the enemy to become extremely tired as they approach the forward edge of our zone of resolute defence; they also have to worry about their rear and their strike power characterised by 'high speed, great depth and broad frontage' will be greatly weakened; even worse, they may become the end part of a highly strung bow. In other words, the linking of the positions of resolute defence and guerrilla areas will greatly increase our resistance territories, and it will facilitate fully our need to trade space for time.

Whilst the Chinese are adhering to active defence as the guiding strategy against the 'stronger' enemy, the US has replaced its doctrine of 'active defence' with 'Air Land Battle' doctrine as enunciated in FM 100–5 and the future concept in Army-21.[48] Nevertheless, one immediately discerns China's need to rely on active defence as a workable strategy to inflict maximum attrition on the enemy. Moreover, they do not have the capabilities of the Americans to launch deep attacks which aim at achieving manoeuvrability as well as attrition.[49] As such, the Chinese have found active defence to be serving a limited but extremely functional purpose in defence of their home territory.

Soviet strategy and capabilities

In examining Soviet strategy and capabilities in a Chinese theatre of war (assuming that the Chinese are not prepared to project their forces beyond their territory), one should be aware of recent changes to Soviet military doctrine and strategy. Since 1970, Soviet doctrine has enunciated the 'no first use' (NFU) principle in refraining from using nuclear weapons, at least at the initial stages of a war.[50] The reliance on conventional warfare to subdue the enemy persisted in 1970s, especially as the Soviets hoped to bring about the collapse of NATO's defence.[51] In the context of a Chinese theatre of war, one would assume that the same Soviet military doctrine applies, although one would also presuppose that Soviet forces in the Far East are inferior to those in Europe. On the other hand, the Soviet commitment in the Far East does not have the complexities of the European High Command which involves the countries of the Warsaw Pact.[52]

Whilst NATO's Forward Defence doctrine necessitates the application of nuclear deterrence and renders NFU irrelevant,[53] the Chinese NFU principle encourages the Soviets to be consistent with their military doctrine in refraining from using nuclear weapons in the initial stage of the war. Naturally, the use of both tactical and strategic nuclear weapons by both sides at some stage during the war cannot be ruled out. It all depends on the particular circumstances at the time. Indeed, there seems to be a particular threshold for theatre nuclear warfare (TNW) before further escalations would occur.[54] For instance, should the Soviets fail to effect a strategic breakthrough, or should the survival of Chinese Main Forces be genuinely threatened, TNW might occur. The threshold for the latter would be deemed to be lower than the former, although it would mean a Chinese renunciation of the NFU principle.

On the assumption that the Soviets would initiate a conventional war, the tradition of a Soviet *blitzkrieg* will apply. The Soviets will hope to launch a massive offensive incorporating the elements of surprise and mobility and the concentration of their forces for operational purposes.[55] Whether the *blitzkrieg* will work as successfully as in the Manchurian Campaign of August 1945 against the Japanese would depend on the Chinese response.[56] At the same time, it should be realised that Soviet military doctrine has been modified since 1945. One way of testing the Soviet *blitzkrieg* model is to examine the effectiveness of the latest Soviet operational principles in the context of a Sino–Soviet confrontation. Should the Soviets invade either China's Northeast or Northwest, the operation would come under the command of the Far Eastern theatre of military operations (*Teatr voyennykh Deystvi* — TVD).[57] China's North and Northeast would seem to be an ideal target analogous to the Western TVD which comprises Western Europe excluding Italy. The Northwest on the other hand would span too vast an area for the Soviets to engage the Chinese with the average three to four fronts of a TVD.

Four strategic operations can be clearly identified in a TVD, all of which integrate artillery and missile systems as well as air and electronic warfare. These are:

1. Air operations
2. Anti-air operations

3. Theatre land (ground forces with air support) operation
4. Naval or coastal operation

These combined capabilities qualify Soviet theatre land operations to be in the same league as the American 'Air Land Battle' in view of the prominent air dimension in the form of both close air support and ground attack.[58]

With these capabilities, including the use of nuclear weapons, the Soviets would aim at moving towards the Chinese operational depth as soon as possible. To achieve this, they would resort to using the Operational Manoeuvre Group (OMG) to effect tactical and strategic breakthroughs deep into the Chinese defence. The strength of the OMG ranges from attack division to a front and is always supported by air and artillery attack as OMGs attempt to move deep into the Chinese defence and take the Chinese by surprise. The intense concentration of fire power (both nuclear and conventional) at the initial phase of the war (in which the Chinese admitted inferiority to the Soviets) would be put to use through the operational art of 'Integrated Fire Destruction of the Enemy' (KOPP) and the Ground-Air Strike Teams (LPZUs).[59] Soviet fire strike applied through KOPP incorporates both nuclear weapons as well as conventional artillery, missiles and air attacks. Troop strike incorporating tanks and motor-rifle troops also forms part of KOPP. All in all, KOPP applies at the tactical, operational and strategic levels and can be deemed to be pre-emptive, retaliatory or meeting. As regards the LPZUs, they act as surprise tactical units either in the initial assault or later as 'mini-OMG' covering 25–30 km.[60]

The implementation of the various Soviet strategic operations is not without problems in themselves. For instance, the insertion of an OMG requires support and protection as it is vulnerable to enemy countermeasures. Further, the relative strength of the adversary and the choice of the TVD matter a great deal.[61] Thus NATO and the Chinese are two rather different adversaries. At a glance NATO's emphasis on Forward Defence, its need to defend West Germany close to the enemy border and its proposed policy on the use of nuclear weapons would seem to differ greatly from the Chinese concept of active defence, the deployment of Main Forces in the rear and the NFU principle. Whilst the Chinese forces could be deemed to be inferior to both the Soviet and NATO ones, the Chinese home terrain and the organic management of the theatre would work to their advantage.[62] Indeed, it could be argued that China's Northwest with its great depth would offer the Chinese such advantages. On the other hand, the Northeast would seem to be vulnerable.

A Soviet scenario in an attack on the Northeast would go as follows: It will be a conventional attack with the option of deploying theatre nuclear weapons. The initial stage will be decisive with massive Soviet forces demonstrating their capabilities in a standard 'Air Land Battle' scenario. The Soviets will hope to destroy Chinese obstacles with conventional and nuclear artillery in order to increase mobility and lighten the logistic burden.[63] The Manchurian plain will be the ultimate objective of the Soviets. This necessitates the deployment of massive airborne forces and Mi-24 gunships behind the Chinese lines to destroy Chinese stockpiles and hold key positions for the advancing armoured forces. Finally, ground strikes launched by the superior Soviet tactical air force will devastate the Chinese Main Forces. The combined OMGs and airborne troops will eliminate all resistance being put up by the Chinese militia and guerilla forces, possibly after chemical/biological attacks are launched against Chinese cities.[64]

As regards the lessons of history, there are reports of Soviet interests being revived in the Soviet Manchurian Campaign of August 1945, when the characteristics of surprise, mobility and concentration of force were well demonstrated. On that occasion, it took the larger-scale Soviet *blitzkrieg* only six days to envelop the Kwantung Army as Soviet forces comprising 1.5 million men descended from the Greater and Lesser Xingan Ranges in three prongs along a 5000km arc.[65] The massive combined arms attack with a numerical superiority of 2:1 (troop strength), 7:1 (tanks and artillery) and 2.5:1 (aircraft) over the Japanese brought about the defeat of the Kwantung Army.[66]

The Soviet Manchurian Campaign in 1945 serves as valuable experience for the Chinese who have studied the Campaign closely with a view to devising an effective strategy to counter an Afghanistan-style *blitzkrieg*. The Sino–Soviet border clashes of 1969 resulted in a steady military buildup on both sides and increased Sino–Soviet tension. The Soviets are reported to have a strength of 53 Divisions on the border comprising artillery and armoured forces as well as tactical air support and mobile IRBM (171 SS-20s).[67] The Chinese strength comprises 87 Divisions which are being modernised for combined arms and joint operations.[68] The following map and chart illustrate the distribution of forces on both sides:

Map 3

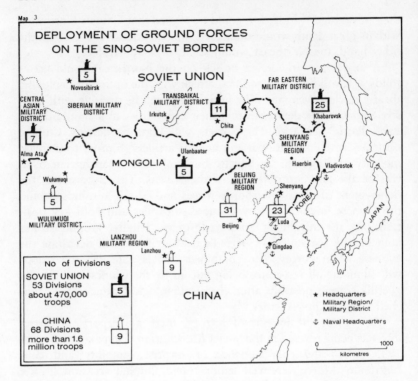

DEPLOYMENT OF GROUND FORCES
ON THE SINO-SOVIET BORDER

Table 5.1 Comparative Strengths of Chinese and Soviet Ground Forces on China's Northern and Northeastern Border*

China	USSR
Shenyang MR	**Transbaykal MD**
2 Missile Divisions	2 Tank Divisions
5 Armoured Divisions	8 Motor Rifle Divisions
23 Infantry Divisions	1 Artillery Division
13 Reserve Force Divisions	
Beijing MR	**Far Eastern MD**
1 Missile Division	2 Tank Divisions
4 Armoured Divisions	22 Motor Rifle Divisions
25 Infantry Divisions	1 Airborne Division
1 Airborne Division	1 Artillery Division
(Air Force)	**Mongolia**
13 Reserve Force Divisions	3 Motor Rifle Divisions

* *The Military Balance 1986–87, pp. 45 and 143.*

It has been estimated that the Soviets have good chances of success should they choose to attack China's Northeast in the next two decades. John Kefner believes that the occupation of the Northeast will not only enable the Soviets to protect the Dzungarian region, but also incapacitate China's development as a credible military and industrial power. Kefner depicts the Soviet scenario to be in three stages:[69]

a. Occupation of Heilongjiang in the Northwest and control of the old Chinese Eastern Railway to improve logistic support by maintaining good links with the Maritime Province.

b. Control of Jilin and North Korea.

c. Extensive control of Liaoning and Port Arthur for the Soviet Navy.

Soviet operational planning for the above scenario will be directed from the Far Eastern TVD in four strategic directions, part of which focuses on Chinese territory:[70]

a. Lanzhou Military Region, especially Wulumuqi Military District.

b. Shenyang and Beijing Military Regions.

c. Japan, Korea and the Philippines.

d. Alaska.

It is believed that strategic operation against Northeast China is the major task for the Far Eastern TVD and it will involve offensive operations by at least three fronts:[71]

1. The Transbaykal Front against the Beijing MR
2. The Second Far Eastern Front against the northern part of Shenyang MR
3. The First Far Eastern Front against the eastern part of Shenyang MR

It is believed that the Far Eastern TVD, like other peripheral TVDs, constitutes a new High Command of Force (HCOF) which meets the need of 'organizing the combat coordination and integration of all five services of the Armed Forces, rather than two to three, as was the case in previous wars'.[72] TVD high command was urged by Soviet Chief of the General Staff Ogarkov to meet the demands which came about with 'the advent of new weapons and delivery systems'.[73] This is especially advantageous to the Soviet preference for large conventional offensives rather than global strategic nuclear missile attacks at the inception of the war. In a word, instituting the HCOF of the Far Eastern TVD provides an improved command system for the Soviets in future confrontations with China.

Defence in depth and the Chinese theatre of war

Although the Chinese have become more relaxed about the Soviet threat, it is quite clear that Chinese war plans have the well-defined objectives of stopping Soviet advances in order to win time for strategic cover (*zhanlue yanhu*),[74] or else the entire process of defeating a superior force with an inferior force for the entire country will be delayed. Given the generally pessimistic assessment of China's deterrence capabilities, it follows that the longer time China has for war-preparedness, the better chance it has in thwarting the enemy. Indeed, war-preparedness during peacetime has since the early 1980s, been regarded as the foundation for a victory over a stronger enemy.[75]

Active defence is the strategy for the Chinese in their determination to fight a protracted war of attrition with the enemy in which heavy casualties will be expected on both sides. A great deal of emphasis is put on the initial phase of the war in which the Chinese aim at the minimum objective of delaying enemy advances and hopefully at preventing a strategic strike by the enemy (*zhanlue tuji*).[76] The Chinese also expect both conventional and nuclear attack although they do not and cannot have a foolproof plan against the latter. On the assumption that the Chinese could hold a series of Soviet conventional attacks, the probable scenario would be:

1. Chinese counterattacks and Soviet withdrawals,

2. Soviet escalation of the war to either the tactical nuclear level or worse still the strategic nuclear level, and

3. A strategic stalemate followed by international mediation and a peaceful settlement.

The second scenario would be initiated by Soviet exposure to Chinese interdiction of its long lines of communication deep in Chinese territory. Should the survival of their Main Forces be threatened by a Soviet strategic breakthrough, the Chinese might resort to TNW.

On the 7500km Sino–Soviet border, and in Chinese military regions adjacent to Soviet territory, the Chinese with 112 divisions have numerical superiority although the task of defending China's vast territory is formidable.[77] By the same token, Soviet *blitzkrieg* and their deep attack strategy may also face difficulties in certain parts of Chinese territory, namely, China's Northwest.

Whether the Chinese can withstand Soviet *blitzkrieg* and intense fire power and strike power depends a great deal on their defence in depth. In turn, appropriate deployment of the Main Forces, Local Forces, the guerrilla forces and the militia in specific theatres of war is a crucial determinant for success. It is not likely that the Chinese are prepared to confront Soviet advances on the border with a significant number of Main Force divisions, although some may be deployed to slow down the enemy. In fact, there is no clear information on the exact location of Chinese forces. Perhaps a good clue in support of Chinese faith in defence in depth is the reorganisation of the eleven military regions into seven.[78] Apart from the general aim of streamlining the PLA and reducing military expenditure, the Central Military Commission would have considered the strategic importance of merging and absorbing former military regions for defence priorities.[79] For instance, the enlarged military regions would be better suited to command and control in a theatre war against both the Soviets and other lesser enemies like the SRV, and other hostile neighbours in the future. Similarly, a case may be made for China's greater reliance on better logistics and command and control systems in each MR (for details, see Chapter 1 and Map 1). Insofar as the Soviet threat is concerned, the enlargement of Lanzhou MR seems to support claims that the Chinese are relying more on in depth defence as an effective strategy against Soviet deep attacks. Had the Chinese been advocating Forward Defence like NATO's strategy, Wulumuqi would have been made the headquarters of the enlarged MR. As it is, the new headquarters in Lanzhou would place the Chinese in a better position in the Northwest to thwart Soviet deep attacks which could initially advance 750km deep into Chinese territory with their Front OMGs. As regards Chinese Main Forces, Main Force divisions are stationed in Wulumuqi Military District. Chinese strategic planners are placing greater reliance on anti-Soviet regional defence. Whenever possible regional command centres should operate away from the border and should be well supported by the Main Forces. Thus Lanzhou and Chengdu are ideally located away from the borders. The enlarged Chengdu MR with its command at Chengdu rather than Kunming would better facilitate inter-MR links in the defence of the Northwest against the Soviets. As regards Beijing and Shenyang MRs, they have been considered as the stalwarts of central defence planning with a heavy concentration of Main Forces and fire power in the southern parts of the MRs. These concentrations in the south reflect the China's attempts to remedy weakness in the Northeast in the face of Soviet deep attacks. For instance, Beijing, which is only 500km from the Mongolian border, is vulnerable to Soviet deep attacks which could penetrate 1200km deep into Chinese territory.[80]

Being aware of this vulnerability, the Chinese strengthened inter-MR coordination in North and Northeast China by redefining the boundaries of Beijing and Shenyang MRs in 1982.[81] The intention was to shift the responsibility of defending the N–S Inner Mongolian corridor west of the greater Xingan Mountains to Beijing MR. This would hopefully result in better command and control for the abovementioned sector under Beijing MR. In turn Shenyang MR will be better equipped for the defence of the Northeast.

Chinese defence in the Northeast will initially be confined to border defence over a prolonged period. The defending Local Forces and any forward Main Force units will then retreat to the first line of defence with the greater Xingan Range in the west and the lesser Xingan Range in the north and east. The objective will be to slow down the Soviet advances. Given China's lack of forward defence capability to launch deep attacks into enemy territory, it is just as well that China's Northeast is less exposed than the West German theatre. In any case, should the Soviet forces effect a breakthrough of the first line of defence by conventional or nuclear means, the Chinese will need to create obstacles by both nuclear and conventional means to impede Soviet armoured advances. Chinese Main Forces will need to conduct mobile warfare in order to delay Soviet operations. At the same time, they will need to avoid major engagements in order to prevent annihilation by the superior Soviet forces.[82]

Chinese success in defence in depth depends on their capabilities under nuclear battle conditions. Specifically the Chinese will need to seal the point of nuclear breakthrough caused by enemy attacks.[83] Since 1983, the Chinese General Staff Department has concentrated on training and exercises with a view to increasing Chinese capabilities under nuclear battle conditions.[84] To start with, inexperience, inadequate equipment and teaching material and the high level of difficulty all work against a good training program.[85] Nevertheless, in 1983 Han Huaizhi as Assistant to the Chief of General Staff identified essential changes to conventional warfare resulting from nuclear battle conditions. These in turn mean that consideration must be given to:

1. Survivability.

2. Varying standard operational procedures.

3. Changing combat groupings and methods of attack.

4. Overcoming damages and contamination caused by nuclear strikes.

5. Securing higher level headquarters.

6. Securing a much more sophisticated combat and logistics system.

7. Political work in the battlefield.[86]

In Fuzhou and Wuhan MRs, exercises were scheduled for 1984 which aimed at training infantry units to seal points of nuclear breakthrough in conjunction with combined arms operations.[87] Chinese calculations point to optimism as they claim that it would take only 16 minutes for the second echelon battalion, mounted on tanks and vehicles, and 31 minutes when it is on forced march to reach the point of nuclear breakthrough. They claim that it would take the enemy 39 minutes to reach the same point. Chinese optimists continue to argue that their anti-tank capabilities can halt Soviet strikes at these points of nuclear breakthrough. In the main, the Chinese claim that they have a numerical superiority of 2.5:1 (the number of Chinese anti-tank resources in the first echelon platoons: the number of enemy armoured vehicles).[88] These Chinese calculations seem to seriously underestimate the high level of radioactivity in battle zones after nuclear blasts. It is interesting to note that the Soviets also seem to have failed to take into account the need for temporary halts, as it takes time for the radiation level to decline.[89]

Thus US Defence Secretary McNamara wrote in 1963 in response to Sokolsky's work:[90]

> It is inconceivable to me how you send troops through an area in which there may have been literally hundreds of nuclear bursts.... It is as though the people who were writing the statements had never really had exposed to them the destructive power of nuclear weapons.

Discussions at the divisional command level have not included the use of Chinese tactical nuclear weapons to seal the point of nuclear breakthrough.[91] Two factors are probably responsible for this. First, given Soviet superiority in nuclear weapons, there is wisdom for the Chinese to refrain from any use of theatre nuclear forces (TNF) which may be answered by a full-scale Soviet TNF strike.[92] Second, should the Soviets make their initial nuclear strike near the border where the Chinese Main Forces would not be threatened, the latter would have less incentive to use TNF. It remains doubtful whether the Chinese can halt Soviet advances by conventional war. Given present limitations in technology and weapon systems, the Chinese response would appear to be the best improvised way to halt the Soviets. Moreover, this response in many ways resembles the NATO response to Soviet nuclear strikes. First, anti-tank guided missiles have been regarded as effective against the Soviet armoured units (regiment size according to the Chinese) which penetrate enemy territory after the nuclear blast.[93] Second, the Chinese disperse their units to the battalion level and below in order to preserve independent command and salvage logistic supplies after the nuclear barrage.[94] NATO battle groups have the same aim.

As a result, the Soviets will need to disperse their troops with a view to 'eliminating' survivors and facing a probable nuclear attack.[95] The major Chinese weakness, as they themselves admit, is inadequate mobility in the 'fire power competition'. One glaring inadequacy is in the area of tactical air strike which has been NATO's strength.[96] Nevertheless, the recent emergence of combined arms and joint operations should somewhat ameliorate the inferior Chinese position.

Three-dimensional defence system of great depth

The only way for the Chinese to prevent a major Soviet breakthrough at this stage is to effect defence in depth by providing a 'shield' in the form of a concentration of their Main Force units against several front OMGs and the Soviet second echelon. Thus positional warfare will apply in the defence of cities against conventional nuclear attacks.[97] However, the Chinese hope that any major confrontation will occur deep into Chinese territory so that a modern version of 'luring the enemy in deep' will take place. This differs a great deal from Mao's alternative to Otto Braun's strategy of 'stopping the enemy at the gate' which emerged during the Kiangsi Soviet period, as cities and territories will be defended.[98] Nevertheless, the principle of wearing the enemy down, and launching counter-attacks against the enemy's lines of communication are the same. Thus, mobile and guerrilla warfare under modern conditions will be used to achieve these objectives. For the strategy to work, the Chinese hope that a three-dimensional defence system of great depth (*dazhongshen di liti fangyu tixi*) can be established.[99]

> In order to enforce thoroughly the strategic directions of active defence under new conditions, we believe that it is necessary to establish a three-dimensional defence system of great depth. This system is composed of individual zones which have frontage and depth. Not only do they have ground defence works, but also air and naval defence in coordination. It should not only cause attrition, annihilate the enemy and resist the enemy's frontal attack, but also perform a supporting function for the battle zone or even the entire theatre. The size of the defence zone depends on the operational principles of our adversaries and their experience and theories in breaking through great depths. For major battles, the frontage and depth of the defence zone should be able to withstand attacks from an enemy front army. For secondary battles, the size of the defence zone should be greater than the attacking frontage and the immediate and designated depth of an enemy army group....

The Chinese discuss at great length problems of command and control in a three-dimensional battlefield. Two major problems are the reduction of the safety margin (*anquanjie*) and the ambiguity of the front line. The first problem requires China to strengthen the building of defence works in order to reduce enemy fire power and air strikes from a high altitude. The second problem concerns the control of air space over the battle area. Zones controlled by one side on the ground may have air corridors, combat bases and mobile airborne units of the opposite side located within them. This makes the identification of the front line rather difficult.[100]

In the setting of an 'Air Land Battle', the Chinese hope that the frontage and depth for major battles can withstand the attacks of a Soviet front army. For secondary battles, the Chinese defence coverage should be greater than the advancing front and depth of a Soviet group army. The concept of a 'ring of defence' comprising a series of tactical supporting points (*zhanshu zhichengdian*) is now considered fundamental to China's ability to withstand enemy airborne and armoured attacks in conventional, nuclear and biological/chemical warfare:[101]

> ... For strategic points in individual battles, several defence zones should be established from front to rear. Each defence zone should be composed of a series of tactical supporting points and each supporting point should possess a ring of defence which comprises the capabilities to strike, hide and manoeuvre. All these are capable of not only resisting continuous strikes by a large number of enemy tanks and APCs, but also handling enemy elements by enemy ground forces. In addition, they can resist enemy air strikes, air-borne attacks, conventional weapons and fierce attacks by nuclear and chemical weapons. In between the various defence zones, we should establish fire zones or mid-way defence zones in order to facilitate the disruption of enemy intentions to develop strategic (*zhanyi*) breakthrough from tactical breakthroughs.

The above specifications represent Chinese efforts in improving their defence capabilities in combined arms, the success of which in turn depends on their latest reforms in force structure and C³I which cannot be taken for granted (see Chapter 1). In any case, the Chinese in their euphoria envisage the successful establishment of a 'shield' which would be able to halt enemy offensives in the first few days of a major war:[102]

> The establishment of a three-dimensional defence system of great depth has to be based on the direction of our strategic defence, the enemies' probable strength of insertion, the terrain and probable *materiel* conditions. We must act according to what we have and must not establish defence and covering zones everywhere as that will disperse the strength of our forces. In border areas and territories adjacent to our main defensive zone, there are many 'dead and harsh grounds' (*sidi*) which are difficult to traverse and which are in themselves capable of delaying and impeding the enemy's advance. We should as far as possible make use of these natural 'shields'.

As Soviet troops move deep into Chinese territory, the PLA will be in a position to launch counterattacks as weaknesses in the advancing Soviet OMGs are identified.[103] Beijing MR's Deputy Commander of the Artillery Corps, Li Jian, identified Soviet attack's strength as a 'hardened head' and their weaknesses as the 'long tail', 'large buttocks' and 'too many intestines'.[104] Li further argues for ways to weaken the 'hardened head'. For Li's plans to work, it would require Chinese Main Forces to withstand the formidable combination of fire strike (mainly missiles and fixed wing aircraft) and troop strike (mainly tanks and artillery). Should Chinese Main Forces succeed in withstanding Soviet attacks deep into Chinese territory, Li Jian's plans may have some success in striking at Soviet weaknesses. These include hitting at the 'long tail' or long lines of communication. The logistic vulnerability of a Soviet motorised division is given as follows:[105]

> The destruction of one of the 20 water-carrying vehicles will cause either 68 tanks or 1367 vehicles to grind to a halt; the destruction of one refuelling vehicle will cause 7–8 APCs to stop (fuel consumption of 1 mechanised division per km is one tonne); the destruction of one of the four oil pipe lines in a Soviet Front Army will paralyse 4 to 5 mechanised divisions.

As for the 'large buttocks', the Chinese claim that the supplies of Soviet forces which traverse too vast an area are vulnerable to Chinese guerrilla attacks:[106]

> One motorised division (MD) advancing along the axis at the speed of 20–30km per 24 hours will cover 2400km. Supplies for 1 MD amount to 3700 tonnes to be transported by nearly 1000 vehicles.

Soviet 'intestines' identified as the third weakness refers to all the complexities of a Soviet deep attack which can be easy prey for Chinese attacks. These include headquarters for C^3I, missile launch sites, artillery, airfields, fuel and ammunition depots etc.[107] On paper the Chinese combined arms operations will have a chance against the 'stronger' enemy should their improved force structure and C^3I make it possible for the Chinese to maximise their defence efforts.[108] The concept of a 'shield' confirms the Chinese faith in defending fixed positions, making the defence of major cities crucial. For instance, in North and Northeast China, which can be considered as one theatre of war, the defence of both Beijing and Shenyang is crucial to China, to the extent that the Chinese may have to drop the principle of NFU should the survival of their concentration of Main Forces be threatened. Thus the defence of cities, which requires the Chinese to rely heavily on positional warfare, emerged in the early 1980s as a crucial element of China's active defence.[109]

It was a City Defence Symposium in 1980 in Jilin which revealed that the Chinese were beginning to take city defence seriously when Wang Enmao, then First Secretary of the Jilin Provincial Party Committee, confirmed the changing concept of Chinese defence:[110]

City defence is very important for war preparedness. City defence construction is a major aspect in the modernisation of national defence. As it is also a part of the general strategic plan — the national defence modernisation programme — we should consider city defence construction as a strategic issue and never underestimate its importance.

To avoid the mistakes made by the Kwantung Army, the Chinese are relying on strategic defence in the initial stage of the war to avoid a major Soviet breakthrough. In real terms, it will be necessary for the Chinese to hold the line of defence on the foothills of the Greater and Lesser Xingan Ranges. In other words, cities like Haerbin and Siping will have to be defended by the Chinese Main Forces. Kefner's second stage scenario mentioned earlier must not be allowed to happen if the Chinese were to survive a major *blitzkrieg*. Should a Soviet strategic breakthrough look imminent, the Chinese may resort to TNW. Following Li Jian's reasoning, the Chinese can deploy low-yield tactical nuclear weapons (when they become available) to hit hard at lines of communication on the Sino–Soviet border, or for that matter, interdict neighbouring Soviet strategic position and cities (see Chapter 2). The longer the time the Chinese have in developing battlefield nuclear weapons, and improving their accuracy and C^2, the greater the deterrent effect will become.

One way of strengthening city defence under discussion by military academics is to increase Chinese capabilities by deploying mobile units in 'axle-style' (*chengzhou shi*) defence. Bearing in mind the Soviet superiority in long-range fire power and high-speed air strike, the design of an inner ring and an outer ring in an axle has been regarded as essential. The inner ring comprises the city and the adjacent suburbs where positional defence will be undertaken. The outer ring comprises the vast countryside where units (up to platoon size) and the militia can combine to conduct 'People's War-style' guerrilla warfare. The key to the success of 'axle-style' defence is the deployment of mobile units between the two rings with their backs to the city where they can obtain logistic support. Being situated in the countryside, there will also be plenty of food supplies. The mobile units are envisaged to possess good anti-air, anti-tank and anti-chemical/biological capabilities and are likened to 'ball-bearings' between the two rings which can resist enemy pressure. When pressure is heavy, the mobile units can operate on the exterior lines against the enemy's complex logistic support system.[111]

Soviet fire power

Although China may feel confident about its reliance on active defence as the answer to Soviet attacks, it is certainly aware of its inadequacies in military capabilities. To compensate for Soviet superiority in fire power and mobility, the Chinese will need to narrow the technological gap wherever possible, whilst at the same time rely on the human factor and strategy to reinforce their capabilities.

As early as 1980, the Chinese had started to realistically face the predicament of superior Soviet fire power as they painted a dismal picture of their defence capabilities against Soviet nuclear attacks.[112]

> Soviet troops are now equipped with tactical nuclear weapons of various sizes, not only the 10 000 ton class, the 1000 ton class and the 100 ton class, but also much smaller ones which could be fired by a conventional cannon. The radius of destruction of such a shell is not much greater than 200 to 700 metres, and they are likely to become more compact. These are designed for use in actual combat zones to kill armed personnel without massive destruction of urban centres and industrial sites.... One tactical nuclear shell could penetrate our defence line and leave a gap several hundred meters long. It could destroy our defence hubs and vital strongholds. A single tactical nuclear shell, when exploded at a low altitude, could kill our troops positioned on any side of a mountain peak. Although troops inside defence shelters would not be killed, they would not be able, due to post-explosion radiation, to take up positions outside the shelter soon enough to intercept enemy tanks and armour units advancing in the wake of the shelling. True, tactical nuclear weapons lose some of their effectiveness in mountainous areas, but this could be compensated for by firing more shells. I don't think any enemy who is set to gain the military initiative would hesitate to pay the price.

The Chinese can also expect much improved Soviet air strike and air support capabilities since 1983 when the Soviet Air Force underwent substantial reorganisation. One of the major features has been restructuring Tactical Aviation (regarded as flying artillery) to achieve greater integration at the theatre level. In substance, long range strike capability has been improved with the SU-24 'FENCER' and TU-16 'BADGER'. Similarly, combat aircraft have become more sophisticated with the development of the Su-25 'FROGFOOT', Su-17 'FLANKER', MiG-29 'FULCRUM' and the MiG-31 'FOX-HOUND', which will make the Soviet Air Force an even more formidable Force in the 1990s. Without doubt, the Far East Theatre again is a poor second in the allocation of Soviet resources, but one would expect the modernisation process to take effect with greater pressure from the 'Far East lobby'.[113]

As regards troop strike, the two formidable Soviet capabilities are the armoured units and artillery supplemented by airborne troops. Soviet domination in Main Battle Tanks (MBT) with its modified T-64 and T-72 have led the Chinese to follow the world trend of resorting to developing Anti-Tank Guided Missiles (ATGM). Nevertheless, the tank remains the most versatile and robust land weapon system, a fact that the Chinese are also well aware of and finding it difficult to counter. Worse still, the T-72 is believed to have improved armour, possibly with ceramic inserts in the cast turret armour, and ceramic backing to the hull armour, making the work for Chinese armour-piercing weapons even harder (for Chinese capabilities, see Chapter 2).[114]

Apart from the contest between the MBT and the ATGM being fairly uneven, the artillery may be the determinant for the land battle. Thus Soviet sub-munitions or improved conventional warheads suitable for their SS-21 'Tochka' would be extremely lethal in attacks against China's deep defence.[115] It is estimated that there are at least 40 launchers for the SS-22s in missile brigades in the Far East and that their accuracy is increased because of improved conventional munitions (ICM). In addition, the Soviets have deployed some 100 SS-1C SCUD SRINF missile launchers in the Far East. All in all, the Soviets would hope that instant minefields created by such warheads would seal the flanks of Soviet OMGs against the Chinese.[116] Another crucial Soviet development is Extended Range Artillery in which the USSR overtakes the West. Thus, the Chinese follow-on echelons would find it difficult defending themselves against the 2S5 152 mm gun (range 35–40km) and the BM-27 (range 35–40km).[117]

Soviet superiority in firepower and mobility will, however, need to be supported by an extremely efficient logistic system. The element of surprise has been eclipsed by much improved Chinese surveillance capabilities which include the availability of satellite communications information. The completion of the BAM railway, despite problems with weather and rugged terrain, undoubtedly improve Soviet logistic support levels, making the Soviets less vulnerable to Chinese interdiction.[118] Nevertheless, it remains true that the Soviet Far Eastern Theatre of War compares less favourably with its European counterpart in terms of logistic support and capabilities.[119]

In a *blitzkrieg* which would drive right into Heilongjiang and Jilin in China's Northeast, the Soviets would aim at controlling the old Chinese Eastern Railway in order to increase logistic support by creating a territorial buffer for the Pacific Maritime Province. Soviet fire power should be assessed in the two classical categories of fire strike and troop strike. In turn, Soviet fire strike can either be conventional or nuclear or both. The Soviet nuclear capabilities are well known. For instance, their tactical nuclear arsenal includes the SS-21, SS-X-23 and SS-22 as well as other nuclear-capable artillery, aviation and longer-range missiles.[120] There is no doubt that the Soviets are confident of their qualitative and quantitative advantages over the Chinese, so much so that they would welcome Chinese first use of nuclear weapons.

Chinese capabilities and operational art: combined arms and joint operations

China hopes to halt Soviet breakthroughs deep in Chinese territory by well-planned operational principles which are supported by much improved fire power. Such improvements, as identified in the military modernisation program are selective, namely weaponry improvements in anti-air strike, anti-armour and anti-airborne attack capabilities (see Chapter 2). The Chinese are well aware of the drawbacks of the 'Just Defence' syndrome, should they choose to remain on the defensive all the time. Thus the strengthening of Chinese manoeuvrability, and mobility in general, would be the crucial factor in putting into effective use the improved weapon system, and in perfecting operational principles which are tailor-made for a Chinese theatre of war and aim at identifiable weakness in the Soviet *blitzkrieg*.

Improvisation and innovation would help to implement mobile and manoeuvre-oriented defence. For instance, even with a four km wall of mines and prelaid sensors, as well as new weapons on order (eg, TOW ATGW and Improved Hawk SAM), the Chinese may find the Soviet artillery force overwhelming.[121] However, Chinese strategic planners can take advantage of Soviet weaknesses in the same way that the NATO High Command would, although they would otherwise be disadvantaged by technological inferiority. But certain essential elements of the operational art are also applicable to the Chinese theatre of war.

Whilst Forward Defence goes against the Chinese principle of defending their own territory and 'assimilating' the enemy on home terrain, it should be clear to the Chinese that deep attack is the answer to halting major Soviet OMGs. The adapted operational art in the Chinese case can therefore be an execution of that art in

Chinese territory rather than on Soviet soil. The prerequisite to the above is that the Chinese theatre of war should have a depth of, say, over 1000km in order to prevent a Soviet strategic breakthrough.

In the defence of the Northeast, the Chinese would be expected to launch deep attacks against advancing Soviet OMGs. The deep attack principle would also test the latest Chinese efforts in combined arms as they would be wise to launch joint air-land attacks on OMGs when they are most vulnerable. It is well known that OMGs require the art of deception to achieve an element of surprise. Nevertheless, they are most vulnerable as they concentrate in an area 30–50km behind the forward Soviet troops before they can insert themselves into the Forward Line of Troops (FLOT).[122] Thus the Chinese have advocated the launching of deep attack against the Soviet second echelon as they believe that it would terminate the Soviet echelon formation's 'source' and 'flow'.[123] They also believe that the Soviet second echelon contains many weaknesses when the first echelon is on the attack. As the former begins to manoeuvre in an area 30–100km from the Chinese frontage, the Chinese believe that it is not vigilant, lacks defensive power and its force structure is too mixed to be well organised.[124] Although they realise that they lack the firepower and mobility of the Americans, the Chinese still hope to deploy specially despatched mobile units to attack the Soviet second echelon in order to create offensive capabilities in defence.[125] Without doubt, militia and guerrilla units can coordinate with the deep attack against the entire Soviet rear echelon by conducting mobile-guerrilla warfare.[126] The question remains whether these mobile units have the necessary firepower and mobility to halt the Soviet second echelon. The development of Chinese combined arms is still at an infancy stage and they will have to strive extremely hard in good time before they can take advantage of a Soviet tactical weakness, especially when OMGs are well protected and supported by air and artillery (eg, a Soviet Front artillery would have the range to cover a Front OMG).[127]

The Chinese are conscious of the rather desperate situation they are in against the 'stronger' enemy and improvements are being made to force structure as well as fire power. Undoubtedly they hope to maximise manoeuvrability against the formidable foe so that they can respond the best way they can to a major Soviet attack. The Chinese are aware of Soviet air superiority which would practically paralyse any Chinese air-land operations. The partial answer to such pessimistic scenarios is for the Chinese to improvise in operational art. Thus the Chinese would need a 'tactical doctrine' to maximise their capabilities in an 'Air Land Battle'. Such doctrine would provide leadership in combined arms operations at brigade level and above in order that improved capabilities and fire power for land operations and associated air support could be maximised. It would also direct the Chinese toward the reform of certain components of their force structure and C³I so that the coordination of the fire of manoeuvre forces, conventional and nuclear artillery, the support of armed helicopters and the tactical aircraft can be achieved (see Chapter 1).[128] It is not likely that the West would know of the existence of such a doctrine, but the Chinese are introducing changes to accommodate combined arms and joint operations.

The establishment of the first mechanised combined arms group army (*hecheng jituanjun*) in August 1986 at Shijiazhuang under Li Jijun's command has set the pace for the Chinese to remodel and modernise its defence force for combined arms and joint operations.[129] In the hope that the Soviet threat is not imminent and in making strategic plans for a long-term solution to the Soviet challenge, the Chinese are moving in the right direction in their recent revolutionary measures to improve their strategic capabilities. The recent symposium on 'Strategic Defence and Systems Engineering for the Year 2000', sponsored by the Military Systems Engineering Commission and attended by over 100 specialists from the three forces in Beijing in July 1986, further suggests that the Chinese are hoping that they can evolve effective deterrent capabilities by the year 2000.[130]

Combined arms operations will indeed strengthen the first few 'rings of defence'[131] in the initial stage of the war should the Chinese be able to apply the new combined arms group army model to restructure the Local Forces and the Reserve divisions and regiments (see Chapter 1 for a standard combined arms group army formation). There are reports that the process has started.[132] Furthermore, the disbanding of the artillery divisions suggests that Local and Reserve Forces will benefit in fire power by the redeployment of resources.[133] In a specific case like the defence of China's Northeast, these improved units charged with the heavy responsibility of delaying enemy advances and preventing any enemy strategic breakthrough, will have to rely on a reasonable early warning/reconnaissance and logistic system. Thus the establishment of the two major Signals Intelligence (SIGINT) stations with HF, VHF and SHF intercept systems at Korla and Qitai in Xinjiang in 1979 signifies that the Chinese have capabilities for missile telemetry regarding ABM missile tests at Sary Shagan and ballistic missile tests from Tyuratam,

Kapustin Yar and Plesetsk.[134] By 1985, China had established a network of twelve sites with SIGINT facilities on the northern border monitoring Soviet military activities and also supplementing the collection efforts of China's other SIGINT facilities and air defence radar systems.[135] Modern air surveillance and long-range radars of Western origin also feed into the Chinese AD system although it is doubtful whether they can adequately cover the northern border where Soviet air interdiction will be heavy in a major war.[136] Chinese logistic support for border defence in the Northeast will continue to improve significantly as the seventh Five-Year Plan invests in electrification and double-tracking for the Manzhouli–Haerbin–Suifen line.[137] The overall effect of improved Chinese capabilities is that the Chinese may be able to significantly halt enemy advances in the initial stage of the war before the 'revolutionalised' Chinese Main Force units take on the Soviet OMGs in positional warfare and in defence of cities, say, on the northern part of the Manchurian plain (eg the defence of Haerbin and/or Siping).

In the meantime, Chinese Local Forces, especially guerrilla units, will move into the rear area to disrupt the enemy's long lines of communication.[138] (Li Jian's description of the complex Soviet logistic system has been examined.) It was Li Jian who as Deputy Commander of the Beijing Artillery Corps proposed the novel idea of increasing the fire power of guerrilla units and assigning Main Force elements to the former. These guerrilla artillery units (*yuji paodui*) comprising ten to a few dozen men organised from either the Main Force or Local units are believed to be capable of interdicting the enemy's armoured units from a distance of 1–10km in well-hidden spots.[139] These units should be equipped mainly with light anti-armour fire power as well as all-weather communications systems, and should operate within a radius of 50km from the Chinese main frontage in the enemy's rear. Li Jian cited the anti-Soviet Afghan and Kampuchean experiences to highlight the advantage of guerrilla units operating in the rear areas. Thus Li believes that capabilities like 'strike' and 'hide' as typified by the guerrilla artillery units will significantly disrupt the enemy's complex logistic system.[140]

As a stalement emerges, the Chinese Main Forces will assume the major burden of active defence when cities are to be defended. It was therefore most appropriate for Wang Enmao, as the first Secretary of the Jilin Provincial Party Committee, to address the problem of the defence of cities.[141] The defence of Haerbin would probably be a test case in future conflicts.

PROSPECTS FOR STRATEGIC DEFENCE

Will the strategy of 'People's War under modern conditions' be capable of defending Chinese territory against Soviet attacks? Whilst there is no definite answer to this question, it is evident that the Chinese believe that the strategy will work, especially if they were given six to seven decades to bring about strategic changes to defence modernisation. Thus far, the Chinese have already made use of revolutionary changes and successes in defence modernisation to support the implementation of strategic defence in the initial stage of the war. The need to undertake active defence which relies on positional warfare supplemented by mobile and guerrilla warfare is a direct response to Soviet superiority in strategy and capabilities. At the same time, the Chinese realise that they need to improve their odds in future confrontations with the Soviets. Whether the Chinese can withstand a Soviet *blitzkrieg* and their deep attack strategy depends on how well they can implement defence in depth. Thus, the seven enlarged MRs not only provide better command and control in a theatre war, but also emphasise greater reliance on regional defence and the concentration of Main Force units deep in Chinese territory. Furthermore, the need to improve capabilities under nuclear battle conditions has encouraged active training and exercises in order to halt Soviet advances after nuclear bursts. The deployment of anti-tank guided missiles against Soviet armoured units and the dispersal of units to battalion level and below have been been identified as ways to improve Chinese survival under nuclear battle conditions. To reinforce defence in depth, the Chinese believe that a three-dimensional defence system which provides both frontage and depth in a theatre of war, and involves good coordination of the three services, will be able to withstand enemy air, airborne and armoured attacks in conventional nuclear and biological/chemical warfare. In addition, well-planned operational principles supported by improved fire power have been evolved to strengthen manoeuvrability and mobility in a Chinese theatre of war. To take the initiative, the Chinese emphasise the need to develop capabilities to launch deep attack against advancing Soviet OMGs and the entire rear echelon. The deployment of militia and guerrilla units to conduct large-scale guerrilla warfare will further increase Chinese mobility and underline the contribution of the populace.

Should the Chinese be able to withstand Soviet attacks by implementing successfully strategic defence in the initial stage of the war, a stalemate would ensue. The deployment of Chinese Main Force units to defend cities deep in Chinese territory would then become critical to Chinese survival. Chinese determination to perfect a system of wartime mobilisation which relies on the Reserve Forces comprising the reserve units as well as the armed basic militia will also be a critical factor in China's active defence efforts. Should the Chinese be able to train modern Reserve Forces in support of Main Force units, their chances of success in halting Soviet advances, say, in the Northeast, will be greatly enhanced. The Chinese have obviously not yet optimised their wartime mobilisation efforts as the new measures were only introduced in 1984–85.[145] Nevertheless, given time and experience, there is no doubt that the Chinese will be able to mobilise their formidable Reserve Forces which will fully support China's strategic defence of key cities and positions. By doing so, the Chinese will have lived up to their claims that 'People's War under modern conditions' is the strategy for all seasons.

6
Chinese Maritime Power

The growth of Chinese maritime power became noticeable in the early 1980s as China began to develop certain 'blue water' capabilities. It denotes clear directions in defence modernisation as the Chinese strive to improve their warfighting capabilities for the three services of the PLA, especially in combined arms operations and joint warfare. In adopting a new strategic outlook in defence modernisation, the Chinese have given themselves six to seven decades to reach advanced world standards in the development of military technology and the modernisation of the PLA in general. No matter whether the Chinese succeed or not in their endeavour, the strategic changes will definitely have a significant impact on China's role in the strategic balance. In turn, its neighbours in the Asia–Pacific region will particularly feel the growth of China's maritime power as it continues to improve naval capabilities as an integral part of its strategic plan for defence modernisation.

Economic modernisation, labelled as China's national priority, has not deterred the development of a modern navy which assumes for itself not merely the responsibility of coastal defence but also the capabilities of projecting itself to protect its strategic and regional interests. Thus China's intention to develop 'blue water' capabilities was evident to the world when the Chinese Navy was capable of supporting the Chinese ICBM Test mission in the South Pacific in May 1980.[1] In turn economic modernisation requires the development of trading interests and the securing of energy resources, which both require a modernised navy which can project its force, at least in the Asia–Pacific region with a view to protecting China's growing economic interest. The growth of China's merchant navy traversing the major sea lines of communication will need greater support and protection, especially in disputed waters, say, in the South China Sea.[2]

Rear Admiral J.R. Hill defines maritime power as the ability to use the sea. In the context of China, the growth of maritime power will benefit the protection of its economic interests, and the projection of its forces against opponents.[3] In the process, China may find it essential to exert political pressure on Taiwan for 're-unification' and this would also be facilitated by China's ability to impose an effective naval blockade on the island. Nevertheless, China is fully aware of the fact that its growth in maritime power has to be gauged in the context of the strategic balance in the Asia–Pacific region, which has been dominated by the superpowers, especially in respect of their naval forces.

Superpower naval rivalry and China's strategic role in the Asia-Pacific region

Superpower naval rivalry in the Asia–Pacific region dominates the strategic balance in East and Southeast Asia. Indigenous nations concerned with their national security problems have to take cognisance of the rivalry, especially in regard to US dominance and increasing USSR naval presence and desire to compete with the US for global maritime supremacy.[4] In this context, China can see the advantage of US naval presence in limiting Soviet expansion despite its 'equidistance' stance *vis-a-vis* the two superpowers. Conversely, the US recognises the role of China, Japan and the Philippines as a strategic factor that 'would weigh heavily in defining both the naval character of war in the Pacific and its ultimate outcome...'.[5] These comments from Admiral S.R. Foley, Commander-in-Chief of the US Pacific Fleet, further confirm the US strategy to sustain and improve a maritime emphasis in defence: 'A fundamental component of the nation's success in deterring war with the Soviet Union depends upon our ability to stabilize and control escalation in Third World crisis.'[6]

The contribution of Japan and the US bases in the Philippines to the US strategic advantage over the USSR in the Pacific is well known. In its role as 'an unsinkable aircraft carrier', Japan is part of the US global nuclear deterrent against Soviet SS-20s and submarine-launched missiles. In securing the conventional defence of Japan and the protection of its sea lines of communication (SLOCs), the US will be able to provide air superiority, offensive counter-air capabilities and assist Japan in its responsibility to protect the 1000nm SLOCS.[7] As regards the US bases in the Philippines, it is important for the US to secure a renewal of the lease in 1991. Given the onerous task the Aquino government has in reconstructing the nation, there is little doubt that it is extremely amenable to accommodating US interests provided that she is able to strike the best bargain. The US will also insist on retaining full operational control of the bases.[8] The presidential commission responsible for drafting a new Philippine Constitution has stipulated that a new treaty is required for foreign bases, troops or facilities to be allowed in Philippine territory beyond 1991. At the same time it has made the renewal of the lease easier for the US by deleting provisions against foreign military forces and facilities, and against nuclear weapons in the Philippines.[9] Should the US lose these bases, and should it secure substitutes further north in the Pacific, it would severely constrain US ability to restrict Soviet activities in the Southwestern Pacific and Southeast Asia.[10]

Foley adheres great importance to the 'salutary strategic implications' of Sino–American relationship:[11]

> A rapprochement between the Chinese and the Soviets would profoundly alter the existing military balance in the Pacific and the world and greatly complicate US unilateral and NATO planning.

Conversely, a growing Chinese Navy with increasing 'blue water' capabilities which is 'on side' with the US, would add to the strength of the nations of the Pacific which are wary of Soviet strategic designs in the Pacific.

With the gradual modernisation of its surface combatants as well as its SSN/SSBN force, China's ability to exert influence on its neighbours increases. In the 1990s it will play a more assertive role over the disputed waters in the South China Sea, the containment of the Soviet detachment (or larger strength in future) in Southeast Asia and the exerting of maritime 'leverage' over Vietnam.[12] In response to the above, some ASEAN states (Indonesia and Malaysia in particular) are suspicious of China's long-term regional interest. Thus, ASEAN's sacrosanct principles of ZOPFAN (Zone of Peace, Freedom and Neutrality) are cherished in order to guard against 'Chinese expansionism' and to secure the region against Soviet and Vietnamese force projection capability.[13]

Should close Sino–American relations persist, the modernised Chinese fleet will intangibly and in varying degrees contribute to the US maritime strategy to destroy the Soviet fleets by 'seizing the initiatives' and 'carrying the fight to the enemy'.[14] As long as the Chinese find it necessary to interdict Soviet SLOCs in the Asia–Pacific region, it will contribute to tilting the naval balance in favour of the US. In addition, these scenarios can take place without a formal understanding or alliance between China and the US.[15] Whilst the Soviets consider the Pacific a secondary maritime theatre which aims at securing their land and sea based strategic missile forces and interdicting enemy shipping and maximising attrition on enemy naval and air forces, the US assumes an offensive strategy of forward deployment to destroy the Soviet Pacific Fleet (SOVPACFLT).[16] Given the existing US superiority over the USSR in this region, any probability of an independent Chinese interdiction of the SOVPACFLT would require Soviet strategists to make due adjustments in force structure and planning. Specifically, Chinese interdictions and strikes from the North and East Sea Fleets may be undertaken by either the surface combatants or the SSN/SSBN.[17] The fact that the SOVPACFLT may need to counter these attacks would add to the strategic advantage of the US, whose ASW offensives pose a significant threat to the Soviet SSBN bastions in the Sea of Japan and the Sea of Okhotsk.[18]

Depending on the extent of these Chinese interdictions and strikes, the US Pacific Command (PACCOM) will find greater flexibility against the SOVPACFLT.[19] Such flexibilities would in turn reactivate the debate on the validity of the US 'swing' strategy which has now been officially abandoned.[20] In other words, increased anti-Soviet naval capabilities in the Pacific may induce the US to admit that the superiority of the US PACCOM to the SOVPACFLT makes it possible for the Third Fleet to be redeployed to the Atlantic via the Panama Canal after the outbreak of war.[21]

Chinese objectives: sea denial and naval presence

In the absence of a US–Chinese military alliance, one may ask what role the Chinese Navy has to play as it begins to take on regional interests. In the first place, China is able to demonstrate sea denial capabilities in Chinese waters, which will be effective against probable Soviet amphibious attacks. Second, China will make its naval presence felt in the Asia–Pacific region. Short of engaging the enemy in combat, Chinese naval presence will demonstrate China's determination and resolve to protect its political and economic interests in the region. Third, China has the option of interdicting Soviet sea lanes should a war break out involving China and the superpowers.[22] Mutual cooperation in such circumstances, although it will fall short of a formal alliance, will indeed benefit the US a great deal in the naval balance, especially if the US still believes in the 'swing' strategy.[23]

It is now pertinent to examine the extent that defence modernisation has been able to support Chinese objectives in demonstrating capabilities in sea denial and naval presence. Coastal defence against probable Soviet attacks is China's top priority as it strengthens its sea denial capabilities. At the same time, shoud its ability to make its naval presence felt in the Asia–Pacific region increase with further strategic breakthroughs in the development of naval technology and armament, the effect of the force multiplier would have to be assessed in the light of how it may change the naval balance in the region. Indeed, Chinese and Japanese objectives to protect their political and economic interests in the next few decades will have significant impact on superpower rivalry in the Pacific.

Sea denial

The Chinese are capable of increasing sea denial capabilities by ensuring that sea-air operations would contribute to preventing the Soviets with any opportunity to launch large-scale amphibious attacks on, say, the Liaodong Peninsula in Northeast China. Similarly, the South China Sea with its disputed waters provides great potential for sea-air operations beyond the limited experience of the Xisha operation in 1974.[24] The most significant projection of naval strength is the SSN and SSBN capabilities which constitute a significant strategic deterrence force and a trump card for the Chinese. The development of joint sea-air operations will indeed enable the Chinese to halt any Soviet plans to launch amphibious attacks on the Liaodong Peninsula. In the first place, the Chinese ROMEO and WHISKEY class submarines will be able to form an adequate ambush platform at the strategic chokepoint in the Tsushima Channel. With the deployment of more HAN class SSNs, the Chinese will adequately provide a second echelon of attack submarines to support the 'wolf pack' of patrol submarines. Finally, the XIA class SSBNs with their base in Qingdao will enhance China's strategic first-strike capabilities which will have Vladivostok and adjacent targets in mind.[25]

The constricted waters of the Tsushima Channels and the Yellow Sea not only provide the Chinese Navy with favourable conditions in facing the SOVPACFLT, but also facilitate the launching of joint operations against probable Soviet amphibious attacks. Thus air divisions from the military air regions in North China are capable of giving air support to both ground and naval forces should Liaodong be attacked.[26] This of course assumes that the Chinese can overcome their C³I problems. It has been reported for instance that recent training emphasised countering low level attacks from many directions, and improving coordination between anti-aircraft, artillery and missile units.[27] In this light, the Chinese J-7s and Q-5s would provide improved air support for the Chinese ground forces in an anti-amphibious attack scenario.[28]

The Chinese have also concentrated on perfecting tactics for anti-amphibious attacks which comprise the integrated defence of estuaries and harbours. They would defend the ports and harbours themselves, their two flanks and the adjacent islands. Capabilities in concentrated fire power and quick response are deemed necessary to counter enemy strikes from surface combatants and the amphibious force, and also submarines and the air force. The use of HY-2 (CSSC-2) land-based SSM also constitutes an integral part of China's coastal defence capabilities in the face of an attempted Soviet invasion from the sea.[29]

In the face of limited, but improving, Chinese joint operations, it is highly unlikely that the Soviets will launch an amphibious attack on the Liaodong Peninsula. They will have much more to gain by concentrating on a large-scale attack on the Northeast, which will include the deployment of their airborne troops. Indeed, it is difficult to envisage what advantage the single division of 7000 strong of the Soviet Naval Infantry (SNI) assigned to the SOVPACFLT may gain should they succeed in landing on the Liaodong Peninsula.[30] In a word, the SNI will be outnumbered and it will not achieve the objectives of concentration, surprise and mobility. Finally, the Soviets cannot dismiss the possibility of an American intervention in any Sino–Soviet confrontation as the US PACCOM assumes a forward deployment strategy in the Northwest Pacific.[31]

Naval presence

With rapidly improved naval capabilities the Chinese will be in a better position to utilise naval diplomacy and naval presence for the rest of the century. The use of warships as a means of 'signalling' to communicate its intentions to other rival nations will indeed strengthen China's bargaining position in naval diplomacy.[32] The next escalatory step is naval presence which is more common with the missions of the superpowers. Nevertheless, Chinese intentions to enforce the principle of 'one country two systems' may motivate them to utilise naval presence as the most efficient way to bring flexible fire power to bear in regions beyond their coasts.[33] Taiwan is the case in point. Naval presence may be costly but the Chinese may keep options open and the cost down. In addition, the political effect of a small-scale presence mission may be strengthened if principles like the territorialisation of the sea are applied.[34] Thus the declaration of specific parts of East and Southeast Asian waters to be TEZ (total exclusion zone), EEZ (exclusive economic zone) or even EFZ (exclusive fishing zone) will facilitate China's implementation of naval missions. The use of Chinese warships will then be deemed to be a continuation of politics.[35]

Maritime disputes and conflicts will be China's concern in the future as fish and oil resources raise disputes over ownership. China's claims to the Spratley Islands 600 miles to the South of the Chinese mainland have been cited as symptomatic of a powerful neighbour leaning on small countries (Vietnam and the Philippines) with claims on oil resources. That China regards its sovereign claims over the Spratley Islands as 'non-negotiable' conforms to 'the fashionable trend of island grabbing' as depicted by Sir James Cable.[36] Another way for China to seek international approval of its rights to exercise claims over adjacent territories would be to become a signatory to the 1982 United Nations Convention on the Law of the Sea (UNCLOS III) which recognises the concept of the 200-mile EEZ.[37] Such a move would entitle China to have 'the exclusive right to manage the living and non-living resources of the sea' in the EEZ.[38]

In Southeast Asia, the PRC has strengthened its signal of resolve in backing its sovereignty claims and indicating determination to the SRV and USSR. It has built up its naval forces in the area and has been engaged in sustained exercises in the South China Sea, the Philippine Sea as well as the Gulf of Thailand. Consistent improvements have been observed in alongside refuelling at sea and logistics transfer, in addition to ASW, AS, rotary-wing and FMPB operations.[39] These advances in PRC naval capability for force projection in the South China Sea are heavily supported by landbased air and missile formations in the adjacent Hainan Military District.[40] Consequently, the PRC has tangibly shown its resolve to enforce its claims in the South China Sea against all comers and, in particular, the Socialist Republic of Vietnam (SRV) and its allies. Table 6.1 below sets out the PRC's claims to the disputed islands:

Indeed, the record of Sino–Vietnamese clashes and Chinese exercises in the region in 1982–84 speaks for itself. In 1982, PRC and

Table 6.1: Island claims in the South China Sea (January 1986)*

Common Name	Claims	Occupied by
(A) 'Spratley Group'	PRC/SRV/ROC/MAL/PHIL	ROC/SRV/PHIL
Amboyna Cay	PRC/SRV/ROC/MAL/PHIL	SRV
Commodore Reef	PRC/SRV/ROC/MAL/PHIL	PHIL
Flat Island	PRC/SRV/ROC/PHIL	PHIL
Itu Aba	PRC/SRV/ROC/PHIL	ROC
Lankiam Cay	PRC/SRV/ROC/PHIL	PHIL
Loaita	PRC/SRV/ROC/PHIL	
Namyit	PRC/SRV/ROC/PHIL	SRV
Nanshan	PRC/SRV/ROC/PHIL	PHIL
Northoist Cay	PRC/SRV/ROC/PHIL	PHIL
Pearson Reef	PRC/SRV/ROC/PHIL	SRV
Sand Cay	PRC/SRV/ROC/PHIL	SRV
SW Cowe	PRC/SRV/ROC/PHIL	SRV
South-East Cay	PRC/SRV/ROC/PHIL	SRV
Spratley Island	PRC/SRV/ROC	SRV
West York Island	PRC/SRV/ROC/PHIL	PHIL
Thitu	PRC/SRV/ROC/PHIL	PHIL
(B) 'Paracel Group'	PRC/SRV/ROC	PRC
(C) Pratas Reef	PRC/ROC	ROC

Key: PRC (People's Republic of China)
    ROC (Republic of China: Taiwan)
    SRV (Socialist Republic of Vietnam)
    MAL (Malaysia)
    PHIL (Philippines)
* Source; Adapted from B. Hahn, 'South-Asia's miniature naval arms race', *Pacific Defence Reporter*, September 1985, p. 22.

SRV ships clashed in the Gulf of Tonkin when the SRV refused to concede control over water boundaries west of 107.3° east longitude. In 1983, another clash occurred in the Paracel Islands occupied by the Chinese and claimed by the SRV. Chinese submarines were deployed in SRV waters on that occasion.[41] As regards China's exercises, in 1984 in the Spratley Islands the PRC Navy demonstrated that it can assault and occupy the islands by manoeuvring a sizeable air and logistically supported surface action group in a major exercise comprising a 2000 man strong amphibious force.[42] A classic demonstration of Chinese capabilities in naval presence would be the blockade of Taiwan.

Lastly, the implications of the 'Iwo Jima Exercise' elaborated in Chapter 1 should be mentioned here as it denotes Chinese progress made in joint operations. Chinese successes in conducting task force level exercises over 1000 miles from the coast will have far reaching consequences for the naval balance in the Pacific. It is easy to imagine the force multiplier effect should China deploy SSNs and SSBNs in these joint operations.

A study of Chinese maritime power should not be confined merely to demonstratations of China's naval capabilities in exercises and operations against its neighbours. Discussions should therefore be devoted to how maritime power can support the advancement of China's political objectives in the near future. Scenarios that demonstrate the effect of the force multiplier should China choose to resolve the Taiwan question or conflict with the SRV are therefore relevant case studies in the assessment of Chinese maritime power. Nevertheless, these studies are not intended to be 'policy-recommendations' but serve to demonstrate the extent that China can harness its naval capabilities to forward its political objectives.

The reunification of China: the Taiwan issue

David Muller's possible and plausible scenarios for the resolution of the Taiwan issue presents readers with an inspiring picture of a probable settlement of China's outstanding issue — the re-unification of China — according to the principle of 'one country two systems' which necessitates the return of Hong Kong and Taiwan to the 'motherland'.[43] In covering probably all contingencies, Muller depicts high levels of conflict and acute political upheavals like Taiwan developing nuclear weapons, special relations with the USSR or claims that Beijing simply runs out of patience with nationalist intransigence. In so doing, Muller quite rightly points to the probable negative consequences of exerting armed *force* effectively to bring about the capitulation of Taiwan. These include US intervention and a USSR–Taiwan *entente*.[44]

Muller correctly advises against an invasion and favours a blockade. Apart from having to face strong ground and air forces, a Chinese invasion will be costly and will cause heavy Taiwanese civilian casualties. In contrast, a blockade strikes at the island's economy. In addition, Taiwan's Air Force is ill-suited to anti-surface and anti-submarine warfare and its 30-odd aging surface combatants would be easy targets for the Chinese submarines.[45] It remains important to examine the feasibility of the blockade scenario, especially in regard to the operational options the Chinese will have.

It is proposed here that whilst the PRC does not need to wait for an acute political situation developing in Taiwan which may threaten its security, its exertion of *force* can be kept to a lower level so that the chances of inviting superpower intervention will be kept to the minimum. In many ways, it makes good sense for the PRC to take the initiative in bringing pressure upon Taiwan instead of waiting for an acute political situation to develop on the island. For instance, its methodical approach to turning Hong Kong into a Special Administrative Region speaks of its determination to apply the principle of 'one country two systems' seriously with a view to 'recovering' Hong Kong, Macao, and particularly, Taiwan. It is true that even at this wave-length, China will need a catalyst to develop in Taiwan, which could be the Guomindang continuing to lose control of a Taiwanese autonomous movement.[46]

The single most effective means in the exertion of force is the disruption of Taiwan's economy which can be brought about by disrupting the crucial sea lanes. Thus Muller correctly points to the effectiveness of a naval blockade comprising submarines and surface forces which would leave the 20-odd Taiwan-owned oil tankers strung out between the Persian Gulf and Taiwan, whilst foreign-flag ships would be inhibited from calling on Taiwanese ports.[47] Nevertheless, if the Chinese were to avoid superpower intervention whilst being keen on taking the initiative in exerting force, there must be a combination of naval options which the Chinese could apply and which could minimise the probability of escalation, as it might provoke the US into taking the side of the Taiwanese. In the first place, the disruption of sea lanes involves not only the cutting off of Taiwan's energy supply line and the import of raw materials, but also creating havoc for the exporting of Taiwan's manufactured goods via either their own carriers or foreign-flag shippers. In turn, the naval blockade would cover sea lanes to the Persian Gulf, northward to Japan and eastward to the US, whilst the major ports of Jilong and Gaoxiong could also be mined. The best Chinese strategy should be a good combination of low intensity operations which could create political and economic instability for the Taiwanese and higher level operations which will least provoke US intervention. The first considerations of low intensity operations include major exercises in the South China Sea and the Yellow Sea which would disrupt Taiwanese shipping. Demonstrations of Rights and Resolve are the two types of operations permissible under international law.[48] Second, a medium-level option that the Chinese may contemplate is to impose a quarantine on Taiwanese carriers and even ships carrying Taiwanese goods in proclaimed exclusive zones along the major sea lines of communication. In choosing the exact zone, the Chinese will have to face the possibility of confronting the Taiwanese F–5 (226 F–5 and 30 F–5F). The closer the Chinese are to the island, the more effective their operations will be. Should these be within the range of the F-5s the Chinese will have to deploy the LUDA-class destroyers which have an effective anti-air defence system.[49] Nevertheless, it should be pointed out that whilst a Chinese quarantine may not be construed as an act of war, Taiwanese F-5s attacking Chinese ships would be so considered.[50]

The best low-level operation for the Chinese to initiate is to claim Quemoy (Jinmen) by enforcing the twelve nautical miles territorial sea claims and cutting off all supplies to the Taiwan Island.[51] As an extension to that, two barriers can be set up by surface combatants, each with a front of 30–60 miles close to Jilong and Gaoxiong. A total of two task groups may be deployed with at least two submarines used for surveillance. Should Chinese ships be attacked by the Taiwanese Air Force, the PRC will have good reasons to impose a full blockade, or mine one or more Taiwanese ports.[52]

A Chinese maritime quarantine may take the form of procedures like 'search and inspect' or the instituting of a clearance system to assist vessels which transit the waters in the vicinity of Taiwan and vessels destined for Taiwanese ports. For those vessels found acceptable, they could be issued a Clearance Certificate (CLEARCERT).[53] The permissibility of the control system could perhaps be justified on grounds of minimum interference of the high sea, minimum violence and precedence.[54] In assessing the maritime quarantine rule, the Chinese would indeed find the US experience of naval interdiction of offensive weapons and associated *materiel* to Cuba in 1962 invaluable.[55] A possible Chinese claim that Taiwan is one of China's provinces may strengthen its claimed sovereign right to search the relevant ships. To exercise control, Chinese surface combat ships may inflict injury on ships. This would include shots over the bow or light damages to the stern or the propeller. To enforce such a quarantine, the Chinese will need to deploy two squadrons of frigates to the north of Taiwan and two more to the south. These would have to be permanently on station, and allowance would have to be made for an adequate standby force which may be undergoing the normal refit process. The Chinese collection of frigates may just be large enough for this kind of operation. The ideal range would be 2500nm at 14–15 knots during operations.[56] Air surveillance will be essential for the identification of shipping targets.[57]

At this point, the question of whether the Chinese would be violating international maritime laws is relevant, although many nations have been known to have violated these laws of the sea, with the US being the most blatant 'violator' in the past.[58] So far, none of these actions could be construed as an act of war. In addition, they would not involve an overly significant number of surface combat ships, especially when the element of surprise is added.

As regards the legal interpretations of the maritime quarantine rule, there is one which the US had adhered to. It states that quarantine is based on the customary principle of international law, as confirmed in Article 51 of the Charter of the United Nations, which stipulates that a nation may engage in self-defence in provocative circumstances.[59] Thus the Chinese may claim that it is its inherent right to engage in self-defence by searching Taiwanese ships which would be carrying goods detrimental to their national interests (for example, shipments of arms to Taiwan).

In 1971 in the India–Pakistan conflict, India claimed that its incursion into East Pakistan was in self-defence as Bengali refugees were threatening its scanty food supply.[60] For those who would wish to justify their maritime quarantine therefore, they would claim that the interdictory action is legally permissible. Nevertheless, others may argue that the spirit of Article 51 of the UN Charter should be interpreted in a restrictive sense, meaning that no defensive action should be undertaken unless an armed attack is initiated.[61]

Beyond the maritime quarantine would be the imposition of a naval blockade of Taiwanese ports and coastline which would constitute an act of war. In addition, it would involve a major Chinese deployment of submarine and surface forces which might escalate to a situation in which the US might face the unpleasant choice of whether it should intervene. A great deal will depend on the political climate at the time and how much it values China's strategic role in the region. It would also be a test of US obligation *vis-a-vis* the Taiwan Relations Act.[62]

The best means of imposing a naval blockade with the least risk of provoking the Americans would be for China to mine one of the ports or a critical part of the coastline by deploying their large submarine force. With the Taiwanese having extremely weak ASW capabilities, the Chinese ROMEO and WHISKEY class submarines would find it easy to accomplish their mission with little resistance.[63] The element of surprise, which is highly feasible, adds to the chances of success. Indeed, a mine blockade effectively avoids 'eyeball to eyeball' confrontation with the enemy. An invisible enemy makes it difficult for reprisals and keeps the risk of escalation to the minimum. Although a mine blockade is generally considered an act of war, nations have opted for it because of the minimum probability of escalatory conflict. Thus Britain mined the Norwegian coast during the Second World War and the US mined Haiphong in 1972.[64] It might therefore prove economical for the Chinese to resort to mining operations although the deployment of surface combatants may keep operations to a relatively low level at the initial stage. Taiwan's weakness in ASW capabilities is reflected in its meagre strength of obsolete coastal mine sweepers, rendering the island vulnerable to mine blockade. The delivery of the two Dutch-built Zwaardvis-class submarines will only marginally improve its ASW capabilities.[65] (See the next section on China's Strategic Mine Offensive for details of Chinese submarine mine-laying capabilities.)

A careful selection of naval operations would hopefully bring about Taiwan's willingness to concede to China's demands. It would induce Taiwan to negotiate with the Chinese once political and economic instability results from that series of Chinese naval operations. As long as the Chinese are prudent in their action in avoiding the risk of American involvement, the hope for 'reunification' would be high.

Nevertheless, the Chinese should be fully aware of the fact that they must be prepared for escalation when challenged by Taiwan and its allies. They should therefore have the capacity to alter the composition of the task force in order to match the level of force predominant in the region. Paradoxically, confrontation with the US should be avoided at all cost.

As regards Soviet intervention on invitation from Taiwan suggested by Muller,[66] it is highly improbable in view of heavy US interest in the region. A withdrawal of US economic and political support may cause Taiwan's economy to collapse. It is also unimaginable for the US to allow another Cam Ranh Bay to emerge in the Pacific. Unless the Chinese adopt a high profile in imposing the naval blockade, the likelihood of US intervention is almost zero although the usual diplomatic protestations will occur. The best that the US can do for Taiwan is to help it bargain for greater autonomous power under 'one country two systems'.

A Chinese strategic mine offensive against the SRV

Another probable situation which would demonstrate the effect of the force multiplier concerns China's efforts to contain further Vietnamese expansion in Indochina. The Kampuchean question constitutes one of China's major security problems and possible diplomatic channels to reduce tension in that region have been discussed in Chapter 4. On the other hand, should the Khmer Rouge collapse and should major SRV invasions into Thailand materialise, the Chinese will be compelled to take certain drastic actions. (See Table 6.2.)

Should the Chinese launch a 'second lesson' attack on the SRV on a scale similar to the first one in 1979, they would find that the chances of 'bleeding the SRV white' would be minimal. It could be further argued that the Sino–Vietnamese stalemate would persist unless the Chinese were to contemplate a large-scale campaign which would challenge the air defence system around the Hanoi-Haiphong sector. Given this probable situation and given China's fear of Vietnamese 'expansionism', it would be to its advantage to open a new front, namely, the launching of a sustained mine blockade against the SRV. This plausible scenario assumes that major SRV incursions into Thai territory would have induced ASEAN to harden its attitude towards the SRV and would have persuaded Malaysia to take part in multilateral operations against the SRV. In this pessimistic scenario, which would be a serious attempt to prevent the fall of the 'domino', the Chinese and ASEAN would be joining hands to at least salvage the situation in Thailand and prevent the collapse of Malaysia. It is envisaged that the Chinese naval blockade would be synchronised with ASEAN blocking action to stop the collapse of southern Thailand at the Kra Isthmus.[67] Without doubt, it would require the parties concerned to appreciate the threat of SRV 'expansionism', should it materialise, before the 'Kra-Mine blockade' scenario would be considered plausible. In turn, should the SRV consider this scenario probable and plausible, it may have to reappraise its strategic position in Southeast Asia carefully in the near future.

PRC responses as indicated on the ladder are not confined to their own escalation level. For example, a PRC punitive campaign against the SRV at Level III could be accompanied by a mine-blockade of the SRV (a Level I option) together with the deployment of Chinese forces to Thailand to support Thai forces. Indeed, it can generally be assumed that the PRC would take up all lower level options at any given point on the ladder to the maximum extent resources would allow.

The SRV is heavily reliant upon the USSR in terms of military, technical and general economic aid.[68] The majority of these supplies are delivered by sea and it would be a desirable objective for the PRC to constrict resupply to the SRV as much as possible during a crisis. This could serve the purpose of restricting the availability of Soviet military hardware and spare parts in addition to 'strangling' the SRV economically.[69] However, a naval blockade involving the PRC surface fleet would involve a prohibitive risk of direct confrontation

Table 6.2: The 'Second Lesson' — an escalation framework

Vietnamese Actions	Possible Chinese (PRC) Response

LEVEL V

Full scale invasion of Thailand involving an attempt to bring down the Bangkok government.	*V Invasion* 13. Move to take SRV capital. 12. Permanent occupation of Northern SRV.

LEVEL IV

An attempt by the SRV to take and hold objectives in Thailand. The purposes may range from attempts to destroy Kampuchean resistance movements to a prelude to full scale invasion of Thailand.	*IV Major Incursion* 11. Devastate economic infrastructure of Northern Vietnam. 10. Threaten SRV capital.

LEVEL III

Consistent SRV incursions into Thai territory causing instability and panic in the Thai population and government. This would probably be supported by a reinforced Soviet Naval presence in the South China Sea.	*III Punitive Campaign* ie repeat of 'first lesson'. 9. Selective destruction of SRV economic infra-structure. 8. Hold limited objectives for a time. 7. Medium scale attacks

LEVEL II

Limited SRV crossings of Thai border at perhaps battalion strength for the purpose of probing Thai defences and testing Thai resolve. Destruction of Khmer Rouge resistance, and collapse of the KPNLF.	*II Limited Assistance to Thailand* on Thai territory 6. Combined Arms operations against SRV units in support of Thais. 5. Limited Ground forces to hold territory. 4. Specialist units, ie Artillery, Airforce etc. 3. Logistics support.

LEVEL I

Likely destruction of Khmer Rouge. Continued 'insolence' of the SRV. Further entrenchment in Kampuchea.	*I Economic Warfare* Designed to make the SRV 'suffer' major economic loss and harrassment. This can involve indirect means such as minewarfare which eliminates escalatory 'eyeball-to-eyeball' contact with the Soviets. 2. Minewarfare Blockade Campaign (act of war). 1. Minewarfare Quarantine Campaign (non-act of war).

Note: This Table is intended to provide a basic framework of appropriate PRC responses to Vietnamese actions. The list of PRC options is not exhaustive but is merely indicative of possible and *proportional* PRC options.

with the Soviets. During the 'first lesson' in 1979 the Soviets supported the SRV by establishing a naval presence in the South China Sea. By the end of the 'first lesson' the force consisted of fifteen warships and four general purpose submarines.[70] This force would probably be increased if the PRC attempted to interdict Soviet supplies. Consequently, engagement of opposing surface naval forces would almost certainly ensue. Obviously this type of risk would be unacceptable to the PRC due to its clear naval inferiority and extreme aversion to antagonising the Soviets. Nevertheless, the PRC does possess a capability which could successfully cripple SRV logistics resupply while not initiating escalatory 'eyeball to eyeball' naval engagements with the Soviet Union.

The PRC has the capability to launch a sustained mine blockade against the SRV for the following reasons:

1. The PRC Navy has over 100 conventional patrol submarines on inventory. This total includes 95 ROMEO and 15 WHISKEY class vessels. The ROMEO class can carry 36 mines while the WHISKEY can carry 28 mines.[71] These vessels have operated in exercises involving forces of 60 boats.[72] A force of 20–30 submarines could mine the approaches to all SRV and Kampuchean ports as well as conduct sustained 'reseeding' operations for a prolonged period.[73] The relatively shallow waters around Vietnam are ideal for the operations of the light (1100–1800 ton) classes of PRC submarines.

2. The major submarine base of Yulin, which is located on the south Hainan Island, would act as an ideal base for such operations. It is only 170 nm from the main SRV northern port of Haiphong and 750 nm from the main southern port of Ho Chi Minh City. Also, the entire Kampuchean coastline is well within range of PRC patrol submarines. Hainan has the facilities to support a large-scale submarine mining operation since it is the base for the PRC South Sea fleet. In addition, extensive repair and maintenance facilities exist on the nearby Leizhou Peninsula.[74] Hainan is also a military district in its own right and substantial air assets are permanently based there.[75]

3. The initial minelaying against northern SRV ports could be undertaken aerially by the Naval Air Force based in the Hainan Military District. This is especially the case if an element of surprise is involved. In general, any aircraft capable of carrying a bomb can carry a mine. The success of aerial mine attacks, even

against extremely potent air defences, was proven during the US mining campaign against three North Vietnamese ports and large stretches of coastline in 1972. Most mines were deployed by carrier-based US aircraft. A total of about 11 000 mines were deployed with the loss of only one A7E aircraft.[76] This is far less than the US losses incurred in attacking land-based targets because fighter-bombers flying low over the water are much less detectable by radar than are planes flying over land at higher altitude. Of course, attrition of PRC air platforms would probably be higher due to less pilot expertise and an improved SRV Air Force. However, a properly mounted operation would yield benefits far outweighing costs, especially if the PRC were willing to lay more mines at slightly longer distances from port entrances. American forces were able to lay fields right down the main channel of Haiphong harbour early in the campaign but this may be an over-ambitious task for the PRC Air Force. However, low flying fighter-bombers and even light-bombers could intensively mine port approaches and coastal areas. Chinese J7 (Mig 21 derivative) and H–5 (11–28) assets could probably be employed in such operations with a minimum of modification.[77]

4. Vietnamese ports have traditionally been highly susceptible to mine blockade. During World War II for example, Haiphong harbour was closed to the occupying Japanese forces for almost two years. In October 1943 a US bomber dropped three mines on Haiphong harbour. A Japanese freighter was soon sunk and the port was closed. This was shortly followed, in November 1943, by the sinking of one more freighter after another US bomber deployed an additional three mines. Another ship was eventually sunk and the port was closed for the duration of the war even though only three mines remained in the harbour.[78]

The 1972 US mine campaign was another outstanding success in that it completely cut off seaborne resupply to North Vietnam. At that stage of the war about 85 per cent of some 2.5 million tons of war material imported annually by North Vietnam arrived by sea, mostly through the harbour of Haiphong.[79] The operation was effective immediately. A small number of vessels exited Haiphong during the announced 72-hour delayed arming setting on the mines (which was announced by President Nixon), but after this no traffic entered or departed from the port for 300 days. A huge burden was placed on overland rail routes from China, and these routes became increasingly susceptible to interdiction by US forces. There is little doubt that the mining campaign was 'a significant impetus' to the Peace Agreement of January 1973.

Rear Admiral McCauley, USN, who commanded US mine-sweeping forces in North Vietnamese waters under the terms of the Peace Agreement, highlighted the vulnerability of the Vietnamese to mines as follows:

> It was an impressive sight on flying over Haiphong in the early days of (Operation) End Sweep to see all 26 ships at anchor behind the minefield. None had moved since May when the first mines were dropped. . . the effectiveness of the campaign demonstrates once again the vulnerability of a country which has little or no mine-sweeping capability to mining. The North Vietnamese ocean shipping was paralyzed until we arrived with the technical knowledge to clear their main channel.[80]

5. The technology involved in launching and sustaining a naval mine blockade against the SRV is not required to be of a high level. Over 95 per cent of the mines deployed by the US against the Vietnamese during the 1972 campaign were 'bomb-mines' of a relatively simple type.[81] These mines were mainly converted Mk 82 (500lbs) General Purpose Low Drag Bombs. These weapons were called Destructors (DST–36). The conversion was accomplished using a US Mk 75 Destructor Adaption kit which consists of a battery, booster charge, arming device and firing mechanism.[82] Effective PRC submarine-deployed minefields would ideally be 'mixed bags' of mines which would include mainly bottom mines with a 'sprinkling' of moored mines, and obstructor devices designed to complicate any Soviet sweeping efforts. The bottom mines would be the main weapons and could have mixed settings in terms of ship counts, activation delay and on-off periods.[83] Such features, which are of World War II technology level, are still extremely difficult to counter and would demand an extremely disproportionate response from Soviet countermeasure forces.[84] The PRC is capable of manu-facturing (if they have not already) adequate Pressure-Magnetic, Pressure-Acoustic or Pressure-Magnetic-Acoustic combination bottom mines which would be more than adequate for the operation of imposing a sustained and 'tight' economic blockade against the SRV.[85] Such mines would be ideal for use in the shallow waters in and around the SRV and Kampuchea and

would have devastating effects in the likely deployment depth of between 20–60 meters.[86]

Mines involving higher technological capabilities could almost certainly be acquired from European arms markets. Higher technology mines are important elements of 'mixed bag' minefields and demand extraordinary countermeasures. In particular, Italy could provide the PRC with advanced mines on which to base eventual Chinese production. The MR 80 combat mine and its training derivative, for example, could be acquired to give the PRC 'Hi-mix' mines on inventory and also provide a firm basis in the development of state-of-the-art mine technology. Italy and the PRC have been enjoying very cordial relations as reflected in the recent agreement for the sale of considerable amounts of defence *materiel* and for military training by the Italians to the PRC. The US and other European countries are also potential suppliers. Consequently, the acquisition of high mine technology by the PRC is not seen as a particularly difficult problem.[87]

6. Given that a large mine-laying effort against the SRV were initiated (involving the use of about 20–30 submarines initially, and perhaps ten to maintain 'momentum'), a massive mine countermeasure effort would be required. Indeed, such an operation would necessarily involve at least the entire SOVPACFLT's mine countermeasures forces for many months if the blockade were to be effectively broken.[88] It should be remembered that the Americans took several months during which to sweep their *own* mines from North Vietnamese areas, despite an intimate knowledge of mine characteristics such as sensitivity settings, sterilisation time and even the positions of minefields. As Rear Admiral McCauley points out:[89]

> ... (Operation) End Sweep was a unique solution to a unique problem and did not present a challenge of nearly the magnitude that can be expected in future... Operation End Sweep was the highest priority in the Pacific Fleet. It commenced with the ceasefire and, as a result, people, ships and aircraft, which in a wartime scenario would have been otherwise occupied were made available. The objective of the mine-sweeping was largely accomplished prior to laying mines when the self-destruct time was set into the fuse. Even with the cooperation of the DRV (Democratic Republic of Vietnam) and knowledge of types, location, settings and expiration dates of mines we were compelled to devote a large force and exercise great caution to ensure that the seas and ports were clear.

Without this information the task would have been infinitely more difficult.

Indeed, McCauley's US Minesweeping Task Force (designated CTF 78) consisted of five large ocean minesweepers (MSO) and five major naval platforms for the support of sixteen CH–53 Sea Stallion MCM helicopters and the numerous support helicopters used in the operation.[90] Thus, the disproportionate response drawn by the mine is clearly evident given that a major US task force was committed for six months to clear its own mines from accurately known locations along a relatively small stretch of coastline. The implications of this for any Soviet-mounted minesweeping effort are obvious.

Political factors

The major factors to be considered by PRC decision-makers when contemplating a mine blockade will be (a) the likelihood and nature of a Soviet response, (b) world opinion and (c) effectiveness against the SRV.

Soviet response to the PRC's operations involving extensive use of mines against SRV harbours and coastal areas will depend chiefly on the perceived degree of US support for the PRC operation and the degree of Sino–Soviet *rapprochement* achieved at the time.[91] The Soviets would not be expected to substantially aid the SRV if its long-term central interests of maintaining stable relations with the US and China were seriously compromised by giving direct assistance to the SRV. This would particularly be the case if the SRV were seen to be acting waywardly and aggressively in the view of world opinion. A naval presence may be exerted by the Soviets together with mine countermeasure forces. But it is unlikely that the USSR would risk serious escalation by direct attack against PRC land-based forces, even though attacks against PRC minelaying aircraft and submarines in SRV territorial waters could not be ruled out. A mining campaign against the SRV would therefore seem to be an effective means of establishing a naval blockade with minimal escalation potential (see Table 6.2). This is indicated by the 1972 US mine campaign precedent.

The offensive mining campaign of 1972 was put forward by the Nixon Administration as a necessary and proportional response to the major attack launched by North on South Vietnam. North Vietnamese forces were supported by heavy imports of war *materiel* delivered through the three main northern harbours. The campaign's object was outlined by Nixon in his speech on 8 May 1972:[92]

> I therefore conclude Hanoi must be denied the weapons and supplies it needs to continue its aggression.... All entrances to North Vietnamese ports will be mined to prevent access to these ports. United States forces have been directed to take appropriate measures within the internal and claimed territorial waters of North Vietnam to interdict the delivery of supplies.... Rail and all other communications will be cut off the maximum extent possible.

He went on to emphasise that the campaign 'was restricted in intent and purpose', stressing that the minefields had been confined to the internal and claimed territorial waters of North Vietnam.[93] This ensured that the operation did not violate the freedom of the high seas and neutral shipping was given ample time to leave the ports at risk. Notices were issued to mariners and vessels heading towards declared danger areas were visited and warned by US and South Vietnamese Naval Forces.[94]

These actions thus satisfied the requirements of international law to a sufficient degree and 'legitimised' the action in terms of the majority of world opinion. The 1907 Hague Minewarfare Convention was satisfied in that neutrals were warned and an indication was made that the conflict was strictly limited to a belligerent's territorial seas, and that territorial seas and the freedom of the high seas was not challenged.[95] A statement to the effect that North Vietnamese naval operations would be interdicted by the mines ensured that the US would not be open to the charge of laying mines with the 'sole object of intercepting commercial shipping'.[96]

Sir Robert Thompson, a major critic of US war management during the Vietnam war, aptly summarised the US position during the mining campaign when commenting that[97]

> (The mining) was aimed at Hanoi's future capability to continue the war at the pace Hanoi itself had set.... A far more important purpose was the message which it conveyed to the Russians: 'If you arm your allies with superior offensive weapons to invade my allies, you must expect appropriate American response which may involve you'. The Russians got the message at once.

It is not beyond the pale of reality that the PRC may find itself in a similar position to that of the United States in 1972. In an effort to support its Thai and Kampuchean 'allies', the PRC must look at ways of reducing Hanoi's means of setting the 'pace' of a war against Thailand and the Khmer Rouge. A maritime mining campaign may again be an important and low-risk adjunct in the achievement of this objective.

Finally, the effectiveness of a sustained mine blockade against the SRV would tend to be considerable. In 1972, the cutting of seaborne resupply was estimated to have reduced land shipment of *materiel* from North to South Vietnam, to a mere tenth of its pre-mining level.[98] Supplies reaching NVA and Vietcong combat areas were reported to be reduced by 800–1500 tons per day.[99] The mining operation also caused a major 'drawing down' of North Vietnamese ammunition and supplies which were estimated to last four months under heavy combat conditions.[100] Consequently, major constriction of Vietnamese war stock resupplies would be of invaluable importance in the blunting of any full-scale Vietnamese incursion into Thailand, and generally reducing their warfighting and war-sustaining capability.

During 1979 over 140 carriers delivered more than 900 000 tons of Soviet ordnance valued at over $US1 billion through Vietnamese ports. If such resupply efforts can be deterred or significantly reduced by minefields the PRC will have done much to maximise the prospects of success in land and air operations. Consequently, the PRC would be wise to consider the advantages of mine warfare in a 'second lesson' scenario as a low-risk/high-gain option which can multiply the effectiveness of other Chinese capabilities. Certainly, the ability to blockade Vietnam would give PRC strategy against Vietnam a more flexible and comprehensive dimension.

Chinese maritime power

Despite constraints on military spending, China has certainly made noticeable progress in the modernisation of the Navy. Chinese maritime power will exert itself on the Pacific region as China develops more 'blue water' capabilities. Proven sea denial and naval presence capabilities will in turn be strengthened by political leverage that China can apply to maintain its economic and security interests. It will not be impertinent to assume that the Chinese Navy will play a much more active role in the waters of East and Southeast Asia. A naval blockade of Taiwan and a mine offensive against the SRV are two probable scenarios in support of such claims. The Navy is a forward-looking service of China's defence force which accepts the concept of 'two surface combatants and one submarine' (*liangjian yiting*) as the main strength of a modern navy.[101] The two surface combatants referred to are the Aircraft Carrier and the Guided Missile

Cruiser. Although the likelihood of China commissioning an aircraft carrier in the next two decades is small, it is not inconceivable that China may increase its force projection capability by developing VSTOL carriers beyond the year 2000. In a word, the Chinese Navy is a growing force to be reckoned with in the Asia–Pacific region.

PART III

Military Leadership

7

The People's Liberation Army (PLA) and Party Leadership, 1979–82

PARTY LEADERSHIP AND THE PLA, 1979–82

Mao Zedong's military science

In the wake of veteran general Huang Kecheng's criticism of Mao's disastrous record in the Cultural Revolution, came the PLA's deliberate move to confirm Mao's contribution to the preservation of the Party-army image. This emerged in the form of declarations attributing the 'greatness of the democratic tradition' of the PLA and the effectiveness of 'People's War under modern conditions' to Mao. Whilst Mao had been systematically stripped of any traits of deification, and his economic policies severely criticised, the Army had on the other hand found it befitting to uphold Mao's military thought in order to ensure stability in the forces. In this respect, Mao's military thought received an unprecedented boost as Mao Zedong's military science (*Mao Zedong junshi koxue*) was being used as a term to summarise Mao's contribution. The PLA attributed the following to Mao:[1]

> He and his comrades-in arms, in accordance with the basic principles of Marxism, and taking into consideration the conditions of our country, created and accumulated unique experiences which provide guidance for the Chinese revolutionary war; through theoretical distillation, (it) became an invincible science in which our people use armed revolution against armed counter revolution — Mao Zedong military science.

201

There seemed to be three levels of assessment of Mao's position in the PLA, with the recognition of Mao's military thought as the ultimate. But each level of assessment represented the firm principles the military wished to lay down in order to ensure that the PLA could be best equipped to defend the nation. These views had also been expressed through a spectrum of representative military figures ranging from a first group of marshals and veteran generals like Huang Kecheng and Ye Jianying, to a second group headed by Yang Dezhi, theoreticians from the military academies and senior cadres from the General Staff Department responsible for strategy and planning, and a third group of Party watchdogs in the PLA represented by the General Political Department (GPD) headed by Wei Guoqing and other leading veteran political commissars like Xiao Hua of Lanzhou Military Region.

It was the first group, which as early as National Day in 1979, started the process of 'de-Maoisation' when Ye Jianying openly criticised Mao for making mistakes in the Cultural Revolution.[2] This line of approach was further reinforced by Huang Kecheng's article to the nation in April 1981. Beyond this basic level of criticism however, the second group of opinions hastened to emphasise the importance of his military thought as an integral part of Mao Zedong's thought which was still considered to be the guiding principle of the Party and the PLA. More importantly, Yang Dezhi believed that the PLA should continue to learn from Mao's philosophical and military writings, and his highly skilled art in building the Army. Yang believed that this was necessary to ensure that the Party provide absolute leadership for the Army. This second group of opinion, therefore, revealed not only the fact that Mao's position and image had not been underplayed, but also that strategic planners had invoked Mao's military thought for practical application. In so doing, China hoped to surge ahead with promotion of the basic strategy for national defence which they unquestionably attributed to Mao — 'People's War under modern conditions'. Yang Dezhi thus wrote:[3]

> As far as our Army is concerned, comrade Mao Zedong's theory on the building of the people's army, his writings on political work in the army and his whole series of strategy and tactics on People's War have in particular been our powerful ideological weapon in overcoming difficulties and obstacles and defeating the enemy.

Furthermore, Song Shilun, Head of the Military Academy, confirmed the undoubted function of Mao's military thought as a guide for future wars. Song Shilun claimed that in future 'anti-aggression wars' against massive invasion by hegemonic powers, China would thus have to rely on People's war because of its inferior equipment facing superior enemies. Song nevertheless went much furrther, to make the point that Mao's military thought must be treated as an arrow on aim at the target which was war in future. In other words, Mao's theories and strategies on People's War should be 'modernised' to take into consideration modern conditions which did not exist in the past, so that new experiences could eventually be incorporated and theorised about in order to enrich Mao's military thought as part of the process of historical development.[4] These new experiences which represented 'modern conditions' imply, first of all that top priority be given to strategic defence, which differed from the past practice of tactical offence from exterior lines. This change was based on the rationale that stability in defence now depended on the strengthening of certain positions and directions in defensive battles, which should in turn be coordinated with offence launched by field army corps from exterior lines.

Second, whilst strategic offence as the last stage of war was clearly recognised (as Mao so defined) to be the decisive factor in defeating the enemy, it was suggested that new problems arising from the development of new weapons and technical equipment would require research and new solutions. According to Song Shilun, systematic research would create new and relevant theories which can be added to the military thought of Mao. At this second level reassessment of Mao, strategists and planners in the PLA were brandishing the banner of Mao's military thought as a vehicle to rally support from commanders at various levels for China's master strategy for national defence, one which reconfirmed the need to apply the principles of People's War. It was also one which nevertheless emphasised the need to take full cognisance of modern technology and systematic strategies which did not contradict but rather added to the very foundation of Mao's military thought.[5]

The third and highest level of reassessment of Mao's military thought was being made by the General Political Department which had the awesome task of maintaining the image of the Party-army nexus intact, and strengthening political work despite the traumatic experience of the Cultural Revolution. Key figures like Wei Guoqing, the Director, and his deputies Fu Zhong and others aimed to revive and strengthen political work, not only through basic groundwork in the political commissar system, but also through a close identification of Party leadership and People's War. To the GPD, Mao Zedong's military thought became relevant because of Mao's assertion that political work was the Army's life line. This was written into the 'Regulations on Political Work in the PLA'.[6] Furthermore, Fu Zhong cited Mao's famous references to 'Man over weaponry' and People's War to underpin the inseparable relationship between war and politics, thus avoiding the mistake of pursuing a 'purely military viewpoint' (*danchun junshi luxian*) without paying any attention to politics, as Lin Biao and the Gang of Four had done.[7] Political work, together with strengthened military training, general logistic work and research on military science were the four criteria for the building of a modern people's army ready for the launching of People's War in defence of China.[8] These four criteria combined a high level of proletarian consciousness with modernised technology and equipment. The GPD took great pains to associate political work with the urgent needs of the day because it claimed that the Party was going through a transitional period. On the eve of the Sixth Plenum on 22 June 1981 for instance, Wei Guoqing reiterated that political work should be improved in accordance with the practical needs of the new historical period.[9] The 'Resolution on CPC History (1949–81)' adopted in the Sixth Plenum undoubtedly forms the basis of Wei's claim that political work should aim at the re-education of those who have been exposed to undesirable political experience since the Cultural Revolution.[10] The exercise was thus seen as a historical transition requiring ideological strengthening and indoctrination. Wei commented:[11]

> Nowadays our young cadres and fighters, who occupy the great majority in our Army, are not only greatly different from those in the period of war and early post Liberation days, but also greatly different from those in the ten years before the internal turmoil. They are full of new spirit, keen on promoting Four Modernisations, willing to think, deeply brave in innovating and positive in advancing their career. This is the main stream. There are nevertheless inevitable weaknesses in them brought about by their experience in life: the lack of basic knowledge in Marxism, the lack of training through hard living conditions and the lack of good judgement which cause them to be easily influenced by erroneous thinkings like anarchism, extreme individualism and bourgeois-liberalism (*zichan jieji ziyou hua*).

To press the point home, the GPD identified strengthened political work, which seemed to have lagged behind, as an integral part of Mao's military thought. Furthermore, it consciously promoted Mao's military thought to the status of military science because it claimed that the former was squarely based on and developed from the theory of knowledge in Marxism, dialectical materialism and historical materialism.[12] In the PLA, the new political orientation definitely stood out as an oasis in the desert at a time when the Chinese bureaucracy seemed to be overly indulged in seeking ways to improve the economy and people's livelihood. The promotion of Mao's military thought to military science was in itself extremely interesting as it was diametrically opposite to certain measures which could be construed as moves in the direction of de-Maoisation; whilst Mao's economic principles and his insistence to foster class struggle were being forsaken, there was an increasing recognition of his contribution in the military arena.

As if to justify Deng's pragmatic line, 'seeking truth from facts', the prevailing principle in the Four Modernisations was identified as the foundation linking the process of the birth and development of Mao Zedong's military science. It was also considered as the concentrated and outstanding demonstration of how Mao applied and developed the Marxist theory of knowledge in the military sphere. 'Seeking truth from facts' was a scientific attitude which linked practice and theory, in the same way that general principles of Marxism were linked to the practical conditions of the Chinese revolutionary war. To Fu Zhong, this scientific approach to the study of war resulted in the correct grasping of the nucleus of Marxist dialectics, that is, the law of the unity of opposites. Mao's military science thus became everlasting truth because of its sound dialectical foundation. Furthermore, 'seeking truth from facts' which had been so closely identified with the present pragmatic line was being seen as the scientific basis of Mao's military science.[13]

Party leadership of the PLA followed from the above as it derived its legitimacy and orthodoxy from the basic principles of Marxism-Leninism, in much the same way that Mao's military science had been recognised and honoured by the military. The GPD therefore hoped that the combination of strengthened political work and a boosted Maoist image would go a long way to restore the revolutionary model of the Party army, and eradicate many of the general problems in the PLA in terms of discipline, corruption, cases of insubordination and varying degrees of local and regional independent tendencies. As for the strategists and planners, they believed that the elevation of Mao's thought to a military science contributed positively to the confirmation of the present strategy for national defence which sought a stronger ideological support. Futhermore, it was claimed that adaptations in the name of technology and modernisations would in no way jeopardise either

Mao's basic principle of man over weaponry or the need for a politicised army supported by the people. Emerging from the entire development was the basis of the present strategy — 'People's War under modern conditions'. Whilst Mao's military science was taken to be the everlasting truth, there was room to take cognisance of modern developments, including the need to investigate and research foreign military developments. Whilst long-range missiles and nuclear weapons should in no way debase the status of Mao's military principles, they would be contributing factors in strengthening China's defence in accordance with the needs of present day developments, so that China could expect to be successful in its war against aggression and hegemony.[14]

Efforts to strengthen ideological work under the General Political Department:

The propagation of Mao Zedong's military science was not the only way to strengthen Party leadership. Through the GPD, the Party also worked to promote the strengthening of ideological work in the PLA to a level which seemed to go beyond what the official Party would expect of the PLA in maintaining orthodox Party spirit and identity. The resolution in the Sixth Plenum categorically declared in Section 35 that class struggle was no longer the major contradiction.[15] However, the Resolution also gave Mao Zedong Thought due recognition not only because Mao developed further the nucleus of Marxist dialectics, that is, the law of the unity of opposites, but also because Mao 'forged philosophy into a sharp weapon in the hands of the proletariat and the people for knowing and changing the world'.[16] To know the world and to change the world would also involve changing one's own thought, for as Mao said in 'On Practice':[17]

> The struggle of the proletariat and the revolutionary people to change the world comprises the fulfilment of the following tasks: to change the objective world and at the same time, their own subjective world — to change their cognitive ability and change the relations between the subjective and the objective world.

The changing of one's subjective world thus required thought reform for the individuals. What seemed ambivalent in the Resolution was that whilst thought reform was seen to be essential in the changing of the objective world, indicating due emphasis put on

Party orthodoxy, Party spirit and Party identity, class struggle was de-emphasised because it no longer constituted the major contradiction in the present stage of socialism. This ambivalence was more distinct when Deng Xiaoping expounded on 'Correcting Party Style' not long after the Sixth Plenum.

Deng Xiaoping's 'Correction of Party Style' contained no reference to the need to reform one's thought nor the need to change one's subjective world view. It stopped short of such strengthening ideological orientation when Deng delivered the message that 'self-criticism' was important in restoring orthodox Party spirit.[18] Deng's attitude seemed clear. The rectification of malpractices in the Party and the State did not involve violent Party struggles of the kind which accentuated class struggle. Self-criticism would thus go a long way without resorting to the rectification of thought through a vigorous process of violent Party struggles. The truth of the matter is of course that Deng's pragmatic urge to launch China on the long and difficult road towards modernisation left no room for violent struggles of any kind. This revelation should in turn be related to the Resolution which remained ambivalent as explained before, suggesting that the Party had no consensus to the extent which ideological work should be strengthened, because of fears of resurrecting the Left.

Contrary to Deng's optimism regarding Party leadership and methods of inculcating Party spirit, the GPD, which had been persistent in urging the strengthening of ideological work and honouring Mao's military thought with the status of science, maintained a rather different stand. Thus Xiao Hua, who as Political Commissar of Lanzhou MR and a Standing Committee Member of the powerful Central Military Commission (CMC) spoke for the GPD and the military who continued to believe that strengthened ideological work was the ultimate answer to maintaining a Party army and Party orthodoxy. To them, political work was the best guard against the emergence of Party deviations and the rise of regional insubordination in the forces, which would have rendered the work of the GDP and political commissars extremely difficult. As if to refute Deng's line, Xiao attacked the following slogan 'This is the time to grasp economics, and it is no use learning theory'.[19]

Xiao believed China was involved in a great historical moment of transition, and faced complicated problems in thought and practice. Problems regarding Party spirit were relevant, for instance. The way to solve these problems was to seek guidance from theory. The level of theory could only be raised if one grasped the basic Marxist principles which should, in turn, be linked with practice.

To achieve the three basic elements of Party spirit a great deal of attention must be paid to thought reform. Such reform did not stop short of self-criticism, but stipulated in the process the need for the Communist to change the objective world and their own subjective world in the same way that Stalin and Mao specified.[20] Thus in the area of maintaining orthodox Party spirit and ideological leadership, Xiao Hua had taken the initiative to become the spokesman for vigorous adherence to the basic principles of Marxism as the best guarantee against over-indulgence in pragmatism which seemed to have beset China with more new problems than it could solve.

Xiao Hua and his associates were not alone in their deliberations. Zhou Enlai's widow, Deng Yingchao, came out strongly in favour of a large-scale rectification campaign as an answer to eradicating deviations. The message coincided with the convening of the Sixth Plenum in June 1981 showing that there was no consensus in the central leadership. Deng Yingchao also went beyond Deng Xiaoping's modest policy of self-criticism to call for the launching of a campaign (*yundong*) similar to the Rectification Campaign of 1942–44. Like Xiao Hua, Deng Yingchao stressed the importance of rectifying one's thought as a life-long mission for a Communist Party member. Because of the present new historical stage, Deng Yingchao believed that China needed a 'learning campaign' (*xuexi yundong*) which should be more penetrating and popular than the rectification campaign of the Yan'an period, the end result of which would guarantee the success of thought reform and the remoulding of oneself.[21]

The reaction from Dengists was almost immediate. In the wake of the Sixth Plenum, they were quick to emphasise that there would not be any need to undertake campaigns (*bugao yundong*), and that they were most unwilling to launch the nation into possible upheavals which might upset the Dengist 'apple-cart'. For instance, Deng claimed in July 1981, that to solve present Leftist problems, past lessons must be accepted and campaigns must not be organised.[22]

Whilst the Dengist stand was understandable and reasonable from their own perspective, it did cause concern to the GPD and some leading political commissars who feared that a weakened, official Party stand on the need for ideological leadership and Party rectification would result in undesirable developments in PLA units to the detriment of China's political stability.

The problem of 'three supports and two militaries'

The issue of 'three supports and two militaries' had bedevilled both Deng Xiaoping and the central military leadership as it continued to affect stability and unity within the PLA, making it difficult for the present leadership to enforce its modernisation programs fifteen years afterwards. The 'three supports and two militaries' made its revolutionary debut as a necessary military intervention to sustain the Cultural Revolution in the interest of the Revolutionaries. It denoted the series of circulars issued by Mao and the Central Committee in December 1966 and early 1967 calling for the PLA to support the Left, agriculture and industry and carry out military control and military training. In particular, Mao pointed out in his 'Directive to Comrade Lin Piao' in January 1967 that 'the army should be sent to support the revolution of the broad masses of the Left'.[23] Such military support for the Left and the PLA's subsequent participation in the three-way revolutionary committees, accounted for the dominance of the military in the Ninth Party Congress in April 1969, signifying the PLA's increasing influence in politics. The Lin Biao affair of September 1971 led to the collapse of Lin's stronghold, as his generals were also disgraced and later put on trial, but the PLA continued to be active and influential when Mao died, and the Gang of Four fell in September–October 1976.[24] Hua Guofeng's ascendancy and Deng Xiaoping's re-emergence and subsequent control of the Party and the PLA by July 1977 brought in different perspectives for the military. At the same time, the Party intended to maintain effective control of the PLA wherever and whenever possible.

In the post-Mao era, it would seem logical that in the name of pragmatism and the Four Modernisations Deng would eliminate ultra-Leftist elements in the PLA in order to eradicate the remnants of the Gang of Four and consolidate his own strength in the new leadership. This was indeed the case, as the Third Plenum of the Eleventh Central Committee in December 1978 saw not only the confirmation of Deng's pragmatic line, but also the demise of some ultra-Leftist commanders. The reshuffles and dismissals of regional military commanders in January–February 1980 further witnessed Deng's 'anti-Left' determination. Chen Xilian, Commander of Beijing Military Region, associated with the Gang of Four, was also dismissed in February 1980 together with other remnants like Wang Dongxing, Wu De and Ji Dengkui.[25]

Nevertheless, it was also in January–February 1980, at a time when major reshuffles were successfully brought about in the military regions, that the Party declared an 'amnesty' for those commanders and commissars who had supported the Left. On 3 February 1980, Beijing Radio declared:[26]

> To strengthen further army-government and army-people unity, we must look upon the 'three supports and two militaries' at work as a thing of the past. During the great cultural revolution, the PLA carried out the 'three supports and two militaries' task in accordance with the decision of the Party Central Committee Chairman Mao and Premier Zhou. At that time the PLA played a role in stabilising the situation. Therefore, its achievements were of primary importance. In carrying out their work, PLA units in various areas made some mistakes which were mainly caused by the interference and sabotage of Lin Biao and the gang of four and by the lack of work experience on the part of the PLA units themselves. In looking at the problems that emerged in the 'three supports and two militaries' work, we should take into consideration the historical conditions in those days. We should not be overcritical of these problems but should try to understand them. We should unite as one, look ahead to the future and work conscientiously for the four modernisations.

In the military regions and provinces, campaigns to consolidate Army-civilian relations in January–February 1980 went further, to 'preach' that the problem of 'three supports and two militaries' was one of the past which should be forgotten so that the PLA could surge ahead with its modernisation program. Two representative examples are cited below from two military districts, the military regions of which were accommodating Leftist commanders/ commissars (see Table 7.1), to indicate the eagerness of the Party to put it on record that there should not be any further revenge on the Leftists.

The first case refers to Jiangsu Military District under Nanjing Military Region. Xu Jiatun, the First Secretary of the Jiangsu CCP Committee, defended the Leftists at a meeting of leading members of the Party, government and the PLA cadres held on 5 January 1980 when Liao Hensheng, First Political Commissar of Nanjing Military Region, criticised some commanders 'who got carried away' and committed mistakes in supporting the Left in the Cultural Revolution. Xu said:[27]

> Most of the comrades who supported the broad masses of the Left were good. The relatively stable situation in Jingsu was directly linked to the military's support of the Left.... In those days, (Chen Peixian) was chief of the Jiangsu political work group, and he protected many good comrades when the order was issued to root out '16th May' elements.

The second case is from Liaoning Military District under Shenyang Military Region which had a notorious record for accommodating Leftists. In January 1980 the Party, government, soldiers and civilians of the Yingkou Municipality in Liaoning met to review the problem of 'three supports and two militaries'. New China News Agency reported thus:[28]

> By means of specific analysis of the cadres who supported the Left, the municipal Party committee tried to help everyone understand that the overwhelming majority of the comrades taking part in the 'three supports two militaries' work were good and comparatively good, and that their problems were mostly caused by the interference and sabotage by Lin Biao and the gang of four and lack of experience in local work. We should concentrate our hatred on Lin Biao and the gang of four and should not be overcritical toward the PLA comrades....

The judgement made by the Party Committee of the Yingkou Municipality that military cadres who supported the Left were good and comparatively good had since been regarded as classic. Whatever mistakes might have been committed were placed squarely on Lin Biao and the Gang of Four.

Why should the Party have declared an 'amnesty' in early 1980? Reshuffles in the military regions did help to eradicate ultra-Leftist elements. However, they did not cause Deng to be complacent about the military situation. On the contrary, he saw the need to launch a nationwide campaign in early 1980 with a view to reviving the prestige that the PLA once enjoyed, and alleviating conflicts between the PLA and the people which had arisen since the Cultural Revolution. The 'amnesty' would thus facilitate the Party's enforcement of its objective of appeasing the Leftists who were not included in major reshuffles and dismissals. The launching of the campaign could also be seen as the Party's response to restlessness in the units which had been brewing since the fall of the Gang of Four. The Party thus responded by calling upon the people to develop a tradition of supporting the Army and giving preferential treatment to the families of revolutionary soldiers and martyrs. At the same time there were conscious efforts to revive the PLA's former prestigious position, when joining the Army meant a promising career for the young and honour for their parents.

In the early 1980s it was reported that the young preferred civilian careers based on a university education. This shift in interest necessitated the Party's Propaganda Department to initiate recruitment exercises, a phenomenon unheard of before as they never made the news.[29] The demand that recruits should finish lower middle school or sometimes even upper middle school in order to make a contribution to the modernisation of national defence, further limited the choice of young people in the eligible age bracket.

Whilst recruitment was becoming more of a task, public opinion did not reflect favourably on the PLA either. *The People's Daily* declared that proper opinion had to be created to ensure respect for the PLA.[30] The erosion of the PLA's prestige obviously stemmed from the lack of respect many civilians have for units which had come into conflict with the interests of residents in the areas in which they were stationed. Friction and conflict arose in the recent past as units continued to occupy civilian properties as might have been deemed necessary in the Cultural Revolution. The occupation of parts of the campus of both Beijing University and the People's University caused the students of the Beijing University to stage a march and sit-in in October 1979, to hit at 'special privilege for the armed forces'.[31] These two examples represent the tip of the iceberg. No doubt the Party was doing what it could to harmonise relations between the people and the PLA.

Whilst the people did not have high regard for the PLA, the latter also expressed dissatisfaction on several fronts which further affected its prestige and morale. The colossal cuts in the defence budget of RMB 21.94 billion and RMB 5.43 billion respectively in 1980 and 1981, necessarily had repercussions on modernisation. At the same time the demobilisation process which had then started in the early 1980s, with an estimated figure of 400 000, began to have an effect on the PLA.[32] The Party kept on urging preferential treatment for the families of the PLA, but demobilised soldiers had no guaranteed and secure jobs apart from access to the military structure which was only capable of absorbing a certain proportion. Worse still, disillusionment had been expressed by units over the Party's new agricultural policy since 1979 which favoured the responsibility system and fixed quotas of production for the household. Units felt that their families were disadvantaged by the fact that the soldiers themselves would not be in a position to contribute to their families' labour force, causing their family production targets to be lower than the norm.[33]

It was no surprise therefore that the Party declared that 'three supports and two militaries' should be looked upon as an issue of the past. In the face of almost insurmountable problems, the Party handed down the 'amnesty' in the hope that stability and unity in units could be maintained. The slogan of *anding tuanjie* or stability and unity[34] thus became the order of the day in 1980, and so was the motto of *shangxia xiangqin* (cordial relations between the ruler and the ruled). The first slogan denotes Deng Xiaoping's continual concern that political equilibrium must be maintained in the name of modernisation, and major reshuffles in the military regions in January–February 1980 reinforced his confidence to be magnanimous to the Leftists. However, the second slogan calling on the rank and file to pay allegiance to the Party came strangely as a well-nigh 'feudal' campaign, as it stressed good human relationships as a supplementary means to effect Party control. Thus in January 1980 the editorial in the *Liberation Army Daily* cited the late Ming political philosopher Wang Fuzhi: 'With cordial relations between the ruler and the ruled, there will be equilibrium in the *tianxia* (empire)'.[35]

The editorial went on to give examples of how unity between the emperor and the people in the reigns of the first emperor *Guangwu* of the Eastern Han and the second emperor *Taizong* of the Tang accounted for stability in society. This historical inference in the form of an appeal to commanders/commissars for stability and unity was in fact Dengist pragmatism of the highest order, showing Deng's various tactical moves with a view to consolidating leadership in the PLA.

The role of the General Political Department: modernisation or Party control?

The duties and functions of the GPD have been understood as three-fold: to promote ideological work, enforce discipline and boost morale, with the last function very much being the end-result of the first two. Political-ideological education has been regarded as of paramount importance, because it serves as the means by which the Party, through the political commissar system and the Party committees and political departments at the various levels, can ensure the loyalty of the PLA to the Party.[36] It goes without saying that this ideal situation is often tested in times of political turbulence. The second task of maintaining discipline within the PLA falls into two categories. First, the GPD's duty is to ensure that the political and ideological quality of high ranking officers is maintained. The second concerns general disciplinary issues which involve the GPD in meticulous work to ensure that the PLA, the Party and the civilian population have cordial relations, and above all, that the families of the rank and file are well cared for and have good relations with their officers. The organisational structure facilitating these functions are well thought out, which undoubtedly has given people the impression that the PLA is a highly motivated and disciplined force capable of enduring great hardship and austerity. Moreover, much has been attributed to Mao Zedong for his work in building up the Party-army model.

It would be incorrect to assume that such an image had been seriously eroded as a result of the tumultuous years China went through during the Cultural Revolution and afterwards, but it would nevertheless be pertinent to examine how the GPD was being confronted with various problems in its latest mission to support the pragmatic Party, and how these objectives might sometimes work against the ideals that the GPD aimed to achieve.

It was Wei Guoqing who subsequently took over from Zhang Chunqiao in September 1977 as Director of the General Political Department, having to face great difficulties in orientating the PLA towards the new leadership's Four Modernisations policy, and in appeasing restless feelings resulting from the collapse of the Gang of Four. In the same way that the resolutions of the Third Plenum of the Central Committee of the 11th Party Congress in March 1978, and the legislation of the Second Plenum of the Fifth National People's Congress justified the Party's pragmatic line for modernisation, the GPD likewise invoked these same resolutions and legislation to steer the PLA solidly behind the Party in support of the Party's enforcement of the various new policies relevant to the PLA. As the All-Army Conference of Directors of Mass Work Department was convened in July 1979, with Wei Guoqing announcing the Party's earliest intention to eradicate past mistakes, three distinct themes emerged as specific GPD objectives.[37]

The First theme emphasised the need for the PLA to maintain stability and unity in the wake of the Party's attempts to eliminate Leftist remnants. The maintenance of stability and unity would require reaching political compromises, and at times even compromising with units which were associated with the Revolutionary Left. The second theme signalled the beginning of a basic shift in the functions of the GPD, as methods for political work were regarded as adaptable according to needs and special circumstances (ie Four Modernisations), a changing view was to take a much more definite shape in 1980–81. The third theme denotes the need for revitalised efforts to educate cadres in democratic practices and the legal system to better equip themselves for the supervision of disciplinary work as well as freeing themselves from the former shackles of excessive Leftist beliefs and feudal practices.[38]

In 1980–81, the GPD continued to take on the almost impossible task of having to adapt political work to the immediate goals of socialist modernisation, as well as attempting to reinforce the traditional role of the GPD as the means to strengthen the Party's control over the Army. These two aims denote the contradiction between the Party's desire to ensure that the PLA (through the work of the GPD) would conform to the various pragmatic policies introduced, including the responsibility system in agriculture, and the need for the GPD to strengthen ideological and political work within the PLA on the other.[39] If the GPD were to be successful with the latter task, it would have to uphold the line that the nation, and hence the PLA, must struggle against class enemies, in order that the dictatorship of the proletariat could be perpetuated. Yet in April 1981 the GPD, via the *Liberation Army Daily*, professed that although class struggle was still relevant, it was no longer the major contradiction in Chinese society.[40]

In its eagerness to woo the support of the PLA for its modernisation policies, the Party undoubtedly had given top priority to the pragmatic approach, including reorientating political work to suit current needs. In other words, the Party required the PLA to support changing Party policies, especially in regard to the rural policy in favour of fixed production quotas for individual households. Such reorientation of political work did not contribute any support to 'the strengthening of Party building' in the PLA, a function which had been associated with past GPD work when 'Redness' was stressed and when political work was very much regarded as the sole means by which ideological indoctrination could be properly administered in the PLA. Paradoxically, Wei Guoqing in the PLA Political Conference in May 1980 still continued to underline the 'strengthening of Party building' and the improvement of the Army's fighting ability as the model for a modernised revolutionary Army.[41] On the other hand, political-ideological work was originally stressed, but no longer conformed to the traditional style which used to have the training of a Party-army as its mission. Instead, the Party had made it a point to dissociate GPD work from ideological overtones affiliated with the 'blood doctrine', continuous revolution and class struggle. Indeed, in its eagerness to maintain an anti-Leftist stand in April 1981 the PLA took great pains to persuade the rank and file that there was no change to the PLA's stand against the Leftist remnants, and that the promulgation of the Four Basic Principles should not be understood as a swing to the Left or as the Party's attempt to launch an anti-Right campaign.[42]

In 1981 political-ideological work was defined and adapted to suit present needs. In the first place, the GPD had claimed in November 1980 that the system of ideological work (*sixiang jidu*), apparently cast aside by the Gang of Four, should be revived; and second, that the Party regarded the realisation of the Four Modernisations as its political line and the greatest political objective.[43]

In addition, the GPD believed that political work and politics could not be entirely separated. To do so would put political work in an improper context. From January 1980 when the Party tolerated 'three supports and two militaries', to the time that the Party assumed a stronger anti-Left attitude (which still persists) a year later, the General Political Department had generally maintained the same line that strengthened ideological work was essential. However, the GPD seemed to have taken the point that Four Modernisations would require the PLA's support as long as it did not jeopardise its basic position on ideological indoctrination. Two representative articles in the *Liberation Army Daily* in November 1980 reflect the rationale of the GPD's support for the pragmatic Party's modernisation program, especially with regard to national defence, as long as it did not contradict the basic principle of fostering ideological work. Thus Guo Zhongyi in his 'an investigation into the "appropriate position" of political work' wrote:[44]

> The Party sees its own political line as the greatest politics in its realisation of Four Moderisations. One who does not see the similarities between politics and political work does not understand clearly the meaning of political work, which may also lead to the downgrading of its position and function. Separating political work and politics completely is tantamount to placing political work in an unsuitable place.

Thus the message was very clear. 'Four Modernisations' was the greatest objective which is inseparable from political work, with the latter serving the former.

Furthermore, in November 1980, the Director of Political Work for the Beijing Armoured Unit, Tian Jisheng, also emphasised that political work should change with changes in circumstances. He claimed that political work should serve as a guarantee for the modernisation of the forces, with the GPD taking the lead in revolutionalising the PLA, and that it would involve drastic measures like retiring old cadres and eliminating 'formalistic reforms' which stood in the way of genuine, revolutionary changes.[45] Nevertheless, it was not certain whether such a new orientation might jeopardise good political work in the traditional Maoist way, and which would otherwise have ensured good ideological indoctrination in the PLA. Pragamatism and modernisation seemed to be poor substitutes for a revolutionised morale-booster which good ideological work might bring about, but the improvement of people's livelihood which modernisation promises might also serve as a morale-booster if the formula in political work were to become effective.

Indeed, pragmatism must also have induced the Party and the GPD to emphasise much less 'Redness' because of the various problems they have inherited, including what had been known as the 'remaining poison'.[46] In general, these refer to the continuing saga of 'three supports and two militaries' as well as worsening disciplinary problems involving in-service as well as demobilised soldiers. Thus, the GPD had to face them squarely with the introduction of legislation, the institution of legal bodies and the launching of public campaigns to ensure that stability is maintained in the PLA. This was by no means an easy task.

Entrenched Leftist influence in the military regions

Given the fact that many military cadres supported the Left and became dominant in the revolutionary committees during 1967–69, and to a lesser extent in the later period, it would be safe to assume that many of them remained in active service in the early 1980s. The blatant culprits like the 'Linists' headed by Huang Yungsheng were put on trial and convicted together with the Gang of Four. Many others were dismissed in 1980–81. However, many remained. The Party was not in a position to eradicate all Leftist remnants as it relied on unity and stability in the Army to maintain political equilibrium and an effective defence program. However, the Party was in a position to distinguish between two categories of Leftists in the PLA. First, there were commanders and political commissars who played a positive role in the seizure of power during the Cultural Revolution, actively supporting the Left and exploiting the situation to advance their own career. Many of them found themselves in positions of power on the revolutionary committees, probably at the expense of other commanders whom they might have persecuted. Whilst the most serious offenders had been punished, numerous others either remained entrenched in their original positions since the

Cultural Revolution or had been transferred to other military regions/districts. They remained in power either because they were protected by senior commanders or because the Party was not in a position to eliminate them. Deng Xiaoping was not keen on upsetting the equilibrium in the PLA, especially when problems facing the PLA needed to be solved.

The second category of commanders and political commissars classified as Leftists were involved in supporting the Left in the Cultural Revolution, but their major objective was to maintain law and order, as the Party itself had explained in the 'amnesty'. Furthermore, there were no blatant and unjust records of brutality or violent persecutions undertaken by them during their careers although their support for the Left was without question. Whilst the two categories are distinct, it should also be noted that the general label of 'three supports and two militaries' has two separate connotations, one denoting support for Lin Biao, and the other support for the Gang of Four, especially Jiang Qing and Zhang Chunqiao.

The complex problem of 'three supports and two militaries' induced Deng Xiaoping to waver between the lenient attitude of early 1980 and the later, anti-Left one, which tended to take a hardline approach. The distribution of entrenched Leftist influence in the military regions and districts in 1982 is as shown in Table 7.1.

Category A in Table 7.1 comprises MRs with the most serious problem *vis-a-vis* 'three supports and two militaries'. Nanjing, in particular, stands out as the most critical in two respects. First, most of the identifiable Leftist commanders and political commissars had remained in Nanjing MR since the Cultural Revolution, although their positions might have varied with the MR. The fact that they were not required to transfer to another MR shows the extent of Leftist entrenchment. Thus Zhou Chunlin, Deputy Commander of Nanjing MR, actively supported Zhang Chunqiao when he was Commander of the Shanghai Garrison in the 'seizure of power' in Shanghai at the beginning of the Cultural Revolution. Likewise Liu Yaozong, Yu Guangmao and Guan Junting remained in Nanjing MR. Similarly, Shenyang and Guangzhou accommodated a fair number of entrenched Leftist commanders/commissars who remained in the same region. Li Desheng stood out as the most senior commander in this category with a conspicuous record of Leftism. Lanzhou exhibited an interesting feature of accommodating Leftist cadres originally from other military regions, some of whom had been openly criticised in the past few years.

Category B comprises four MRs with a lesser number of

Table 7.1: Identifiable Leftist Commanders/Political Commissars in the Military Regions (May 1982)

Military regions	Commanders/political commissars with ultra-Leftist records	Commanders/political commissars with active Leftist records
Category A (Acute Leftist Problems)		
Nanjing MR		
1 Nanjing MR	Zhou Chunlin DCdr*+Cdr, Shanghai Gar. Du Ping PC*2 and PC	
2 Anhui MD	Yu Guangmao Cdr+DCdr. Shanghai Gar. Liu Yaozong 2ndPC*PC, Shanghai Gar.	
3 Zhejiang MD		Guan Junting Cdr+Nanjing
Shengyang MR		
1 Shengyang MR	Li Desheng Cdr×+Ch, Anhui RC Jiang Younghui DCdr&MRCOGS Xie Zhenhua DCdr+Shanxi RC	Li Huamin DCdr+Wuhan DCdr
2 Jilin MD	He Youfa Cdr×+Cdr Ding Chi DPC+Jilin MD	
3 Liaoning MD	Yang Dayi Cdr+DCdr, Hunan	
Guangzhou MR		
1 Guangzhou MR	Jiang Xieyuan DCdr+MRDCOGS Huang Ronghai DCdr×+VCh, Guangdong RC Ou Zhifu DCdr×+VCh, Guangxi RC	
2 Guangdong MD	Hao Shengwang Cdr×+Cdr, 43A Corps	
3 Hunan MD	Zhang Lixian 2ndPC×+DPC	
Lanzhou MR		
1 Lanzhou MR	Li Yuan DCdr+47A Corps, Changsha Huang Jingyao DCdr×+Heilongjiang RC Chen Kang DCdr*+VCh, Yunnan RC Duan Siying DPC+DPC, Kunming MR Lin Shan PC+VCh, Qinghai RC	
2 Ningxia MD		

Table 7.1 (cont'd):

Military regions	Commanders/political commissars with ultra-Leftist records	Commanders/political commissars with active Leftist records
Category B (Leftist Problems)		
Chengdu MR		
1 Chengdu MR	Kong Shiquan 1stPC[+]3rdPC, Guangzhou MR Ren Rong DPC[+]PC, Sichuan MD Tian Bao 2ndPC[×][+]VCh, Sichuan RC	
2 Xizang MD		
Wuhan MR	Yan Zheng PC[+]DPC, Fuzhou MR Wang Huaixiang DCdr[*][+]Ch, Jilin RC	
Beijing MR		
1 Beijing MR		Yuan Shengping PC[+]DPC, Wu Lie DPC[+]DCdr, 2nd Artillery Yang Junsheng PC[+]16A corps
2 Beijing Garrison	Cao Zhongnan PC[+]DPC, Shanxi MD	
3 Tianjin Garrison	Liu Haiqing DCdr[+]DCdr, Hebei MD	
Wulumuqi MR	Wang Fuzhi DCdr[+]Gen Staff Dept.	
Category C (Negligible Leftist Problems)		
Fuzhou MR	. . . .	Liu Jianting 2nd PC[*]2ndPC Fu Kuiqing PC[+]DPC, Shenyang Zhang Haitang DCdr[+] Liaoning MD
Kunming MR		
Jinan MR		. . . .

Key:
+ Different position in the Cultural Revolution
† Present location the same as that in the Cultural Revolution
* Criticised by name in the post-Mao period
× Associated with Mao and Lin in the Cultural Revolution

Abbreviations:
Cdr   Commander
CoGs Chief of General Staff
MD   Military District
PC   Political Commissar
V   Vice-
Ch   Chairman
Gar   Garrison
MR   Military Region
RC   Revolutionary Committee

identifiable Leftists than category A, although they accommodated some blatantly Leftist commanders. Wang Huaixiang of Wuhan MR for instance had a notorious record in Jilin in the Cultural Revolution. Category C represents three MRs with negligible Leftist influence, accommodating some 'exiles' from other MRs.

The extent of Leftist influence in the military regions should also be studied in relation to power shifts and power distribution, especially with reference to their high command. As early as 1974, during the era of the Gang of Four, a major reshuffle of the MRs involving six commanders in pairs of exchanged postings went some way to minimise regional entrenchment. With Deng Xiaoping's effective reshuffle and dismissal of regional military leaders in January–February 1980, power distribution in the MRs moved distinctly in favour of Deng's leadership. His chairmanship of the CMC was confirmed in June 1981 in the Sixth Plenum, and this further equipped him with extra ammunition to tackle the problem of 'three supports and two militaries'. In MRs where the commanders and first political commissars were loyalists (eg originally from the 129th Division) who did not have a confirmed record of supporting the Left in the Cultural Revolution, the work of eradicating or at least controlling Leftist elements in these MRs would be easier.[47] Nevertheless one sometimes finds that a balance of power exists when a loyalist MR commander, for instance, is being checked by a Leftist first political commissar, or *vice versa*, making the eradication of Leftist elements a tedious task for Deng's supporters. This factor should also partly explain the continuation of entrenched Leftist influence in the MRs.

Criteria used in Table 7.2 include not only Whitson's theory of affiliations and alignments in the Field Army systems, but also factors since the Cultural Revolution which identify the political stand of commanders and political commissars in regard to military modernisation, political work and their attitude towards the Cultural Revolution itself.[48] Their participation in the Korean War is also identified, wherever relevant, as a factor of experience in 'modern' warfare which proves useful in China's modernisation program. As for Whitson's theory, military affiliations and alignments are still extremely relevant where Deng Xiaoping's commanders of the former 129th Division or Second Field Army are on record as having been in support of his Four Modernisations. There are naturally exceptions, as is apparent in the case of Li Desheng who was from the Second Field Army. In such cases, military alignments naturally cross the boundaries of Field Army systems, a feature which also

Table 7.2: Deng Xiaoping and the regional command, May 1982

Military Regions	Commanders	First Political Commissars/ Political Commissars
Category A (pro-Deng)		
Beijing	Qin Jiwei 129D	Yuan Shengping 4
	2	Ko
	Ko	L(+)
Chengdu	You Taizhong 129D	Tan Qilong *
	2	3
	MM	P
	P	
Guangzhou	Wu Kehua 4	Wang Meng 38A Corps
	Ko	NP
	MM	
	P	
Wuhan	Zhang Caiqian 129D	Li Chengfang *
	4	129D
	Ko	2
	L(+)	P
Category B (balance of power)		
(i) Kunming	Zhang Zhixiu 3	Liu Zhijian *
(marginally pro-Deng)	L	129D
		2
		Ko
		P
Wulumuqi	Xiao Quanfu 4	Wang Enmao *
(marginally pro-Deng)	Ko	1
	MM	NP
	L	
(ii) Jinan	Rao Shoukun 3	Xiao Wangdong *
(balance of power)	Ko	3
	L	P
	Navy	
(iii) Nanjing	Nie Fengzhi 3	Guo Linxiang *
(under Xu Shiyou)	P	129D
		2+NC
		P
Category C (independent)		
Fuzhou	Yang Chengwu NC	Fu Kuiqing 3
	Ko	
	L	
Lanzhou	Du Yide 2	Xiao Hua *
	P	4
	Navy	L
		P
Shenyang	Li Desheng 129D	Liao Hansheng *
	2	1
	Ko	P
	MM	
	L	

Key:
*	First Political Commissar	L(+)	Leftist-turned pro-Deng
1–4	Field Army system	MM	Military modernisation record
Ko	Korean War experience	NC	North China Field Army
L	Leftist supporter in the Cultural Revolution	NP	Not Purged
		P	Purged

applies to the new central military leadership, as is obvious in Yang Dezhi's support for Deng and possibly Hu Yaobang. Indeed, realignments since the Cultural Revolution emerge as a result of Deng's success in persuading some commanders and political commissars to support his pragmatic policies. This is so despite the lack of historical affiliations and sometimes despite Leftist records in the Cultural Revolution. The obvious examples are Yang Dezhi and his associate Yuan Shengping.

In Category A in Table 7.2 Beijing is considered pro-Deng, not merely because it would seem important for the Party to maintain a guaranteed political stability in the capital, but also because of the Party's success in dismissing Chen Xilian. Furthermore realignments in favour of Deng and Hu Yaobang as mentioned earlier are relevant to Beijing, as Yuan Shengping was transferred there in early 1980 at the same time as his close associate in Jinan, Yang Dezhi, was transferred from Kunming to become the Chief of General Staff in Beijing.

Similarly, Wuhan is considered loyal, as Zhang Caiqian (despite his Leftist background) went with Deng Xiaoping and Liu Zhijian of Kunming in February 1982 to Guangzhou with the vital mission of appeasing the military in that region.[49] Chengdu and Guangzhou remained loyal to the Party under Deng and Hu. Although both Zhao Ziyang and Xi Zhongxun were transferred to the Party centre from Chengdu and Guangzhou respectively, the Party's institutionalised control over the two MRs continue with the appointment of Tan Qilong and Wang Meng to succeed Zhao and Xi respectively. Sichuan, where Deng came from was naturally a loyalist stronghold. As for Guangzhou, the loyalist command faced Leftist entrenchment in the MR.

Category B comprises three groups. Whilst they represent a balancing force with either a loyal commander checking a Leftist political commissar, or *vice versa*, there is sometimes evidence to show that pro-Deng commanders or commissars actively supported Deng's attempts to appease the military. Thus Group (i) includes Kunming where in February 1982 Liu Zhijian's active support for Deng Xiaoping when they went south to Guangzhou confirmed the growing influence of the loyalists. Similarly Wang Enmao's transfer back to Xinjiang from Jilin in November 1981 represents Deng's determination to solve many of the political and social problems which were very often relevant to the minorities in that region.[50] Group (ii) comprises Jinan, where Rao Shoukun's Leftist record was balanced by that of Xiao Wangdong, who was a victim of the

Cultural Revolution in 1966. Group (iii) is unique as Nie Fengzhi was still very much under the wings of Xu Shiyou, his comrade in arms and former superior, who stationed himself in Nanjing MR despite his transfer from Guangzhou to become a Standing Committee Member of the CMC in February 1980. Xu's political attitude was at best ambiguous and at worst hostile to Deng, making any attempt on the part of Nie Fengzhi to eradicate Leftist influence extremely difficult.[51]

Category C comprises three military regions exhibiting a great deal of 'independent tendencies' either because of the region's associations with the Mao-Lin group in the Cultural Revolution or because of outspoken views expressed by commanders/political commissars which were rather critical of Deng Xiaoping's pragmatic line. Li Desheng and Yang Chengwu (before his purge as Chief of General Staff in March 1968) belonged to the first group and Xiao Hua to the second.

In comparing Tables 7.1 and 7.2, it should be possible to identify more closely the Party's prospects of eradicating Leftist elements from the military regions, a move consistent with its persistent anti-Leftist attitude, and vital to stability in the future. It follows that in MRs where the regional command was pro-Deng, there was great incentive to solve the problem of 'three supports and two militaries' should there be a strongly entrenched Leftist influence. When the latter was prevalent, as in the case of Nanjing MR, the extent of success for any anti-Leftist measures would depend on the political attitude of the regional command. Table 7.3 summarises the Party's anti-Leftist efforts.

The central military leadership

Hu Yaobang's ascendancy as Chairman of the Chinese Communist Party in June 1981 did not carry with it the Chairmanship of the CMC despite stipulations in Clause XIX of the Constitution of the PRC which says: 'The armed forces of the Chinese People's Republic should be led by the Chairman of the Central Committee of the Chinese Communist Party'. Instead, Deng Xiaoping was made Chairman of the CMC. Hu's rapid ascendancy reflects Deng's intention to inject 'new blood' into the top echelon of the leadership, conspicuous examples being Zhao Ziyang's Premiership and Geng Biao's appointment as Minister of Defence. Nevertheless, the fact that Hu's predecessor Hua Guofeng concurrently held the post of Chairman of the CMC which was denied to Hu, suggests that Hu was not yet accept-

Table 7.3: Prospects for the eradication of Leftist influence in the Military Regions, 1982

Military Regions	Extent of Leftist influence	Prospects for eradicating Leftist influence
Category A (pro-Deng)		
Beijing	moderate	good
Chengdu	moderate	good
Guangzhou	acute	marginally fair
Wuhan	moderate	good
Category B (balance of power)		
Kunming	negligible	good
Wulumuqi	moderate	good
Jinan	negligible	good
Nanjing	acute	poor
Category C (independent)		
Fuzhou	negligible	good
Lanzhou	acute	marginally fair (Xiao Hua was an independent figure but he was keen on political work)
Shenyang	acute	poor

able to the PLA as its 'spiritual' leader. There might have been opposition from either the Left-inclined generals or veterans like Ye Jianying. In the realm of politics in the PLA, Deng could not have afforded to retreat to the 'secondline', although in Party affairs he seemed to have been successful in so doing.

Deng Xiaoping's general intention to nurture the second generation in the PLA should not be doubted as he had been quite successful in 'rejuvenating' the top Party leadership. Deng's efforts to 'rejuvenate' the PLA were not so successful as it was a more complex organisation with long traditions and factional affiliations and alignments. The principle of *chuan, bang, dai* (to pass on, to assist and to lead) designed to nurture the second generation[52] also failed to convince the PLA that a civilian Party Chairman (later General Secretary) with a weak military background should hold the concurrent post as Chairman of the CMC. Whilst the Party was continuing to pursue Deng's pragmatic policy, and being confident of leadership in the post-Deng period, the PLA did not seem to be as stable.

Since his reemergence after the fall of the Gang of Four and his appointment as Chief of General Staff in July 1977, Deng Xiaoping had however been successful in strengthening the central military elite under the principle of collective leadership. Two major landmarks signal Deng's successes in strengthening military support for his pragmatic leadership. First, the convening of the Fifth Plenum of the Eleventh Central Committee in February 1980, which coincided with the transfer of many regional commanders to the centre, witnessed the successful application of Deng's principle of collective leadership, resulting in the bolstering of his position in the CMC. This also represented Deng's preparation for the removal of Hua Guofeng from the Chairmanship of the Party and the CMC. At the same time, the urge to modernise the PLA for national defence, especially against the Soviet Union, and eagerness to promote the principle of 'People's War under modern conditions', obliged Deng to cross Field Army boundaries to enlist support. And he succeeded in doing so. At the same time, the dismissal of Chen Xilian, Commander of Beijing MR, together with others like Wang Dongxing and Ji Dengkui, further strengthened Deng's hand. The second landmark was the convening of the Sixth Plenum in June 1981 which marked the fall of Hua Guofeng from the Chairmanship of the Party and the CMC. The ascendancy of Hu Yaobang as Chairman of the Party, and the assumption of the Chairmanship of the CMC by Deng himself in the Plenum further strengthened Deng's position in the party, and for that matter, in the PLA.

In the strengthened central military leadership, there were also two interesting features suggestive of Deng's deliberate policy to reinforce national defence and to contain the excessive influence of certain independent veteran generals. In the first place, two commanders were transferred to the centre in order to strengthen China's military modernisation. Zhang Aiping, who had been Director of the Science and Technology Commission for National Defence since December 1975, was made Deputy Chief of General Staff in September 1977, only two months after Deng assumed the post of Chief of General Staff. Zhang's modernisation efforts were further strengthened when Yang Dezhi was transferred from Kunming to become Chief of General Staff, and when Hong Xuezhi was appointed Director of the General Logistics Department in February 1980. Yang's experience as Commander of Kunming MR during the Sino–Vietnamese border war in February 1979 no doubt made him the best qualified to plan the finest strategy for defence. Hong's immaculate record in Korea as a logistics commander, where he was reported to have been responsible for successes against offensives launched by the US General Michael Clark in North Korea in 1952, no doubt convinced Deng that he would help improve China's logistic capabilities in the context of 'People's War under modern conditions'. The fact that Hong was purged as early as 1959 along with his seniors like Peng Dehuai and Huang Kecheng also exonerated him politically.[53]

The second feature suggests Deng's attempts to maintain a certain balance within the Field Army systems, and the case in point being the Third Field Army system. Whilst alliances of military factions sometimes cross Field Army boundaries in Deng's collective leadership model, it remains true that senior and venerable marshals/ generals of a particular Field Army system commanded the respect of their subordinates within their respective systems. Thus the well-known independent and entrenched influence of Xu Shiyou seemed to be balanced, at least partially, by the presence of Zhang Aiping and Su Yu in the central military elite. As Xu's peers, the latter two were not without weight in the Third Field Army system. Table 7.4 summarises the position of the strengthened central military leadership.

With his reinforced central military leadership as chairman of the CMC, Deng wished to maintain greater support for his pragmatic policies and greater strength to contain Leftist influence in Beijing. It was not Deng's intention to eliminate all commanders with a Leftist record or whose political stand was Left-inclined despite the Party's continuing anti-Left position. Deng was not in a position to eliminate all of them. The policy of *anding tuanjie* applied to the situation in which Deng was in a much better position than before to contain Leftist influence, and at the same time face independent individuals like Ye Jianying and Xu Shiyou. By virtue of his seniority in the CMC, his Chairmanship of the Standing Committee of the People's Congress and his entrenched position in Guangzhou, Ye Jianying had been rather indifferent to Deng's pragmatism. Xu's entrenched position in Nanjing, despite his official posting to Beijing as a Member of the Standing Committee of the CMC, remained an obstacle in the eradication of Leftist influence in the MR. Yang Chengwu seemed to be the most innocuous individual in this group as there was no evidence of any strong views he had expressed against Deng's pragmatism. In addition, his dismissal as Chief of the General Staff in March 1968 during the Cultural Revolution brought him into less conflict with the pragmatists.

The remaining power group which Deng faced was the 'conscience' of the PLA, that is, the General Political Department headed by Wei Guoqing. Wei continued to speak out in favour of strengthened political work and the importance of Mao Zedong's military science in the PLA, which sometimes went contrary to the pragmatic goals of Deng's leadership. Moreover, politically minded commanders/

Table 7.4: Deng Xiaoping and the strengthened central military leadership (July 1977 to May 1982)

	Chairman/Minister/Chief	Members (July 1977–Feb 1980)	Additional Members (March 1980–May 1982)
Central Military Commission	Hua Guofeng* (to 1981.6) Deng Xiaoping (from 1981.6)	Li Xiannian† 77.7 Xu Shiyou* 70.2 Han Xianchu* 80.2 Wang Ping 80.2 Xiao Ke 80.5 Chen Xilian* 77.7 Xiao Hua*	Hu Yaobang† 81.2 Wang Zhen† 80.10 Yang Shangkun† 81.7 Wei Guoqing* 81.7 Song Renqiong 81.7
Ministry of Defence General Staff Dept	Geng Biao Yang Dezhi	Yang Dezhi*# 80.2 Yang Yong†* 77.9 Zhang Aiping*# 77.10 Zhang Zhen 80.2 Chi Haotian 77.11 Liu Huaqing 80.1	Geng Biao# 81.3
General Political Department	Wei Guoqing#	Gan Weihan 80.4 Huang Yukun 75.9 Yan Jinsheng 77.10 Zhu Yunqian 78.10 Hua Nan 80.4	
General Logistics Department	Hong Xuezhi	Hong Xuezhi 80.2 Wang Ping 78.4	
Navy	Ye Fei	Ye Fei 79.3 (Cdr & 1st PC)	
Air Force	Zhang Tingfa	Zhang Tingfa 78.1	
Railway Corps	Chen Zaidao	Chen Zaidao† 76.7	

Key:
† Staunch supporter of Deng Xiaoping
* Independent/leftist cadre
# Member of Central Military Commission

Table 7.5:   The Challenge to Deng Xiaoping in the central military leadership (July 1977 to May 1982)

Deng and his Collective Leadership

Leftists in CMC	Independent Marshal/ Commanders	General Political Department
Hua Guofeng*	Ye Jianying*	Wei Guoqing*
Chen Xilian	Xu Shiyou*	
Li Desheng*	Yang Chengwu	
	Xiao Hua	
	(in favour of strengthened political work)	

Key:
*   Politburo Member
CMC   Central Military Commission

commissars sometimes echoed Wei Guoqing's firm stand. Xiao Hua as the First Political Commissar of Lanzhou holding the concurrent post as member of the CMC was the most distinctive example. Table 7.5 analyses the challenge to Deng's position in the central military leadership.

On the eve of the Twelfth Party Congress which was convened in September 1982, Deng Xiaoping's China had moved from the stage of *transitional crisis system* to that of *transitional conflict system*. The basic reason for this claim is that most opponents to Deng's leadership, especially Hua Guofeng and his 'whateverists', were not completely purged or physically eliminated after the revolution of a successor conflict.[54] Furthermore, the threats posed by 'three supports and two militaries', especially in the military regions, still constituted conflicts that existed between concurring groups, 'where terms of incumbency and transition of power from incumbent to successor are not yet completely regularised, but where succession conflicts do not result in a thorough shake-up and ensuing *crises* for the whole political system'.[55]

8

The PLA and Party Leadership since the Twelfth Party Congress

If the Third Plenum of the Eleventh Party Congress in 1978 could be considered as Deng Xiaoping's launching pad for his pragmatic line for the Four Modernisations, then the convening of the Twelfth Party Congress in September 1982 should definitely be hailed as the confirmation of increased success that he had managed to achieve in making the Chinese style of socialism work. Deng was able to confirm the correctness of his line since the Third Plenum, introduce the new Party Constitution and establish a revitalised Party structure which would tackle all the problems of modernisation with new vigour.[1]

The introduction of the new Party Constitution was necessary to condemn and eliminate Leftist problems remaining from the Cultural Revolution. Furthermore, the new Constitution provided the strengthened Party leadership with a machinery that would optimise the efforts of Deng's pragmatists. First of all, Hu Yaobang as General Secretary endorsed the document entitled 'Resolution on Certain Questions in the History of Our Party since the Founding of the People's Republic of China'. The resolution was passed in the Sixth Plenum of the Eleventh Party Congress in June 1981. Hu hailed the document as a landmark in ideological guidance as it rectified past Leftist mistakes in the Party.[2] To close the chapter on the negative effect of the Cultural Revolution, the new Party Constitution in the Preamble stipulated that the Party must 'oppose all "left" and "right" incorrect tendencies'. It also contained the important but 'revisionist' message that class struggle was no longer the major contradiction in the Chinese society.[3]

On the positive side, the new Party Constitution replaced the Chairmanship of the Party with the General Secretariat. The Central Secretariat of the Party Committee was strengthened with the injection of new blood, some of whom were third-echelon cadres.[4] The newly established Central Advisory Committee and the Central Discipline Inspection Committee facilitated the retirement of veteran cadres and the launching of Party rectification respectively.[5]

The new situation created by the Twelfth Party Congress affected the PLA in many ways. Firstly, Party leadership of the Central Military Commission was further confirmed despite the fact that there were two organisations, ie the Party Central Military Commission and the State Central Military Council. In addition to the fact that the memberships were identical, it was Hu Yaobang's reassuring words that confirmed the Party's control over the military:[6]

> Once the new draft Constitution has been discussed and passed by the National People's Congress, the Party Central will continue to lead our nation's armed forces through the State's Central Military Commission.

In substance, the Chairman of the Party Central Military Commission has the final say regarding all important decisions made by the State Central Military Council. Nevertheless, the creation of the Party Central Military Commission is in accordance with Deng's general direction to distinguish more clearly between the functions of the Party and the State. Through the new Council, greater coordination of defence industries and commissions, as well as more efficient tactical decisions in procurement, research and development can hopefully be made. These improvements in turn would contribute to greater efficiency in economic planning.[7]

The Party Congress also reinforced the principle that the development of economic construction was the foundation for all modernisation programs. Thus defence modernisation could only be developed with a view to the general objectives of China's economic development. Nevertheless, Hu Yaobang's speech in the Twelfth Party Congress underlined the importance of building a regularised revolutionary army which would increase China's defence capabilities under modern conditions. Furthermore, the Party reiterated the need to improve ideological and political work and maintain good discipline within the PLA, paving the way for the launching of Party rectification which is still under way.[8]

As regards the introduction of the Central Advisory Committee (CAC) and the Discipline Inspection Committee (DIC), the PLA as a branch of the State also benefited from these new establishments. Thus veteran military personnel could retire and join the ranks of the CAC. Furthermore the All-Army DIC was subsequently established under Guo Linxiang's Secretariat to launch rectification in earnest.[9]

Finally, the new Party Constitution stipulated under Section VI the need to reform the leadership organisations and the cadre system with a view to turning the cadres into a revolutionised, younger, better educated and specialised force.[10] This general objective again applied to the PLA and the subsequent streamlining, structure reforms and reorganisations introduced in 1984–85 were very much in line with this general objective.

Whilst the Central Military Commission as the power-house of the army building exercise was poised to further strengthen Deng Xiaoping's leadership in the PLA after the Twelfth Party Congress, some of the problems that had been plaguing the PLA continued to persist. Needless to say, some of these problems were also common to other government organisations. For instance, the question of 'liberal and democratic thinking' as indicated by the Bai Hua case[11] and the effect of the responsibility system in agriculture on the PLA are issues which also occur in other government establishments. Nevertheless, it was the Leftist problem of 'three supports and two militaries' which continued to be of grave concern to the PLA. It therefore became one of the major objectives of the revitalised Central Military Commission in late 1982 to continue with the battle against residual Leftist problems. For the subsequent four years this objective has become part of the Party rectification exercise which deals with both existing as well as emerging new problems in the Party and the PLA. As far as 'three supports and two militaries' is concerned, Table 8.1 shows that it had continued to plague the PLA up to the end of 1984 although indications were that it was not as acute as it had been before the Twelfth Party Congress.

One significant feature in Table 8.1 is that the number of military cadres with unknown postings (as far as one can tell) suggests that 'three supports and two militaries' will become a diminishing issue in the future. First of all, the Party has launched a large-scale exercise to retire veteran cadres, many of whom found themselves obliged to join the Central Advisory Committee (CAC) instead of having the option of remaining in their postings either in the military regions or in the general departments. Furthermore, the launching of major plans to streamline, restructure and reorganise the PLA in 1984–85

Table 8.1: Identifiable Leftist commanders/political commissars in the Military Regions, 1984

Military Regions	Commanders/political commissars with ultra-Leftist records	Commanders/ political commissars with active Leftist records
Category A (Acute Leftist problems)		
Nanjing MR		
(1) Nanjing MR	Zhou Chunlin DCdr Du Ping CAC	
(2) Anhui MD	Yu Guangmao Cdr Liu Yaozong PC	
(3) Zhejiang MD		Guan Junting PU
Shengyang MR		
(1) Shengyang MR	Li Desheng Cdr Jiang Yonghui TR Cdr, Fuzhou MR Xie Zhenhua TR PC Kunming MR	Li Huamin DCdr
(2) Jilin MD	He Youfa PU Ding Chi DPC	
(3) Liaoning MD	Yang Dayi Cdr	
Guangzhou MR		
(1) Guangzhou MR	Jiang Xieyuan DCdr Huang Ronghai PU Ou Zhifu PU	
(2) Guangdong MD	Hao Shengwang PU	
(3) Hunan MD	Zhang Lixian 2nd PC	
Lanzhou MR		
(1) Lanzhou MR	Li Yuan PU Huang Jingyao DCdr Chen Kang DCr Duan Siying DPC	
(2) Ningxia MD	Lin Shan PC	
Category B (Leftist problems)		
Chengdu MR		
(1) Chengdu MR	Kong Shiquan PU Ren Rong TR Adviser, Wuhan MR	
(2) Xizang MD	Tian Bao PU	
Wuhan MR	Yan Zheng PC Wang Huaixiang PU	
Beijing MR		
(1) Beijing MR		Yuan Shengping CAC Wu Lie DPC & 2nd PC, Beijing Garrison

Table 8.1 (cont'd):

Military Regions	Commanders/political commissars with ultra-Leftist records	Commanders/ political commissars with active Leftist records
(2) Beijing Garrison		Yang
(3) Tianjin Garrison	Cao Zhongnan TR 2nd PC	Yunsheng PC
Wulumuqi MR	Liu Haiqing DCdr Wang Fuzhi DCdr	
Category C (Negligible Leftist problems)		
Fuzhou MR		Liu Jiangting TR PC, Fujian MD Fu Kuiqing PC
Kunming MR		Zhang Haitang PU
Jinan MR	. . . .	. . . .

Abbreviations:

Cdr	Commander	CAC	Central Advisory Committee
DCdr	Deputy Commander	TR	Transfer to
PC	Political Commissar	PU	Posting Unknown
MD	Military District	MR	Military Region

greatly facilitated the dismissal and retirement of entrenched Leftist PLA cadres. This is not to say that Leftist influence had disappeared, as the present Party rectification exercise in 1986 still points to the need to eliminate problems. However, it does mean that 'three supports and two militaries' will no longer be the focus of attention in the Party's positive efforts to strengthen army-building and defence modernisation.

Central military leadership 1982–86

In the period 1982–85, Deng Xiaoping succeeded in strengthening his control of the Party and proceeding with his modernisation program, and also separating the power of the Party and that of the military. In so doing, the Central Military Commission has become a power-house which attends to the major tasks of enforcing the new program of structural reforms and reorganisations. The Party's control over the military lies squarely with the Deng Xiaoping–Yang

Shangkun team, (under which are the two veteran marshals Xu Xiangqian and Nie Rongzhen) and the four heads of the general departments and the Ministry of Defence. At the same time, the separation of power has brought with it the demise of the military in the Party's hierarchial structure as evidenced by the diminution of the power of the military in the Politburo.

Amongst the many major decisions made in the Twelfth Party Congress, Deng broke all past links by turning the CMC into a small but efficient task force, the singular objective of which is to realise defence modernisation. At present, it would appear that the two marshals are too senile to be effective. The workforce in the CMC forms a caucus represented by the four heads of department/ministry who execute the policies laid down by the Deng–Yang leadership.

The demise of the military in party politics is borne out by a comparison of the membership of the military in the Politburo in thhe Twelfth Party Congress in 1982 and that in the Conference of Party Delegates in September 1985. In 1982 the military had ten members and one alternate member (including Deng) on the Politburo. In 1985, there were only four members and one alternate member from the military on the Politburo. The decline of the military in the party hierarchy is due to the retirement of the three veteran marshals and former Air Force Chief, Zhang Tingfa, and the dropping of the dissenters (Li Desheng and Wei Guoqing). In addition, only two of the four heads of the general department/ ministry managed to gain seats in the Politburo. They were Yu Qiuli and Yang Dezhi. The situation remains the same in 1986. The diminution of PLA influence in the Politburo and other major decision-making organisations has been spurred on by the lesson of 'three supports and two militaries' and the phasing out of interlocking directorates. As leftist influence in the military gradually tapers off, the Party is keen to urge the PLA 'to reestablish the ethic that the military has no role to play in civilian political or economic decision making'.[12] The dissolution of overlapping power in Party, civilian and military institutions also steer the PLA towards becoming increasingly apolitical.

The PLA's general departments 1985–86

Streamlining the PLA general departments had started as early as 1982. One of the major steps taken was to reduce of the number of deputies in the three general departments from nine to five in the General Staff Department (GSD), from eight to five in the General

Political Department (GPD) and from twelve to four in the General Logistics Department (GLD).[13] The first two departments now have only four deputies. The streamlining exercise was accompanied by the injection of new blood into the three departments. With two exceptions, all the deputies were appointed in September 1985, which coincided with Deng Xiaoping's second major personnel reshuffle since 1982. Another new thrust in the three departments is that they seem to be prepared for a long process of military modernisation as new blood from third-echelon cadres is injected, many of whom are from PLA units in the military regions. There is now a good mixture of experience and modernisation incentives.

In the GSD, Xu Huizi and He Qizong are the two prominent third-echelon cadres who have received a great deal of media attention. They provide a good balance in the department and compliment the experience of the two veteran deputies (Xu Xin and Han Huaizhi). Xu Huizi, at 54, was commander of the 39th Group Army and had long combat experience dating back to the Civil War and the Korean War. In addition, he was reported to have written authoritative articles on problems in combined arms operations. In 1983, he was reported to have organised anti-airborne and anti-encirclement exercises under nuclear conditions. His prominent record no doubt justifies his position as the first deputy.[14]

He Qizong, at 43, was Commander of the 11th Army and a seasoned field commander as he had taken part in the Sino–Indian border war in 1962. In 1979, he participated in the Sino–Vietnam border war as Deputy Commander of a regiment. In 1984, He was in charge of a major operation there.[15] In the GPD, Zhou Keyu, at 50, took up the Secretariat of the All-army Discipline Inspection Commission. Zhou is another example of the promotion of outstanding cadres from military regions to key positions in the general departments. He was Political Commissar of the 67th Army in Jinan before taking up his new post.[16] Zhou Wenyuan at 45 is in the same category, having had tertiary education and experience, and was the Director of the Political Department in the Dalian Military Academy. He was transferred from Shenyang MR where he was Deputy Director of the Political Department of a division. In the GLD, the appointments of all four deputies were made in April–June 1985, with two being promotions from within the ranks in the GLD (Zhang Bin and Liu Mingpu) and two from the military regions (Zhao Nanqi and Zong Shunliu).[17] Those from the military regions seem to be in the category of third-echelon cadres, judging by their former rank. Zong was Chief of Staff of the 39th Army whilst Zhao was briefly Political Commissar of Jilin Military District.[18] In addition to his concurrent post as Deputy Political Commissar, Zhao is the first deputy in the GLD.[19]

The longer the time that China is given in maintaining a stable military leadership under Deng Xiaoping and Yang Shangkun, the greater the chance of success it will have in realising structural reforms and reorganistion within the PLA. The Central Military Commission has now been working since the Twelfth Party Congress as a professional power-house in preparing China for contingencies and external threats at a pace that is unprecedented. The entire defence modernisation program stands a greater chance of reaching targeted goals as continuity is provided by the emergence of an efficient hierarchy of third-echelon cadres in the central military leadership. It appears that Deng Xiaoping's principle that there should be a fair distribution of the age groups of 60:50:40 for senior military cadres is beginning to work with the injection of substantial new blood into key positions both in the general departments and the military regions.[20] The major question is whether the leadership provided by the Deng–Yang team would be very much weakened after their deaths. To remedy this situation, Deng Xiaoping has done his best to turn the PLA into a western-style defence force through the current army-building exercise so that it would serve China as a loyal arm of the State in the same way that armies do in Western democratic countries. It would therefore be to China's advantage to see Deng in command for a much longer time. (Subsequent events in 1987 reveal Deng Xiaoping's plan to prepare Zhao Ziyang for the formidable task of leading the PLA. As Party General Secretary and Vice-Chairman of the CMC, Zhao will be expected to command, in due course, the respect of the entire PLA. See Epilogue in this Chapter).

Deng Xiaoping and the Regional Command, 1982–86

It has been claimed that Deng Xiaoping has outdone Mao Zedong in his ability to exercise greater control over the military. If one were to compare Mao's personnel reshuffles of the MRs in 1974 with Deng's recent reshuffles in 1982 and 1985, it would appear that Deng's ability to control the military has been much greater. Mao's 1974 reshuffle was characterised by the exchange of postings of commanders in MRs[21], whilst Deng's reshuffles in 1982 and 1985 involved retirements, dismissals and the new appointments of enter-prising and relatively young commanders of the third-echelon so

Table 8.2: Deng Xiaoping and the regional command 1982–85

Military Regions	Commanders		First Political Commissars/Commissars	
	Sept 1982–Jan 1983	June–Sept 1985	Sept 1982–Jan 1983	June–Sept 1985
(A) The stabilisation of the pro-Deng leadership				
Beijing	Qin Jiwei 81.7	same	Fu Chongbi	Yang Baibing
Guangzhou	You Taizhong	same	Wang Meng 81.7	Zhang Zhongxian
Nanjing	Xiang Shouzhi	same	Guo Linxiang 80.2	Fu Kuiqing
(B) The emergence of pro-modernsation third-echelon leadership				
Jinan	Rao Shoukun 80.2	Li Jiulong	Xiao Wangdong 80.1	Chi Haotian
Shenyang	Li Desheng 74.1	Liu Jingsong	Liu Zhenhua	same
(C) Changing leadership in the NW–SW frontier MRs				
Chengdu	Wang Chenghan	Fu Quanyou	Wan Haifeng	same
Lanzhou	Zheng Weishan	Zhao Xianshun	Xiao Hua 77.7	Li Xuanhua
			(Tan Youlin 83.11)	
(D) The demise of the four military regions				
Fuzhou	Yang Chengwu 77.11		Fu Kuiqing 81.2	
Kunming	Zhang Zhixiu 80.2		Liu Zhijian 79.2	
Wuhan	Zhou Shizhong		Li Chengfang 78.1	
Wulumuqi	Xiao Quanfu 80.2		Wang Enmao	

essential for continuity and modernisation. In the Twelfth Party Congress in September 1982, Deng further strengthened his leadership by exercising greater control over the military regions. Thus the CMC under his leadership appointed five new commanders and four new political commissars.[22]

Of the five new commanders, You Taizhong (Guangzhou), Xiang Shouzhi (Nanjing) and Wang Chenghan (Chengdu) were staunch supporters of Deng with a history going back to the 129th Division and the Second Field Army. The first two were charged with the task of handling Leftist problems in Nanjing and Guangzhou MRs which have been beset with problems remaining frrom the Cultural Revolution. Thus Deng has been able to rely heavily on these three commanders for unfailing support. Qin Jiwei of Beijing MR is Deng's additional strong bastion. The Political Commissars of these four MRs on the other hand have no record at all of supporting Deng. The other two new appointments of commanders have no bearing on increased support for Deng either. Both Zhou Zhizhong (Wuhan) and Zheng Weishan (Lanzhou) were of the Third and First Field Army generations respectively and did not seem to work in favour of Deng either.

It was not until the summer of 1985 just prior to the convening of the Conference of Party Delegates in September 1985 that Deng Xiaoping introduced major personnel changes to the MR in line with major PLA reforms. The only interim changes were the appointment of Tan Youlin as Political Commissar for Lanzhou MR in November 1983 to succeed Xiao Hua and that of Jiang Yonghui as Commander for Fuzhou MR in November 1983 to replace the dissident Yang Chengwu.[23] In mid-1985, Deng further strengthened his leadership by promoting third-echelon commanders to carry on with long-term commitments to military modernisation. The appointments of Li Jiulong (Jinan MR) and Liu Jingsong (Shenyang MR) represent the CMC's determination to ensure that the strategy of 'People's War under modern conditions' and the newly organised combined arms and joint operations can be realised.[24] In Jinan MR, Chi Haotian as the new Political Commissar at the age of 59 has had experience in the Korean War and has been a central organ cadre as Deputy Chief of the General Staff in 1977.[25] His appointment certainly helps the general cause. Table 8.3 provides the general picture of Deng's leadership in the military regions in 1986.

The reduction of the number of MRs from eleven to seven also results in the demise of most of the commanders and political commissars of the four 'defunct' MRs of Fuzhou, Kunming, Wuhan

Table 8.3: Deng Xiaoping and the regional command 1985–86

Military Region	Commanders	First Political Commissars/Political Commissars
(A) Pro-Deng leadership		
Beijing	Qin Jiwei 129D 2 KO	Yang Baibing — Dep. Dir. P.D. Beijing; Dep. Coms. Beijing '82
Guangzhou	You Taizhong 120D 2 MM P	Zhang Zhongxian — 4; Dep. Coms. Jilin MD; Coms. Shenyang MR Artillery
Nanjing	Xiang Shouzhi 2 KO MM (2nd Artillery)	Fu Kuiqing — Coms. 23A '66; Coms. Shenyang '77; Coms. Fuzhou '82
(B) Pro-modernisation third-echelon leadership		
Jinan	Li Jiulong KO 54A	Chi Haotian — Dep. Coms. Beijing '75; Dep. C of GS '77
Shenyang	Liu Jingsong MM (mechanised D) 64A	Liu Zhenhua — Reg. Coms. NE China '48; Coms. Shenyang '82
(C) Independent leadership in the NW–SW frontier MRs		
Chengdu	Fu Quanyou 1 Dep. Com. 3D'73 1A '82	Wan Haifeng — L; Dep. Coms. Beijing '76
Lanzhou	Zhao Xianshun Heilongjiang MD '76 Dep. Com. Shenyang '82	Li Xuanhua — Dep. Dir. P.D. Beijing '80; Dir. P.D. Wulumuqi '81

Key:
1–4   Field Army system
A   Army Corps
D   Division
KO   Korean War experiences
L   Leftist support in the Cultural Revolution
MM   Military Modernisation Record
P   Purged
Com./Dep.Coms.   Commander/Deputy Commander
Coms./Dep.Coms./Reg.Coms.   Commissar/Deputy Commissar/Regimental Commissar
Dir.P.D./Dep.P.D.   Director, Political Department/Deputy Director, Political Department
Dep.C. of GS   Deputy Chief of General Staff

and Wulumuqi.[26] It seemed that Deng had anticipated the merging of the MRs in the early 1980s and had left the regional command in the four MRs relatively unchanged. The only new appointees in 1982 were Zhou Shizhong as Commander for Wuhan MR and Wang Enmao as Political Commissar for Wulumuqi MR. Wang was then charged with the task of handling problems that had been plaguing the Northwest.[27] Many of the commanders and political commissars in the four MRs had reached retirement age and their demise in the summer of 1985 can be regarded as Deng's relaxed way of phasing out elements who were very often not from his own camp. In any case, the retirement of aged cadres contributes to modernisation and provides the opportunity for the third-echelon cadres to promote their ideals. Of the eight senior cadres in the four MRs, only Fu Kuiqing remains as he was transferred from Fuzhou MR to become the Political Commissar for Nanjing MR.

The power base for the supporters of Deng continues to come from Beijing, Nanjing and Guangzhou MRs. However, it has to be emphasised that Nanjing and Guangzhou continue to inherit the problems of the Cultural Revolution as many senior commanders are still linked to the 'three categories of people' who are at present targets of rectification in the current exercise of criticism and self-criticism in the PLA. It has been Deng's wish that his staunch supporters at the head of the two MRs will continue to reduce and eliminate such residual problems (see Category A, Table 8.3).

Finally, it is worth noting the development of the four enlarged MRs. Guangzhou MR remains a source of strength under You Taizhong's leadership whilst Jinan MR would give Li Jiulong greater room for manoeuvring in his modernisation attempts as Henan Military District (formerly under Wuhan MR) is under his jurisdiction now. The enlarged MRs of Chengdu and Lanzhou are charged with the crucial task of ensuring war-preparedness on the southwestern and northwestern frontiers. Leadership in the two MR appears to be fairly independent as there is no conspicuous supporter of Deng Xiaoping's. Most of the leaders have been transferred from other regions. For instance, Lanzhou Commander Zhao Xianshun has a career mostly associated with the northeastern provinces whilst Political Commissar Li Xuanhua was transferred to the northwest from Beijing in 1980.[28] Li's posting to Wulumuqi in 1981 at least provides continuity to the leadership as the two MRs of Wulumuqi and Lanzhou were merged in the summer of 1985 (see Category C, Table 8.3).[29] For Chengdu MR, Commander Fu Quanyou has a long association with the First Field Army generation on the western frontier and he seems to be the key man experienced in frontier defence.[30]

PARTY RECTIFICATION AND THE PLA

For six years after the convening of the Twelfth Party Congress in September 1982, China's reinvigorated Communist Party under Deng Xiaoping has been striving hard to preserve the fruits of modernisation. It is aware of the hazards of China's open door and relaxed economic policy, and what they may bring to bear on the Chinese society at large. To remedy the problems created by modernisation policies, the Party introduced party rectification in various forms in order to prevent the 'germs' of modernisation from infecting the socialist society.[31] Thus since September 1982, goals have been to bring about 'a fundamental change for the better in party style. Party rectification was carried out by stages and in groups from the central to the basic levels to strive to bring about an improvement in party style as scheduled'.[32]

The cherishing of a model Party style will continue until the Party is certain of success. A great deal of effort in this respect has been devoted to rectifying past mistakes and new problems associated with a more relaxed society. These include unhealthy tendencies like corruption, fraud, factionalism and favouritism.[33] The magnitude of these problems and the increased intensity of the Party's investigations of its members suggest that a significant degree of success is still eluding the Party.

Party rectification has the pragmatic goal to eliminate both historical and new problems which stand in the way of modernisation. Party style as understood by members of the Party would appear to be the weapon to get rid of unhealthy tendencies and to help Party members adapt to whatever major changes and reforms have been introduced in the name of economic construction and the well-being of modernisation. If a Party member were to ask what the ideological basis which sustains the reinvigorated Party style is, the answer would probably be that it is the cherishing of socialist spiritual civilisation which promotes socialist ideology and culture and the training of leading cadres who have ideals, high moral standards and good discipline.[34] In addition, cadres will be expected to take positive action to eliminate bourgeois, feudal ideas and unhealthy tendencies in order to improve the spiritual environment.[35] Socialist spiritual civilisation embodies both cultural and ideological aspects.

The fields of art, literature, education and science dominate the cultural whilst the promotion of Marxist revolutionary ideals, morality and discipline sums up the ideological. The Party has set about emulating models and examples of socialist spiritual civilisation. These include 'the five stresses, four beauties and three loves' (decorum, manners, hygiene, discipline, morality; mind, language, behaviour, environment; Party, motherland, socialism), National Ethics and Courtesy Month (in the month of March since 1982), 'civility villages' and 'five-good families' (diligent at work and study; considerate of family members and neighbours; practise family planning and attention to children's education; observe the law and discipline; courteous public behaviour).[36] The Party also claims that the improvement of Party style is reflected in 'the restoration and development of the Party's democratic centralism, its principle of collective leadership, and the normalisation of inner party life'.[37]

A sound understanding of the fundamentals of Marxism-Leninism constitutes the basis for good Party style. Nevertheless, Party rectification, launched since 1982, has not been emphasising the sacrosanct ideological principles of Marxist-Leninism and Mao Zedong Thought. While the Party still cherishes the four basic principles of upholding the socialist road, the people's democratic dictatorship (ie, the dictatorship of the proletariat), the leadership of the Communist Party, and Marxism-Leninism and Mao Zedong Thought, it has taken a pragmatic attitude towards 'raising the level of Marxism'.[38] Hu Qili, a member of the Politburo and the Secretariat of the CPC Central Committee, has been the most outspoken in confirming that certain outdated and specific principles of Marxism could be done away with so long as its basic ones are upheld. The Party regards this approach to be scientific and developmental.[39] A scientific approach toward Marxism is one of upholding its basic principles while doing away with certain outdated specific principles or those that have proved not entirely valid in practice, and replacing them with new principles. This means enriching and developing Marxism in the light of practical experience derived from the new era and the new historical period. In adhering to the basic direction of theoretical work, the theorists should clearly combine theory with practice and apply the Marxist stand, views, and methods in studying problems concerning China and the world. This should be the basic principle for theoretical work.[40]

The Party's pragmatism persists both in its interpretation of Marxism and its ways of solving residual and new problems. Hu Qili called upon theoretical workers (theoreticians) 'to combine theory and practice, and apply the Marxist stand, views and methods in studying problems concerning China and the world'.[41] Thus the best way of cherishing Marxism is to ensure that 'China's immediate problems are solved, and the vehicle for that was to promote a healthy Party style'.[42]

The PLA is part and parcel of Party rectification as unhealthy tendencies relevant to the Party exist in varying degrees at all levels in the PLA. The positive efforts to promote good Party style and spirit have been especially relevant to the PLA as its success is crucial to the PLA's acceptance of major changes and reforms brought about in the last two years. It will be a long and sustained process of ideological education before the PLA can become adjusted to the full impact brought about by the reduction-in-strength, reorganisation, and structural reforms since 1985.

Rectification within the PLA began to pick up momentum in 1982–83, followed by the two scheduled stages of rectification in 1984 and 1985. The CMC claimed that rectification work at the army corps and divisional levels had been completed by 1985. The year 1986 has been devoted to investigations and examinations of grass-roots rectification at the regimental level and below. The inculcation of good Party style and the elimination of unhealthy tendencies remain the consistent theme for rectification.[43]

Yang Shangkun, Vice-Chairman of the CMC, had been supervising rectification in the PLA all along. Together with him, Yu Qiuli, Director of the GPD, Yang Dezhi, Chief of the General Staff and Guo Linxiang, Secretary of the All-Army Discipline Inspection Commission (and Deputy Director of the GDP), constitute the caucus of the CMC which has the task of reinforcing 'revolutionalisation, modernisation and regularisation' through party rectification.[44] In his all-important speech to the Conference of Cadres of Central Organs on 9 January 1986 entitled 'The Army Should March in the Vanguard of Rectifying Party Style', Yang Shangkun pinpointed the PLA's efforts in tackling two major issues.[45] First, the PLA needs several years to handle problems arising from reduction-in-strength, reorganisation and structural reforms. Second, the campaign against unhealthy tendencies will continue for quite some time. To the Party, an improvement in Party style and the inculcation of good Party spirit constitute the remedy. It has been a painstaking task for Yang Shangkun and his team propagating the importance of Party style and instructing PLA units to study key documents by Party cadres on the subject. In addition, they also set about organising the machinery to conduct investigations of units both in the central military organs and the military regions.[46]

Party rectification in the PLA 1982–84: overtures

Party rectification in the PLA in 1982–83 was a preliminary exercise setting the pace for the two-stage campaign in 1984 and 1985 respectively. The Twelfth Party Congress further consolidated Deng's control of the PLA but dissident voices still loomed large at the various levels of the military and the problem of 'three supports and two militaries' still plagued the PLA.[47] Party rectification therefore served as an extremely important weapon for Deng to ensure that the PLA conform to his pragmatist line which gives top priority to economic construction.

With the central organs of the CMC and senior cadres of the military regions as targets, the Party identified for their benefit deviations and the ways that these should be rectified. The Beijing MR Commander, Qin Jiwei, commented on the three difficulties in rectification. These were difficulties in eliminating the 'three categories of people' (sanzhongren), rectifying unhealthy tendencies and launching self-criticism exercises. The 'three categories of people' refers to those who supported the Leftists in the Cultural Revolution, those who were seriously factionalist in their ideas, and those who indulged in beating, smashing and looting.[48] These Leftist tendencies were still entrenched in certain military regions, and were to be eliminated wherever possible. Objections were also raised about the lack of confidence in Communism as many cadres were ambivalent about their ideological orientation. Worse still, many cadres began to pursue self-seeking goals, and some claimed the right to enjoy special privileges because they felt they had contributed much to the Revolution.[49]

Rectification started in earnest in 1983 although the Party had not envisaged a nationwide campaign as yet. Nevertheless, the machinery was set in motion as many central organs like the Standing Party Committee of the Second Artillery Corps were instructed to review their unhealthy tendencies by examining documents on rectification.[50] It was hoped that confidence in rectification could then be increased. The importance of studying documents was likened to the monumental rectification campaign of 1942–44 as the General Logistics Department cherished the Yan'an spirit in undertaking in-depth discussions on the basis of Party documents. Although the scope and intensity of these review sessions could not be compared with the Yan'an experience, the Party had set the required pace for later purposes.[51] Thus the first batch of six party rectification liaison groups was established in January 1984 in order to investigate unhealthy tendencies and improve work on Party style in the General Staff Department, the Navy, the Political Work Academies at Shenyang, Lanzhou and Kunming MRs.[52] One conclusion the CMC had reached by the beginning of 1984 was that investigation work was important, especially in the form of collective investigation (*jiti jiancha*), as the means to maintain a high standard in rectification, so that self-criticism, the eradication of factionalism and other unhealthy tendencies could be eliminated.[53]

Party rectification in 1982–83 ushered in a systematic two-stage campaign which had specific objectives and well-identified units and institutions in mind. The spirit of thorough and collective investigation was extended to the first-stage of the campaign which had the central organs of the CMC and the top leadership in military regions as targets. Thus large-scale discussion sessions were launched to stimulate criticism and self-criticism as the Party was most persistent in eradicating Leftist factional tendencies. Yang Shangkun pointed out that many cadres had been used to the 'Leftist way of doing things' as the norm.[54] The investigations were to be undertaken on the basis of a sound, theoretical framework which could be established as a result of the thorough studies of relevant rectification documents. As if to highlight the Party's determination, in August 1984 leaders of the CMC announced that several senior cadres were criticised for their unhealthy tendencies, and they claimed that the event caused quite a commotion amongst grass-roots units. There were cases of corruption, larceny, and violations of rules and regulations in units in Shenyang, Guangzhou and Lanzhou.[55]

Whilst the CMC was eager to intensify its work on strengthening improvements to Party style and eradicating Leftist tendencies, it also wanted to establish a good image and show that it was not being excessive in its rectification efforts. Thus the principle of 'synchronising rectification and change' (*bianzheng biangai*) was adopted and made prominent as the CMC would not wish to cause undue alarm in those units which had indelible records of 'three supports and two militaries'.[56] Similarly, Beijing MR stressed the principle of 'four don'ts and four permissions' to allay fears of excessive action during investigation and allowed for the opportunity to turn over a new leaf.[57] In February 1985, Yang Shangkun summarised rectification work of 1984, and claimed that the level of political consciousness of cadres had, in general, been raised so that they had a good understanding of the Party line. Second, he claimed that the Cultural Revolution had been thoroughly negated and that factionalism and Leftist tendencies had been eliminated.[58] The fact that the second-stage of party rectification was launched in early 1985 revealed that Yang's pronouncement was more one of euphoria than a definitive statement.

During this period, the Party concentrated on the elimination of spiritual pollution in the PLA, both on the theoretical, the literary and artistic fronts. Deng Xiaoping defines the substance of spiritual pollution as disseminating all varieties of corrupt and decadent ideologies of the bourgeoisie, and other exploiting classes, and disseminating sentiments of distrust towards the socialist and Communist cause, and to the Communist Party leadership. Deng's pronouncement on the occasion of the Second Plenum of the Twelfth Party Committee on 11–12 October 1983, officially launched the campaign against spiritual pollution, which aimed at the rectification of Rightist tendencies and strengthening Party leadership.[59] The scope of the campaign was later broadened to address the question of alienation of the socialist society. In the process, both literary bureaucrats like Zhou Yang and intellectuals were criticised. They were therefore required to positively support the elimination of spiritual pollution. In other words, there was to be no more indulgence in bourgeois liberalisation.[60] Hu Qiaomu, the Party theoretician, blamed the random use of concepts of humanism and alienation as the source for individualism and scepticism in a socialist society. The remedy for that was that individuals should follow the Party's definition of truth rather than their own.[61] These words represent the Party's reaction to intellectuals' enthusiastic response to Deng Xiaoping's support for freedom of creation, theory and variety in 1979.[62] The process of liberalisation of thought unleashed by Deng Xiaoping indeed created problems for the PLA. The cases of Bai Hua and Zhao Yiya are classic examples.

It was the GPD which upheld the banner of socialist spiritual civilisation, and in 1982 started to criticise bourgeois liberalisation within the PLA. Thus Bai Hua's famous film *Bitter Love* (*kulian*) was criticised by the Party mainly because it symbolised excessive liberalisation (*ziyouhua*), especially when the challenge came from such close quarters — Bai Hua is a cadre in the PLA. It is therefore no wonder that most of the criticism of Bai Hua's film was published either in the *Liberation Army Daily* or in related journals in 1981–82.[63] Excessive liberal thinking committed by Bai Hua in his film, which he then criticised himself for such mistakes in December 1981, can be summarised as follows:[64] First, in depicting the continuous sufferings of hero Ling Chenguang in the Cultural Revolution and after, the film mistakenly attributed all failures in China to the personal worship of Mao Zedong. Second, excessive liberal thinking in the film exhibited bourgeois ideas that challenge the Four Basic Principles upon which Chinese socialism is based.

Yet again, liberal-thinking intellectuals were restrained by the Party when they became excessive. This is not surprising in Chinese Communist history. Nevertheless, Bai Hua's case is all the more interesting because it took the Party some time before it condemned the writer in the *Liberation Army Daily*. At the same time, the closing of this case did not lead to any purges: Bai Hua was reported to be in Yunnan writing on the minorities.[65] It was well known that Deng Xiaoping and Hu Yaobang did not encourage the launching of campaigns to rectify Party deviation, and in December 1981 Hu Yaobang declared that the Bai Hua case should be closed. After the writer had criticised himself, he was still regarded as a Party member and a writer.[66] At the same time, there was reason to believe that the Army, which had been surpervising Bai Hua's work, did not take kindly to Bai Hua's liberalised thinking as the man was a 'bad influence' in the Army. The volume of attacks on him in PLA-related journals bears witness to the determination of the Army (ie, the GPD) to identify the case of Bai Hua as the very epitome fo the anti-Right campaign.[67] It is equally obvious that the Party was not willing to take a hard line for the sake of political equilibrium. Thus the end result was that Bai Hua was required to criticise himself, and he did. But there was no purge.

The second case regarding the Zhao Yiya 'scandal' in August 1982 denotes bourgeois liberalisation of the highest order as Zhao's criticism of Deng Xiaoping's policies were allowed to be published in the *Liberation Army Daily* on 28 August 1982.[68] It also reflects problems Deng had with the General Political Department under Wei Quoqing's leadership and suggests the lack of unanimity of support for Deng's open-door policy. Zhao Yiya raised four points in his article entitled 'Communist Thought is the Core of Socialist Spiritual Civilisation'. First, Zhao maintained that Party cadres tended to ostensibly emphasise 'civilisation' at the expense of neglecting 'spirit' in the sponsorship of socialist spiritual civilisation.

Second, Zhao objected to the claim that there could not be high ideals without culture, and cited model heroes including Lei Feng to support the point as they did not have high cultural standards. Third, he believed that the cherishing of Communist thought from a leadership position did not constitute 'ultra-Leftism'. Finally, Zhao criticised certain senior cadres on the ideological, literary and media front for committing mistakes in bourgeois liberalisation and acting against the four basic ideological principles.[69] With one month's delay, the embarrassed Party reacted vehemently by labelling Zhao Yiya as propagandising Leftist ideas in the name of opposing bourgeois liberalisation. In turn, these ideas were contrary to Marxism. The *Liberation Army Daily*, which launched the counterattack, admitted to the seriousness of Leftist thoughts as Zhao's article was permitted to be published in the paper earlier.[70]

Party rectification and PLA reforms since 1985

To subordinate the PLA to the overall needs of national economic construction, the CMC had been contributing to balancing the national budget since 1981 when the defence expenditure, like many other sectors, began to experience cuts. It was also realised since the early 1980s that the oversized PLA (which then stood at 4.2 million men) should be reduced. It became a reality in July 1985 when the CMC announced the reduction-in-strength of one million troops to be realised in stages over two years. Associated with this traumatic experience were significant changes pertaining to structural reforms and adaptations like the merging and reduction in the number of MRs from eleven to seven.[71] The CMC had been giving a great deal of publicity to the smooth execution of these policies, but not all was well. Yang Shangkun observed that it would 'require several years and a lot of complicated work to thoroughly fulfil the reduction-in-strength and reformative tasks put forward by Comrade Xiaoping'.[72] More specifically, Yang Shangkun also publicly denounced factionalism in PLA Academies which was in the way of reforms and the promotion of Party style. In this connection, Yang was referring to the continuation of Leftist problems which had bedevilled the Cultural Revolution, plaguing the Academies in their work to improve themselves.[73]

Targets set for reduction-in-strength could be achieved through retirement, resignation, transfers to other units and to civilian jobs (that is, demobilisation).[74] One notices a great deal of publicity has been given to how cadres and commanders of units had extended to the CMC full cooperation. On the other hand, there is ample literature on problems that have emerged. In the first place, the execution of such policy, to say the least, has been traumatic because of the sheer size involved, and the impact on the daily life of cadres and commanders in units all over China when adaptations to a new civilian lifestyle may prove difficult.[75] Quite understandably, evidence of resistance to these changes is ample. There are also obscurantists and opportunists who have found the fluid situation to work to their advantage as they resort to means of advancing their own causes and benefits. These are the problems that the CMC has devoted a great deal of effort trying to rectify serious mistakes, and to help achieve those specific targets *vis-a-vis* reforms and changes withi the PLA.[76]

The PLA and the 'Anti-Bourgeois Liberalisation' Campaign

In conducting rectification in the PLA, the Party had made it clear that political work should ensure that the so-called 'Anti-Bourgeois Liberalisation' campaign could exert itself in the army. As early as July 1985, Yu Qiuli announced his support for Anti-Bourgeois Liberalisation in an article in the *Red Flag* entitled 'Communist Members Must Consciously Strengthen Party Spirit When Conducting Reform'. He maintained that:

> Some party members were badly affected by the 'Cultural Revolution' and corroded by the corrupt thinking of capitalism and feudalism; individualism, liberalism, anarchism and sectarianism have not been properly overcome and the emergence of a new trend of deviatiations is a striking reflection.[77]

According to Yu the strengthening of Party spirit was responsible for successes in bringing about military reforms and rectifying deviations amongst new Party Members who had not undergone vigorous training.[78] Basically, Yu believed that the strengthening of Party spirit required Party members to emphasise the following: (1) follow the general policy in favour of economic construction; (2) take initiatives in executing Party and government policies; (3) give priorities to the interests of the Party and the people; (4) observe Party principles in work and oppose favouritism and corruption; and (5) strictly observe Party discipline.[79]

Yu's directive highlighted the objectives of Party rectification in the PLA for the period 1985–87, emphasising the need to oppose Anti-Bourgeois Liberalisation. In January 1987, the Central Military Commission issued a bulletin entitled 'Concerning the Resolution on Political Work in the Army in the New Era', which reasserted the need to 'insist on the four basic principles, oppose Bourgeois Liberalisation and strengthen construction of Socialist Spiritual civilisation'.[80] The Resolution was initially discussed at the Enlarged Conference of the CMC held in mid-December 1986, where Yu Qiuli explained its meaning. Whilst the Resolution itself emphasised the continuing need to oppose Bourgeois Liberalisation, Yu Qiuli's explanation underlined the need to educate Party members rather than conduct struggles against them, and to use political work to support defence modernisation.[81]

Yu asserted that political work constituted the army's life-line, the function of which should be 'to serve' and 'to guarantee'.[82] Political work, particularly, 'should serve the construction of Socialist modernisation and of a modernised and professionalised revolutionary arm, (it should) guarantee the Party's absolute leadership of the army and the quality of the people's army. The construction of Socialist spiritual civilisation in the army and the people and between the army and the administration, the raising of warfighting capabilities and the completion of various tasks in the army.'[83] After three years of rectification in the army, the CMC has formulated the view that political work should ensure that Bourgeois Liberalisation be eliminated, and that the objectives of defence modernisation should be supported so that the PLA can quicken its pace in transforming itself into a genuinely modernised and professional defence force.[84] The tide has apparently turned in 1987 as the need to quicken defence modernisation seems to have eclipsed the drive to intensify Party rectification.

A detailed study of some of the typical problems the CMC encountered in conducting Party rectification in 1985 is now in order. Guangzhou MR seemed to have more than a fair share of these problems in 1985. A meeting of secretaries of Party committees at army and divisional levels in December 1985 revealed 'ideological unrest among officers and slackness in work style of the Army'.[85] Here, it seemed that senior cadres were deliberately resisting these new reforms as they would affect their own status either because they themselves had to be transferred or demobilised. It could also be that they would be losing ground in their power structure as they might have to accept officers transferred from other units, or that their units had to be incorporated with others or substantially cut in size and funding. In December 1985 it was reported in Guangzhou MR, that some units were challenging the Party's principle of 'democratic centralism in party committees, of unity among party committees, and the problem of failure to investigate and deal with new unhealthy practices and certain leading cadres' use of power for personal gain'.[86] The acuteness in Guangzhou MR must have alarmed the

CMC as the whole contingent of senior cadres comprising Deng Yingchao, Chairman of the Central People's Political Consultative Council, veteran Xu Xiangqian, Vice-Chairman of the CMC, Yu Qiuli and He Changgong, former member of the Standing Committee of the Central Advisory Commission, all descended upon Guangzhou and met with Party committee members of the Military Region.[87]

Apart from the sheer trauma of facing tremendous reduction in funding, and the demand for greater efficiency, senior commanders would have to adapt themselves to changes brought about by significant measures like the reduction of the number of military regions from eleven to seven, and the transfer of power of the People's Armed Forces Department (PAFD) from dual leadership (Party-PLA) to control under the local Party committees. The first measure had relegated the status of the former Fuzhou, Wulumuqi, Kunming and Wuhan MRs to that of military districts. The full implications of such changes would require further research. The second measure effectively empowers local Party committees and their secretaries to supervise and train not only the militia but also the new system of reservists with which China hopes to strengthen its war-preparedness since the new Military Service Law was introduced in May 1984.[88] Although PLA cadres still participate in the program, there is no doubt that the Party wants to be in full control of the situation. Again, one expects backlashes to have occurred at the local levels where PLA cadres in the PAFDs had been charged with important duties of supervising and training the militia. It is therefore not surprising that He Qizong, Deputy Chief of the General Staff, identified the restructuring of the PAFDs at the county level as one of the three objectives of PLA reforms for 1986.[89]

The most positive way for the Party to rectify deviations was to be persistent in promoting good work in Party style and Party spirit. Thus Yang Shangkun commented on the need to strengthen education in Party spirit as follows:[90]

> As regards party spirit, it is in practice to insist on the four principles, to possess ideals and to have high morals, culture and discipline.

In March–April 1985, units at the division and corps level in Guangzhou, Kunming and Shengyang MRs concentrated on investigation work to promote Party spirit. In Kunming MR, investigations emphasised cadres' attitudes toward Party affairs and their understanding of the overall situation.[91] In Guangzhou MR, investigations covered disciplines, ideological work and Party style in which these investigations were supported by requirements for cadres to study the relevant documents thoroughly.[92] These documents would include important pronouncements on Party policies since the convening of the Twelfth Party Congress in September 1982. Circulars regarding major PLA reforms and changes since 1984 were especially relevant. The important speeches by leading cadres in the National Conference of Party Delegates in September 1985 and the subsequent Conference of Cadres of Central Organs on 6–9 January 1986, all provided the basis for the PLA to conduct thorough Party rectification.[93] Yang Shangkun's speech on 9 January on 'The Army Should March in the Vanguard of Rectifying Party Style' highlighted the PLA's role in the exercise. Emerging out of these important deliberations were three documents which provided the basis for debates in plenary sessions of the All-Army Discipline Inspection Commission of the CMC which had been led by Guo Linxiang, the Secretary. These include 'The Outline for the Report on Issues about Rectifying Party Style', 'A Draft Resolution on Certain Issues concerning the Rectification of Party Members' Ideology and Work Style under the New Situation' and 'A Draft Circular on Strengthening Discipline'.[94] Although these documents were not as sophisticated as the 22 documents which launched the Party Rectification Campaign of 1942–44, they were the products of several years of experience in Party efforts in eliminating unhealthy tendencies and deviations. All in all, the Yan'an spirit of Party rectification had been present in some respects. In both cases, the promotion of Party spirit was considered significant in maintaining uniformity in Party leadership.[95] In both situations, the Party was in urgent need of reform and for specific goals to be achieved. Both encountered problems in the form of unhealthy tendencies or deviations which made it necessary for rectification to be undertaken through investigations and the process of criticism and self-criticism. Both stressed the importance of avoiding excessive Leftist tendencies in rectification. Where the present exercise appeared to be less effective was due to the absence of charismatic leadership and the inculcation of a well-defined ideological line that Mao Zedong was responsible for initiating in the 1940s. By the same token, whilst the present rectification efforts would be fairly effective in minimising unhealthy tendencies and educating cadres to accept the various PLA reforms and change, they would probably fall short of inculcating a strong sense of political consciousness among PLA cadres which the Party fears might lead to ideological overtones. Instead, the Party would be content with achieving pragmatic targets of eliminating unhealthy tendencies and obstacles to modernisation, and of promoting high morals, culture and discipline.[96] An additional impact of Party rectification and PLA reforms launched since July 1985 has been the diminution of the problem of 'three supports and two militaries'. Through natural attrition as a result of requirements to dismiss or retire senior cadres in the Party's general exercise to streamline the PLA, many commanders with Leftist history must have been withdrawn from active service (see Table 8.1).

Investigation work in the Military Regions: Rectification at the grass-roots level

Yang Shangkun remarked in 1983 that Party rectification would take at least three years to complete, implying that major success would not be achieved before the Party could launch its successive, scheduled campaigns to rectify past mistakes, unhealthy tendencies, and to solicit support for the recent reforms and changes introduced into the PLA.[97] In the wake of the two-stage Party rectification program in 1984 and 1985, which extended from the central organs of the CMC subsequently to units at the army corps and division levels, the Party immediately reinforced rectification efforts at the end of 1985 and early 1986 by launching an investigation exercise.[98] Work groups/teams were dispatched by military regions to units at the regiment level and below. A great deal of publicity has been given to 'serving the real needs at the grass-roots level',[99] with a view to understanding and solving practical problems. It is also quite obvious that these investigations are the means to intensity rectification and to ensure that grass-roots units can also be 'cleansed' of deviations and be receptive to reforms. It is too early to gauge the extent of success of these recent measures, but it is apparent that all military regions have been given detailed schedules of these operations. The Party hopes that investigation work will turn out to be an effective exercise in controlling PLA excesses vis-a-vis factionalism, obscurantism, deviations and resistance to reforms.

Guangzhou, Beijing and Nanjing MRs set about establishing the vertical linkage between the regional command and grass-roots units in late 1985 in accordance with a well-planned machinery which involved the entire offices of the regional commands over an extended period, reflecting the intensity and magnitude of the investigations. Work groups or teams have been established, comprising senior commanders and commissars who would spend as long as one month with grass-roots units attempting to identify and solve problems. These groups have the authority to bypass bureaucratic channels and make decisions which would strengthen ties between the regional command and the units.[100] As the head of these investigations teams is often the MR commander himself, or his deputy, prompt and useful decisions can be made, contributing to the solidarity of the military region.[101] For instance, Wang Chengbin, Deputy Commander of Nanjing MR, boasted of the record of having solved 148 out of 154 problems presented to him by PLA units over a span of one month in October 1985.[102] As regards cases where no immediate solutions could be found, the heads of these work groups/teams would ask for instructions from higher authorities.[103]

The magnitude and intensity of investigations undertaken by Nanjing MR for the entire month of October 1985 are reflected in the establishment of 24 work groups which comprised 260 senior cadres.[104] As military regions went about their tasks, it became quite obvious that units took advantage of these opportunities to establish two-way communications with a view to making their opinions on rectification heard as well as improving their general conditions. For instance, in visiting the 9th Company of a certain armoured infantry regiment (one of the ten companies involved), Qin Jiwei, Commander of Beijing MR, was told that 100 suggestions and proposals on rectification were presented to their superiors. In response, Qin encouraged their democratic style as long as the correct work style was followed.[105] In Nanjing MR, Xiang Shouzhi, Commander of the MR, and other senior cadres, were confronted in their investigations with requests to improve general conditions. These included mundane matters ranging from inadequate supply of vehicles arising from retrenchment, to a request for a movie projector.[106] Whilst there is no evidence that these requests and appeals had overshadowed the intended objectives for Party rectification, the CMC would certainly not wish to allow these activities to eclipse the main thrusts of the investigations. The performance of work group investigations in Guangzhou MR definitely confirmed the CMC's determination to undertake thorough Party rectification. This Military Region probably had the worst case of unhealthy tendencies reported, prompting senior cadres to send task forces to rectify unhealthy tendencies. Unlike other military regions which involved a fair number of work groups (up to 24) in the investigation exercise, Guangzhou MR concentrated on intensive investigation work which involved only four work groups, headed by the five leading cadres in the MR.[107] But it was clear that the CMC had selected well-identified units which were black spots for rectification.

These included four units at the army level and eight at the divisional level, some of which had violated political and economic policies, pursued unhealthy trends because of self-seeking interests and committed crimes like fraud.[108] The intensity of the investigation was reflected in the elaborate preparatory work. Discussions were held between the five leading cadres (headed by Commander You Taizhong and Commissar Zhang Zhongxian) and the Party Committee of the relevant units in order to identify the specific problems and promote ideological education. Thus the study of Marxist theories, the analysis of positive and negative cases, the learning of heroes and models and the undertaking of criticism and self-criticism were the four areas in the education for senior cadres in units which were plagued by ideological unrest and a slack work style.[109] The four work groups involved the Party committees of the twelve units in enlarged meetings in order to conduct serious sessions of criticism and self-criticism. These soul-searching investigations are fully justified in view of the seriousness of unhealthy tendencies in Guangzhou MR since the uncovering of the notorious and illegal motor vehicle sales by units of Hainan Military District.[110]

Acute cases uncovered in October 1985 included the violation of production and business operation policies by the Guilin City People's Armed Forces Department, the illegal conversion of a hotel into residental homes for individuals by Shaoguan Military Sub-district and the promotion, against regulations, of the wife of a certain senior cadre at the divisional level who worked in a service cooperative.[111] The most serious case involved leaders of a certain division who set about fraudulently purchasing imported cars and vans against MR regulations and resold them for profit in Xi'an. When it resulted in the death of a battalion instructor at the hands of a certain car owner, they falsified the date of a certain contract on two occasions. When these scandals were uncovered, four work teams on four occasions under the MR Commander and Commissar held heart-to-heart talks with the seven members of the standing Party committee of that particular division.[112] The commander and commissar were asked to make self-criticism and the Party committee made a self-examination report to the higher authorities. It was thus reported that Guangzhou MR punished the former two on 31 October 1985 'by giving them a warning and a serious warning within the Party respectively'.[113] What seemed questionable was that despite the tremendous efforts put into the investigations of this particular case, the two involved seemed to have got away quite lightly. The warnings issued would seem too mild as punishment for mistakes which were so serious in nature. It makes one wonder whether the entire Party rectification exercise might appear futile if the Party is not resolute in its efforts to cleanse the hierarchy of unhealthy tendencies.

Deng's PLA 1986

Ever since 1979 when Deng Xiaoping allowed more freedom of expression, creation and theory and less of Party control in China, Party-Army relations have experienced various changes in accordance with the major political trends. The interaction of Party-Army relations has been characterised by Deng's preference for economic modernisation and his increasing success in dominating the Party with his pragmatic line. In the process Deng intends to transform the PLA into a modernised and professional defence force which will be given greater autonomy in deliberating its defence strategy against China's enemies. At the same time, Deng expects that the PLA with its newly acquired identity will refrain from meddling with politics. Over the period 1979–86, the Party has through different stages and various manoeuvres re-exerted its influence on the PLA.

The first landmark of success is the Twelfth Party Congress in September 1982 when Deng was able to clear China of Hua Guofeng's innuendoes. Nevertheless, entrenched Leftist influence in the PLA persisted. This was compounded by the major problem faced by China — the backlash of its open-door policy which the Party labelled as spiritual pollution. In the ensuing Party rectification launched in 1983, the PLA has been educated as well as modernised to become more apolitical. Reforms and streamlining in the PLA since July 1985 have continued to represent the Party's wish to build up the PLA's image as a professional defence force which looks to the Party for political guidance. This process of transformation is still taking place. Despite problems, Deng Xiaoping seems to have gone from strength to strength in steering the PLA in the right direction in support of efforts to institutionalise 'Dengism' in China.

Both the 'pragmatist' Deng and the 'visionary' Mao have been able to use their grand ideological visions and the cravings of the Chinese people 'for a better life that promise miraculous changes just around the corner'.[114] Deng Xiaoping's paternalistic authority and his promise of a prosperous economy have worked in favour of the Deng regime. The rectification campaign in the PLA has further confirmed the Party's successes in exercising social control. As China continues to steer a relatively even course between exercising authority and liberalising controls at a time when the citizens seem to be uncritical of the rulers, one finds the PLA to have made significant contribution to the stable political climate as it has become itself more subservient to the Party.[115]

To western observers, the risk of instability in the PLA power structure is often brought out as a concern for China's future as most of the military leaders are in their seventies. They therefore fear the creation of a political vacuum as a result of imminent deaths and retirement which may prove to be a destabilishing factor.[116] It is hoped that this chapter has demonstrated that the second and third echelon cadres have emerged as a significant political force in the military regions, and more so in the general departments. Given time, they will definitely be capable of taking over from the Long March veterans. Their task is also made easier by the way that the PLA is now perceived as a loyal arm of the State and an institutionalised model of meritocratic standards and policies.[117] It is apolitical and is an effervescent proponent of what modernisation stands for.

Epilogue: October – December 1987

The convening of the Thirteenth Party Congress in October 1987 has revealed new developments in Party–Army relations which witnessed the emergence of a younger military leadership and indicated Chinese emphasis on professionalisation. Whilst Deng Xiaoping has retired from both the Politiburo and the Party Central Committee, he remains Chairman of the CMC. Despite Yang Shangkun's advanced age and reports that he may take up either the Presidency or Chairmanship of the Standing Committee of the People's Congress, it is now confirmed that Yang Shangkun remains Permanent Vice-Chairman of the CMC. In addition, Zhao Ziyang, the Party General Secretary, has been appointed Vice-Chairman of the CMC. The intention to establish Zhao Ziyang's position in the PLA is obvious, although it will take some time before he can replace Deng, who has found it necessary to remain at the helm. As regards the three general departments under the CMC, all three heads have been replaced by younger people, two of whom were transferred from the military regions. Thus Chi Haotian, formerly Political Commissar of Jinan MR, has been appointed Chief of the General Staff in the place of Yang Dezhi, who retired from both the Politburo and the Party Central Committee. Yang Baibing, formerly Political Commissar of Beijing MR, has replaced Yu Qiuli as Director of General Political Department, whilst Hong Xuezhi's Deputy, Zhao Nanqi, has replaced the former to become Chief of the General

Logistics Department. It is important to note that both Chi Haotian and Yang Baibing were transferred to the General Departments from the military regions. It signifies greater reliance on commanders and cadres who have been exposed to the practical needs of the military regions at a time when the pace of defence modernisation has been quickened. The last transfer was made when Yang Dezhi was appointed Chief of General Staff. Chi Haotian at the age of 61 is probably the best person there is for the important position of Chief of General Staff. His experience in the Korean War and previous appointment as Deputy Chief of General Staff must have accounted for his selection. His appointment will probably bring about stronger ties between the central military elite and commanders of the MRs. With the appointments of the three new heads of the General Departments, it means that a more youthful leadership and greater determination to foster defence modernisation are guaranteed. In the meantime, Zhang Aiping's position as Minister of Defence has been taken over by Qin Jiwei, who has also been made a member of the Politburo.

Memberships of the military on the Politburo and the Party Central Committee reveal a significant trend in development. Whilst the number of Politburo members has significantly decreased, that on the Party Central Committee has conversely increased. There is probably dissatisfaction expressed by the old guard who would regard recent developments as the erosion of military influence on the Party. Nevertheless, the retirement of numerous commanders and commissars in recent years has certainly led to the emergence of a more youthful military leadership which favours professionalism and believes in the separation of responsibilities for the Party and the PLA. These younger commanders seem to have received their rewards as they become either full or alternate members of the Central Committee.

Conclusion

Long term economic modernisation will guarantee for China a prominent role in the world and will lead to the growth of its economic and trading interests. To secure these interests in the context of international rivalry, China will need to develop adequate warfighting capabilities and a workable defence strategy against external threats. The priority given to economic modernisation rather than defence development in the 1980s might have disappointed PLA leaders, but an economically stronger China will provide a powerful infrastructure for developments in defence technology, and will support the evolution of a modernised defence force capable of resisting an invading enemy.

CHINA AND THE STRATEGIC BALANCE

As a nuclear power with limited second-strike capability, China has reinforced its position as a force to be reckoned with by the superpowers. Its professed independent foreign policy is a forceful vehicle in the exertion of influence on the regional strategic balance. China also claims that its foreign policy is determined independently on the merits of each case and in the interest of the Chinese people. In dealing with the Sino–Soviet border conflict and the Kampuchean question, China has demonstrated its skill in prudent crisis-avoidance as well as in playing a 'semi-US' and a 'semi-Soviet' card. Increased US technological and economic assistance, which includes cooperation in nuclear energy matters and the transfer of military technology, is adequate evidence of China's tilt toward the US. Weinberger's tour of China in October 1986 and the port visit of three US naval vessels to Qingdao in November 1986 further confirm that ties between the two countries have been closely maintained. As if to compensate for any backlash arising from the tilt, China has chosen to respond favourably to Gorbachev's 'peace offensive' launched from Vladivostok on 28 July 1986. Soviet announcements of troop withdrawals from Afghanistan and Mongolia, and of the continuation of border talks at the deputy ministerial level could have long term positive effects on Sino–Soviet relations. As regards the Kampuchean question, the wind of change seems to have put pressure on the SRV to be more responsive to proposals from interested parties for a possible solution. China seems to have succeeded in making the USSR realise that this particular obstacle is standing in the way of Gorbachev's grand plan to host a Helsinki-style Asian forum and to get the USSR accepted as a member of the Pacific community. Indeed, Moscow may realise by now that conflict in Cambodia has outlived its usefulness, and is detrimental to the recent Soviet peace initiatives.

Progress toward the normalisation of Sino–Soviet relations will add to China's prestige in the Asia-Pacific region. Recent Chinese diplomatic initiatives have continued to illustrate China's efforts to play a prominent role in international politics. At this stage China feels obliged to be responsive to Gorbachev's peace initiatives, and the prospects for greater stability in the Asia-Pacific region are good.

NEW WARFIGHTING CAPABILITIES: THE MODERNISED PLA 1986–87

Given its commitments to global and regional security interests, China needs to improve its warfighting capabilities and evolve a workable defence strategy so that it can conduct itself competently as the pivot in the great power triangle.

With its defence force being maintained at 6–8 per cent of GNP after it has undergone a major reduction in strength and restructuring exercise, there are good prospects for China to develop warfighting capabilities that would best prepare the PLA for a future war against aggression. A consistent balance of foreign technology and self-reliance has contributed significantly to defence modernisation, although it does not necessarily narrow the technological gap between China and the USSR, the 'stronger' enemy. China's war-preparedness has also been improved as a result of recent efforts to strengthen its war mobilisation system. Thus the enforcement of the revised Military Service Law introduced in May 1984 has steered China closer to its objective of maintaining a leaner, younger, better educated, modern army which is in turn supported by the large and well-trained Reserve Forces. Nevertheless, China is experiencing similar problems to those facing western countries that rely on the mobilisation of large Reserve Forces to support their regular formations when war breaks out. Prospects will look better in the 1990s when China can be more confident of its combat-ready Reserve Forces.

Emerging out of the reform process is the development of skills in combined arms and joint operations as the foundation for improved warfighting capabilities. The reorganisation of field armies into group armies sets in motion basic changes to force structure and C^3I which are still under development. Arising from this process are encouraging improvements in the various arms and services of the defence force.

Specific measures to meet the presumed goals of this process have been indicated over the past few years. The appearance of a new range of AFVs (mainly APCs and upgraded main battle tanks), and gradual increases to tactical logistic and general purpose transport vehicles fleets, coupled with the re-organisation of field armies into group armies, have clearly placed the ground forces on the path to an enhanced tactical mobility. At the same time, the ground force's anti-armour capability is being improved through the deployment of first generation ATGM, and the fitting of more effective main gun systems to its tanks. Improvements in long-range and self-propelled artillery will enable the ground forces to strike deeper into the enemy's combat zone, while the gradual upgrading of offensive air support capabilities in both equipment and procedures should raise the PLA's level of battlefield survivability and combat power over the battlefield. The strenuous efforts being made to improve the vital areas of C^3I and EW will undoubtedly achieve a 'combat multiplier' effect during the PLA's operations.

Yet the pace and scale of these developments is the critical factor in assessing the degree of capability enhancement that can be achieved, while innovative concepts such as active defence in selected forward areas, and guerrilla artillery operations, highlight fundamental problems that the PLA does not seem to have resolved. These include the provision of effective logistic support to formations isolated from the mainstream support system. Likewise, the ability of the PLA's reconnaissance and intelligence resources to rapidly and accurately identify developing threats far beyond the FLOT, such as the concentration of Soviet OMGs in their assembly areas, is also in doubt. Even if this ability were to be achieved, there is little to indicate that the PLA has developed the air and ground resources required in the air-land battle concept to effectively attack such targets in the face of formidable Soviet air defences. Moreover, weaknesses in the PLA's repair and logistics systems will take time to overcome. Thus there are considerable doubts as to the ability of the PLA, and the Air Force in particular, to sustain operations at the high intensity that could be expected during a major confrontation with Soviet forces.

The recent history of China's force development has been characterised by protracted negotiations over selected importations of foreign technology, laborious indigenous research and development programs, and exhaustive revision of operational concepts. This suggests that, even if defence expenditure were to be raised sharply (an unlikely event in the near to mid-term), the attainment of enhanced tactical capabilities on a force-wide scale will take a long time to accomplish. Nevertheless, progress at even a slow pace should help raise the PLA's capability in continental defence, thus contributing to China's overall strategic deterrence.

At the strategic level, force development has also been a gradual process, but more impressive in relative terms. The attainment of a second-strike capability for the PLA's strategic nuclear forces, the extension of missile ranges, and the emergence of the SLBM arm, place increasing restraints on any would-be aggressor. Supported by improved satellite reconnaissance systems, these forces are increasing their effectiveness and survivability. At the same time, modest conventional strategic forces are being created through developments in the Navy's surface warfare, naval aviation strike, submarine and amphibious warfare capabilities. If the Navy can match these developments with improvements to ASW, logistic support, long range maritime reconnaissance and air defence, China's ability to deter attack from the sea and to project its own power into the Western Pacific and Southeast Asian regions will be greatly enhanced. Although certain improvements seem imminent, such as construction programs for new principal surface combatants and the acquisition of in-flight refuelling aircraft, once again financial constraints and accessibility to foreign technology are largely determining the pace of development. Thus no 'quantum leap' is currently in sight. The direction of China's efforts indicate, however, that it has identified the major deficiencies, and intends to redress them in its own good time.

As newly acquired capabilities, focused mainly on the ability to conduct combined arms and joint operations, open up a new dimension in power projection, China's Navy becomes an effective means to preserve its regional interests. The Navy is the forward looking service of the Chinese defence force, keen to quicken the pace of modernisation in order to defend china's sovereign and maritime rights. Liu Huaqing has identified developments in missiles, electronic warfare and automation as evidence of China's success in naval modernisation.

In the context of the Asia-Pacific region, a growing Chinese Navy with increasing 'green water' and some 'blue water' capabilities which is 'on side' with the US will add to the strength of the nations of the Pacific littoral in countering Soviet strategic designs. The persistence of close Sino–US relations will guarantee that the modernised Chinese fleet will contribute in varying degrees to the US maritime strategy to destroy the Soviet fleets by 'seizing the initiative' and 'carrying the fight to the enemy'. On the other hand, the Sino–Soviet *rapprochement* could profoundly alter the existing military balance in the Pacific and the world, according to US Admiral Foley.

China's present sea denial capabilities are effective against probable Soviet amphibious attacks whilst Chinese naval presence will continue to demonstrate China's resolve to maintain its economic and political interests, especially in the disputed waters of the South China Sea. Any Soviet amphibious attack on the Liaodong Peninsula would therefore be met by Chinese submarines in constricted waters, an improved Chinese joint operations capability and effective coastal defence. Should China become a signatory of UNCLOS III in order to establish claims to the 200-mile EEZ, its involvement in maritime disputes and conflicts would increase. The nine-day exercise near Iwo Jima in May 1986 reveals the Chinese Navy's latest development in strategic doctrine and combat capability. The Task Force exercise, involving different Task Groups and the coordination of various operational elements, suggests considerable improvements have been made in the Navy's C^3I system.

Looking into the future, China may contemplate imposing a naval blockade on Taiwan and launching a strategic mine offensive against the SRV in order to achieve important political objectives. The Taiwan case would comprise a combination of naval operations aimed at minimising any probable escalation or US intervention. Thus the options of a wartime quarantine, a naval blockade and a mine blockade would be open to the Chinese who could decide on the exact formula to achieve 're-unification'. A probable mine offensive against the SRV could be achieved by initial minelaying against northern SRV ports, undertaken by the Naval Air Force despite the challenge from SRV air defence. The Chinese submarine force can also conduct sustained 'reseeding' operations for a prolonged period.

Despite financial constraints, the Chinese Navy has made significant progress in modernisation and will continue to acquire more 'green water' and 'blue water' capabilities as well as playing a more active role in the waters of East and Southeast Asia.

The support base provides China with resources which sustain its warfighting capabilities. Two significant components of the support base are the transportation system and the Reserve Forces. Whilst the former primarily guarantees the 'new construction' of industrial bases, the Chinese believe that it is half military in nature and that it serves the military directly during wartime. The Reserve Forces guarantee the country's war-preparedness and make it possible for China to maintain a smaller, though modernised, defence force. Since China's success in reorganising its original eleven military regions into seven, railway connectivity has become more prominent as the means to improve the level of cost-effectiveness and self-sufficiency in logistics and combat power in the military regions. Double-tracking and electrification will further improve the military regions' defence in depth capabilities and linkage with neighbouring MRs. Lanzhou and Chengdu MRs are classic examples.

The Chinese Reserve Forces support the country's sensible development of a 'leaner, meaner' defence force. China seems determined to ensure that the estimated 5.3 million reservists are war-prepared. The newly formed Reserve Divisions are expected to reach a satisfactory standard in combined arms and joint warfare capabilities. Guangzhou MR's record of achieving the M+2 day objective and training about 1000 men in units of the three services in June 1984 may remain for some time a model the State hopes all military regions can follow for the mobilisation of individual reservists. Leadership and training for reservists also appear to resemble western models, especially the Swiss one. The speed and procedures for mobilisation, the retention of reservist ability and the training of reserve officers are the main features of this similarity.

Bringing the People's Armed Forces Department under Party leadership nation-wide in 1986 signals China's determination to integrate economic construction and militia work. Training has become a part of the responsibility system. Rich provinces like Jiangsu and Liaoning find that they can adequately accommodate this system. In less well-to-do provinces like Gansu and Guangxi, however, militia training has to be curtailed to make way for economic construction. Integrating productive labour with militia duties is now seen as a way for the militia to become wealthy, when one-third of the time of the militiamen can be devoted to acquiring production skills and actual production. Despite constraints, the capabilities of the armed basic militia have been enhanced as both urban and rural militia units are expected to take part in air defence, anti-tank and anti-airborne operations in the future war. Training has also been centralised to improve efficiency. Improved militia capabilities in combat and logistics are demonstrated in the defence of the Sino–Vietnamese border, as well as in exercises in which the militia artillery units are expected to become an integral part of the strategic defence in Chinese territory.

Improved warfighting capabilities as demonstrated in the various arms and services of the PLA and in the support base, provide the foundation for China's defence against external threats. The result is that the Chinese are now more confident in their strategic defence against the 'stronger' enemy.

China's defence modernisation has undergone strategic changes since 1985 when 'Strategic Changes to the Guiding Thoughts on National Defence Construction and Army Building' were introduced. Peacetime war preparation is envisaged now as a step by step improvement of defence capabilities, which should in turn be integrated with the economy. The Chinese are not only optimistic that no global war will break out in this century, but also confident that defence modernisation will improve their warfighting capabilities. They anticipate that long term defence modernisation, characterised by strategic breakthroughs in high-technology, will achieve advanced world standards by the middle of the twenty-first century. At the same time, China hopes that strategic defence against an invading enemy will be successful, as it incorporates the significant human factor of People's War vintage with advances in defence modernisation. In the process, the strategy of 'People's War under modern conditions' is evolved.

A NEW DEFENCE STRATEGY

People's War is no longer considered by China in the 1980s in the same politicised and belligerent manner as it was conceived by Lin Biao in 1965. Instead, it has evolved into a strategy that prepares the Chinese for the worst in a future war against the 'stronger' enemy. Thus 'people's War under modern conditions' stands out as the solution, having inherited the essence of People's War, which encompasses China's ability to block the enemy in Chinese territory and to bring about a stalemate so that the enemy is denied any prospect of victory. While the human factor remains important as China continues to rely on the large reservoir of Reserve Forces, significant improvements to warfighting capabilities in both conventional and nuclear warfare are China's best guarantees for ensuring that a stalemate can be followed by counter offensives.

Changing conditions in modern warfare have induced the Chinese to adapt People's War to suit strategic defence in Chinese territory. The strategy of active defence, which favours positional warfare supported by secondary mobile and guerrilla operations to defend strategic positions and cities, is now the cornerstone for the design of the future battlefield. To increase mobility in active defence, it has been proposed that mobile warfare should be conducted within the main defensive position and in adjacent areas. Similarly the Chinese claim that positional guerrilla warfare, which relies on coordination with the Main Force units and the local terrain, generates initiatives in active defence.

Given formidable Soviet fire power and airstrike in launching massive offensives that incorporate the elements of surprise, mobility and concentration of forces, the Chinese will need to halt Soviet advances and strategic strikes in the initial stage of the war. Specifically, Chinese defence in depth may succeed in preventing the Soviet OMGs from effecting strategic breakthroughs. The appropriate deployment of the Main Force, Local and guerrilla units in particular theatres of war would be a crucial determinant for success. The reorganisation of the original eleven military regions into seven larger ones suggests improved Chinese capabilities in C^3I. The heavy concentration of the Main Forces and fire power in the southern parts of Shenyang-Beijing MRs and the designation of Lanzhou city as headquarters for the enlarged Lanzhou MR (incorporating the former Wulumuqi MR) suggest that the Chinese are implementing active defence in order to block an enemy thrust from the Northwest.

As the war may escalate to nuclear battle conditions, the Chinese have recently devoted a great deal of effort to organising exercises and training units to seal points of nuclear breakthrough in conjunction with combined arms operations. In the main, the Chinese rely on anti-tank rockets and the dispersion of units to the battalion level and below in order to preserve C^2 and as an effective means to halt the advance of Soviet armoured units after tactical nuclear blasts. Nevertheless, the Chinese are aware of their inadequacies *vis-a-vis* the 'fire power competition', but are relying on combined arms and joint operations to ameliorate their inferior position.

The future theatre of war will by and large be dictated by the

Soviets who have induced the Chinese to devise a three-dimensional defence system of great depth as an answer to the Soviet *blitzkrieg* as sustained by OMGs. It has been compared to a 'shield' which resembles a ring of defence comprising a series of tactical supporting points. The Chinese hope that the frontage and depth of their defence zones can withstand enemy air, airborne and armoured attacks in conventional, nuclear and biological/chemical warfare. Specifically the Chinese claim that weaknesses in the Soviet OMGs can be identified and that the Soviet lines of communication are vulnerable as the latter advance deep into Chinese territory.

The Chinese are aware that Soviet OMGs are well prepared and supported by the artillery and from the air, but they believe that the Soviet second echelon lacks defensive power and that its formation is not well organised when it approaches an area 30–100km from the Chinese frontage and when the first echelon is on the attack. Chinese militia, guerrilla and reservist units can also create greater havoc by conducting mobile guerrilla warfare. Thus deep attacks against Soviet OMGs in Chinese terriroty should be launched as improved Chinese combined arms and joint operations capabilities terminate the 'source' and 'flow' of Soviet echelon formations. To avoid strategic breakthroughs, the defence of cities becomes crucial. In the Northeast for instance, cities like Haerbin and Siping will have to be defended, and the use of TNF will have to be contemplated despite China's belief in the no-first-use principle. Strategic positions can further be improved by deploying mobile units in strength to provide an 'axle-style' defence between the inner ring of city defence and outer ring where guerrilla warfare can be undertaken in the countryside. The main aim to be achieved is to maximise mobility in active defence.

The combined arms group army will become the new model for China's modernised defence force as military regions regroup their Main Force units according to this new concept. To make the best of new warfighting capabilities, Chinese strategic planners are looking ahead to the year 2000 when they hope to perfect China's strategic defence under the umbrella of 'People's War under modern conditions'. In this ideal situation, the Chinese will not be content with a stalemate, but will seek ways to launch strategic counter offensives against the invader.

DENG XIAOPING'S DEFENCE FORCE

In 1986–87 the Party's control over the military has laid squarely with the Deng Xiaoping-Yang Shangkun team which oversees the small but efficient task force in the Central Military Commission as China strives to fulfill the objectives of defence modernisation. The demise of military influence in the Politburo and other leading political institutions reflects Deng's grand plan to transform the PLA into a professional and loyal arm of the State no longer prone to meddling in politics. This process of 'depoliticisation' and modernisation is the very epitome of Dengism. In the four years since the convening of the Twelfth Party Congress, Deng has made tremenduous progress in stabilising the PLA, something Mao Zedong could not have dreamed of achieving. At the same time, great care has been taken to nurture second and third echelon cadres in the general departments and the military regions in order to perpetuate the fruits of Dengism in the PLA.

The Party has also succeeded to a large extent in transforming the PLA into an apolitical institution. The Twelfth Party Congress initiated major political changes which gradually eliminated 'Leftist' opposition and consolidated Deng's control of the PLA. Party rectification, retrenchment and major reforms have brought about significant changes to the defence force. Reduction-in-strength across the board has led to the retirement or dismissal of veteran Leftist cadres and the negation of the former 'three supports and two militaries' policy followed by the PLA during Cultural Revolution. Hu Yaobang's pronouncement at the Twelfth Party Congress that the Party Central would continue to lead the nation's armed forces through the State's Central Military Commission has also worked in favour of the PLA's support for the State's economic modernisation. In addition, Party rectification in recent years signifies China's efforts to eliminate spiritual pollution and cherish spiritual civilisation in all government institutions, including the PLA. It has been the Central Military Commission's task to reinforce 'revolutionisation, modernisation and regularisation' through party rectification. The inculcation of Party spirit through intensive investigation work which aims at eliminating unhealthy tendencies constitutes the primary objective. High morals, culture and discipline are the targets to be achieved in the absence of a compelling ideology and the charismatic inspiration of Mao Zedong, but rectification efforts in the PLA seem to have fallen short of instilling a strong sense of political consciousness among cadres. In any case, the pragmatists are wary of ideological overtones. In addition, despite the fanfare and intensity in rectification work, the Party does not appear to have been resolute in imposing punishment and penalties on cadres who have committed serious mistakes. On the positive side, Party rectification has served a useful purpose in educating the PLA to accept the need to reduce the strength of the defence force by one million and to introduce structural reforms. In this respect, rectification in the PLA has taken on a distinctive dimension as senior commanders need to be convinced that the traumatic changes that affect their careers or performance are crucial to China's modernisation efforts. This process of education continues as the Chinese hope that fruitful results can be achieved. In 1985, Yang Shangkun had already warned that it would take several years and complicated work to fulfill the tasks of reform in the PLA.

There is hope that the PLA will be further modernised in view of Deng Xiaoping's success in nurturing second and third echelon cadres in the general departments, the central military institutions and the military regions. Given time, these younger and better educated cadres in the elite force will take over from the Long March veterans without leaving a political vacuum. Xu Huizi, He Qizong, Zhou Keyu and Zhou Wenyuan in the general departments represent the cream of younger cadres who have already attained the status of deputies in the general departments. Similarly, the appointments of Liu Jingsong and Li Jiulong as commanders of Shenyang and Jinan MRs respectively demonstrate the successful injection of new blood into military regions in support of defence modernisation. The transformation of the PLA into an institutionalised model of meritocratic standards well sustained by second and third-echelon cadres will contribute to the perpetuation of Dengism after Deng.

The dismissal of Party General Secretary Hu Yaobang in January 1987 and prominence given to sceptics of economic reforms like Chen Yun, Hu Qiaomu and Deng Liqun prior to the convening of the Thirteenth Party Congress seemed to have threatened what Dengism stands for. Nevertheless, the Thirteenth Party Congress, convened in October 1987, reconfirmed China's determination to surge ahead with economic modernisation. Zhao Ziyang, officially appointed General Secretary, announced that China's socialist society was still in its primary stage, and that the Chinese should not jump over stage. At the same time, Zhao reiterated that China was determined to undertake economic reforms. The influence of the old guard was further diminished as many senior cadres retired from the Politburo and the Central Committee. (Deng himself retired from both.)

Deng and Yang Shangkun remain Chairman and Permanent Vice Chairman of the Central Military Commission respectively, indicating that both octogenarians are still indispensable to defence modernisation and stability in the PLA. The perpetuation of Dengism in the PLA will depend on Zhao Ziyang, who has been appointed Vice Chairman of the CMC and will most likely assume leadership in the post-Deng era. It is also apparent that Zhao as a civilian in the CMC does not command the same respect as Deng. Nevertheless, should the depoliticised PLA continue to sustain its development in favour of professionalisation and meritorious standards, it would gladly accept the leadership of Zhao Ziyang in the post-Deng era and genuinely live up to the Party–army image.

The modernised PLA has become closely identified with the objectives of Deng's socialism. Propensity brought about by modernisation overrides whatever political insensitivity the Chinese leadership may have been accused of. Likewise Deng's success in transforming the PLA into a younger, better educated and more modern defence force is the best guarantee for the PLA's allegiance to a Party that preaches modernisation. The relative lack of stature of the new leadership of the PLA's general departments, and the weakening of military representation on the Politburo also enhance the Party's ability to assert authority over the PLA, at least in the short term. Long term prospects for the new generation PLA depend on the degree to which its expectations concerning the development of China's socialist system are met and, in particular, the development of China's defence capabilities. Whilst the PLA is sensitive to the nation's priority being given to economic reforms, sometimes at the expense of defence modernisation, the younger military commanders now represented in the Central Committee can be expected in the post-Deng period to demand positive results. Failure to meet these expectations in economic development and defence modernisation, because of either economic setbacks or political instability, may result in the PLA attempting to reassert its influence in the political arena. This may be particularly the case should the PLA conceive the security of the Party and the State to be under threat, a situation reminiscent of its intervention in the Cultural Revolution.

Notes

INTRODUCTION

1. Qi Zhengjun, 'To Be the "Designer" of the Future Battlefield', *Jiefangjun Bao* (Liberation Army Daily; hereafter *JFJB*), 22 July 1983, p.3.
2. Huang Huamin and Xiao Xianshe, 'A Summary Report of Major Views Expressed in the Conference on "Strategic Changes to the Guiding Thoughts for Our Army Building"', *JFJB*, 20 December 1986, p.4.
3. Qi Zhengjun, 'To Face Reality and Forecast the Future', *JFJB*, 6 January 1984, p.3. *See also* Zhu Songchun, 'Chinese Scholars Discuss Strategy for the Development of National Defense', Hong Kong *Liaowang* Overseas Edition, No.29, 21 July 1986, pp.6–8, in Foreign Broadcast Information Service, Daily Report-China, (hereafter FBIS–CHI), 25 July 1986, K3.
4. Qi Zhengjun, 'To Face Reality and Forecast the Future', *JFJB*, 6 January 1984, p.3.
5. *Ibid*. See also Zhang Taiheng, 'Ascertaining the Campaign Objective Is the Primary Issue in the Study of Campaign Concepts', *JFJB*, 19 September 1986, p.3.
6. Mao Tse-tung, *Basic Tactics*, (Praeger Publishers, New York, 1966), pp.6–7.

CHAPTER 1

1. Xin Yang and Wei Bing, 'What Is the Way to Understand Strategic Changes to the Guiding Thoughts on National Defence Construction?', *JFJB*, 5 September 1986, p.3.
2. For several years in the early 1980s some China specialists

believed that the PLA was reducing its personnel strength and trimming its organisational structure. One source used to support this thesis was the growing references in Chinese media to reductions in the ages of the PLA's officer corps. A typical example towards the end of this process appeared in the *Renmin Ribao* (People's Daily; hereafter *RMRB*) reporting that between early 1984 and June of that year 'readjustment of leading groups at army, division and regiment levels' had resulted in reductions in average ages of between 3.9 and 7.9 years: see *RMRB*, 19 June 1984, p.7. Later in 1984, following the announcement of the retirement of 40 very senior officers, CGS Yang Dezhi was reported to have stated that the PLA would thin its ranks further, for economic reasons: see *South China Morning Post*, 7 January 1985, p.6. The inference drawn was that a lot of 'dead wood' was being retired or moved to the inactive list. More tangible evidence came in the form of the transfer of the Railway Engineer Corps and Capital Construction Engineer Corps to civilian control in 1983, and the reorganisation of armour, artillery and engineer elements in the high command structure: see *Handbook of the Chinese People's Liberation Army*, (Defence Intelligence Agency, Washington, November 1984; hereafter *Handbook 1984*), p.8. A reorganisation that may have entailed a net force expansion was the formation of the Marine Corps in about 1982 (see Note 99 in Chapter 2), but it is possible that this was accomplished by the straightforward transfer of assets from existing formations. Probably the most substantial force reduction during this period occurred during the formation of the People's Armed Police (PAP). According to some sources the decision to establish an internal security force separate from the PLA was taken in 1982, and was in part related to the 'regularisation' and reorganisation of the PLA. By 1984 some 25 internal defence divisions of the PLA were reported to have been transferred to the PAP: see *Handbook 1984*, p.23; Xinhua (New China News Agency; hereafter XH), 5 April 1983, in FBIS–CHI, 6 April 1983, K5; and R.H. Ward and D.H. Bracey, 'Police Training and Professionalism in the People's Republic of China', in *the Police Chief*, (International Association of Chiefs of Police, Gaithersberg, Maryland, May 1985), p.36. All these reductions occurred before the more recent cut-back of one million personnel announced in 1985.

3. Xin Yang and Wei Bing, 'What is the Way to Understand Strategic Changes to the Guiding Thoughts on National Defence Construction?', *JFJB*, 5 September 1986, p.3.
4. *Ibid.*
5. *Ibid.*
6. 'Grasp the Construction of Professionalism and Strengthen the Might of the Nation and the Army', *JFJB*, 18 September 1986, p.1.
7. Huang Huamin and Xiao Xianshe, 'A Summary Report of Major Views Expressed in the Conference on "Strategic Changes to the Guiding Thoughts for Our Army Building"', *JFJB*, 20 December 1986, p.4.
8. Xin Yang and Wei Bing, 'What Is the Way to Understand Strategic Changes to the Guiding Thoughts on National Defence Construction?', *JFJB*, 5 September 1986, p.3.
9. *Ibid.*
10. *Ibid.* In the Enlarged Conference of the CMC in June 1985, Deng Xiaoping maintained that there were three major reasons which contributed to long-term peace and that it was possible for global war not to break out in this century. First, the United States of America and the Soviet Union which were the two nations capable of conducting a global war, would be maintaining a military balance for a long time, so that neither one would wish to initiate a war. Secondly, neither side was ready with its global strategic deployment. Thirdly, the growth of the 'force of peace' far exceeded that of the 'force of war', and contributed to either delaying or stopping the outbreak of war.
11. *Ibid.*
12. Li Qianyuan, 'A preliminary Analysis of the Characteristics of Limited War in the Future', *JFJB*, 19 December 1986, p.3 and Huang Huamin and Xiao Xianshe, 'A Summary Report of Views Expressed', *JFJB*, 20 December 1986, p.4.
13. Xin Yang and Wei Bing, 'What Is the Way to Understand Strategic Changes?', *JFJB*, 5 September 1986, p.3.
14. Yang Dezhi, 'To Make Military Theories Prosper in National Defence Construction', *JFJB*, 11 September 1986, p.1.
15. *Ibid.*
16. *Ibid*, p.4.
17. *Ibid.*
18. 'Full Text of Report on Implementation of State Budget for 1985 and on Draft State Budget for 1986', XH, 15 April

1986, in FBIS–CHI, 22 April 1986, K7.

19. Yang Dezhi, 'An Important Guideline in Constructing Our Army in the New Era', *JFJB*, 16 July 1983, p.1.

20. See *The Economist*, 25 January 1986, p.23 and Rita Tullberg, 'World Military-Expenditure', *World Armaments and Disarmament: SIPRI Yearbook 1986*, (Oxford University Press, Oxford and New York, 1986), pp.218–19. The Central Intelligence Agency tends to argue that reduced military expenditure represents 'diminished priority' for defence in the modernisation program. This is not necessarily the case as 'other sectors of the economy carry considerable military burdens, ranging from improved health programmes to updated industrial machinery'. See *The Military Balance 1986–1987*, (The International Institute for Strategic Studies, London, 1986), p.142.

21. Carl G. Jacobsen, 'Soviet Military Expenditure and the Soviet Defence Burden', *World Armaments and Disarmament: SIPRI Yearbook 1986*, pp.263–267. See also *The Economist*, 25 January 1986, p.23.

22. 'Yang Shangkun on Restructuring the Army and Reduction-in-Strength', *RMRB*, 6 July 1985, p.1.

23. Zhang Aiping, 'Several Problems Concerning Defence Modernisation', *Hongqi*, (Red Flag; hereafter *HQ*), No.5, 1983, pp.21–24.

24. *Ibid.*

25. See Appendix 1.

26. It has been reported that Pakistan was suspected of supplying China with the model for the Chinese-built version of the French EXOCET. See Mary Lee, 'Two-way Street for Arms', *Far Eastern Economic Review* (hereafter *FEER*), 12 December 1985, p.25. Similarly, there have been reports of secret military cooperation between China and Israel in the fields of tactical missiles (SSM), EW, RPV and tank AFV. See *Foreign Report*, (*The Economist* publications, London), 12 December 1985, p.5.

27. Zhang Aiping, 'Several Problems Concerning Defence Modernisation', p.22. See also 'Zhang Aiping on Reform Problems Concerning Defence Technology and Industry', *JFJB*, 20 November 1984, p.1.

28. Zhang Aiping, 'Several Problems Concerning Defence Modernisation', p.22.

29. *Asian Aviation*, May 1986 p.42 and *BBC World Round Up*, 4 November 1986.
30. See Appendix 1.
31. *Jane's Defence Weekly* (hereafter *JDW*), 14 December 1985, p.1317.
32. Tullberg, 'World Military Expenditure', pp.217–218 and 'Army Paper Supports Economic Construction before National Defence', XH, 9 July 1985, in *BBC Summary of World Broadcasts* (hereafter *SWB*), 11 July 1985, FE8000/BII/1.
33. Tullberg, 'World Military Expenditure', p.219.
34. 'Yang Shangkun Discusses Cuts in PLA Forces', XH, 7 July 1985, in *SWB*, 9 July 1985, FE/7998/BII/I.
35. *The Military Balance 1986–87*, p.142. IISS estimates that the Chinese Reserves have a strength of 5 377 000 with the following breakdown: Army 5 000 000; Navy 144 000; Marines 135 000; Air (AD) 200 000.
36. 'PLA's He Qizong Discusses Reduction Work', Beijing International Service, 30 January 1986, in FBIS–CHI, 31 January 1986, K1.
37. 'Yang Shangkun on Restructuring the Army and Reduction-in-Strength', *RMRB*, 6 July 1985, p.1.
38. 'Smooth Development in Army Restructuring and Reduction-in-Strength', *RMRB*, 18 July 1985, p.1.
39. 'Chief of General Staff Yang Dezhi on the Completion of Army Restructuring in Two Years', *Ta Kung Pao* (Hong Kong), 29 July 1985, p.3.
40. 'China's Budget', *JDW*, 13 July 1985, p.72. According to Xinhua, 1 000 million yuan would be spent on resettling the one million to be demobilised. 30 000 apartments were reported to have been built for retired officers.
41. 'To Take Care of the Overall Situation and to Actively Strive to Secure the Smooth Completion of Resettlement Work', *Zhongguo Fazhi Bao* (Chinese Legal System Daily), 8 March 1985, p.1. It was reported that incidents involving refusals to resettle demobilised soldiers happened occasionally. The CMC appealed to individual units to overcome difficulties they might confront in resettling demobilised soldiers.
42. 'Measures to Ease Return of Soldiers to Civilian Jobs', XH, 10 March 1985, in *SWB*, 14 March 1985, FE/7899/BII/10. The CMC intended to resettle 47 000 demobilised cadres at the battalion and regiment levels who had formed the PLA during

the Sino–Japanese War and the Civil War respectively. See *Wen Hui Pao* (Hong Kong), 6 March 1985, p.1.

43. Yang Dezhi, 'To Quicken the Pace and To Strive for the Construction of a Standardised and Revolutionary Army', *Sixiang Zhanxian*, (Ideological Front; Chinese PLA Political Academy), No.9, 1984, p.4.

44. 'Deng Xiaoping on Domestic Policy in CBS Interview', Beijing XH, 14 September 1986, in FBIS-CHI, 16 September 1986, B1–2.

45. 'Full Text of Report on Implementation of State Budget for 1985 and on Draft State Budget for 1986', in FBIS–CHI, 22 April 1986, K8–15.

46. William T. Tow, 'Science and Technology in China's Defense', *Problems of Communism*, Vol.XXXIV, July–August 1985, pp.19–21.

47. 'Science, Technology and Industry for National Defence Should Strive to Serve the National Economy (editorial)', *JFJB*, 23 August 1983, p.1. The Editorial claims that the integration benefits both sectors. In particular technological teams in military industries gain valuable experience. Profits can be set aside for R & D and production of new weapon systems.

48. Tow, 'Science and Technology in China's Defense', p.19.

49. *Defence Modernisation*, (Chinese People's Liberation Army Fighters' Press, Beijing, 1983), pp.22–23.

50. Tow, 'Science and Technology in China's Defense', p.28.

51. *Ibid.*

52. *Ibid.*

53. *Ibid.*, pp.19–21. See also Denis Fred Simon, 'The Challenge of Modernizing Industrial Technology in China', *Asian Survey*, (hereafter *AS*), Vol.XXVI, No.4, April 1986, pp.423–430 and Tai Ming Cheung, 'China Switches from Defence to Development', *Pacific Defence Reporter*, November 1986, pp.27–8.

54. N. Lee, *The Chinese People's Liberation Army 1980–82: Modernisation, Strategy and Politics*, (Canberra Papers on Strategy and Defence No.28, Australian National University, 1983), pp.32–48.

55. See Appendix 1.

56. Simon, 'The Challenge of Modernizing Industrial Technology in China', pp.432–39. See also Tow, 'Science and Technology in China's Defense', pp.28–30. There has been a relaxation of

export control in the COCOM (Coordinating Committee of the Consultative Group on Export Controls to Communist Nations) list as a result of US initiatives. Whilst China benefits from the relaxation, 'six special mission areas' remain inaccessible to the Chinese over the short term. These are nuclear weapons, nuclear delivery systems, anti-submarine warfare, electronic warfare, intelligence gathering systems and power projection capabilities.

57. Cao Yuguang, 'A Significant Measure in Strengthening the Reserve Forces for National Defence', *RMRB*, 8 June 1984, p.7 and He Zhengwen, 'The Basic Law for Building Defence Modernisation in our Nation', *RMRB*, 8 June 1984, p.7. See also Ellis Joffe and Gerald Segal, 'The PLA under Modern Conditions', *Survival*, Vol.XXVII, No.4, July/August 1985, pp.146–68.

58. 'Yang Dezhi Explains the "PRC Military Service Law (Revised Draft)"', *JFJB*, 23 May 1984, p.1.

59. 'To Do a Good Job in Reserve Service Training', *JFJB*, 29 July 1984, p.2 and Xu Peng, 'To Do a good Job in Two Combinations and to Strengthen Defence Capability', *JFJB*, 9 January 1983, p.4.

60. 'NCP Discusses Draft Law on Military Service', XH, 22 May 1984, in *SWB*, 23 May 1984, FE/7650/CI/1.

61. 'Military Service Law Expounded', *China Daily*, 20 June 1984.

62. Alan N. Sabrosky, 'Defence with Fewer Men? The American Experience', in G. Harries–Jenkins (ed.) *Armed Forces and the Welfare Societies: Challenges in the 1980s*, (International Institute for Strategic Studies, Macmillan Press, London, 1982), pp.196–7.

63. *Ibid.*, p.190.

64. *Ibid.*

65. J. Chester Cheng (ed.), *The Politic of the Chinese Army: A Translation of the Bulletin of Activities of the People's Liberation Army*, (Hoover Institution of War, Revolution and Peace, Stanford University, California, 1966), p.713.

66. Sabrosky, 'Defence with Fewer Men?', p.194.

67. See Table 1.4.

68. 'Conscription in Jiangxi', Nanchang Provincial Service, 3 August 1985, in *SWB*, 10 August 1985, FE/8026/BII/7.

69. 'Circular Concerning "Conscription Work Regulations", *Bulletin of the State Council of the PRC* (The State Council and

the Central Military Commission, Beijing), No.31, 20 November 1985, p.1053.

70. The figure given for 1985 is 410 000 men and officers. See note 23. China intended to resettle 830 000 demobilised soldiers in 1986. See 'PLA to Resettle 830 000 Ex-servicemen in 1986', Beijing Zhongquo Xinwenshe, 15 January 1986, in FBIS–CHI, 17 January 1986, K7.

71. Bulletin of the State Council of the PRC, 20 November 1985, p.1047 and Xinhua Monthly, November 1985, p.45.

72. Bulletin of the State Council of the PRC, 20 November 1985, pp.1048–49.

73. The Military Balance 1986–87, pp.142 and 145. See also E. Hall, 'An Army that "Wears Its Enemy Down"', South China Morning Post, 1 March 1984.

74. 'Conscription in Jiangxi', in SWB, 10 August 1985, FE/8026/BII/7.

75. 'Reportage on New Military Service Law', XH, 4 June 1984, in FBIS–CHI, 6 June 1984, K3.

76. 'The Completion of Adjustment and Reform Work for Nation-wide Militia Organisations', JFJB, 17 March 1983, p.1.

77. Liberation Army Daily (hereafter LAD) Commentator, 'To Make Contribution to Building Strong Reserve Forces', JFJB, 8 January 1984, p.4.

78. Gai Yumin, 'People's Armed Forces Departments Reorganised', XH, 2 May 1986, in FBIS–CHI, 6 May 1986, K17 and FBIS–CHI, 4 March 1986, K21.

79. 'On Perfecting the System of Combining the Militia with Reserve Service', XH, 8 December 1985, in SWB, 13 December 1985, FE/8133/BII/10–11.

80. 'Yang Shangkun on Reforming Militia Work', Peking Home Service, 25 February 1985, in SWB, 1 March 1985, FE/7888/BII/10 and 'Completing Adjustment and Reform Work', JFJB, 17 March 1983, p.1.

81. 'Yang Shangkun on Cuts in Militia Training', Zhengzhou, Henan Provincial Service, 20 October 1985, in SWB, 26 October 1985, FE/8092/BII/11.

82. 'City and County Army Units to be Placed Under Local Jurisdiction', Peking Home Service, 28 August 1985, in SWB, 31 August, FE/8044/BII/7.

83. Liu Dizhong, 'Beefed-up Militia Aims to Improve Defence Strategy', China Daily, 29 January 1985, p.1.

84. 'Reserve Division Established in Capital', XH, 1 February 1985, in *Ming Pao*, 2 February 1985.

85. XH, 1 August 1984, in *SWB*, 8 August 1984, FE/7716/BII/7– 8. It was reported that a certain RD in Hubei for the first time successfully participated in a military exercise with a certain army of Wuhan MR. Tactics of attack in field operations and railway transport were practised.

86. 'Training Centres for Reservists on Rotation', *Liaoning Ribao*, 5 October 1984, p.4.

87. 'Training Officers of Reserve Divisions', XH, 25 June 1984, in *SWB*, 28 June, FE/768/BII/3 and 'Why Does the Reserve Officer System Develop Rapidly?', *JFJB*, 9 May 1984, p.3.

88. 'Strive Hard to Build the Artillery in the Militia', *JFJB*, 14 September 1983, p.3.

89. *Handbook 1984*, p.76.

90. *Ibid.*, p.78.

91. *Xinhua Ribao*, 2 August 1983.

92. For example, some outdated communications equipment provided difficulties, C^3I generally suffered deficiencies that caused problems in co-ordinating ground force operations, and infantry-tank co-operation was inadequate: see L. Buszynski, 'Vietnam Confronts China', *AS*, Vol. XX, No.8, August 1980, p.841, and *Handbook 1984*, pp.76 and 78.

93. Xu Xiangqian, 'Strive to Achieve Modernization in National Defence', *HQ*, No.10, 2 October 1979, pp.28–33.

94. Beijing Domestic Service, 21 November 1980, in FBIS–CHI, 25 November 1980, L24–25.

95. *CONMILIT*, (Hong Kong), May 1981, pp.7–11.

96. XH, Beijing Domestic Service, 15 January 1982, in FBIS–CHI, 19 January 1982, K5 and K11.

97. AP, Beijing, 2 August 1983, in *South China Morning Post* (hereafter *SCMP*), 3 August 1983.

98. *Ibid.* See also Table 1.5.

99. *Ta Kung Pao*, 21 November 1983.

100. *Wen Hui Pao*, 6 April 1984, p.3 and *Ming Pao*, (Hong Kong), 30 January 1984, p.6.

101. *Memorandum of the Ministry of Foreign Affairs of the SRV on Chinese War of Escalation and Aggravation of Tension Along the Vietnam-China Border*, (Hanoi), 4 July 1984.

102. Yang stated that the whole of the armed forces would 'further develop in the direction of ... a composite force', and that efforts would be increased to form combat (formations) 'com-

bining several services'. See XH, 7 July 1985, in *SWB*, 9 July 1985, FE/7998/BII/I.

103. The Beijing Garrison Command contains at least one division of People's Armed Police, as well as PLA units. See XH Domestic Service, 29 September 1985, in FBIS–CHI, 1 October 1985, K14.

104. *Wen Hui Pao*, 6 April 1984, p.3 and Beijing Domestic Service, 28 September 1985, in FBIS–CHI, 2 October 1985, K4.

105. *Ming Pao*, 20 June 1986, p.7 and 24 August 1986, p.5. The role of the air element is not defined beyond providing 'support to the ground units', but its aircraft are described as belonging to the Army's aviation troops. This may refer to aviation units operated by the ground forces, possibly for reconnaissance, liaison and battlefield transport purposes. China's Super Puma and S–70 helicopters would be suitable for these tasks. It is also possible but less likely, that Air Force strike elements have been integrated into group armies.

106. By May 1987, some 730 000 personnel had been retrenched, leaving about 300 000 still to be demobilised by the end of the year: see XH, 26 May 1987, in FBIS–CHI, 27 May 1987, K1.

107. *Ming Pao*, 24 August 1986, p.5; *FEER*, 7 August 1986, p.23; XH, Beijing, in FBIS–CHI, 25 August 1986, K10–11, XH Domestic Service, 26 January 1987, in FBIS–CHI, 2 February 1987, K19 and XH, 27 March 1987, in FBIS-CHI, 1 April 1987, K24. In the course of this troop reduction, regiments and divisions have been disbanded and others have been partly disbanded, then amalgamated with elements of other units to form new formations. In one case elements of an infantry division amalgated with two tank regiments to form a tank brigade, a somewhat disparate mix. See FBIS–CHI, 15 May 1987, K12–13 and 20 May 1987, K10.

108. *JFJB*, 26 October 1984, p.2.

109. NCNA, Beijing, 28 January 1986, in FBIS–CHI, 5 February 1986, K13–15; and CNA, 27 March 1986, in *SWB*, 1 April 1986, FE/8221/A3/3.

110. XH Domestic Service, Beijing, 22 April 1986, in FBIS–CHI, 24 April 1986, K9; NCNA Beijing, 26 April 1986, in *SWB*, 29 April 1986, FE/8245/BII/1; and *FEER*, 7 August 1986, p.23.

111. CNA, 10 June 1986, in FBIS–CHI, 10 June 1986, K12.

112. XH, 24 July 1984, in SWB, 27 July 1984, FE/7706/BII/1–2; and *Ming Pao*, 11 June 1986, p.5.

113. Zhongxin She, Beijing, 19 June 1986, in *Ming Pao*, 20 June 1986, p.7.
114. *Ming Pao*, 11 June 1986, p.5.
115. *FEER*, 7 August 1986, pp.22–23.
116. Beijing Domestic TV Service, 18 January 1986, in FBIS–CHI, 24 January 1986, K10–11. The fulfilment of this program was partially indicated in a media report in late 1986 concerning the holding of large-scale exercises of mechanised combined arms group armies somewhere in North China. Air Force bombers and ground attack fighters also participated: *Hsin Wan Pao*, (Hong Kong), 26 October 1986, p.4, in FBIS–CHI, 27 October 1986, K14.
117. In 1985 a training regiment was established in each group army, but as this proved inadequate, it was expanded to a division in 1987. In addition, combat support arms such as engineers and signals have formed specialist training organisations. See *JFJB*, 19 May 1987, p.1, in FBIS–CHI, 3 June 1987, K26.
118. Zhang Taiheng, 'Firm Guiding Principles and Flexible Tactics', *JFJB*, 27 May 1983, p.3.
119. See in particular note 38 in Chapter 3.
120. 'Strive to Raise Our Army's Fighting Capabilities under Modern Warfare Conditions, (editorial)', *JFJB*, 8 January 1984, p.1.
121. 'A Certain Mechanised Division Took Measures to Cultivate "Staff Officer in Combined Arms" in Order to Raise Efficiency in Command', *JFJB*, 30 May 1984, p.3.
122. 'Strive to Raise Our Army's Fighting Capabilities', *JFJB*, January 1984, p.1.
123. Special *LAD* Commentator, 'Strive to Raise Our Army's Coordinated Fighting Capabilities', *JFJB*, 8 April 1984, p.2.
124. 'A Certain Motorised Division's Reform in Joint Tactical Training Achieved Outstanding Results', *JFJB*, 18 September 1984, p.1 and 'A Certain Group Army Experimented New Fighting Methods and Tested New Theories', *JFJB*, 5 November 1984, p.1.
125. 'Our Army's Campaign Training is Prepared for a New Breakthrough', *JFJB*, 1 December 1984, p.1.
126. *Ibid.*
127. Electronic Warfare (EW) is included in this section because of its overlap with Intelligence.
128. Defence Intelligence Agency, *Handbook on the Chinese*

Armed Forces, (Government Printing Office, Washington, D.C., 1976; hereafter *Handbook 1976*), p.2–1.

129. See Carlyle A. Thayer, 'Regularization of Military Bureaucratic Regimes: From Symbiosis to Coalition — The Case of Vietnam', (a paper prepared for the Asian Studies Association of Australia's Sixth Biennial Conference, Sydney, May 1986).

130. *Handbook 1984*, p.8.

131. *Foreign Report*, 25 July 1985, p.5.

132. *SWB*, 8 July 1985, FE/7997/BII/1, and 9 July 1985, FE/7998/BII/1.

133. See *Heilongjiang Ribao*, 1 May 1987, p.3, in FBIS–CHI, 15 May 1987, S4, and Shanghai City Service, 8 May 1987, in FBIS–CHI, 29 May 1987, 02.

134. *Ta Kung Pao*, 25 July 1985, p.1. In April 1987 the Chinese media reported that the Navy had completed its force reduction and had eliminated more than 80 units of various sizes: *Sunday Morning Post* (Hong Kong), 12 April 1987, p.8.

135. J. Bussert, 'China's C^{3}I Efforts Show Progress', C^{3}I *Handbook*, (First Edition, EW Communications Inc., Palo Alto, 1986), p.174.

136. SWB, 31 July 1984, FE/7709/BII/12, and *RMRB*, 2 June 1987, p.3, in FBIS–CHI, 5 June 1987, K9.

137. Zhongxin She, Beijing, 19 June 1986, in *Ming Pao*, 20 June 1986, p.7.

138. *FEER*, 7 August 1986, pp.22–23. The National Defence University offers, inter alia, a three year instructors' course: XH, 17 May 1987, in FBIS–CHI, 18 May 1987, K23.

139. SWB, 27 July 1984, FE/7706/BII/1–2, FBIS–CHI, 10 June 1986, K12, FBIS–CHI, 10 June 1986, K12, FBIS–CHI, 18 May 1987, K23 and ABC 'Report from Asia', 2 August 1987.

140. *FEER*, 7 August 1986, p.23.

141. SWB, 5 July 1984, FE/7687/BII/1 and FBIS–CHI, 12 August 1985, K7.

142. For an example of this in a group army HQ in Beijing Military Region see *JFJB*, 6 February 1987, in FBIS–CHI, 17 February 1987, R1.

143. *Jing Bao* (Hong Kong), No. 2, 5 February 1986.

144. *FEER*, 7 August 1986, p.22.

145. *JFJB*, 26 October 1984, p.2.

146. For example, in 1984 an artillery army in Fuzhou Military Region (MR), using microcomputers, developed its own software to provide data to assist in the planning of unit and

vehicle movements. The system developed also provided for the automated dissemination of orders, reduced dramatically the time taken under manual arrangements for planning and direction, and enabled the staff in command posts to be reduced by two thirds (*SWB*, 3 August 1984, FE/7712/BII/6–7). Another army in Jinan MR seems to have developed an even more sophisticated ADP-based C^3 system that includes the above-mentioned features, plus graphic displays of the movement of forces, and accurate information on unit readiness states, locations etc. (*SWB*, 3 August 1984, FE/7712/BII/7–8).

147. Zhongxin She, Beijing, 23 August 1986, in *Ming Pao*, 24 August 1986, p.5.
148. The automation of C^3I systems is described in XH, 9 November 1986, in *Ming Pao*, 10 November 1986, p.5; Beijing Domestic Service, 29 July 1986, in FBIS–CHI, 31 July 1986, K37, Zhongguo Xinwen She, Hong Kong, 18 February 1987, in FBIS–CHI, 20 February 1987, K39, and Nanjing, Jiangsu Provincial Service, 16 February 1987, in FBIS–CHI, 20 February 1987, 02–3.
149. The US Defence Department continues to oppose the sale of networking technology for fear that it would enhance China's capacity for C^3I integration: see *FEER*, 6 August 1987, p.13. In February 1987 Zhongguo Xinwen She described the status of the all-Army project as a 'preliminary framework' for the whole Army: FBIS–CHI, 20 February 1987, K40.
150. Buszynski, 'Vietnam Confronts China', *AS*, August 1980, p.841.
151. Bussert, 'China's C^3I Efforts', p.177.
152. *Ta Kung Pao*, 15 February 1986, p.3.
153. J.C. Donnell, 'Vietnam 1979: Year of Calamity', *AS*, January 1980, p.23.
154. Bussert, 'China's C^3I Efforts', p.176.
155. *Ibid.*, p.179.
156. *Ibid.*
157. For example, see E. Hall, 'An Army that "Wears Its Enemy Down"', *SCMP*, 1 March 1984, p.8.
158. *SWB*, 31 July 1984, FE/7709/BII/9.
159. *SWB*, 3 August 1984, FE/7712/BII/7–8.
160. FBIS–CHI, 20 February 1986, W3 and Zhongguo Xinwen She, Hong Kong, 18 February 1987, in FBIS–CHI, 20 February 1987, K39.
161. *JDW*, 14 December 1985.

162. XH, 1 February 1987, in FBIB–CHI, 2 February 1987, K19, and *Ming Pao*, 15 June 1987, p.9.

163. *FEER*, 2 January 1986, p.9.

164. Zhongguo Xinwen She, Hong Kong, 18 February 1987, in FBIS–CHI, 20 February 1987, K39. In May 1987 the US decided not to sell fibre optics to China as part of a telecommunications protocol, following strong opposition from the US SIGINT organisation, the National Security Agency, which feared such sales would lead to a decrease in its ability to intercept Chinese communications. Britain, however, wrested agreement from the White House for British companies to sell the very technology to China that US firms were forbidden to sell: *FEER*, 6 August 1987, p.12. See also *Ming Pao*, Hong Kong, 15 June 1987, p.9.

165. US Joint Chiefs of Staff, *US Military Posture for FY 1978*, (US Government Printing Office, Washington D.C.), p.118, cited in R.W. Fieldhouse, 'Chinese Nuclear Weapons: An Overview', *SIPRI Yearbook 1986*, p.105.

166. FBIS–CHI, 23 January 1978, E4, cited in B. Swanson, 'An Introduction to Chinese Command, Control, Communications and Intelligence', *Signal*, May/June 1978, p.52.

167. D. Wagner and D. Barlow, 'National Defence', in *China, A Country Study*, (Department of Army pamphlet 550–60, US Government Printing Office, Washington D.C., 1981), p.465, cited in R.W. Fieldhouse, 'Chinese Nuclear Weapons', p.105. Among the indications of a direct command relationship in peacetime between the PCMC and the Strategic Nuclear Forces are the upgrading of the C³I link from the PCMC through a new high-capacity microcomputer system (the JH series), and a shift in responsibility for logistic support from the Military Regions to the Strategic Nuclear forces themselves in 1985. See *Liaowang* (Overseas Edition), No.23, Hong Kong, 8 June 1987, pp.8–9.

168. Bussert, 'China's C³I Efforts', p.175.

169. *Ibid.*, p.178 and Zhongxin She, Beijing, 14 June 1987, in *Ming Pao*, Hong Kong, 15 June 1987, p.9.

170. FBIS–CHI, 3 June 1987, K24–25.

171. Bussert, 'China's C³I Efforts', p.178.

172. Current US policy restricts China's access to advanced US technology in the intelligence processing and electronic warfare fields: see *FEER*, 6 August 1987, pp.12–13.

173. Tactical air reconnaissance missions are probably carried out

at altitudes between 1000 and 6000 metres: *Handbook 1984*, p.34. One type of aircraft used in the air photo reconnaissance role is a variant of the F–6, which is generally similar to the Soviet MiG–19R, with cameras mounted in the lower forward fuselage: *JDW*, 14 December 1985, p.1317. Capabilities, and the scale of effort that can be provided have not been revealed, but they are unlikely to meet all the needs of the Ground Forces.

174. For Naval Air Force shortcomings in this field, see Li Jing, 'Functions of Naval Aviation and Development of Weapons and Equipment', in *Hangkong Zhishi*, Beijing, June 1983, pp.2–4. China has developed several types of RPV, at least one of which, the D–4 can carry a 25kg camera payload on sorties of over two hours duration. *Defence Attache*, (Diplomatist Associates Ltd. London), No.1/1986, pp.41–42. China is also developing the Yun-8 (a modified An-12 CUB) to provide a long-range maritime patrol (LRMP) capability. One aircraft cleared 'technical qualification tests' in late 1985, which probably equate to air-worthiness tests. A Swedish air surveillance package, including SLAR and cameras, was planned to be fitted to this aircraft in late 1986, and China may add an IR scanner of its own manufacture. See *JDW*, 28 September 1985, p.679 and 25 January 1986, p.114; *Aviation Week and Space Technology*, 19 May 1986, p.18.

175 Early warning of an enemy attack by missiles or bombers is a critical element of China's strategic intelligence system. There is no evidence that China operates AEW aircraft yet, but the SIGINT network established with US assistance, which doubtless provides both communications intelligence (COMINT) and electronic intelligence (ELINT), will contribute significantly to China's early warning system. The product of these facilities no doubt also covers other Soviet military activities, and supplements the collection efforts of China's other SIGINT facilities and air defence radar systems. See *US News and World Report*, 29 June 1981, p.10; *Washington Post*, 18 June 1981, p.34; *FEER*, 4 April 1985, p.18; and Bussert, 'China's C³I Efforts', pp.173 and 175.

176. Bussert, 'China's C³I Efforts', pp.173 and 175.

177. Areas of China's air space, such as the Beijing-Shanghai corridor, are served by modern air surveillance and long-range radars of Western origin. These also feed into the Chinese air defence system: Bussert, 'China's C³I Efforts', pp.173–175.

178. China has revealed even less about its electronic counter-countermeasures (ECCM) capabilities.
179. Zhongxin She, Beijing, 23 August 1986, *Ming Pao*, 24 August 1986, p.5.
180. *SWB*, 1 April 1986, FE/8221/A3/3.
181. *Handbook 1984*, p.25.
182. G. Jacobs, 'China's Submarine Force', *JDW*, 9 February 1985, pp.220–224; 'China's Frigate Classes', *JDW*, 5 January 1985, pp.28–32; and 'China's Destroyers', *JDW*, 23 February 1985, pp.322–324.
183. Bussert, 'PRC Electronics' in *Defence Electronics*, March 1985, p.130.
184. *Asian Aviation*, May 1986, p.42.
185. *Handbook 1984*, pp.58–9.
186. The early warning radar network, operated by the Air Force, may be a weak link in China's strategic defence system, at least in human terms. Deployed mainly in isolated frontier and coastal areas, the Radar Service seems to be the Cinderella of the Air Force, offering very limited career prospects for its personnel. See FBIS–CHI, 11 May 1987, K13.
187. Bussert, 'China's C³I Efforts', p.174.
188. *Ta Kung Pao*, 25 August 1985, p.1, in FBIS–CHI, 26 August 1985, W2.
189. Bussert, 'China C³I Efforts', p.179.

CHAPTER 2

1. Huang Huamin and Xiao Xianshe, 'A Summary Report of Major Views Expressed', *JFJB*, 20 December 1986, p.4.
2. *Ibid.*
3. *Ibid.*
4. 'Our Combined Army Corps of the Ground Forces Showing Their Strength', *JFJB*, 13 September 1986, p.1. See also 'Reforms in Tactical Training in Joint Operational Setting in a Motorised Division Achieve Outstanding Results', *JFJB*, 8 September 1986, p.1.
5. Li Qianyuan, 'A Preliminary Analysis of the Characteristics of Limited Wars in the Future', *JFJB*, 19 December 1986, p.3. *See also* Zhang Qinsheng et al., 'Limited War: the Major Threat at Present and in the Future', *JFJB*, 26 September 1986, p.3.

6. *Ibid.*
7. Zhang Taiheng, 'Ascertaining the Campaign Objective Is the Primary Issue in the Study of Campaign Concepts', *JFJB*, 19 September 1986, p.3.
8. *Ibid.*
9. *Ibid.*
10. 'Reforms in Tactical Training in Joint Operational Setting in a Certain Motorised Division Achieve Outstanding Results', *JFJB*, 18 September 1986, p.1.
11 *Ibid.*
12. *Ibid.*
13. 'To Adapt to Strategic Changes and Do Well in War preparation', *JFJB*, 1 November 1986, p.2.
14. *Ibid.*
15. *Ibid.*
16. Zhou Yushu, 'Military Training Should Adapt to Strategic Changes', *JFJB*, 5 December 1986, p.3.
17. 'Specialised Elements Have Become the Main Strength of the Ground Forces', *JFJB*, 26 September 1986, p.1.
18. *Ibid.*
19. 'Our Army's Various Reforms Have Achieved Fruitful Results', *JFJB*, 24 December 1986, p.1. See also 'A Certain Group Army Attempted to Build "A New Training Base for the Arms of the Reserve Forces"', *JFJB*, 5 April 1986, p.1.
20. 'A Motorised Regiment Conducted Base-Oriented Rotational Training on a Trial Basis', *JFJB*, 5 April 1986, p.1.
21. *Ibid.*
22. 'A Certain Group Army Organises Commanding Officers for Temporary Appointments in Other Arms', *JFJB*, 22 July 1986, p.2 and 'Reforms Have Made Training Filled with Life', *JFJB*, 19 December 1986, p.1.
23. *Handbook 1984*, p.19.
24. In these armies, the Chinese claim that 66 per cent of the combat battalions are tank and APC–borne infantry battalions: Zhongguo Xinwen She, Hong Kong, 31 May 1987, in FBIS–CHI, 3 June 1987, K25.
25. The US Defence Intelligence Agency's (DIA) estimate of cargo and general service trucks in the division did not alter between 1976 and 1984: see *Handbook 1976*, pp.A–3 and A–17, and *Handbook 1984*, pp. A–3, and A–5. By way of contrast, since 1976 a typical tank regiment of a MF infantry division received an increase of about 14 APC, probably for reconnaiss-

ance purposes, and the number of tanks increased from 32 to about 80. See D.C. Jones (1980), *US Military Posture for FY 1981*, (Government Printing Office, Washington D.C.), p.77, cited in Lee, *The Chinese People's Liberation Army 1980–82*, p.9; *Handbook 1976*, Annex C, and *Handbook 1984*, Appendix C. When unopposed, troops marching on foot can move at a rate of 40 km a day in open terrain. See *Handbook 1984*, pp.25–26.

26. *JDW*, 10 May 1986, p.848.

27. *JDW*, 10 May 1986, p.846; *Bingqi Zhishi* (Beijing), No.6, 1984, front cover and inside front cover. More recently, China advertised for export a new MICV, the WZ–501, a vehicle very similar to the Soviet BMP–1, equipped with a 73–mm gun and an AT–3 SAGGER ATGM system. Presumably, this vehicle will also be issued to the PLA (see *JDW*, 1 February 1986, p.161). A communist newspaper in Hong Kong has also claimed that the PLA has 'motorized infantry units' equipped with APC with a 90–mm gun (*Ta Kung Pao*, 15 February 1986, p.3, in FBIS–CHI, 20 February 1986, W3). The APC was not identified further, but this report is one of several that have referred to APCs mounting various calibre guns. An indigenous ACV has also been developed (see *RMRB*, 21 September 1984), and an agreement has been signed with Vickers Defence Systems (UK) for the co-production of a new MICV based on the H–1 APC chassis (see *JDW*, 11 January 1986, p.5).

28. For example, one major agreement has been with Austria's Steyr-Daimler-Puch. See *JDW*, 11 August 1984, p.179.

29. Total motor vehicle production for all purposes in 1981, for example, was only 190 000. See 'State Council Praises Hubei Automobile Production', in FBIS–CHI, 10 January 1986, K15–16. A subsequent increase to about 300 000 in 1984 still could not keep up with demand: *FEER*, 23 May 1985, p.74. Recently announced plans for a major increase in vehicle production should lead eventually to the upgrading of the gound forces tactical mobility, and also to a certain extent, their strategic mobility: FBIS–CHI, 10 January 1986, K15–16.

30. *Ta Kung Pao*, 15 February 1986, p.3, in FBIS–CHI, 20 February 1 W3.

31. XH, Beijing, 30 July 1985, in FBIS–CHI, 5 August 1985, K5–6.

32. *Handbook 1984*, pp.A–4 and A–24. Artillery anti-tank ranges are quite good, although mobility in action is somewhat limited as most weapon systems are towed.

33. NCNA, 15 October 1984, in *SWB*, 18 October 1984, FE/7777/BII/2; *Beijing Review*, No.31, 30 July 1984, p.21 and *Ta Kung Pao*, 15 February 1986, p.3. This may be the Type 70–1 light anti-tank weapon. Similar to the US M–72 and probably acquired through the SRV some years ago, a new production program was reported in 1984: *JDW*, 11 August 1984, p.179. Its range, however, is only about 150m: *Handbook 1984*, p.A–24. On the other hand, a new vehicle-mounted ATGM system took part in the National Day Parade in Beijing, 1984. See *CONMILIT*, No.95, October 1984, p.80. It was not identified by the Chinese.

34. NCNA, 15 October 19984, in *SWB*, 18 October 1984, FE/7777/BII/2.

35. Unless the Chinese intend to repeat it later, such a small order is probably intended to familiarise the PLA with a state-of-the-art system, and possibly to provide Chinese engineers with a reverse engineering opportunity. See AFP, Hong Kong, 2 April 1987, in FBIS–CHI, 3 April 1987, G1.

36. Discussion about the improved TOW have been conducted since at least 1983, when US teams visited China to consider this and other military aid possibilities: *FEER*, 4 April 1985, pp.17–18. Difficulties in reaching agreement seem to centre on the US desire to sell the complete TOW system, while China only wants to buy a few components, suggesting that the Chinese have made some progress in developing a similar system of their own, but need additional Western technology for completion: *FEER*, 27 May 1986, p.32; *FEER*, 8 March 1984, pp.12–13, and *Time*, 10 February 1986, p.43. Indigenous anti-tank minelaying systems include the M–1979 hasty minelaying MRL system (see Lee, *The Chinese People's Liberation Army 1980–82*, pp.9–10), and another type that scatters from helicopters: *Handbook 1984*, p.65.

37. *The Military Balance 1986–1987*, p.143.

38. On 5 October 1984 *Liaoning Ribao* reported the establishment of Reserve tank divisions which had been incorporated into the PLA Order of Battle. They appear to be manned by ex-servicemen. See Joint Publications Research Service (hereafter JPRS), *China Report*, (Political, Sociological and Military Affairs, Arlington, Va), 21 November 1984, p.66.

39. *Handbook 1984*, pp.19 and A–3.
40. The most numerous type of tank in service is the Chinese version of the Soviet T–54 main battle tank (MBT), the Type 59. Its 100–mm gun has only limited effectiveness against the latest Soviet tanks. As an interim measure, these tanks are gradually being upgraded with various European IR systems, laser range-finders, and the US M68 105–mm gun (licensed in Israel and sold to China) among other improvements. See *JDW*, 27 July 1985, p.173 and 1 February 1986, p.161; also *Ta Kung Pao* 15 February 1986, p.3, in FBIS–CHI, 20 February 1986, W3. There is also a lesser but growing number of the more modern Type 69 (in two versions). Based on the Type 59, this tank has a laser range-finder, an improved main gun (possibly a 115–mm smooth bore for the Type 69–1 and a 100–mm smooth bore for the type 69–2; both firing fin-stabilised ammunition), and IR night vision equipment. A tank simplified fire control system (TSFCS) enables the Type 69 to engage moving targets with a much increased first round hit probability over earlier Chinese tanks. The Type 69 has the added protection of a complete NBC system, and side skirts, although advanced armour does not seem to be used in its construction. See *JDW*, 1 February 1986, p.161 and 8 February 1986, p.205. The type and calibre of the main gun fitted to the Type 69–1 have been in doubt since its first public appearance in 1984. Some sources suggested it was the 115–mm smooth bore as described, perhaps produced with British technological assistance. Others have held it to be a 105–mm rifled gun produced with Israeli assistance. See *Handbook 1984*, p.A–21; *JDW*, 14 December 1985, pp.1307–1312 and *The Economist*, 25 January 1986, p.24. Other tank types include the light Type 62 (designed for use in rough terrain), and the Type 63 amphibious reconnaissance tank. Some obsolete T–34 and possibly JS–3 are utilised in Local Force and training units. Although the Type 59 and possibly the Type 62 are being upgraded, with the possible exception of the Type 69, it is doubtful that Chinese tanks can match the range, firepower and protection of the Soviet tanks facing them across the border. Other improvements to the type 59 are believed to include armoured side skirts, gun stabilizer, computerised fire control, increased power traverse, and man-oeuvrability, plus rubber track pads. See Lee, *The Chinese People's Liberation Army 1980–82*, p.11; CNA, 10 Decem-

ber 1984, in *SWB*, 12 December 1984, FE/7826/BII/10 and *Ta Kung Pao*, 15 February 1986, p.3, in FBIS–CHI, 20 February 1986, W3. In numerical terms, the Chinese now claim to have one of the three largest tank forces in the world, and to have increased the proportion of armoured elements within combat formations (see under 'Mobility'): Beijing Domestic Service 19 May 1987, in FBIS–CHI, 26 May 1987, K13–15, and Zhongguo Xinwen She, Hong Kong, 31 May 1987, in FBIS–CHI, 3 June 1987, K25. The size of the Chinese tank force comes as no surprise. For a number of years Western authorities have estimated it to be the third or even the second largest. For example see *The Military Balance 1978–79*, pp.6, 9 and 56, and *The Pacific Defence Reporter 1987 Annual Reference Edition*, (Peter Isaacson Publications, Victoria), pp.92, 99 and 144.

41. FBIS–CHI, 15 May 1987, K12 and 26 May 1987, K15, and *Handbook 1984*, Appendix G.

42. Beijing Domestic Service, 19 May 1987, in FBIS–CHI, 26 May 1987, K13–15. Improvements to the PLA's APC and MICV inventory are noted under Mobility, and developments in self-propelled (SP) artillery, including AD systems, are considered under Fire Support for the Land Battle – Conventional Artillery. The majority of tank units, however, probably still have to operate in coordination with motorised or even dismounted infantry, and with towed artillery. Even in APC equipped units, there are insufficient APCs to lift all the infantry.

43. XH, 30 July 1984, in *SWB*, 3 August 1984, FE/7712/BII/3 and Beijing Domestic Service, 20 May 1987, in FBIS–CHI, 26 May 1987, K14–16.

44. *JFJB*, 20 October 1984, p.2 and FBIS–CHI, 26 May 1987, K15–16.

45. Reference to the development of a new MBT was contained in CNA, 10 December 1984, in *SWB*, 14 December 1984, FE/7826/BII/10 and Beijing Domestic Service, 19 May 1987, in FBIS–CHI, 26 May 1987, K14.

46. For example, the 85–mm Type 56 gun has considerable potential in the anti-tank role. See *JDW*, 8 December 1984, p.1008.

47. *Handbook 1984*, pp.A–3, A–7, A–16, A–25 and A–27.

48. For example, the 130–mm Type 59–1 gun has a range in excess of 27 000 m: see *Handbook 1984*, p.A–25.

49. *Soviet Military Power 1985*, (US Government Printing Office, Washington D.C., 1985), p.88.

50. 160–mm mortars and 107–mm towed MRL have been replaced by 122–mm howitzers and 122–mm vehicle-mounted
MRL respectively. See *JDW*, 27 July 1985, p.171. In addition,
a gradually increasing number of 130–mm tracked MRL and
122–mm SP howitzers is probably being provided to enhance
the mobile fire-power of mechanised and motorised formations. The introduction of new SP and towed 152–mm gun
systems contribute to an improvement in long-range artillery
capability: see *JDW*, 10 May 1986, pp.849–851. The latter
system, which is believed to have been developed with the
assistance of Western specialists, may fire base-bleed ammunition that could extend its range to over 34 000 m. See *JDW*,
10 May 1986, p.850, and *Handbook 1984*, p.A–25. A new,
30-tube truck-mounted 130–mm MRL system has also been
produced, with a reported maximum range of 10 217m: *JDW*,
10 May 1986, p.851. This system is no doubt used in the close
support role, and thus has a somewhat longer range than
other close support MRLs. The Chinese version of the Soviet
BM–21 122–mm MRL has an even longer range — up to
20 500m: see *Handbook 1984*, p.A–27 — but would probably
be allocated to non-divisional units for long-range, 'breakthrough' tasks.

51. 17 200m is the range of the Type 66 152–mm gun-howitzer, a
weapon system previously held in artillery divisions. See
Handbook 1984, p.A–25.

52. Such temporary artillery groups can include support groups of
lesser range weapons in direct support of infantry or tank
regiments; long-range groups of heavier weapons, either in
direct support of divisions, or for tanks controlled by army
HQ; and destruction groups of heavy artillery to destroy
obstacles and defences. See *Handbook 1984*, p.35.

53. *Ming Pao*, 24 August 1986, p.5 and FBIS–CHI, 25 August
1986, K10–11. The guided missiles could be mobile long-
range SSM, which would help redress the PLA's serious deficiency in its capability to attack enemy third echelon and
follow-on forces, such as Soviet OMGs in their assembly
areas. Improvements to ammunition have been achieved by
means of foreign assistance. In 1984–85 a PRC–US agreement was implemented concerning the sale of US equipment,
reported to cost US$98 million, for the manufacture of
improved artillery ammunition. See *FEER*, 4 April 1985,
pp.17–18 and *Time*, 10 February 1986, p.43.

54. *SWB*, 3 August 1984, FE/7712/BII/6–7 and *SWB*, 10 July 1984, FE/7691/BII/7. The Chinese also claim that the first mechanised group army to be formed uses a computer-based command and control system to direct a 'multi-layered network of fire' encompassing 'tanks, large calibre artillery and guided missiles': *Ming Pao*, 24 August 1986, p.5.

55. *Handbook 1984*, p.35.

56. For example, during a large skill-at-arms competition held in Guangzhou MR in 1984, the winner of the artillery event was a regiment that had 'computerized ... [its] firing data'. See XH, 11 October 1984, in JPRS–CPS–84–0788, p.68. In 1980 the Chinese also purchased a few sets of British-made Field Artillery Computing Equipments: see Karen Berney, 'Dual-Use technology Sales', in *China Business Review*, Vol.11, No.4, July–August 1980, p.25. Whether they can exploit this technology remains to be seen.

57. *Handbook 1984*, pp.69–71.

58. See Table in R.W. Fieldhouse, 'Chinese Nuclear Weapons: An Overview', *SIPRI Yearbook 1986*, p.102.

59. *Handbook 1984*, p.36.

60. Fieldhouse, 'Chinese Nuclear Weapons: An Overview', *SIPRI Yearbook 1986*, p.104.

61. *Soviet Military Power 1985*, p.36.

62. This is the case with the Soviet FROG–7 and SS–21 (divisional-level systems with ranges no more than 120km), the US LANCE and HONEST JOHN systems, and Shorter Range Intermediate Range Nuclear Force (SRINF) missiles such as the Soviet SCUD–B and SS–23. See *Soviet Military Power 1985*, pp.39, and 67–68.

63. China claims that mechanised elements of combined arms formations are equipped with 'guided missiles': for example see *Wen Hui Pao*, 24 August 1984, p.3; FBIS–CHI, 25 August 1986, K10–11; and *Ming Pao*, 24 August 1986, p.5. It is possible, however, that this refers to ATGM such as the HJ–73 (SAGGER) or to other non-nuclear SSM or SAM, although a solid propellant land-based nuclear SSM is probably being developed: *Handbook 1984*, p.71.

64. China's eventual choice of delivery systems is yet to be revealed, but one option it could adopt is the development of a nuclear-armed cruise missile to serve theatre and tactical roles. According to Arkin and Fieldhouse, the US Tomahawk sea-launched cruise missile (SLCM) is 'emerging as the most im-

portant nuclear strike system in the Pacific Command and other naval forces'. See W.M. Arkin and R.W. Fieldhouse, *Nuclear Battlefields: Global Links in the Arms Race*, (Ballinger Publishing Company, Cambridge, Massachusetts, 1985), p.125. China has already developed an operational air-launched cruise missile for its B–7 aircraft, and SLCM systems for its submarines (see later section on the Navy). There are no strong indications that these missile systems are nuclear-armed, but the development of such missiles in air, land and sea-launched configurations would greatly enhance China's deterrent capabilities against the powerful Soviet forces it faces.

65. *Foreign Report*, 12 December 1985, p.5 and 6 March 1986, p.6.

66. *Handbook 1984*, p.A–36.

67. According to the Chinese media, the Chemical Defence Corps, which was founded in 1950, conducts nuclear, biological and chemical (NBC) training. It has participated in all of China's nuclear tests, guarding the test sites. It has also conducted 'various surveys and tests', probably referring to both defensive and offensive chemical warfare activities. It is represented on major headquarters by a Chemical Defence Branch, which seems to provide technical direction for Chemical Defence units in the formation, and to coordinate the development of NBC warfare techniques and equipment: Zhongguo Xinwenshe, 14 February 1986, in FBIS–CHI, 18 February 1986, K2–3. See also an example of local initiative in Wulumuqi MR, where the Chemical Defence Branch developed new anti-nuclear flash goggles: *Jiefangjun Huabao* (hereafter JFJHB), November 1983, p.42.

68. According to the Tel Aviv daily newspaper *Yediot Aharanot* of 18 July 1984, quoting British Intelligence sources, Israel was helping China to re-evaluate its (conventional and) chemical weapons capability. China was also concerned about the 'sale of chemical weapons to Taiwan': *JDW*, 11 August 1984, p.178 and *Foreign Report*, 12 December 1985, p.5. Overt references to the Chemical Defence Corps' offensive role are very rare, but one appeared in the Chinese media in early 1986, in which it was claimed that Chemical Defence units had cooperated with the infantry during the 'self-defence battles against Vietnam' to 'wipe out the enemy at short range', and to destroy 'over 1500 enemy forts and strongholds'.

Moreover, during the current re-organisation, the Chemical Defence Corps was being strengthened. It was upgrading its capabilities and training, studying enemy doctrine and techniques, and was providing an expanded protective service to 'whole units' as well as to individuals: Zhongguo Xinwenshe, 14 February 1986, in FBI–CHI, 18 February 1986, K2–3.

69. *Handbook 1984*, p.36. See also 'To Do Well Two Kinds of Preparations and Grasp Two Sets of Skills', *JFJB*, 14 March 1984, p.2 and Special Commentator of *LAD*, 'Strive to Raise Our Army's Electronic Warfare Capabilities', *JFJB*, 12 April 1984, p.2.

70. *Ibid.*

71. The A–5 FANTAN ground attack aircraft, for instance, is considered to be as fast with weapons carried as most modern strike aircraft. See Bill Sweetman, 'Air Forces', in G. Segal and W.T. Tow (eds), *Chinese Defence Policy* (Macmillan, London, 1984), p.78.

72. *Handbook 1984*, p.36.

73. Sweetman, 'Air Forces', p.78.

74. *Handbook 1984*, p.37.

75. *Asian Aviation*, May 1986, p.42.

76. *Ibid.*

77. *JFJHB*, No. 8, August 1982, pp.30–33; *JFJB*, 17 June 1983, p.4; XH, 20 July 1985, in FBIS–CHI, 5 August 1985, K5–6, and *China Daily*, Beijing, 1 August 1986, p.1.

78. For example, the Mi–8 HIP, which the Soviets have used in the gunship role, and the recently acquired S–70C civilian version of the US Blackhawk. See *CONMILIT*, No.95, Hong Kong, October 1984, p.64. For the establishment of the ground force's air arm see XH, Domestic Service, 26 January 1987, in FBIS–CHI, 2 February 1987, K20.

79. *Handbook 1984*, pp.A–2, A–7, A–10, A–27/28, and *JDW*, 22 December 1984, p.1100.

80. The Ground Force's medium and heavy AAA resources have tactical ranges from only 10 000m to 12 000m. Rates of fire are low — 15 to 20 rounds per minute — but these weapons are radar-controlled. They have traditionally been grouped in AAA divisions which could be deployed to support field armies. See *Handbook 1984*, p.A–28.

81. Air Force and naval AA units are largely armed with heavy AAA weapons, and are supplemented by Reserve and Militia AAA units for what appears to be urban and industrial AD

tasks. Some Chinese variants of the 1950s vintage Soviet SAM — the SA–2 GUIDELINE — are also in service. This SAM is of limited tactical value, for while portable, it is not mobile (needing prepared, fixed sites, which are difficult to conceal), is ineffective at low altitudes, and is doubtless vulnerable to Soviet ECM: see Sweetman, 'Air Forces', p.79. Air Force and naval AA weapons are radar-controlled. As in the case of the Ground Force's medium and heavy AAA units, radar and fire-control systems are based mainly on early Soviet designs, perhaps updated in some cases. See *JDW*, 3 November 1984, p.764.

82. *Defence Electronics*, January 1984, p.22 and *FEER*, 28 June 1984, pp.11–22.

83. *RMRB*, 16 September 1984, in FBIS–CHI, 18 September 1984, K6.

84. *Jingji Ribao*, 15 October 1984, in *SWB*, 18 October 1984, FE/7777/BII/2; *JDW*, 15 January 1985, p.1132 and *CONMILIT*, No.98, January 1985, inside front cover.

85. For example, information provided to potential overseas buyers shows that the HN–5 can be fitted to the BMP–1 look-alike, the Type WZ501 MICV. See *JDW*, 15 December 1984, p.1063.

86. NCNA, 15 October 1984, in *SWB*, 18 October 1984, FE/7777/BII/2. In February 1986 a communist newspaper in Hong Kong revealed that Jiangdong-class frigates had been equipped with the Hongqi-61 SAM, which was similar to the Sea Sparrow missile system: see *Ta Kung Pao*, 15 February 1986, p.3.

87. *JDW*, 15 June 1985, p.1132.

88. *JDW*, 10 May 1984, p.849.

89. The tactical AA range of the Type 80 SP AA gun is reported to be the same as the towed Type 59 AA gun, and as no fire-control system is fitted, it is limited to clear-weather operations only. See *JDW*, 10 May 1986, p.849.

90. *JDW*, 22 December 1984, p.1099.

91. Media reports indicative of these aspects include Gansu Provincial Service, 20 June 1984, in *SWB*, 23 June 1984, FE/7677/BII/5; Shaanxi Provincial Service, 21 July 1984, in *SWB*, 25 July 1984, FE/7704/BII/5 and *Liaoning Ribao*, 5 October 1984, p.4, in JPRS, *China Report*, 21 November 1984, p.66.

92. Frequent references to training in the 'Three Defences' and the 'Five Defences', which include defence against air and air-

borne attacks, reflect the emphasis on air defence measures in the field.

93. Beijing Domestic Service, 29 July 1985, in FBIS–CHI, 12 August 1985, K4–6. The Chinese expect that the new SAM technical training centre will train 1000 personnel a year 'capable of performing combat readiness duties': *RMRB* Overseas Edition, 18 February 1987, p.4, in FBIS-CHI, 20 February 1987, K39.

94. Under the new semi-automated system, microcomputers have replaced manual processes: XH, Beijing Domestic Service 5 May 1987, in FBIS–CHI, 7 May 1987, K19.

95. The BJ 7104 has a speed of only 250kph, but the Changkong No.1 has an average speed of about 900kph, and a range of 600–900km. The B–2 can tow two main targets plus four others representing descending paratroops. See *JDW*, 3 March 1984, p.307; *Defence Attache*, No.1/1986, p.41 and *JDW*, 4 March 1986, p.426. In addition, Shenyang Military Region produced a working rotary-wing RPV for training units in defence against armed helicopters: see *JFJHB*, No.11, November 1983, p.42.

96. In the latter stages of the civil war against the Nationalists, the PLA learned to its cost the risks of launching an amphibious assault without adequate support against well-prepared defences. A disastrous failure to seize the island of Jinmen in 1949 demonstrated that proper air and naval protection and fire support were essential to success. A much better-conducted series of operations was the Dachen Islands compaign of 1954–55. The high point of this campaign was an amphibious assault by 6000 ground force troops, supported by artillery and air strikes, to seize Yijiang Island, while PLA naval units dealt with opposing Nationalist ships. US observers reported that the PLA carried out the complex operation in flawless textbook fashion: see D.G. Muller, *China as a Maritime Power*, (Westview Press, Boulder, 1983), pp.26–27. The threat of US intervention in the event of an invasion of Taiwan seemed, however, to convince the PRC of the futility of attempting to develop the force levels and specialist skills required to conduct such a large enterprise, and contributed to the dominance of the strategy of continental defence, in which the Navy was assigned a subsidiary role, mainly that of coastal defence. This perception was no doubt strengthened by the action of the US Seventh Fleet in breaking the PLA's blockade

of Jinmen in 1958. Thus apart from maintaining limited efforts to train Ground Force units in amphibious landings, little was done to develop a credible capability until the late 1970s, when a combination of strategic and internal political circumstances resulted in a revival of interest in maritime affairs.

97. Muller, *China as a Maritime Power*, p.166. Under these programs, by 1986 three Yukan-class large LST and over 20 Yuliang-class LSM had reportedly been built. See *JDW*, 22 March 1986, p.529. The Qiong Sha assault transports also made their appearance during this period. The PLA itself traces the development of the Marine Force to the same period. See *JFJB*, 8 September 1986, p.1.

98. *Wen Hui Pao*, 6 August 1981, in FBIS–CHI, 11 August 1981, W4, cited in Muller, *China as a Maritime Power*, p.166.

99. In 1982 the PLA's newspaper, *Jiefangjun Bao*, listed some of the Marine's major equipments, and identified the force's tasks as being to:

   a. attack islands and conduct landings in conjunction with naval operations;

   b. seize and secure forward bases for the Navy;

   c. study and develop techniques, tactics and equipment for use in amphibious warfare.

JFJB, 12 May 1982, p.1. *See also Liaowang* Overseas Edition, No.23, Hong Kong, 8 June 1987, pp.10–11. The Marines' main training base is in the South Sea Fleet area, probably on the Leizhou Peninsula or possibly on Hainan Island. Recently the Marines have paid increasing attention to developing combined arms, joint service and rapid response capabilities. See *JFJB*, 8 September 1986, p.1.

100. *Handbook 1984*, p.56 and *The Military Balance 1986–87*, p.144.

101. *Handbook 1984*, pp.47–59.

102. *The Military Balance 1986–87*, p.144 and *JFJB*, 8 September 1986, p.1.

103. This limitation may be overcome in the not too distant future, as in 1985 China was reported to be negotiating with Britain, France and other countries for in-flight refuelling equipment. See *Foreign Report*, 25 July 1985, p.5.

104. *JFJHB*, No.4, April 1984, pp.16–17.

105. *Handbook 1976*, p.4–47.

106. *Handbook 1984*, p.47.

107. *Ibid.*, pp.47, 66 and A–33; *JFJHB*, No.1, January 1984, pp.2–5; *JFJHB*, No.4, April 1984, pp.16–19, and XH, 4 June 1987, 10 June 1987, K8.
108. For example, see *Ta Kung Pao*, 3 November 1983, p.1 and Beijing Domestic Service, 29 July 1985, in FBIS–CHI, 12 August 1985, K6.
109. XH, Wuhan, 18 May 1983 and Beijing Domestic Service, 29 July 1985, in FBIS–CHI, 12 August 1985, K6.
110. *JDW*, 27 April 1985, p.703.
111. An earlier non-nuclear system — the DF–1 — was probably scrapped or converted to a nuclear system in the early 1970s. See *Handbook 1984*, p.70.
112. Zhongguo Xinwen She, Hong Kong, 28 May 1987, in FBIS–CHI, 28 May 1987, K16 and *Liaowang* Overseas Edition,. Hong Kong, No.23, 8 June 1987, pp.8–9.
113. *JDW*, 15 February 1986, p.233. See also *JDW*, 12 October 1985, p.771 and 7 December 1985, p.1218.
114. *Handbook 1984*, p.70. China developed a MIRV capability through the CZ–3 satellite launch program, and reportedly conducted the first successful DF–5 MIRV test in September 1985. See *FEER*, 24 April 1986, p.14.
115. Muller, *China as a Maritime Power*, p.103.
116. Bussert, 'PRC Electronics', March 1985, map on p.136 and A. Preston, 'The PLA Navy's Underwater Deterrent', *JDW*, 28 April 1984, p.659.
117. *Ibid*, p.659.
118. B. Swanson, *Eighth Voyage of the Dragon*, (Naval Institute Press, Annapolis, 1982), p.251.
119. Preston, 'The PLA Navy's Underwater Deterrent', p.659.
120. *Ming Pao*, 5 June 1986, p.41.
121. For example, see *Handbook 1984*, p.71.
122. *Ming Pao*, 5 June 1986, p.41.
123. Preston, 'The PLA Navy's Underwater Deterrent', p.660; *The Economist*, 25 January 1986, p.24; G. Jacobs, 'China's Auxiliary Ships', *JDW*, 8 March 1986, p.436 and *The Military Balance 1986–87*, pp.142–143.
124. *Handbook 1984*, p.A–44.
125. *Handbook 1984*, p.71. Some sources speculate that there is another class of SSBN, sometimes termed the Daqingyu: for example see *The Military Balance 1986–1987*, pp.141 and 143. If this is correct it could account for the differences in the reported number of missile tubes. It is also possible that the

Daqingyu, if it exists, is in fact a modification of the original XIA design, and not a different class.

126. For example, see *Handbook 1984*, p.A–44; Preston, 'The PLA Navy's Underwater Deterrent', p.660 and *The Military Balance 1986–1987*, p.142.

127. *SCMP*, 16 November 1984; *JDW*, 7 December 1985, p.1218 and *RMRB*, 25 January 1986, in *SWB*, 26 January 1986, FE/8168/BII/1.

128. *JDW*, 22 May 1986, p.529.

129. *Handbook 1984*, pp.72–73; Fieldhouse, 'Chinese Nuclear Weapons: An Overview', p.104 and Zhongguo Xinwen She, Hong Kong, 28 May 1987, in FBIS–CHI, 29 May 1987, K14.

130. *JFJB*, 10 January 1984, p.1.

131. XH, 12 June 1984, in *Wen Hui Pao*, 13 June 1984.

132. *Ibid*; *FEER*, 28 June 1984, p.10; *JDW*, 8 December 1984, p.1016; FBIS–CHI, 5 August 1985, K7; *JDW*, 7 December 1985, p.1218; *JDW*, 15 February 1986, p.233 and *Ming Pao*, 21 June 1986, p.5, in FBIS–CHI, 24 June 1986, W1.

133. XH, 30 July 1984, in SWB, 3 August 1984, FE/7712/BII/2–3 and *RMRB*, 29 October 1984, in *SWB*, 1 November 1984, FE/7789/BII/3.

134. R.S. Wang, 'China's Evolving Strategic Doctrine', in *AS*, Vol. XXIV, No.10, October 1984, p.1050.

135. *The Military Balance 1986–87*, p.144. The 114 diesel submarines listed include two MING–class modified ROMEOs and one GOLF–class guided missile submarine (SSG).

136. In 1985 the Commander of the PLA Navy, Liu Huaqing, observed that the number of major combatants had increased tenfold since the 1950s. See *CONMILIT*, No. 98, January 1985, p.66.

137. *The Military Balance 1986–1987*, p.144.

138. *Ibid*; *Handbook 1984*, p.56; *Ming Pao*, 5 June 1986, p.41 and *The Economist*, 25 January 1986, p.24.

139. *Handbook 1984*, p.A–1.

140. *The Military Balance 1985–1986*, p.112 and *Ta Kung Pao*, 25 August 1985, p.1, in FBIS–CHI, 26 August 1985, W2.

141. G. Jacobs, 'Bringing China's Navy Up to Date', *JDW*, 25 January 1986, p.113.

142. *China Daily*, Beijing, 11 April 1987, p.1.

143. The overall standard of the PLA Navy's electronic equipment has been described as about equivalent to that of late Korean War vintage ships in the West, although improvements are

currently in hand. See G. Jacobs, 'China's Frigate Classes', *JDW*, 5 January 1985, p.31 and G. Jacobs, 'China's Destroyers', *JDW*, 23 February 1985, p.324.

144. The endurance of the Chengdu FFG, Jiangnan FF and Anshan DDG vary between 1670nm and 2800nm at economical speed. The Luda, Jiangdong and Jianghu classes can steam economically from 4000 to 5000nm: Jacobs, 'China's Frigates' and 'China's Destroyers', pp.31 and 323 respectively. The good sea-keeping qualities and endurance of the Luda class attested to by Bruce Swanson in *Eighth Voyage of the Dragon*, pp.255, 265 and 276, reflect the gradual but successful development program of this class since the basic engineering problems encountered in the early 1970s with the lead ship of this class, DDG–105. See JPRS, *China Report*, 17 March 1983, pp.103–107.

145. Jacobs, 'China's Frigate Classes', p.31.

146. *Ming Pao*, 29 November 1983, p.21; *FEER*, 4 April 1986, pp.17–18; *JDW*, 27 July 1985, p.160; *Ta Kung Pao*, 15 February 1986, p.3, in FBIS–CHI, 20 February 1986, W3 and *Ming Pao*, 3 June 1986, in FBIS–CHI, 5 June 1986, W2.

147. *Ta Kung Pao*, 15 February 1986, p.3, in FBIS–CHI, 20 February 1986, W3; Lieuts J. Goldrick and P. Jones, 'The Far Eastern Navies', *US Naval Institute Proceedings*, March 1986, p.65; *Ming Pao*, 3 June 1986, p.10, in FBIS–CHI, 5 June 1986, W2 and *JDW*, 25 January 1986, pp.113–114. Two new FFG were observed recently fitting out in a Shanghai shipyard. They appear to be developments of the Jianghu class, but it is uncertain whether they are part of the abovementioned new construction program. Photographs of these FFG show two distinct configurations: Pennant No.544 has a helicopter landing pad and hanger mounted aft (and thus will be the first PRC combatant to have a helicopter embarked) and a single group of SSM launchers, apparently for STYX-derived Hai Ying 2 anti-ship missiles. Its forward main gun position is unoccupied. Pennant No.535 has two pairs of what appears to be C–801 missile launchers, twin 100mm gun mounts fore and aft, flush sides in the midship section up to 01 deck, and an absence of portholes along the hull, suggesting some NBC protection. Neither ship appears to have a modern electronics fit. See *International Defence Review*, (Interavia SA, Cointrin-Geneva), Vol.19, No.6/1986, pp.718–719. Pennant No.535 is most likely the FFG reported

by Xinhua as having been commissioned on 14 December 1986. Its official description as the 'first Chinese naval vessel to be completely sealed and airconditioned' strengthens the likelihood of an NBC protective system. See XH Domestic Service, 14 December 1986, in FBIS–CHI, 18 December 1986, K1.

148. *Ta Kung Pao*, 15 February 1986, p.3, in FBIS–CHI, 20 February 1986, W3. There has been speculation for several years concerning the origin of this missile. Some observers have suggested that China was supplied a French Exocet by a third country, which it has somehow reproduced. Reverse engineering unaided would, however, be a difficult and lengthy process. It is more likely that Western assistance in design and guidance systems has enabled China to build a missile similar to Exocet. There have been persistent reports since 1984 that Israel has secretly assisted China to develop modern military equipment, including missiles. See *JDW*, 11 August 1984, p.84; *JDW*, 13 April 1985, p.620; *FEER*, 12 December 1985, p.25 and *Foreign Report*, 12 December 1985, p.5 and 6 March 1986, p.6.

149. *Foreign Report*, 25 July 1985, p.5 and *Ta Kung Pao*, 15 February 1986, p.3, in FBIS–CHI, 20 February 1986, W3.

150. Goldrick and Jones, 'The Far Eastern Navies', p.65.

151. *FEER*, 4 April 1985, pp.17–18; *Ta Kung Pao*, 15 February 1986, p.3, in FBIS–CHI, 20 February 1986, W3 and Goldrick and Jones, 'The Far Eastern Navies', p.65.

152. *JDW*, 5 October 1985, p.717.

153. For example, BMB–1, BMB–2, RBU–1200 and FQF–2500 12-barrel depth charge mortars.

154. The article was written by the Deputy Chief of Naval Staff. See Li Jing, 'Functions of Naval Aviation', pp.2–4.

155. See subsequent section on the Air Force.

156. *Ta Kung Pao*, 15 February 1986, p.3, in FBIS–CHI, 20 February 1986, W3.

157. *Asian Aviation*, May 1986, p.42.

158. K. Munson, 'Fishbed, Finback and the Chinese Future', *JDW*, 21 December 1985, p.1369.

159. This is inferred in Li Jing, 'Functions of Naval Aviation'. See also *JDW*, 25 January 1986, p.114 and Goldrick and Jones, 'The Far Eastern Navies', p.66. The Chinese claim that this aircraft can be employed in ASW, anti-shipping, search and

rescue and maritime reconnaisance roles. See XH, Beijing, 21 April 1987, in FBIS–CHI, 21 April 1987, K23.

160. *FEER*, 4 April 1985, pp.17–18.

161. In May 1986 the Chief of the General Staff (CGS), Yang Dezhi, while on a 16 day visit to the US, discussed the purchase of ASW torpedoes, sonar and helicopters: *FEER*, 27 May 1986, p.32.

162. The number of helicopters converted so far has been reported variously from three to seven: *JDW*, 13 April 1985, p.620; *JDW*, 25 January 1986, p.114 and *Ming Pao*, 5 June 1986, p.41. The Chinese may intend to arm some of these helicopters. In 1983 the Deputy Chief of Naval Staff stated that testing was being successfully conducted into firing rockets (huo jian) from naval helicopters, but did not mention the role envisaged: Li Jing, 'Functions of Naval Aviation', pp.2–4.

163. *Aviation Week and Space Technology*, 28 October 1985, p.24, cited in A. Hinge and N. Lee, 'Naval Developments in the Asia-Pacific Region', (Strategic and Defence Studies Centre, Australian National University), a paper prepared for the Asian Studies Association of Australia Biennial conference, May 1986, p.10 and footnotes 23 and 24; G. Jacobs, 'Bringing China's Navy Up to Date', in *JDW*, 25 June 1986, p.114 and *Ming Pao*, 3 June 1986, p.10, in FBIS–CHI, 5 June 1986, W2. On the new Zhi-8 helicopter, see XH, 4 June 1987, in FBIS–CHI, 10 June 1987, K8.

164. *Ta Kung Pao*, 15 February 1986, in FBIS–CHI, 20 February 1986, W3.

165. *JDW*, 24 March 1984, p.436.

166. Reuters, Hong Kong, 26 November 1983; *Ming-Pao*, 29 November 1983, p.21 and *Ta Kung Pao*, 15 February 1986, p.3, in FBIS–CHI, 20 February 1986, W3. See also a *JFJB* article that strongly advocates a force comprising three types of combatants as the prerequisite for securing control of the sea in modern naval warfare — large guided missile ships, submarines armed with guided missiles and cruise missiles, and aircraft carriers: 'New Method for Securing Control of the Sea', *JFJB*, 20 July 1984, p.3. It is interesting to note that since the article was published, China has acquired or taken positive steps towards acquiring the first and second types. Can the aircraft carrier be far behind?

167. When the Commander of the Air Force, Zhang Tingfa, visited

Britain in 1985, he showed great interest in long-range operations and in-flight refuelling, which have relevance for both the Air Force and the Naval Air Force. See *Foreign Report*, 25 July 1985, p.5.

168. In 1983 the Deputy Chief of Naval Staff described these requirements as 'urgent'. He seemed to give the next priority to strengthening the NAF's strike capability, including the acquisition of air-launched guided missiles. The NAF also needed a stronger fighter force to ensure control of airspace, including aircraft with a greater combat radius, look-down, shoot-down capability, and better AAM that could 'attack several targets simultaneously'. The NAF's ASW capability was, however, to be only 'gradually developed'. See Li Jing, 'Functions of Naval Aviation', pp.2–4.

169. In 1985, although not referring specifically to aircraft, Liu Huaqing claimed that the Navy's ECM had greatly improved; *CONMILIT*, No.98, January 1985, p.66. In the previous year a Chinese correspondent described how ECM had been used during a SSF exercise: *Ban Yue Tan* (Half-monthly Discussion), No.24, 1984, p.28. It seems reasonable to assume that both ships and aircraft are being fitted with ECM equipment.

170. *Jane's All the World's Aircraft 1983–84*, p.737; *Ming Pao*, 5 June 1985, p.41 and *JDW*, 15 June 1985, p.1132. The Chinese claim that, this aircraft the B–6D, carries two ASM 'with special targetting functions': XH, Beijing, 21 April 1987, in FBIS-CHI, 21 April 1987, K23.

171. This aircraft, based on the An-12 CUB design, has a claimed maximum combat radius of 2500km and a maximum (cruising) endurance of 10 hours. See *JDW*, 28 September 1985, p.679 and 25 January 1986, p.114.

172. The Swedish Space Corporation's package is reported to include SLAR, a micro-wave radiometer, camera system and processing/data storage units. See *Aviation Week and Space Technology*, 19 May 1986, p.18.

173. The International Institute for Strategic Studies, London, lists 90 ROMEO class, two Ming and 15 WHISKEY class in operational service, with five WHISKEYs in reserve and one GOLF class used for trials: The *Military Balance 1986–1987*, p.144.

174. Preston, 'The PLA Navy's underwater Deterrent', *JDW*, 28 April 1984, p.660 and Jacobs, 'China's Auxiliary Ships', *JDW*, 8 March 1986, p.436. Some sources consider that the

HAN boats have each been fitted with six cruise missiles, having a reported range of 1600km, and have thus reclassified them as SSGN. See *The Military Balance 1986–1987*, pp.141, 142 and 144, and Clare Hollingworth, 'Massive Streamlining and Reorganization of the Armed Forces', in *Pacific Defence Reporter*, Vol.XIII Nos.6/7, December 1986/January 1987, p.45. While such conversions may be in hand, it is doubtful that any have yet reached operational status.

175. Hinge and Lee, 'Naval Developments in the Asia-Pacific Region', p.11.
176. G. Jacobs, 'China's Submarine Force', *JDW*, 9 February 1985, pp.221–222.
177. XH, 26 September 1985, in FBIS-CHI, 1 October 1985, K10–12.
178. The original SSM involved in the WUHAN program is believed to have been a STYX-derived missile, but later reports suggest that the C-801 a more capable weapon, may have replaced it. Goldrick and Jones, 'The Far Eastern Navies' *Ming Pao*, 3 June 1986, in FBIS-CHI, 5 June 1986, W2; *Ming Pao*, 5 June 1986, p.41, and *RMRB*, 28 July 1986, p.4, in FIBS-CHI, 6 August 1986, K9–10.
179. *Handbook 1984*, p.57 and Jacobs, 'China's Submarine Force', pp.220 and 222.
180. *JFJHB*, No.9, September 1982, pp.18–19.
181. *Handbook 1984*, p.57.
182. In 1982 the Chinese claimed, however, that SS299 of the SSF carried out 'a long mission of over 3000nm', and in 1985 Liu Huaqing stated that the scope of submarine operations had extended to sea areas in the West Pacific and around the Xisha and Nansha islands: see *JFJHB*, No.7, July 1982, pp.28–31 and Zhongquo Xinwenshe, Beijing, 26 September 1985, in FBIS-CHI, 1 October 1985, K10–12. Nevertheless, long missions of about 3000nm seem to be exceptions to normal operating practice. On the new records for nuclear submarine operations, see Beijing Domestic Service, 25 March 1987, in FBIS-CHI, 1 April 1987, K28.
183. For example, the replacement of the current diesel-electric propulsion systems with more modern units availiable in the West: see Jacobs, 'China's Submarine Force', p.224. The possibility also exists that modern sonar equipment will be obtained: see *FEER*, 4 April 1985, pp.17–18 and *JDW*, 25 January 1986, p.114.

184. According to some sources, French technicians have been in-
      volved. See Jacobs, 'China's Submarine Force', p.224.

185. *Ta Kung Pao*, 15 January 1986, in FBIS-CHI, 20 February
      1986, W3.

186. *The Militiary Balance 1986–1987*, p.144.

187. *JDW*, 10 August 1985, p.278.

188. *JDW*, 8 February 1986, p.188.

189. Hinge and Lee, 'Naval Developments in the Asia Pacific Re-
      gion', p.11. The Chinese are not confident, however that the
      technical and tactical levels of their offensive minewarfare
      capability can withstand the advanced MCM of modern
      navies, and recognise the need to reform these aspects. At the
      same time, they are prepared to use minewarfare defensively
      to protect the homeland, such as in the defence of Chinese
      straits. See *JFJB*, 6 April 1984, p.3. and note 191.

190. Muller, *China as a Maritime Power*, pp.108–109. The Navy
      regards its shore-based SSM network as one of its major assets
      in coastal defence. See *JFJB*, 2 June 1983, p.4.

191. Swanson, 'Naval Forces', in G. Segal and W.T. Tow (eds),
      Chinese Defence Policy, p.91 and *JFJB*, 6 April 1984, p.3.

192. These are STYX-derived Hai Ying SSM mounted on modified
      Type-63 amphibious tank chassis. See *CONMILIT*, No.88,
      March 1984, p.25.

193. For example a bridge simulator has been developed, and a
      special-to-arm college covering over 40 specialities in sub-
      marine warfare has been opened. See Zhongguo Xinwenshe,
      26 September 1985, in FBIS-CHI, 1 October 1985, K10–12.

194. *JDW*, 12 January 1985, p.51.

195. XH, 29 June 1984, in SWB, 3 July 1984, FE/7685/BII/11 and
      SWB, 4 July 1984, FE/7686/BII/1.

196. For example, see XH, 29 January 1984, in SWB, 2 February
      1984, FE/7556/BII/4; *Ming Pao*, 30 January 1984, p.6 and an
      interview with Liu Huaqing in *Wen Hui Pao*, 31 July 1984,
      p.3.

197. *SWB*, 2 February 1984, FE/7556/BII/4.

198. As at January 1984, efforts in nuclear and chemical warfare
      training were still described as 'basic' and 'experimental', but
      the intention was to improve training for higher command
      elements and tactical headquarters, as well as to boost training
      in all ships and naval establishments. See *JFJB*, 10 January
      1984, p.1.

199. For an account of these operations, see B. Hahn, 'PRC Policy

in Maritime Asia', *Journal of Defence and Diplomacy*, (Defence and Diplomacy Inc., McLean, Va.), Vol.4, No.6, June 1986, pp.19–21.

200. The ships involved were not combatants. The 1983 cruise covered 6000nm, and the 1984 cruise 8600nm. See *RMRB*, 13 June 1983; *Ming Pao*, 14 June 1983 and *CONMILIT*, No.93, August 1984, p.60.

201. Hahn, 'PRC Policy in Maritime Asia', p.20 and *Ming Pao*, 5 June 1986, p.41.

202. So far, major working-level contacts between the PRC and US navies have been confined to a ship passing and signals exercise between the Chinese ships returning from the South Asian cruise and US Seventh Fleet units in the South China Sea, and a port visit to Qingdao by a US Navy task group in November 1986, with the Commander-in-Chief US Pacific Command embarked. This visit by three US combatants led by the Leahy class guided missile cruiser 'Reeves', was the first such visit to China by the US Navy since 1949. The possibility of the PLA Navy conducting training visits to foreign ports was hinted at in a Chinese announcement in 1986 concerning the launching of a new class of training ship. According to Xinhua News Agency, the ship would be used for training 200 cadets 'on the high seas', and would be equipped to standards that would permit foreign port-calls. See Hahn, 'PRC Policy in Maritime Asia', p.21; Taipei International Service, 22 January 1986, in FBIS-CHI, 22 January 1986, V1; XH, 12 July 1986, in FBIS-CHI, 17 July 1986, K29; *Chung Yang Jih Pao*, Taipei, 28 October 1986, in FBIS-CHI, 3 November 1986, Vl; XH, 5 November 1986, in FBIS-CHI, 5 November 1986, B1, and Jinan, Shandong Provincial Service, 7 November 1986, in FBIS-CHI, 10 November 1986, B1.

203. *Ming Pao*, 3 June 1986, p.3 and *Wen Hui Pao*, 10 June 1986, p.2, in FBIS-CHI, 10 June 1986, W1.

204. *Ming Pao*, 4 June 1986, p.3.

205. Beijing Domestic Service, 26 March 1987, in FBIS-CHI, 1 April 1987, K28 and Beijing Domestic Service, 9 June 1987, in FBIS-CHI, 11 June 1987, K13.

206. *The Military Balance 1986–1987*, p.145. Some 200 transport aircraft, most of which have not yet reached their mid-life of type point, are being sold to local and provincial civil air transport services. See Shanghai City Service, 18 August 1985, in FBIS-CHI, 19 August 1985, K9. Some of these surplus

aircraft may be among those the Air Force is to assign to a new civil airline to be established jointly by the Air Force and United China Airlines; *China Daily*, 11 June 1986, p.1.

207. *The Military Balance 1986–87*, pp.141 and 145, and *Handbook 1984*, p.63.

208. For example, the definition of an air campaign (kung zhong zhanyi), also termed an air force campaign, given in the Chinese People's Liberation Army Military Glossary is: 'The totality of a series of operations conducted independently by one or a number of Air Force campaign army groups or campaign tactical regiments according to a unified plan, in order to achieve a given strategic campaign aim'. See Zhao Falin, 'The Status of the Air Campaign Grows Ever Mightier', *JFJB*, 25 November 1983, p.3.

209. *Liaowang*, Overseas Edition, No.8, Hong Kong, 24 February 1986, pp.19–20, in FBIS-CHI, 4 March 1986, K12.

210. *Ibid.*; FBIS-CHI, 5 August 1985, K3 and NCNA, 21 August 1985, in FBIS-CHI, 22 August 1985, K1.

211. *JFJB*, 25 November 1983, p.3. The model suggested here uses the organisational terms applied to the Soviet air forces before their restructuring in the late 1970s. While the Chinese may try to emulate the present Soviet organisation, their current inventory of aircraft seems more suited to the former Frontal Aviation, LRA and Air Defence Forces structure. Whatever organisational solution the Chinese settle on, it is unlikely to be an exact copy of any other nation's, but can be expected to have 'Chinese characteristics'.

212. NCNA, 21 August 1985, in FBIS-CHI, 22 August 1985, K1.

213. *China Daily*, Beijing, 1 August 1986, p.1.

214. *Ibid.* and NCNA, 23 August 1985, in FBIS-CHI, 22 August 1985, K1.

215. XH, 24 May 1983, in FBIS-CHI, 26 May 1983, K4. Presumably, this committee will also provide input to the PLA Air Force's own research and planning into operational requirements. For air traffic control responsibilities see FBIS-CHI, 11 February 1987, K18.

216. *Handbook 1984*, pp.63–64.

217. *JFJB*, 15 June 1984, p.3.

218. *Jane's All the World's Aircraft*, 1983–1984, p.737.

219. Sweetman, 'Air Forces', in Segal and Tow (eds), *Chinese Defence Policy*, pp.77–78.

220. *Asian Aviation*, May 1986, p.42.

221. The PL-7 is reported to have a maximum lock-on range of 14 400m: *JDW*, 22 February 1986, p.311.

222. *Ibid.*

223. Sweetman, 'Air Forces', p.79.

224. These include British GEC Avionics head-up display and weapons aiming computer (HUDWAC), GEC Skyranger or improved Chinese ranging radar with enhanced ECM capability, new air data computer and radar altimeter, new digital IFF, and more secure GEC Avionics VHF/UHF communications. See K. Munson, 'Finback and the Chinese Future', *JDW*, 21 December 1985, p.1367.

225. *Ibid*; *Aviation Week and Space Technology*, 1 September 1986, p.37 and 20 October 1986, p.180, and *Time*, 10 February 1986, p.43.

226. British and French consortia are also reported to be competing for contracts to upgrade the F-8. See *Asian Aviation*, May 1986, p.42.

227. *JDW*, 22 March 1986, p.529; *Asian Aviation*, May 1986, p.42 and *Aviation Week and Space Technology*, 20 October 1986, p.180.

228. Sweetman, 'Air Forces', p.77.

229. *JDW*, 22 March 1986, p.529.

230. For example, an Italian firm (Aeritalia) is reported to be involved in a program to update the A–5, to give it an all-weather capability: *BBC World Round Up*, 4 November 1986 and *FEER*, 18 December 1986, p.24.

231. *Foreign Report*, 6 March 1986, p.6.

232. *JFJB*, 25 November 1984, p.3.

233. XH, 25 July 1984, in *SWB*, 28 July 1984, FE/7707/BII/5–6. New efforts to raise the educational standards of new aircrew entrants and direct recruitment by Air Force Staff from colleges began in 1987: XH Domestic Service, 5 February 1987, in FBIS-CHI, 12 February 1987, K21. The specialist training centres provide instruction in subjects such as aircraft maintenance, SAM operation, radar, logistics and telecommunications: *RMRB* Overseas Edition, 18 February 1987, in FBIS-CHI, 20 February 1987, K39.

234. *China Daily*, 1 August 1986, p.1.

235. *Ibid.*; XH, 30 July 1985, in FBIS-CHI, 5 August 1985, K5–6; XH, 5 January 1986, in FBIS-CHI, 6 January 1986, K23; *Liaowang* Overseas Edition, No.8, Hong Kong, 24 February 1984, pp.19–20, in FBIS-CHI, 4 March 1986, K13 and XH,

28 July 1986, in FBIS-CHI, 29 July 1986, K5–6. In mid-1987 the Commander of the Air Force stated that there were 16.4 times more pilots qualified for all-weather operations than in 1967: XH, Beijing, 12 June 1987, in FBIS-CHI, 12 June 1987, K14.

236. XH, 12 June 1987, in FBIS-CHI, 12 June 1987, K14.

237. *Liaowang* Overseas Edition, No.8, Hong Kong, 24 February 1984, pp.19–20, in FBIS-CHI, 4 March 1986, K13 and XH, 5 January 1986, in FBIS-CHI, 6 January 1986, K23. According to the Commander of the Air Force, nearly 1000 simulators had been used to replace traditional flying training methods: XH, Beijing, 12 June 1987, in FBIS-CHI, 12 June 1987, K14.

238. *China Daily*, 1 August 1986, p.1.

CHAPTER 3

1. Staff Correspondent, 'The First Step Taken in the Seventh 5-Year Plan', Beijing *Liaowang*, No.2, 13 January 1986, pp.6–7, in FBIS-CHI, 31 January 1986, K13.

2. C.K. Leung and Claude Comtois, 'Transport Reorientation towards the Eighties', in C.K. Leung and S.S.K. Chin (eds), *China in Readjustment*, (Centre of Asian Studies, University of Hong Kong, 1983), p.230. See also Gao Yan, 'The Growth of Chinese Railways, 1949–1983, Part I', in *Ming Bao Monthly*, No.3, 1986, p.45.

3. See 'A New Strategic Outlook in Defence Modernisation' in Chapter 1 and 'The Mobilisation of the Reserve Forces' in Chapter 3.

4. *The Military Balance 1986–1987*, pp.141–2. See also note 17.

5. Liu Guoguang (ed.), *A Study on Strategic Problems of China's Economic Development*, (Shanghai People's Press, Shanghai, 1984), p.198.

6. *Chinese Statistical Year Book 1985*, (State Statistical Bureau, People's Republic of China, 1985), p.389.

7. *Defence Modernisation*, (Chinese People's Liberation Army Fighters' Publication), p.256. An example is given here on the heavy demands a motorised division makes on road transport.

8. Ting Xun, 'How Do Military Specailists Make Use of Rail-

ways?,' *Tiedao Zhishi* (hereafter *TDZS*), No.2, March 1984, p.19.

9. *Ibid.*

10. The PRC now has 180 units turning out cars and trucks. Output has risen from 190 000 motor vehicles in 1981 to 439 000 in 1985. The target for 1990 is 2 000 000 as tourism and rail costs increase. See 'State Council Praises Hubei Automobile Production', 10 January 1986, in FBIS-CHI, 3 March 1986, K.3.

11. *Chinese Statistical Yearbook 1985*, p.389.

12. *China Reconstructs*, February 1981, p.22.

13. *Chinese Statistical Yearbook 1985*, p.385.

14. For Ground Force deployment in the two MRs, see Map 3 in Chapter 5.

15. FBIS-CHI, 31 January 1986, K13.

16. Office of the Statistical Planning Bureau, Railway Ministry, 'The Great Achievement of Railway Building in the Sixth Five-year Plan Period', *TDZS*, No.2 March 1986, pp.2–3.

17. Harlan Jencks, *From Muskets to Missiles: Politics and Professionalism in the Chinese Army, 1945–1981*, (Westview Press, Boulder, 1982), p.201.

18. Jiang Chenglu, 'Multiple Tracks being Constructed on the Haerbin-Suifen Line', *TDZS*, No.1, January 1986, pp.2–3.

19. Beijing XH, 6 September 1986, in *Ming Pao*, 7 September 1986. China announces the construction of 16 000km of railways along the coasts to be completed in 1990. The major concern is in East and Northeast China. *See also* note 16.

20. Feng Jinqu, 'The Electrification of the Middle Section of the Longhai Line', *TDZS*, No.5, November 1985, pp.8–9.

21. Yu Qizhong, 'The Artery to Our Country's Northwestern Border — the Lanzhou-Xinjiang Line', *TDZS*. No.2, January 1986, pp.6–7 and Wang Mingkui, 'The Important Trunk Line to the Northwestern Border — the Northern Xinjiang Line', *TDZS*, No.6, November 1985, p.6.

22. Feng Jinqu, 'The Electrification of the Longhai Line', pp.8–9.

23. Feng Jinqu, 'The Electrification of the Chengdu-Chongqing Line', *TDZS*, No.2 March 1985, pp.4–5 and Feng Jinqu, 'The Electrification of Railways on the Yunnan-Guizhou Plateau', *TDZS*, No.1, January 1984, pp.2–3.

24. Wu Qunjian and Han Mei, 'The Important Way Linking the Southwest and Central South — the Hunan-Guizhou Line', *TDZS*, No.3, May 1985, pp.2–3.

25. Zho Wenyuan and Li Zhenxing, 'Double-track Construction Work for the Hengyang-Guangzhou Section of the Beijing-Guangzhou Line', *TDZS*, No.5, September 1985, pp.2–5 and Qi Yaokun, 'The Guangzhou-Maoming Line', *TDZS*, No.2, March 1984, pp.14–15.

26. FBIS-CHI, 6 May 1986, K17 and 4 March 1986, K21.

27. 'Sichuan PLA Leaders Explain Change in Administration of Local Armed Forces', in SWB, FE/8044/B II/7.

28. 'Guangdong Prepares Transfer of Armed Forces', Guangdong Provincial Service, 14 April 1986 in FBIS-CHI, 21 April 1986, p.1 and 'Liaoning Holds Meeting on Army Transfer Work', Liaoning Provincial Service, 8 May 1986, in FBIS-CHI, 14 May 1986, S2.

29. 'Shandong: Liang Buting Speaks on Armed Forces Transfer', Shandong Provincial Service, 23 May 1986, in FBIS-CHI, 29 May 1986, p.2–3. See also *JFJB*, 17 March 1983, p.1.

30. *Bulletin of the State Council of the PRC*, 20 November 1988, pp.1948–9.

31. Sabrosky, 'Defence with Fewer Men?', pp.190–4 and Morris Janowitz, *The US Forces and the Zero Draft*, (Adelphi Paper No.94, IISS, London, 1973), p.20.

32. See Table 1.4 in Chapter 1.

33. Tian Ming, 'All Regions Are Establishing Reserve Divisions in the Ground Forces', *Ta Kung Pao*, 3 July 1984, p.2.

34. 'The Capital Established a Reserve Division', *Ming Pao*, 2 February 1985, p.5.

35. Sabrosky, 'Defence with Fewer Men?', pp.165–9.

36. R.A. Werner, 'The Readiness of US Reserve Components', in Louis A. Zurcher and Gwyn Harries-Jenkins (eds), *Supplementary Military Forces: Reserves, Militias, Auxiliaries*, (Sage Research Progress Series on War, Revolution and Peacekeeping, Sage Publications, Beverly Hills/London, 1978), p.88.

37. XH, 1 August 1984, in *SWB*, 8 August 1984, FE/771 6/BII/7–8.

38. Tian Ming, 'All Regions Are Establishing Reserve Divisions in the Ground Forces', *Ta Kung Pao*, 3 July 1984, p.2.

39. Anthony S. Bennell, 'European Reserve Forces: England, France and West Germany', in Zurcher and Harries-Jenkins (eds), *Supplementary Military Forces: Reserves, Militias, Auxiliaries*, p.44.

40. *JFJB*, 20 May 1983, p.3.

41. Robert C. Hasenbohler, 'The Swiss Militia Army', in Zurcher and Harries-Jenkins (eds), *Supplementary Military Forces*, p.246. See also *JFJB*, 20 May 1983, p.3
42. 'Active Reserve Service Officers and Civilian Cadres', *JFJB*, 29 July 1984, p.2.
43. Bennell, 'European Reserve Forces', p.59.
44. 'NPC Discusses Draft Law on Military Service', XH, 22 May 1984, in SWB, 23 May 1984, FE/7650/CI/1.
45. Jencks, *From Muskets to Missiles*, pp.122–3.
46. *Ibid.*
47. FBIS-CHI, 11 September 1979, R6.
48. *Ibid.*
49. *Ibid.*
50. 'Guangdong People's Armed Forces, Committee Discusses Militia Building', in JPRS, *China Report*, No.74875, 7 January, pp.80–2.
51. *Ibid*, p.81.
52. 'The Current Phase of Chinese Communist Militia Work', *Issues and Studies* (Taiwan), Vol.XV, No.6, June 1979, pp.81–97.
53. 'Regulations on Militia Work', *Issues and Studies*, Vol.XVI, No.2, February 1980, p.77.
54. 'The Current Phase of Chinese Communist Militia Work', *Issues and Studies*, June 1979, p.83.
55. 'Full-Time Militia Cadres Aging, Youth Needed', in JPRS, *China Report*, No.77144, 12 January 1981, p.21.
56. JPRS, *China Report*, No.74875, 7 January 1980, p.81.
57. *Ibid.*
58. 'Having Communes Train Militia Leaders Work out Well', in JPRS, *China Report*, No.76072, 18 July 1980, p.71.
59. XH, 3 March 1986, in FBIS-CHI, 4 March 1986, K21.
60. XH, 2 May 1986, in FBIS-CHI, 6 May 1986, K17.
61. 'National Forum of Advanced Cadres of County People's Armed Forces Departments', XH, 5 March 1986, in *SWB*, 10 March 1986, FE/8203/BII/5.
62. *Ibid.*
63. 'Heilongjiang Carries Out Transfer of Armed Forces', Heilongjiang Provincial Service, 23 April, 1986, in FBIS-CHI, 1 May 1986, S1.
64. *Zhejiang Ribao*, 25 April 1986, p.1, in FBIS-CHI, 7 May 1986, O5.
65. Beijing, XH, 2 May 1986, in FBIS-CHI, 6 May 1986, K7.

66. 'Shift of Hebei Armed Forces Department Progresses', Hebei Provincial Service, 3 April 1986, in FBIS-CHI, 18 April 1986, R2.
67. FBIS-CHI, 6 May 1986, K7.
68. 'Yang Shangkun on Reforming Militia Work', Peking Home Service, 1 March 1985, in *SWB*, FE/7888/B II/10.
69. *Shanxi Ribao*, 30 January 1986, p.1, in FBIS-CHI, 13 February 1986, R1.
70. 'Jiangsu's Achievements in Paying for Military Training Praised', XH, 25 December 1985, in *SWB*, FE/8145/B II/4.
71. *Ibid.*
72. 'Jiangsu Militia Engage in Commodity Production', Jiangsu Provincial Service, 3 March 1985, in *SWB*, FE/7893/B II/12.
73. *Ibid.*
74. Gansu Provincial Service, 26 April 1985, in *SWB*, 2 May 1985, FE/7940/BII/12–13.
75. *Ibid.*
76. Nanning, Guangxi Regional Service, 2 March 1985, in *SWB*, 6 March 1985, FE/7982/BII/8 and XH, 26 March 1985, in *SWB*, 4 April 1985, FE/7917/BII/5.
77. 'Hunan: Mao Zhiyong Stresses the Need for Militia and Reserve Work', Hunan Provincial Service, 13 January 1986, in *SWB*, FE/8166/BII/10.
78. *Ibid.* See also William de B. Mills, 'Leadership Change in China's Provinces', *Problems of Communism*, Vol.XXXIV, May–June 1985, pp.35–7.
79. 'Yunnan Military District Helps Militiamen to Get Rich', Yunnan Provincial Service, 18 March 1985, in *SWB*, FE/7905/BII/12.
80. Shandong Provincial Service, 23 May 1986, in FBIS-CHI, 29 May 1986, 02–3 and 'Further Strengthen Militia and Reserve Work Around the Central Task of National Economic Construction', *Anhui Ribao*, 27 March 1986, p.4, in FBIS-CHI, 14 April 1986, 01.
81. *Liaoning Ribao*, 16 April 1984.
82. 'Militia Training Should Achieve the Integration of the Responsibility System and Ideological Education', *Xinhua Ribao*, 9 May 1983.
83. *Ibid.* See also 'Raising the Standard of Specialism amongst Militia Work Cadres', *Dazhong Ribao* (The Masses Daily), 27 November 1982, p.3 and 'Suzhou Military District Organise the Militia', *Xinhua Ribao*, 18 April 1984, p.4.

84. 'Raising the Standard of Specialism Amongst Militia Work Cadres', *Dazhong Ribao*, 27 November 1982, p.3.

85. 'A Simple Rod Cannot Penetrate the Stars in the Sky', *Liaoning Ribao*, 28 February 1983, p.3.

86. N. Lee, 'The Militia in People's War under Modern Conditions, 1979–1983', in Leung and Chin (eds), *China in Readjustment*, pp.350–52.

87. 'To Solve New Problems According to New Situations', *Dazhong Ribao*, 9 September 1981, p.3.

88. 'Reform Militia Work and Lighten the Peasants' burden', *Liaowang*, No.43, 28 October 1985, p.7 and *Xinhua Ribao*, 15 May 1984.

89. 'The Armed Militia Doing Good Work in Enforcing Specialist Contract', *Dazhong Ribao*, 19 October 1981, p.3.

90. *Liaoning Ribao*, 16 April 1984 and 'Suzhou Military District Organise the Militia', *Xinhua Ribao*, 18 April 1984, p.4.

91. *Ibid.*

92. 'Regulations on Militia Work', *Issues and Studies*, Vol.XVI, No.2, February 1980, pp.79–95.

93. 'Jilin First Secretary Wang Enmao at City Defense Symposium', in FBIS-CHI, 28 March 1980, S1.

94. Lee, *Chinese People's Liberation Army*, p.81.

95. *Ningxia Ribao*, 27 June 1982, in *SWB*, 9 July 1982, FE/7873/BII/4.

96. *Ibid.*

97. FBIS-CHI, 28 March 1980, S1.

98. 'Regulations on Militia Work', p.92.

99. 'Ordnance Cadre Training Unit', JPRS, *China Report*, No.76910, 1 December 1980, p.90.

100. XH, 26 March 1985, in *SWB*, 4 April 1985, FE/7917/BII/5.

101. Jencks, 'China's "Punitive" War on Vietnam', p.813.

102. Lee, *Chinese People's Liberation Army*, p.82.

103. *Ibid*, p.83.

104. XH, 6 July 1984, in *SWB*, 11 July 1984, FE/7692/BII/7.

105. 'Communique on the Chinese Crimes against Vietnam over Past Two Years (1979–80)', in *Viet Nam News Bulletin*, No. 3/81, 20 November 1981, p.5.

106. Hanoi Home Service, 12 May 1985, in *SWB*, 15 May 1985, FE/7951/A3.

107. *Ibid.*

108. *Viet Nam News Bulletin*, No. 3/81, p.5.

109. *Ibid.*, p.4.

CHAPTER 4

1. Coral Bell, 'How Have We Survived the Crisis?', in Coral Bell (ed.), *Forty Years On: Studies of World Change in the Four Decades After 1945*, (Department of International Relations, Australian National University, 1985), pp.47–8.
2. Gerald Segal, *The Great Power Triangle*, (Macmillan, London, 1982), pp.152–55.
3. 'Interview with Zhu Qizhen, Vice Minister of Foreign Affairs of the People's Republic of China', *Journal of Notheast Asia Studies*, Vol.III, No.2, 1984, p.75.
4. *Ibid.*
5. K.K. Nair, *ASEAN-Indochina Relations Since 1975: The Politics of Accommodation*, (Canberra Papers on Strategy and Defence, No.30, Strategic and Defence Studies Centre, Australian National University, Canberra, 1984), pp.92–107.
6. See under Air Force in Chapter 2.
7. Jonathan D. Pollack, 'China's Changing Perceptions of East Asian Security and Development', *ORBIS*, Winter 1986, pp.778–9.
8. For China's attitude towards Afghanistan, see Yaacov Vertzberger, 'Afghanistan in China's Policy', *Problems of Communism*, Vol.XXXI, No.3, May–June 1982, pp.1–23.
9. N. Chanda, 'Superpower Triangle', *FEER*, 4 April 1985, pp.17–19.
10. 'Gorbachev 28 July Speech in Vladivostok', Moscow Television Service, 28 July 1986, in FBIS, Daily Report, Soviet Union (hereafter FBIS–SOV), 29 July 1986, R1–20.
11. 'Interview with Zhu Qizhen', *Journal of Northeast Asian Studies*, Vol.III, No.2, 1984, p.74.
12. LAD Commentator, 'To Learn from the Ideology of People's War and to Continue with the Strengthening of Militia Building', *JFJB*, 24 July 1983, p.3.
13. For a representative Chinese article, see Jun Yan, 'Objective Reality Is the Basis for Determining Strategic Guidelines', *JFJB*, 14 January 1983, p.3.
14. *Jetro China Newsletter*, No.60, January–February 1986.
15. Tass News Agency, Moscow, 10 July 1986.
16. *Beijing Review*, 6 January 1986, p.15, in FBIS–CHI, 6 January 1986, A3.
17. 'Report on Communique', Beijing XH, 14 April 1986, in FBIS–CHI, 15 April 1986, C2.

18. Eduard Shevardnadze and Wu Xueqian had announced their countries' intention to resume border talks when they met in the United Nations General Assembly in September 1986. See FBIS–CHI, 15 October 1986, C2.

19. Pollack, 'China's Changing Perceptions', p.777.

20. *Ibid.*, p.62.

21. 'Gorbachev 28 July Speech', in FBIS–SOV, 29 July 1986, R14, 17–19.

22. *Ibid.*, R17.

23. 'Deng Xiaoping Interviewed by Mike Wallace', Beijing XH, 6 September 1986, in FBIS–CHI, 8 September 1986, B2.

24. Alan J.K. Sanders, 'Mongolia in 1984', *AS*, Vol.XXV, No.1, January 1985, p.122 and *The Australian*, 7 August 1986.

25. *Financial Review*, 12 September 1986 and 'USSR Plans Complete Troop Withdrawal from MPR', Kyodo, 3 September 1986, in FBIS–CHI, 3 September 1986, C1.

26. 'New Atmosphere Seen for Sino–Soviet Normalization', Hong Kong AFP, 16 October 1986, in FBIS–CHI, 16 October 1986, C1–2.

27. 'Further Reportage on Sino–Soviet Consultations', Hong Kong AFP, 14 October 1986, in FBIS–CHI, 15 October 1986, C1–2.

28. 'PRC Announces US Naval Visit to Qingdao', Beijing XH, 9 October 1986, in FBIS–CHI, 10 October 1986, B1.

29. *Ibid. See also* 'US Navy to Make Port Call in Qingdao', Kyodo, 30 September 1986, in FBIS–CHI, 10 October 1986, B1.

30. 'US Secretary of Defence Continues Visit', Beijing XH, 9 October 1986, in FBIS–CHI, 10 October 1986, B1.

31. F.A. Mediansky and D. Court, *The Soviet Union in Southeast Asia*, (Canberra Papers on Strategy and Defence, No.29, Strategic and Defence Studies Centre, Australian National University, 1984), p.78.

32. *Ibid.*, p.78.

33. *Ibid.*, pp.39–40.

34. Nair, *ASEAN-Indochina Relations Since 1979*, p.209 and D. Chandler, 'Strategies for Survival in Kampuchea', *Current History*, Vol.82, No.483, 1983, p.153.

35. N. Chanda, 'Preparing the Ground', *FEER*, 14 March 1985, pp.26–7. In February 1985, Sihanouk was reported to have said that the Khmer Rouge had lost against the Vietnamese army and that Son Sann's forces had been wiped out. How-

ever, all seemed to be well again when Sihanouk was later reported on 21 February to have stiffened his position.

36. Chandler, 'Strategies for Survival', p.153. For instance, Chandler maintains that 'Vietnam will not allow a non-Communist government to come to power in Phnom Penh...'.

37. 'Different Views on Kampuchea', *Problems of Communism*, March–April 1985, pp.138–40. Controversies over Vietnam settlers in Kampuchea and the claim that the only forces resisting the return of the genocidal Khmer Rouge are Vietnam and Heng Samrin's regime, are two examples.

38. Nair, *ASEAN-Indochina Relations*, p.208.

39. *Ibid.*

40. *Ibid.*

41. Pollack, 'China's Changing Perceptions', p.778.

42. Richard Nations, 'A Mild Chill in Moscow', *FEER*, 11 July 1985, pp.10–11.

43. Pollack, 'China's Changing Perceptions', pp.777–80.

44. Richard Nations, 'Moscow's New Tack', *FEER*, 14 August 1986, pp.33–4.

45. FBIS–CHI, 8 September 1986, B2.

46. FBIS–SOV, 29 July 1986, R17.

47. 'USSR Declines Deng-Gorbachev Meet', Tokyo Kyodo, 15 October 1986, in FBIS–CHI, 15 October 1986, C3.

48. 'Rogachev Leaves for Home', Beijing XH, 15 October 1986, in FBIS–CHI, 15 October 1986, C4.

49. Nair, *ASEAN-Indochina Relations*, p.208.

50. Fieldhouse, 'Chinese Nuclear Weapons', pp.99–100.

51. Gerald Segal, 'Nuclear Forces', in Segal and Tow (eds), *Chinese Defence Policy*, pp.107–8.

52. Gregory Treverton, 'China's Nuclear Forces and the Stability of Soviet–American Deterrence', in Christopher Bertram (ed), *The Future of Strategic Deterrence*, (Macmillan, London, 1981), pp.40–42.

53. See Chapter 5.

54. Treverton, 'China's Nuclear Forces', pp.40–1.

55. *Ibid.*, p.42.

56. *Ibid.*, p.43.

57. Han Huaizhi, 'To Underline the Characteristics of Modern Warfare and to Raise the Warfighting Capabilities of Units under Modern Conditions', *JFJB*, 8 November 1983, p.2.

58. Treverton, 'China's Nuclear Forces', pp.40–1.
59. See Chapter 5.
60. Xiao Fengmei, 'The Building of City Development and Its Protection', *Baike Zhishi*, (Encyclopaedic Knowledge), No.3, 1984, p.16.
61. Special Commentator, 'To Do Well in Two Preparations and to Grasp Two Sets of Skills', *JFJB*, 11 March 1984, p.1.
62. Treverton, 'China's Nuclear Forces', p.42.
63. *Ibid.*
64. *Ibid.*
65. Fieldhouse, 'Chinese Nuclear Weapons', pp.98–101.
66. *Ibid.*, p.97 and 'Chinese Delegate Qian Jiadong Addresses First Committee in UN on Disarmament', *RMRB*, 25 October 1984. p.6.
67. Fieldhouse, 'Chinese Nuclear Weapons', p.97.
68. G. Segal, 'China and Arms Control', *The World Today*, Vol.41, Nos.8–9, August/September 1985, pp.165–6.
69. Bonnie S. Glaser and Banning N. Garrett, 'Chinese Perspectives on the Strategic Defense Initiative', *Problems of Communism*, Vol.XXXV, No.2, March–April 1986, p.42.
70. *Ibid.*, p.28. See also 'Liaowang on International Disarmament Situation', in FBIS–CHI, 18 September 1986, A5.
71. Segal, 'China and Arms Control', p.164 and 'Chinese Delegation Attending IAEA Conference', *RMRB*, 26 September 1984, p.6.
72. Jozef Goldblat and Reginald Fern, 'Arms Control Agreements', in *SIPRI Yearbook 1986*, p.578.
73. Richard Nations, 'Joining the League', *FEER*, 14 April 1986, p.14.

CHAPTER 5

1. 'The Sixth Plenum of the Eleventh Party Congress is Convened in Beijing', *RMRB*, 30 June 1981, p.1.
2. Chalmers Johnson, 'Lin Piao's Army and Its Role in the Chinese Society', *Current Scene*, Vol.IV, No.13, 1 July 1966, p.9.
3. Paul Dibb, 'China's Strategic Situation and Defence Priorities in the 1980s', *The Australian Journal of Chinese Affairs*, No.5, October 1980, p.104.
4. Huang Kecheng, 'On Assessing Chairman Mao and Attitudes

towards Mao Zedong Thought', *RMRB*, 11 April 1981, pp.1–2.

5. Su Yu, The Great Victory of Chairman Mao's Guideline on Warfare', *RMRB*, 6 August 1977, pp.1–2.

6. *Ibid.*

7. Xiao Hua, 'Chairman Mao's Revolutionary Line Was the Beacon that Led to the Victory of the Long March', *HQ*, No.9, September 1977, p.81.

8. *Ibid.*

9. 'Strive to Achieve Modernization in National Defence — in Celebration of the 20th Anninversary of the Founding of the People's Republic of China', in FBIS-CHI, 18 October 1979, L15.

10. *Ibid.*

11. Xiao Ke, 'The Great Principles in Army Building', *HQ*, No. 8, August 1979, p.14.

12. *Ibid.*

13. ' "Liberation Army Daily" New Year's Editorial', in JPRS, *China Report*, No. 75841, 9 June 1980, pp.86 and 88.

14. JPRS, *China Report*, No.786002, 7 July 1980, p.29.

15. *Handbook 1984*, pp.5–6.

16. *New York Times*, 4 January 1980.

17. 'Official PRC Statistics: 1977–1978', *The China Business Review*, July–August 1979, p.45.

18. FBIS-CHI, 2 September 1980, L22.

19. Harlan Jencks, 'Ground Forces', in Segal and Tow (eds), *Chinese Defence Policy*, p.66 and H. Jencks, ' "People's War under Modern Conditions": Wishful Thinking, National Suicide, or Effective Deterrent?', *China Quarterly*, No. 98, June 1984, p.316.

20. Jencks, ' "People's War under Modern Conditions" ', p.312.

21. Wang Kefu, et al, 'To Establish the "Shield" under Modern Conditions', *JFJB*, 3 April 1981, p.3.

22. Wang Fuji, 'Development Should be Borne in Mind when Giving Full Play to Superiority — My Views on Guerrilla Research', *JFJB*, 27 March 1981, p.3.

23. Paul H.B. Godwin, 'Towards a New Strategy?', in Segal and Tow (eds), *Chinese Defence Policy*, p.48.

24. Segal and Tow (eds), *Chinese Defence Policy*, xvii–xviii. See also Ngok Lee, 'Dimensions of China's Defence Policy for the 1980s and Beyond', *ASAA Review*, Vol.9, No.2, November 1985, pp.133–41.

25. 'Possibility of Enemy Nuclear Attack Must be Considered', in JPRS, *China Report*, No. 75825, 4 June 1980, pp.97–9.
26. See 'Wartime Mobilisation', Chapter 1.
27. See 'Combined Army and Joint Operations', Chapter 1.
28. Gerald Segal, 'Nuclear Forces', in Segal and Tow (eds), *Chinese Defence Policy*, pp.106–8.
29. *Ibid.*, pp.108–9.
30. Richard K. Betts, *NATO Deterrence Doctrine: No Way Out*, (University of California, Los Angeles, 1985), pp.53–55.
31. Jencks, ' "People's War under Modern Conditions" ', pp.316–9; Segal, 'Ground Forces', pp.98 and 105–09 and P.H.B. Godwin, 'Mao Zedong Revised: Deterrence and Defence in the 1980s', in P.H.B. Godwin (ed)., *The Chinese Defence Establishment*, (Westview Press, Boulder 1983), pp.21–39.
32. Zhang Hongxian and Chai Yuqiu, 'On the Coordination of Resolute Defence and Guerrilla Warfare', *JFJB*, 10 April 1981, p.3.
33. Wang Kefu, 'To Establish the "Shield" under Modern Conditions', *JFJB*, 3 April 1981, p.3.
34. Zhang Hongxian and Chai Yuqiu, 'On the Coordination of Resolute Defence and Guerrilla Warfare', *JFJB*, 10 April 1981, p.3.
35. *Handbook 1984*, p.38.
36. Wang Fuji, 'Development Should be Borne in Mind when Giving Full Play to Superiority', *JFJB*, 27 March 1981, p.3.
37. Zhang Taiheng, 'Firm Guiding Principles and Flexible Tactics', *JFJB*, 27 May 1983, p.3.
38. 'On Protracted War', *Selected Military Writings of Mao Zedong*, (Foreign Languages Press, Peking, 1966), pp.187–267.
39. Zhan Jingwu, 'The Development of Positional Warfare', *JFJB*, 11 March 1983, p.3.
40. Chen Hongwu, 'Do not Despise Defence', *JFJB*, 20 March 1981, p.3.
41. *Ibid.*
42. Chen Chaoxian, 'To Do Research and Develop "Cross-breed" Style Tactics', *JFJB*, 6 May 1983, p.3.
43. Chen Huibang, 'To Insist on the Integration of "Three Warfares" ', *JFJB*, 28 February 1983, p.3.
44. Chen Yangping, 'To Understand Mobile Warfare from a Developmental Point of View', *JFJB*, 18 March 1983, p.3.

45. Chen Chaoxian, 'To Do Research and Develop "Cross-breed" Style Tactics', *JFJB*, 6 May 1983.
46. Jun Yan, 'To Insist on Extensive Guerrilla Warfare', *JFJB*, 1 April 1983, p.3.
47. Zhang Hongxian and Chai Yuqiu, 'On the Coordination of Resolute Defence and Guerrilla Warfare', *JFJB*, 10 April 1981.
48. Cris Bellamy, 'Trends in Land Warfare: The Operational Art of the European Theatre', in *RUSI and Brassey's Defence Year Book 1985*, (Brassey's Defence Publishers, London, 1985), p.258.
49. *Ibid.*
50. Stephen M. Meyer, *Soviet Theatre Nuclear Forces, Part II: Capabilities and Implications*, (Adelphi Paper No.188, IISS, London, Summer 1986), pp.11–12.
51. Boyd D. Sutton, et al, 'New Directions in Conventional Defence?', *Survival*, Vol.XXVI, No.2, March/April 1984, p.52.
52. Viktor Suvorov, 'Strategic Command and Control, the Soviet Approach,' *International Defence Review*, 12/1984, pp.1818–20.
53. Sutton, 'New Directions in Conventional Defence?', p.52.
54. Meyer, *Soviet Theatre Nuclear Forces*, pp.50–52.
55. C.J. Dick, 'Soviet Operational Manoeuvre Groups, A Closer Look', *International Defence Review*, 6/1983, pp.769–76.
56. Roger Beaumont, 'The Soviet Command Structure: The Three Headed Serpent', *Signal*, Vol.39, No.4, December 1984, p.12 and Yoseff Bodansky, 'Reorganizing the Soviet High Command for War', *Defense and Foreign Affairs*, August 1985, pp.29–30.
57. *Soviet Military Power 1986*, (Department of Defense, Washington, D.C., 1986), p.13.
58. Bellamy, 'Trends in Land Warfare', p.231.
59. *Ibid.*, pp.236–40. See also Dick, 'Soviet Operational Manoeuvre Groups', pp.774–75.
60. Bellamy, 'Trends in Land Warfare', pp.236–7.
61. *Ibid.*, pp.235–6.
62. Zhan Jingwu, 'Positional Warfare is Developmental', *JFJB*, 11 March 1983, p.3.
63. Jin Ximin, 'The Future Battlefield under High Pressure', *JFJB*, 31 December 1983, p.3.
64. Dick, 'Soviet Operational Manoeuvre Groups', pp.771–6.
65. Lilita I. Dzirkals, *Lightning War in Manchuria: Soviet Mili-*

tary Analysis of the 1945 Far East Campaign, (The RAND Paper series, Santa Monica, 1976), pp.8–11.

66. *Ibid.*, p.26.
67. *The Military Balance 1986–1987*, p.45.
68. *Ibid.*, p.143.
69. John Kefner, 'Will the Soviets Attack China?', *America*, 15 May 1976, pp.421–23 and 'The Dragon and the Bear: Asian Perception of a Sino–Soviet War', *America*, 24 September, pp.162–4.
70. *Soviet Military Power 1986*, p.63.
71. *Ibid.*, pp.13 and 63.
72. Michael Deane, et al, 'The Soviet Command Structure in Transformation', *Strategic Review*, Vol.XII, No.2, Spring 1984, p.64.
73. *Ibid.*, p.63.
74. Chen Huibang, 'To Make War Preparations according to Strategic Guiding Principles', *JFJB*, 3 June 1983, p.3.
75. *Ibid.*
76. Chen Hongwu, 'Do not Despise Defence', *JFJB*, 20 March 1981, p.3.
77. *The Military Balance 1986–1987*, p.143.
78. Yang Dezhi, 'A Strategic Decision on Strengthening the Building of Our Army in the New Period', *HQ*, No.15, 1 August 1985, K3–4.
79. *The Military Balance 1986–1987*, p.141. The IISS believes that the seven MRs serve largely an administrative function during peacetime but frontier MRs might become Fronts or be combined into Strategic Sectors (*zhanluequ*). *See also* Chapter 3.
80. William E. Odom, 'Soviet Force Posture: Dilemmas and Directions', *Problems of Communism*, Vol.XXXIV, July–August 1985, p.7.
81. *Handbook 1984*, p.20. Note new boundary between Shenyang and Beijing MRs. See also old boundary in the 1976 edition, p.1–12.
82. Chen Yangping, 'To Understand Mobile Warfare from a Developmental Point of View', *JFJB*, 18 March 1983, p.3.
83. Wu Xiangqing, 'An Exploratory Discussion of the Nuclear Breakthrough Point', *JFJB*, 11 February 1983, p.3.
84. 'To Strengthen Training under Nuclear Conditions and to Grasp Two Sets of Warfighting Skills (from the editor)', *JFJB*, 10 January 1984, p.1.

85. Special LAD Commentator, 'To Do Well in Two Kinds of Preparations and to Grasp Two Sets of Skills', *JFJB*, 10 January 1984, p.1.

86. Han Huaizhi, 'To Underline the Characteristics of Modern Warfare and to Raise the Warfighting Capabilities of Units under Nuclear Conditions', *JFJB*, 8 November 1983, p.2.

87. 'To Strengthen Training under Nuclear Conditions and to Grasp Two Sets of Skills', *JFJB*, 10 January 1984.

88. Wu Xiangqing, 'An Exploratory Discussion of the Nuclear Breakthrough Point', *JFJB*, 11 February 1983, p.3.

89. In 1968, Chief Marshal of Tanks Rominstrov believed that 'under conditions of a missile and nuclear war, the armour of the modern tank protects the crew from the light radiation of the nuclear blast and significantly weakens the penetrating radiation'. See Trevor Cliffe, *Military Technology and the European Balance*, (Adelphi Paper No.89, International Institute for Strategic Studies, London, 1972), p.32.

90. *Ibid.*, p.33

91. Wu Xiangqing, 'An Exploratory Discussion of the Nuclear Breakthrough Point', *JFJB*, 11 February 1983, p.3. Wu was divisional Chief of Staff and his solution to the problem was confined to anti-tank weapons and the deployment of small units to guarantee independent command. No mention was made of probable use of TNF.

92. Meyer, *Soviet Theatre Nuclear Forces*, pp.35–6.

93. Wu Xiangqing, 'Nuclear Breakthrough Point', *JFJB*, 11 February 1983, p.3.

94. *Ibid.*

95. *Ibid.*

96. *Ibid.* 'Fire power competition' was identified by Wu Xiangqing as the process denoting a struggle between sealing and anti-sealing at the nuclear breakthrough point. The Chinese therefore conducted exercises to address the problems. For NATO tactical air strike capabilities, see *The Militiary Balance 1986–1987*, p.55.

97. Jun Yan, 'Discussing Active Defence from Ancient to Modern Times', *JFJB*, 7 January 1983, p.3.

98. For the defence of Chinese cities, see Shang Mingfang, 'The Perspective of City Defence Should be Expanded to the Air', *JFJB*, 20 January, 1984, p.3. See also note 111.

99. Wang Kefu, 'To Establish the "Shield" under Modern Conditions', *JFJB*, 3 April, 1981, p.3.

100. Li Jianghe, 'The Multi-layer, Three-dimensional Battlefield', *JFJB*, 23 April 1984, p.3.
101. Wang Kefu, 'To Establish the "Shield" under Modern Conditions', *JFJB*, 3 April 1981, p.3.
102. *Ibid.*
103. Jiang Qinhong, 'The Attacker Avoids Shortcomings and Develops Strengths during Successive Penetrations', *JFJB*, 2 September 1983, p.3. Jiang argues that the OMGs may not necessarily be overextended in Chinese territory as modern conditions have raised Soviet warfighting capabilities. Nevertheless, he believes that OMGs would eventually expose their weaknesses.
104. Li Jian, 'Reliance on Present Equipment Can Overcome Tank Groups', *JFJB*, 27 March 1981, p.3. Li was Deputy Commander of the Beijing Artillery Unit when he wrote this article. He continued to contribute articles on the artillery to the *JFJB* in 1983 and 1984.
105. *Ibid.*
106. *Ibid.*
107. *Ibid.*
108. See 'Combined Arms and Joint Operations', Chapter 1.
109. Shang Mingfang, 'The Perspective of City Defence Should be expanded to the Air', *JFJB*, 20 January 1984, p.3.
110. 'Jilin First Secretary Wang Enmao at City Defence Symposium', in FBIS-CHI, 28 March 1980, S1–2.
111. Zhu Hongjun, 'To Gain Vigour from Mobility', *JFJB*, 11 March 1983, p.3. Zhu is from the Higher Ordnance School and proposes 'axle-style' defence of the city in the context of resistance against Soviet long-range fire power and high speed air strike.
112. 'Possibility of Enemy Nuclear Attack Must be Considered', in JPRS, *China Report*, No.75825, 4 June 1980, p.97.
113. Odom, 'Soviet Force Posture', pp.8–11.
114. *Ibid.*, p.11.
115. Bellamy, 'Weapon Development 1984: Land', in *RUSI and Brassey's Defence Year Books 1985*, p.219.
116. *Ibid.*, p.210.
117. *Ibid.*, pp.210 and 217.
118. *Soviet Military Power 1986*, p.100.
119. *Ibid.*, p.98. See also Dibb, *The Soviet Union: Incomplete Superpower*, p.177.
120. *The Military Balance 1986–1987*, p.36.

121. It has been claimed that the Soviets remain in the lead with conventional artillery systems with the 255 152mm gun (range 35–40km). See Bellamy, 'Weapons Development 1984: Land', p.217.

122. Bellamy, 'Trends in Modern Warfare', pp.238–40.

123. Zhu Hongjun, 'To Gain Vigour from Mobility', *JFJB*, 11 March 1983, p.3.

124. Jiang Wenyu and Wu Weirui, 'To Widen the Horizon of Defensive War', *JFJB*, 11 May 1984, p.3.

125. *Ibid.*

126. *Ibid.*

127. Jiang Qinhong, 'The Attacker Avoids Shortcomings and Develops Strengths during Successive Penetrations', *JFJB*, 2 September 1983, p.3. Jiang spoke highly of the capabilities of the OMG.

128. Chinese strategic planners' forward looking attitude is reflected in the convening of the Conference on Strategic Defence and Systems Engineering in the Year 2000. See note 130.

129. Xu Jiangyao, 'Li Jijun on New Stage of PLA Modernization', XH, 23 August 1986, in FBIS-CHI, 25 August 1986, K10–11.

130. Zhu Songchun, 'Chinese Scholars Discuss Strategy for the Development of National Defense', Hong Kong *Liaowang* Overseas Edition, No.29, 21 July 1986, pp.6–8 in FBIS-CHI, 25 July 1986, K3.

131. Wang Kefu, 'To Establish the "Shield" under Modern Conditions', *JFJB*, 3 April 1981, p.3.

132. *Liaoning Ribao* reported the establishment of Reserve tank regiments in 1984. See JPRS, *China Report*, 5 October 1984, p.142.

133. See Chapter 1.

134. Jeffrey Richelson, 'Monitoring the Soviet Military', *Arms Control Today*, Vol.16, No.7, October 1986, pp.14–16 and *Washington Post*, 18 June 1981, p.34.

135. J. Bussert, 'China's C³I Efforts Show Progress', pp.173 and 175.

136. See Chapter 1, note 148.

137. Jiang Cheglu, 'The Building of Double-tracks for the Haerbin-Manzhouli Line', *Tiedao Zhishi*, No.1, January 1985, pp.4–5.

138. Jun Yan, 'To Insist on Extensive Guerrilla Warfare', *JFJB*, 1 April 1983.

139. Li Jian, 'The Propostion to Develop Guerrilla Artillery Unit Activities in the enemy's rear', *JFJB*, 8 May 1981, p.3.
140. *Ibid.*
141. See note 111.
142. For details, see Chapter 3.

CHAPTER 6

1. Fieldhouse, 'Chinese Nuclear Weapons', *SIPRI Yearbook 1986*, p.107 and Swanson, 'Naval Forces', p.85.
2. Lee and Hinge, 'Naval Developments in Southeast Asia', *Naval Forces*, Vol.VII, No.1, 1986, pp.33–4.
3. J.R. Hill, *Maritime Strategy for Medium Powers*, (Croom Helm, London and Sydney, 1986), p.48.
4. James D. Watkins, 'The Maritime Strategy', *The Maritime Strategy*, (Supplement, US Naval Institute Proceedings), January 1986, pp.4–15 and Donald and Gael Tarleton, 'The Soviet Navy in 1985', *US Naval Institute Proceedings*, Vol.112/5/999, May 1986, pp.98–108.
5. S.R. Foley, 'Strategic Factors in the Pacific', *US Naval Institute Proceedings*, Vol.111/8/989, August 1985, p.36.
6. Watkins, 'The Maritime Strategy', p.5.
7. William M. Arkin and Richard W. Fieldhouse, *Nuclear Battlefields: Global Links in the Arms Race*, pp.117–29 and *Defense of Japan 1985*, pp.83–88.
8. N. Lee and A. Hinge, 'The US Bases in the Philippines (Comment)', *Naval Forces*, Vol.VII, No.3, 1986, pp.8–10.
9. Jose Marte Abueg, 'Aquino Gets Final Draft Constitution', *Financial Review*, 16 October 1986, p.12.
10. Lee and Hinge, 'The US Bases in the Philippines', p.10.
11. Foley, 'Strategic Factors in the Pacific', p.36.
12. Lee and Hinge, 'Naval Developments in Southeast Asia', pp.33–4.
13. *Ibid.*
14. Watkins, 'The Maritime Strategy', pp.11–14.
15. Muller, *China As a Maritime Power*, pp.228–9 and Foley, 'Strategic Factors in the Pacific', p.36.
16. Watkins, 'The Maritime Strategy', pp.13–15.
17. Neil Munro, 'Keeping Watch on the Amur and the Sea of Okhotsk', *Pacific Defence Reporter*, October 1986, p.18.

18. *Ibid.* and Arkin and Fieldhouse, *Nuclear Battlefields*, pp.117–27.
19. *Ibid.*, p.122 and Muller, *China As a Maritime Power*, pp.228–9.
20. John F Lehman, 'The 600-Ship Navy', *The Maritime Strategy*, January 1986, p.33.
21. Watkins, 'The Maritime Strategy', p.10. Watkins' Table 1 on Combatant Repositioning Steaming Times makes provisions for the 'swing' strategy. Thus it takes 27 days for surface combatants to 'swing' from the Western Pacific to the Northern Atlantic via the Panama Canal.
22. An example of improved Chinese naval capabilities is the Naval Air Force which the Chinese claim are effective in ASW and air interdiction against the future enemy. See Li Jing, 'The Function of the Naval Air Force and the Development of Its Weapons and Equipment', *JFJB*, 2 June 1983, pp.2–4. Li was Deputy Commander of the Navy when he presented this paper on the Naval Air Force to the Third All-China Conference of the Aeronautical Society.
23. Jan S. Breemer, 'US–Chinese Cooperation: The Naval Dimension', *US Naval Institute Proceedings*, Vol.109/2/960, February 1983, pp.70–73. *See also* under Navy, Chapter 2 for latest Sino–US cooperation in naval development. Prospects for cooperation are also encouraged by limited SOVPACFLT capabilities. See Dibb, *The Soviet Union: The Incomplete Superpower*, p.173.
24. See Table 1.5 in Chapter 1.
25. Arkin and Fieldhouse, *Nuclear Battlefields*, pp.128–29 and 290–91.
26. *The Militiary Balance 1986–1987*, p.145.
27. See under Navy in Chapter 2.
28. Paul Rogers, *Guide to Nuclear Weapons 1984–85*, (University of Bradford School of Peace Studies, 1986), p.93 and 'Finback-A Revealed', *International Defence Review*, Vol.17, No.12/1984, p.1789.
29. Liu Yong and Qinhong, 'Outlook on Battlefields at River Mouths', *JFJB*, 16 November 1984, p.3.
30. *Soviet Military Power 1986*, p.13.
31. Watkins, 'The Maritime Strategy', pp.13–15.
32. James Cable, *Diplomacy at Sea*, (Macmillan, London, 1985). Coercive diplomacy which resorts to direct threats or overt

acts is regarded by Cable as an active principle in international relations. See pp.16–35.

33. Hill, *Maritime Strategy for Medium Powers*, pp.96–99. One of the major functions of naval presence is to permit operational exercises over a protracted period, especially in a relatively uncluttered environment. Presence is also a clear expression of interest in the region in question.

34. Ken Booth, *Law, Force and Diplomacy at Sea*, (George Allen and Unwin, London, 1985), pp.137–40.

35. *Ibid.* pp.137–68.

36. *Ibid.*, p.174.

37. *Ibid.*, pp.137 and 218–9.

38. *Ibid.*, p.22.

39. Lee and Hinge, 'Naval Developments in Southeast Asia', p.34.

40. Arkin and Fieldhouse. *Nuclear Battlefields*, pp.290–91.

41. See under Navy in Chapter 2.

42. See Table 1.5 in Chapter 1.

43. Muller, *China As a Maritime Power*, p.229–31.

44. *Ibid.*

45. *The Military Balance 1986–1987*, pp.169–70.

46. Carl Goldstein, 'KMT Power Grows Out of a Holstered Gun', *FEER*, 8 May 1986, pp.25–6.

47. David G. Muller, 'A Chinese Blockade of Taiwan', *US Naval Institute Proceedings*, Vol.110/9/979, September 1984, pp.54–55.

48. The 'Iwo Jima Exercise' of May 1986 demonstrates Chinese Improved naval capabilities.

49. For Chinese DDG capabilities, see under Navy in Chapter 2.

50. For the utility of warships as instruments of diplomacy, see Booth, *Law, Force and Diplomacy at Sea*, pp.175–82.

51. Rules emerging from the Third United Nations Conference on the Law of the Sea (UNCLOS III) in 1982 have made it easier for coastal nations to claim rights to the 12-mile territorial sea and the recognition of a special status for waters lying between the islands of archipelagoes. Nevertheless, China's position would be strengthened if it decided to be a signatory of UNCLOS III. See Booth, *Law, Force and Diplomacy at Sea*, pp.63–6.

52. For Chinese capabilities, see *Jane's Fighting Ships 1984–85*, pp.94–7. For Fleet Configuration Changes relating to Task-force section, see Table II (The Inputs of Naval Suasion) in

Edward N. Luttwak, *The Political Uses of Sea Power*, (Johns Hopkins University Press, 1974), pp.76–7.

53. D.P. O'Connell, *The Influence of Law on Sea Power*, (Naval Institute Press, Annapolis, 1975), pp.101–2.

54. *Ibid.*, p.122.

55. *Ibid.* p.56.

56. See note 52.

57. For Chinese air surveillance capabilities, see under Air Force in Chapter 2. See also, Luttwak, *The Political Uses of Sea Power*, pp.78–9 for 'Intrusive reconnaissance by naval aircraft'.

58. O'Connell, *The Influence of Law on Sea Power*, pp.124–9.

59. Booth, *Law, Force and Diplomacy at Sea*, p.143.

60. Kenneth R. MacCruther, 'The Role of Percepton in Naval Diplomacy', *Naval War College Review*, September–October 1974, p.4.

61. O'Connell, *The Influence of Law on Sea Power*, p.95.

62. Kenneth Chern, 'The Impact of the Taiwan Issue on Sino-American Relations, 1980–82', in Leung and Chin (eds), *China in Adjustment*, pp.376–97.

63. For Taiwan's limited ASW capability, see *The Military Balance 1986–1987*, pp.169–70. Taiwan will acquire 10 ASW helicopters and ASROC. For Chinese submarine capabilities, see Navy, Chapter 2.

64. O'Connell, *The Influence of Law on Sea Power*, pp.92–6.

65. *The Military Balance 1986–1987*, p.170.

66. Muller, 'A Chinese Blockade of Taiwan', p.55.

67. Lee and Hinge, 'Naval Developments in Southeast Asia', pp.38–42.

68. 'The Cam Ranh Syndrome', *ASEAN Forecast*, June 1984, p.100. Soviet aid is said to be averaging $US3 million per day or $US1.1 billion annually. This situation is exacerbated by the increasing reliance of PAVN units on conventional operations and Soviet spares for the relevant vehicles and arms.

69. J. Cowie, *Mines, Minelayers and Minelaying*, (Oxford University Press, London, 1949). Captain Cowie, RN, played a leading role in the British offensive minelaying campaign against Germany in World War II. He worked closely with the British Ministry of Economic Warfare, '...to whose strangulatory processes the laying of mines was well attuned'. See p.122.

70. *ASEAN Forecast,* June 1984, p.99.
71. *Jane's Fighting Ships 1984–85,* p.93.
72. Swanson, 'Naval Forces', p.91.
73. G. Hartmann, *Weapons That Wait,* (Naval Institute Press, Annapolis, 1979), pp.69–70. The mining scenario could be similar to the experience of 10-submarine-loads of German mines (338) deployed along the east coast of the US in the Second World War. Immense damage was inflicted on the Americans.
74. Swanson, 'Naval Forces', p.92 and Arkin and Fieldhouse, *Nuclear Battlefield,* pp.290–1.
75. *Ibid.*
76. R. Hoffmann, 'Offensive Mine Warfare: A Forgotten Stragegy?', *US Naval Institute Proceedings (Naval Review),* 103/891, May 1977, p.152.
77. *The Military Balance 1986–1987,* p.145. The H-5 can carry eight 500lb. mines.
78. W. Greer and J. Bartholomew, *Psychological Aspects of Mine Warfare,* (Professional Paper 365, October 1982, Centre for Naval Analyses, USA), p.2.
79. Hoffmann, 'Offensive Mine Warfare', p.150.
80. B. McCauley, 'Operation Endsweep', *US Naval Institute Proceedings,* Vol. 100/3/853, March 1974, p.25.
81. *Ibid.,* p.23.
82. 'Navsea Mine Familiarizer', *Naval Mine Engineering Facility,* (Yorktown, Virigina, 1977), p.22. A detailed description of the DST mine is given here.
83. See under Navy in Chapter 2 for Chinese capabilities.
84. Swanson, 'Naval Forces', pp.93–4.
85. Western technology is now readily available to the Chinese provided that they are able to afford it. DST type mines can be effective in depths of up to 30 metres and should be laid aerially. Submarine laid mines could be deployed in the 30–60 metre depth region. Though the charge weight of submarine laid mines would be effective at greater depths, mine pressure sensors are only reliable to a depth of about 60 metres. Pressure charge on the seabed exerted by a passing ship becomes barely measurable at depths in excess of 60 metres.
86. U. Luckow, 'Victory Over Ignorance and Rear: The US Mine-laying Attack on North Vietnam', *Naval War College Review,* Vol.XXXV, 1/289, January-February 1982, p.24.

87. 'Navsea Mine Familiarizer', *Naval Mine Engineering Facility*, p.17. See also under Navy in Chapter 2.

88. B. Hahn, 'Maritime Dangers in the South China Sea', *Pacific Defence Reporter*, May 1985, p.13. The 71 minewarfare platforms under SOVPACFLT are mainly minesweepers which are ineffective against bottom combination mines. Minehunters would be required in large numbers to counter such mines.

89. McCauley, 'Operation Endsweep', p.23.

90. *Ibid.*, pp.19–20.

91. Probable Sino–Soviet *Rapproachement* would suggest that the Soviets would refrain from taking drastic action. In 1972, Soviet interest in establishing *detente* inhibited Moscow from actively supporting North Vietnam.

92. Luckow, 'Victory Over Ignorance and Fear', p.19.

93. George Bush, 'To Security Council', *The New York Times*, 9 May 1972, p.A–10.

94. *Ibid.*

95. See Cowie, *Mines, Minelayers and Minelaying*, pp.168–80 for a comprehensive discussion of the articles of the Convention Relative to the Laying of Automatic Submarine Contact Mines (No.VIII), signed at The Hague in 1907. This Convention remains the main international agreement despite new technological deveopments.

96. *Ibid.*, p.172 (Article II of Hague Convention VIII refers).

97. R. Thompson, *Peace Is Not at Hand*, (Chatto and Windus, London, 1974), p.115.

98. J.D. Taylor, 'Mining: A Well Reasoned and Circumspect Defence', *US Naval Institute Proceedings*, Vol.103/11/897, November 1977, p.42.

99. Luckow, 'Victory Over Ignorance and Fear', p.24.

100. *ASEAN Forecast*, June 1984, p.99.

101. Hai Yuan and Chen Hongwu, 'The New Formula to Grab Sea Control', *JFJB*, 20 July 1984, p.3.

CHAPTER 7

1. Fu Zhong, 'Mao Zedong Military Science is Forever the Chinese People's Treasure — In Celebration of the 60th Founding Anniversary of the CCP and the 54th Founding Anniversary of the PLA', *HQ*, No.15, 1 August 1981, p.1.

2. Ye Jianying, 'Speech at the Meeting Celebrating the 30th

Anniversary of the Founding of the People's Republic of China', *Beijing Review*, No.40, 5 October 1979, pp.7–32.

3. Yang Dezhi, 'Unswervingly Uphold Our Party's Absolute Leadership over the Army — In Commemoration of the CCP's 60th Founding Anniversary', *HQ*, No.13, 1 July 1981, p.116.

4. Song Shilun, 'Mao Zedong's Military Thinking is the Guide to Our Army's Victories', *HQ*, No.16, 16 August 1981, p.13.

5. *Ibid.*, p.14.

6. Fu Zhong,' Mao Zedong Military Science', p.2.

7. *Ibid.*, p.4.

8. *Ibid.*

9. Wei Guoqing, 'The Power of Political Work Developed in the Period of Historical Transition', *RMRB*, 22 June 1981, p.3.

10. *Resolution on CCP History*, (Foreign Languages Press, Beijing, 1981), pp.3–86.

11. Wei Guoqing, 'The Power of Political Work', p.4.

12. Fu Zhong, 'Mao Zedong Military Science', p.6.

13. *Ibid.*, p.9.

14. *Ibid.*, p.10 and *JFJB*, 14 May 1982.

15. *Resolution on CCP History*, p.78.

16. *Ibid.*, p.69.

17. Mao Tse-tung, *Selected Works of Mao Tse-tung*, Vol.I, (Foreign Languages Press, Peking, 1967), p.308.

18. Deng Xiaoping, 'Comrade Deng Xiaoping Talks on Rectifying the Problem of Party Style', *HQ*, No.21, 1 November 1981, pp.7–8.

19. Xiao Hua, 'To Enhance Party Spirit and Party Style', *HQ*, No.22, 16 November 1981, p.11.

20. *Ibid.*, p.5.

21. Deng Yingchao, 'Celebration and Memories', *RMRB*, 29 June 1981.

22. Deng Xiaoping, 'Rectifying the Problem of Party Style', p.8.

23. Union Research Institute, *Glossary of Chinese Political Phrases*, (Union Press Ltd., Hong Kong, 1977), p.359.

24. See note 1, in Lee, *Chinese People's Liberation Army*, p.142.

25. Chien Tieh, 'Reshuffles of Regional Military Commanders in Communist China', *Issues and Studies*, Vol.16, No.3, March 1980, pp.1–4.

26. 'Peking Radio on the "Three Supports, Two Militaries"', in *SWB*, 7 February 1980, FE/6339/BII/9.

27. 'Jiangsu Leaders Discuss PLA "Support the Left" Campaign', in *SWB*, 31 January 1980, FE/6333/BII/15.

28. 'Solving Problems of "Three Supports, Two Militaries" in Yingkou, Liaoning', in *SWB*, 18 January 1980, FE/6322/BII/1.

29. 'Heilongjiang Begins 1980 Conscription', in *SWB*, 31 October 1980, FE/6563/BII/16.

30. 'Army: Murmurs, Worries', *China News Analysis*, No.1203, 27 March 1981, p.5.

31. David Bonavia, 'The Parade against the Army', *FEER*, 19 October 1979, pp.15–16 and 'PLA Unit "Agrees to Return Some People's University Building"', in *SWB*, 18 October 1979, FE/6284/BII/3.

32. See Notes 22, 23 and 24 in Chapter 1.

33. Jurgen Domes, 'New Policies in the Communes: Notes on Rural Societal Structures in China, 1976–1981', *Journal of Asian Studies*, Vol.XLI, No.2, pp.253–67.

34. *LAD* Commentator, 'Stability and Unity Concerning the Overall Situation', *RMRB*, 30 January 1980, pp.1 and 4.

35. *Ibid*.

36. Harvey W. Nelsen, *The Chinese Military System*, (Westview Press, Boulder, 1977), pp.54–5 and 102–7.

37. 'PLA Conference on Mass Work', *SWB*, 3 August 1979, FE/6184/BII/7–8.

38. '"*Liberation Army Daily*" on Elimination of Feudal Influence in the PLA', in *SWB*, 25 November 1980, FE/6584/BII/1–2 and 'Speech by Wei Guoqing at PLA Political Conference', in *SWB*, 15 May 1980, FE/6420/BII/5–6.

39. Domes, 'New Policies in the Communes', pp.253–67.

40. 'Using the Four Basic Principles as Weapons To Overcome Erroneous Ideological Influence', *RMRB*, 27 April 1981, p.4.

41. *SWB*, 15 May 1980, FE/6420/BII/5–8.

42. *RMRB*, 27 April 1981, p.4.

43. Wei Guoqing, 'Director Wei Guoqing's Speech in the Eleventh Conference of Military Academies and Institutions', *JFJB*, 8 November 1980.

44. Guo Zhongyi, 'An Investigation into the "Appropriate Position" of Political Work', *JFJB*, 13 November 1980.

45. Tian Jisheng, 'Some Thoughts on the Improvement of the System of Ideological-Political Work', *JFJB*, 3 November 1980.

46. Wang Jining and Huang Zhenchun, 'To Go Further on Liberating Thoughts and Eliminating the Ultra-Leftist Line', *JFJB*, 5 November 1980.

47. William W. Whitson, *The Chinese High Command*, (Praeger Publishers, New York, 1973), Chart C.

48. *Ibid.* pp.513–7.
49. 'Deng "in Canton to Wield Axe"', *SCMP*, 7 February 1982 and *Ming Pao*, 11 February 1982, p.1.
50. Donald H. McMillen, *Chinese Communist Power and Policy in Xinjiang, 1949–1977*, (Westview, Press Boulder, 1979).
51. *Wen Hui Pao*, 25 May 1980 and David Bonavia, 'The Heroe's Last Stand', *FEER*, 17 April 1981, pp.17–8.
52. *RMRB*, 27 April 1981, p.4.
53. Huang Zhenxia, *Mao's Generals*, (Research Institute of Contemporary History, Hong Kong, 1968), pp.223–4.
54. Eberhard Sandschneider, 'Political Succession in the People's Republic of China', *AS*, Vol.XXV, No.6, June 1985, p.658.
55. *Ibid.*

CHAPTER 8

1. Deng Xiaoping, 'Opening Speech to the Twelfth National Congress of the Chinese Communist Party', *HQ*, No.18, September 1982, pp.3–5. See also *Wen Hui Pao*, 6 September 1982, p.1.
2. Hu Yaobang, 'Fully Initiating the New Situation in the Construction of Socialist Modernisation', *HQ*, No.18, September 1982, pp.6–30.
3. 'The Constitution of the Chinese Communist Party', *HQ*, No.18, September 1982, pp.31–3 and 'To Split Thoroughly with the Theory of Continuous Revolution under Dictatorship', *Wen Hui Pao*, 10 September 1982, p.9.
4. 'The Constitution of the Chinese Communist Party', p.37. See also *Wen Hui Pao*, 6 September 1982, p.1.
5. 'The Establishment of the Central Advisory Committee Is an Innovation in Chinese Communist History', *Wen Hui Pao*, 12 September 1982, p.1.
6. Hu Yaobang, 'Fully Initiating the New Situation', p.20.
7. Lee, *The Chinese People's Liberation Army*, pp.136–8 and Alastair I. Johnston, 'Changing Party–Army Relations in China, 1979–1984', *AS*, Vol.XXIV, No.10, October 1984, pp.1020–1.
8. See last Section in this Chapter.
9. 'Nanjing PLA Region Improves Grass-roots Work', *Jiefang Ribao*, 7 November 1985, p.1, in FBIS-CHI, 15 November 1985, K15.

10. 'The Constitution of the Chinese Communist Party', p.40.

11. See notes 67, 68, 69 and 70.

12. M.R. Bullard and E.C. O'Dowd, 'Defining the Role of the PLA in the Post-Mao Era', *AS*, Vol.XXVI, No.6, June 1986, p.712.

13. *China Directory 1984*, (Radio Press Inc., Japan, 1984), pp.272, 274 and 276.

14. 'New Senior Military Officers of the Military Region', *Kuang Chiao Ching*, Hong Kong, 16 July 1985, in *SWB*, 20 July 1985, FE/8008/BII/4.

15. Li Wei, 'He Comes from the Battlefields — An Invitation with He Qizong, Deputy Chief of Staff of the PLA', Zhongguo Xinwen She, 28 January 1986, in FBIS-CHI, 5 Feburary 1986, K13–14.

16. *SWB*, 20 July 1985, FE/8008/BII/3.

17. Guang Hua, 'The Way That Deng Xiaoping Rectifies the Army', *Kuang Chiao Ching*, 16 September 1985, p.16. For GLD appointments, See *SWB*, 20 July 1985, FE/8008/BII/3–4.

18. *SWB*, 20 July 1985, FE/8008/BII/3–4.

19. Guang Hua, 'The Way That Deng Xiaoping Rectifies the Army', p.16.

20. Zhang Chunting, 'Making the Leading Squad of the Chinese Army Younger in Average Age', *Liaowang* Hong Kong Edition, No.2, 7 October 1985, pp.11–12, in FBIS-CHI, 6 December 1985, K5–6.

21. See Appendix E in Lee, *The Chinese People's Liberation Army*, p.159.

22. *China Aktuell/Official Activities*, June 1984, p.364/16.

23. For a list of leading cadres of the seven military regions, see *Ban Yue Tan*, No.16, August 1985, p.19.

24. Guang Hua, 'Liu Jingsong, Newly Appointed Commander of the Shenyang Military region', *Liaowang*, Hong Kong Edition, 13 January 1986, p.31 in FBIS-CHI, 23 January 1986, S3–4.

25. Guang Hua, 'The Way that Deng Xiaoping Recitfies the Army', p.17.

26. Of the eight leading cadres of the four 'defunct' MRs, only Fu Kuiqing, Political Commissar for Fuzhou MR, remained in office when he was transferred to Najing MR to become Political Commissar for Nanjing MR.

27. *China Aktuell/Official Activities*, May 1983, p.333/25.

28. Guang Hua, 'The Way that Deng Xiaoping Rectifies the

Army', p.17. For recent activities of Zhao and Li in Lanzhou, see Beijing XH Domestic Service 15 November 1985, in FBIS-CHI, 26 November 1985, T1.

29. *China Directory 1983*, p.196.
30. *China Directory 1986*, p.204 and Whitson, *Chinese High Command*, Chart A.
31. James T. Myers, 'China — The "Germs" of Modernizaiton', *AS*, Vol.XXV, No.10, October 1985, pp.981–97.
32. *LAD* Commentator, 'Actively Take Part in the Party Recitification with a High Degree of Consciousness', *JFJB*, 28 November 1983, p.1.
33. Myers, '"Germs" of Modernization', pp.990–6.
34. *Ibid.*, pp.982–90.
35. *Ibid.*
36. Thomas B. Gold, '"Just in Time!": China Battles Spiritual Pollution on the Eve of 1984', *AS*, Vol.XXIV, No.9, September 1984, p.965.
37. Wang Zhaoguo, 'Issues Regarding the Improvement of Party Style in Central Organs', Beijing, XH Domestic Service, 12 January 1986, in FBIS-CHI, 14 January 1986, K2.
38. 'Hu Qili Stresses Ideological, Political Work', Beijing XH, 18 January 1986, in FBIS-CHI, 21 January 1986, K3 and Myers, '"Germs" of Modernisation', pp.984–5.
39. FBIS-CHI, 21 January 1986, K3.
40. *Ibid.*
41. *Ibid.*
42. *Ibid.*, K2–3.
43. 'Yang Shangkun Advises at Rectification Forum', Beijing Domestic Service, 21 January 1986, in FBIS-CHI, 24 January 1986, K9–10.
44. Yang Shangkun, 'The Army Should March in the Vanguard of Rectifying Party Style', Beijing XH, 13 January 1986, in FBIS-CHI, 14 January 1986, K9.
45. *Ibid.*, K9–13.
46. *Ibid.*
47. 'Actively Take Part in Party Recitification', *JFJB*, 28 November 1983, p.1.
48. Gold, '"Just in Time!", p.949 and 'Qin Jiwei Emphasises that Party Rectification Must Have the Strength to Conduct Simultaneous Rectification and Change', *RMRB*, 9 January 1984, p.1.
49. 'Party Style Rectification Emerges with New Atmosphere in

the Party Committee of a Certain Unit in Beijing', *RMRB*, 19 July 1983, p.4.

50. 'Analyse Favorable Conditions and Increase Confidence in Party Rectification', *RMRB*, 24 December 1983, p.5.

51. 'Party Committee Members of the General Logistics Department Correcting Learning Style during Party Rectification', *RMRB*, 5 January 1984, p.1.

52. 'The Central Military Commission Sends out the First Batch of Liaison Groups for Party Rectification', *RMRB*, 21 February 1984, p.4.

53. *LAD* Commentator, 'The Emphasis Should be on Conducting Collective Investigation well', *RMRB*, 24 May 1984, p.1.

54. 'Yang Shangkun Says that the Army Units Must be Willing to Spend Time on Studying Documents in the Second Phase of Party Rectification', *RMRB*, 16 February 1985, p.1.

55. 'Party Rectificationin in the Army Must Insist on High Standards and High Quality', *RMRB*, 21 August 1984, p.1.

56. 'To Seriously and Thoroughly Enforce the Guiding Principle of Conducting Rectification and Changes Simultaneously', *RMRB*, 1 April 1984, p.4.

57. 'To Take the Lead in Extending Activities in Frank Discussions', *RMRB*, 9 March 1984.

58. *RMRB*, 16 February 1985.

59. Gold, '"Just in Time!"', pp.951–4.

60. *Ibid.*, p.968.

61. *Ibid.*, pp.967–8.

62. Robert Delfs, 'Cool Gusts Menace the Warm Mood of Liberalism', *FEER*, 26 December 1985, pp.85–6.

63. *RMRB*, 24 December 1981.

64. *Ibid.*

65. 'Hu Yaobang, Xi Zhongxun and Hu Qiaomu Encouraging Workers in the Film Industry', *RMRB*, 30 December 1981, p.1.

66. *Ibid.*

67. Fan Ping, 'An Identification of Inclinations and Objective Effects of "Bitter Love"', *Jiefang Wenyi*, No.6, June 1981, pp.71–77.

68. Zhao Yiya, 'Communism Is the Core of Socialist Spiritual Civilisation', *Jiefang Ribao*, 28 August 1982, pp.1–2.

69. *Ibid.*

70. Office of Liberation Army Daily, 'An Article Which Has

Serious Errors', *Jiefang Ribao*, 28 September 1982, pp.1 and 3.

71. See Chapter 3.

72. Yang Shangkun, 'The Army Should March in the Vanguard of Rectifying Party Style', Beijing XH, 13 January 1986, in FBIS-CHI, 14 January 1986, K10.

73. 'Yang Shangkun Says Failure to Eliminate Factionalism in Military Academies Affects Party Rectification', *Wen Hui Pao*, 10 November 1985, p.3, in FBIS-CHI, 12 November 1985, W1.

74. Beijing *Liaowang*, 8 July 1985, in *SWB*, 20 July 1985, FE/8008/BII/6 and 'Demobilised PLA Officers and Men "A Vital Force" in Rural Areas', XH, 25 July 1985, in *SWB*, 29 July 1985, FE/8015/BII/1−3.

75. '"Problems Emerge among Army Officers": Circular Issues', *Ming Pao*, 23 July 1985, in *SWB*, 25 July 1985, FE/8012/BII/1−2.

76. 'Stand up against Intercessional Trend', *JFJB*, 20 January 1986, in FBIS-CHI, 4 February 1986, K4−5.

77. Yu Qiuli, 'Communist Members Must Consciously Strengthen Party Spirit When Conducting Reform', *HQ*, No.13 July 1985, p.3.

78. *Ibid.*

79. *Ibid.*, pp.3−5.

80. 'The Central Military Commission's Resolution Concerning the Army's Political Work in the New Era', *JFJB*, 26 February 1987, pp.1−2.

81. *Ibid.*

82. *Ibid.*, p.1.

83. *Ibid.*

84. *Ibid.*

85. 'Guangzhou Rectifies Leadership of Armies and Divisions', *Ming Pao*, 3 December 1985, in FBIS-CHI, 4 December 1985, W2.

86. 'Guangzhou PLA Solves Problems in Party Conduct', Beijing XH, 4 December 1985, in FBIS-CHI, 6 December 1985, P1.

87. 'Deng Yingchao, Others Meet Guangzhou PLA Cadres', Guangdong Provincial Service, 22 December 1985, in FBIS-CHI, 24 December 1985, K12.

88. See Chapter 3.

89. 'PLA's He Qizong Discusses Reduction Work', Beijing Inter-

national Service, 30 January 1986, in FBIS-CHI, 31 January 1986, K1.

90. 'Yang Shangkun Stresses that the Army Must Strengthen Education in Party Style in the Second Phase of Party Rectification', *RMRB*, 26 August 1985, p.1.

91. 'Corps and Divisional Leadership Cadres Heading Discussion on Party Style, the Overall Situation and Discipline as They Participate in the Second Phase of Party Rectification in the Guangzhou MR', *RMRB*, 17 April 1986 and 'Units in the Second Phase of Party Rectification in Kunming MR Seriously Enforcing Party Style Education', *RMRB*, 29 April 1986.

92. *RMRB*, 17 April 1986.

93. 'Hu Yaobang on Work Style', Beijing XH, 10 January 1986, in FBIS-CHI, 10 January 1986, K2–3 and 'Central Organs Must Set An Example in Rectifying Party Style', Beijing *Liaowang*, No.3, 20 January 1986, p.4, in FBIS-CHI, 5 February 1986, K2.

94. 'CPC Discipline Commission Issues Communique', Beijing XH, 2 February 1986, in FBIS-CHI, 3 February 1986, K12.

95. 'Yang Shangkun Speech at Conference of Cadres of Central Organs on 9 January', Beijing XH, 13 January 1986, in FBIS-CHI, 14 January 1986, K9–13.

96. 'It is Necessary to Boost the Building of Spiritual Civilization', *HQ*, No.20, 16 October 1985, p.2, in FBIS-CHI, 12 November 1985, K3.

97. Yang used Deng Xiaoping's Literary works to boost the morale of the PLA as rectification began to get underway. See Yang Shangkun, 'The Model of Unity between Revolutionary Bravery and Pragmatic Spirit', *JFJB*, 12 July 1983, p.1.

98. FBIS-CHI, 5 February 1986, K3.

99. 'Yang Dezhi on Grass-roots-Level Army Building', Beijing XH, 12 November 1985, K20–1.

100. *Ibid.*

101. 'Leadership Organs Doing Practical Work for Grassroots Levels with High Efficiency', *Jiefang Ribao*, 7 November 1985, p.1.

102. *Ibid.*

103. *Ibid.*

104. *Jiefang Ribao*, 7 November 1985, p.1, in FBIS-CHI, 15 November 1985, K15.

105. Beijing XH, 11 November 1985, in FBIS-CHI, 15 November 1985, K14–5.

106. *Ibid.* K15–6.
107. 'Guangzhou Military Region Educates Cadres', Beijing XH, 29 November 1985, in FBIS-CHI, 3 December 1985, P1.
108. 'Guangzhou Rectifies Leadership of Armies and Divisions', *Ming Pao*, 3 December 1985, p.5, in FBIS-CHI, 4 December 1985, W2–3.
109. FBIS-CHI, 3 December 1985, P1.
110. 'Guangzhou PLA Solves Problems in Party Conduct', Beijing XH, 4 December 1985, in FBIS-CHI, 6 December 1985, P1–2.
111. *Ibid.*, P2 and FBIS-CHI, 4 December 1985, W2.
112. 'Division Leaders Resold Autos for Profits; Instructor Murdered', *Ming Pao*, 6 November 1985, p.6.
113. *Ibid.*
114. Lucian W. Pye, *Asian Power and Politics: the Cultural Dimensions of Authority*, (Harvard University Press, Cambridge, Massachusetts, 1985), p.207.
115. Bullard and O'Dowd, 'Defining the Role of the PLA', pp.711–2.
116. Michel Oksenberg and Kenneth Liberthal, 'Forecasting China's Future', *The National Interest*, No.5, Fall 1986, p.23.
117. Bullard and O'Dowd, 'Defining the Role of the PLA', p.714.

Bibliography

'A Certain Group Army Attempted to Build "A New Training Base for the Arms of the Reserve Forces"', *JFJB*, 5 April 1986.

'A Certain Group Army Experimented New Fighting Methods and Tested New Theories', *JFJB*, 5 November 1984.

'A Certain Group Army Organises Commanding Officers for Temporary Appointments in Other Arms', *JFJB*, 22 July 1986.

'A Certain Mechanised Division Took Measures to Cultivate "Staff Officer in Combined Arms" in Order to Raise Efficiency in Command', *JFJB*, 30 May 1984.

'A Certain Motorised Division's Reform in Joint Tactical Training Achieved Outstanding Results', *JFJB*, 18 September 1984.

'A Motorised Regiment Conducted Base-Oriented Rotational Training on a Trial Basis', *JFJB*, 5 April 1986.

'A Simple Rod Cannot Penetrate the Stars in the Sky', *Liaoning Ribao*, 28 February 1983.

Abueg, Jose Marte. 'Aquino Gets Final Draft Constitution', *Financial Review*, 16 October 1986, p.12.

'Active Reserve Service Officers and Civilian Cadres', *JFJB*, 29 July 1984.

'Actively Take Part in Party Rectification', *JFJB*, 28 November 1983.

'Analyse Favourable Conditions and Increase Confidence in Party Rectification', *RMRB*, 9 January 1984.

Arkin, William M. and Fieldhouse, Richard W. *Nuclear Battlefields: Global Links in the Arms Race*, (Ballinger Publishing Company, Cambridge, Massachusetts, 1985).

Armstrong, David. 'The Soviet Union', in G. Segal and W.T. Tow (eds), *Chinese Defence Policy*, (Macmillan, London, 1984), pp.191–2.

'Army: Murmurs, Worries', *China News Analysis*, No.1203, 27 March 1981, p.5.

'Army Paper Supports Economic Construction before National Defence', XH, 9 July 1985, in *SWB*, 11 July 1985, FE8000/BII/1.

ASEAN Forecast, June 1984, p.99.

Asian Aviation, May 1986, p.42.

Australian Broadcasting Corporation, *Report from Asia*, 2 August 1987.

Aviation Week and Space Technology, (McGraw Hill, New York): 28 October 1985, p.24; 19 May 1986, p.18; 1 September 1986, p.37; 20 October 1986, p.180.

Ban Yue Tan (Half Monthly Discussion; Beijing), No.24, 25 December 1984; No.16, August 1985.

Beaumont, Roger. 'The Soviet Command Structure: The Three Headed Serpent', *Signal*, Vol.39, No.4, December 1984, p.12.

Beijing Review, 6 January 1986, p.15 in FBIS-CHI, 6 January 1986, A3.

Beijing Review (Beijing), No.31, 30 July 1984, p.21.

Beijing, XH, 11 November 1985, in FBIS-CHI, 15 November 1985, K14–15.

Beijing, XH, 15 November 1985, in FBIS-CHI, 26 November 1985, T1.

Beijing, XH, 2 May 1986, in FBIS-CHI, 6 May 1986, K7.

Beijing, XH, 6 September 1986, in *Ming Pao*, 7 September 1986.

Bell, Coral. 'How Have We Survived the Crisis?', in Coral Bell (ed), *Forty Years On: Studies of World Change in Four Decades after 1945*, (Department of International Relations, Australian National University), pp.47–8.

Bellamy, Cris. 'Trends In Land Warfare: The Operational Art of the European Theatre', in *RUSI and Brassey's Defence Year Book 1985*, (Brassey's Defence Publishers, London, 1985), pp.227–263.

———. 'Weapon Development 1984: Land', in *RUSI and Brassey's Defence Year Book 1985*, pp.209–226.

Bennell, Anthony S. "European Reserve Forces: England, France and West Germany', in Louis A. Zurcher and Gwyn Harries–Jenkins (eds), *Supplementary Military Forces: Reserves, Militias, Auxiliaries* (Sage Research Progress Series on War, Revolution and Peace Keeping, Sage Publications, Beverly Hills/London, 1978), pp.39–68.

Berney, Karen. 'Dual-Use Technology Sales', *China Business Review*, Vol.11, No.4, July–August 1980.

Betts, Richard K. *NATO Deterrence Doctrine: No Way Out*, (University of California, Los Angeles, 1985).

Bingqi Zhishi (Weapons Knowledge; Beijing), No.6, 1984 (front cover and inside front cover).

Bodansky, Yoseff. 'Reorganizing the Soviet High Command for War', *Defence and Foreign Affairs*, August 1985, pp.29–30.

Bonavia, David. 'The Parade against the Army', *FEER*, 19 October 1979, pp.15–16.

Booth, Ken. *Law, Force and Diplomacy at Sea*, (George Allen and Unwin, London, 1985).

Breemer, Jan S. 'US–Chinese Cooperation: the Naval Dimension', *US Naval Institute Proceedings*, Vol.109/2/960, February 1983, pp.70–73.

British Broadcasting Corporation, *Summary of World Broadcasts*, Part 3, Far East: see under *Summary of World Broadcasts*.

British Broadcasting Corporation, *World Round Up*, 4 November 1986.

Bullard, M.R. and O'Dowd, Edward C. 'Defining the Role of the PLA in the Post-Mao Era', *Asian Survey*, Vol.XXVI, No.6, June 1986, pp.706–720.

Bulletin of the State Council of the PRC, 'Circular Concerning "Conscription Work Regulations"', *The State Council and the Central Military Commission*, No.31, 20 November 1985.

Bush, George. 'To Security Council', *The New York Times*, 9 May 1972, p.A–10.

Bussert, J. 'China's C^3I Efforts Show Progress', *C^3I Handbook*, (First Edition, EW Communications Inc., Palo Alto, 1986).

——. 'PRC Electronics', *Defence Electronics*, March 1985, pp.129–136.

Buszynski, Les. 'Vietnam Confronts China', *Asian Survey*, Vol.XX, No.8, August 1980, pp.829–843.

Cable, James. *Diplomacy at Sea*, (Macmillan, London, 1985).

Cao Yuguang. 'A Significant Measure in Strengthening the Reserve Forces for National Defence', *RMRB*, 8 June 1984.

'Central Organs Must Set An Example in Retifying Party Style', in Beijing *Liaowang*, No.3, 20 January 1986, p.4, in FBIS-CHI, 5 February 1986, K2.

Chanda, N. 'Preparing the Ground', *FEER*, 14 March 1985, pp.26–7.

———. 'Superpower Triangle', *FEER*, Hong Kong, 4 April 1985, pp.17–19.

Chandler, D. 'Strategies for Survival in Kampuchea', *Current History*, Vol.82, No.483, 1983, p.153.

Chen Chaoxian. 'To Do Research and Develop "Cross-breed" Style Tactics', *JFJB*, 6 May 1983.

Chen Hongwu. 'Do not Despise Defence', *JFJB*, 20 March 1981.

Chen Huibang. 'To Insist on the Integration of "Three Warfares"', *JFJB*, 18 February, 1983.

———. "To Make War Preparations according to Strategic Guiding Principles', *JFJB*, 3 June 1983.

Chen Yangping. 'To Understand Mobile Warfare from a Developmental Point of View', *JFJB*, 18 March 1983.

Cheng, J. Chester (ed). *The Politics of the Chinese Army: A Translation of the Bulletin of Activities of the People's Liberation Army*, (Hoover Institution of War, Revolution and Peace, Stanford University, California, 1966).

Chern, Kenneth. 'The Impact of the Taiwan Issue on Sino–American Relations, 1980–82', in C.K. Leung and Steve S.K. Chin (eds), *China in Adjustment*, (Centre of Asian Studies, University of Hong Kong, 1983), pp.376–97.

Cheung, Tai Ming. 'China Switches from Defence to Development', *Pacific Defence Reporter*, November 1986, pp.27–8.

'Chief of General Staff Yang Dezhi on the Completion of Army Restructuring in Two Years', *Ta Kung Pao* (Hong Kong), 29 July 1985.

Chien Tieh. 'Reshuffles of Regional Military Commanders in Communist China', *Issues and Studies*, Vol.16, No.3, March 1980, pp.1–4.

China Aktuell/Official Activites, (1983–84).

China Daily, Beijing. 20 June 1984; 6 March 1986; 11 June 1986; 1 August 1986; 11 April 1987.

China Directory 1984–86, (Radio Press Inc., Japan 1984–88).

China Reconstructs, February 1981, p.22.

China Report: see under Joint Publications Research Service.

"China's Budget', *JDW*, 13 July 1985, p.72.

'Chinese Delegate Qian Jiadong Addresses First Committee in UN on Disarmament', *RMRB*, 25 October 1984.

'Chinese Delegation Attending IAEA Conference', *RMRB*, 26 September 1984.

Chinese Statistical Yearbook 1985, (State Statistical Bureau, People's Republic of China, 1985).

Cliffe, Trevor. *Military Technology and the European Balance*, (Adelphi Paper No.89, International Institute for Strategic Studies, London, 1972).

'Communique on the Chinese Crimes against Vietnam over Past Two Years (1979–80)', in *Vietnam News Bulletin*, No.3/81, 20 November 1981, p.5.

CONMILIT, (Conmilit Press Ltd., Hong Kong): May 1981, pp.7–11; March 1984, p.25; May 1984, p.61; August 1984, p.60; October 1984, pp.64, 80, 110; January 1985, inside front cover, pp.66–67.

'Conscription in Jiangxi', Nanchang Provincial Service, 3 August 1985, in *SWB*, 10 August 1985, FE/8026/BII/7.

'Corps and Divisional Leadership Cadres Heading Discussion on Party Style, the Overall Situation and Discipline as They Participate in the Second Phase of Party Rectification in Guangzhou MR', *RMRB*, 17 April 1986.

Cowie, J. *Mines Minelayers and Minelaying*, (Oxford University Press, London, 1949).

'CPC Discipline Commission Issues Communique', Beijing XH, 2 February 1986, in FBIS-CHI, 3 February 1986, K12.

Daniel, Donald C. and Tarleton, Gael. 'The Soviet Navy in 1985', *US Naval Institute Proceedings*, Vol.112/5/999, May 1986, pp.98–108.

Deane, Michael et al. 'The Soviet Command Structure in Transformation', *Strategic Review*, Vol.XII, No.2, (Spring 1984), p.64.

Defence Attache. No.1, 1986 (Diplomatist Associates Ltd., London).

Defense Intelligence Agency. *Handbook on the Chinese Armed Forces 1976*, (Government Printing Office, Washington D.C., 1976).

Defense Intelligence Agency. *Handbook on the Chinese Armed Forces 1984*, (Government Printing Office, Washington D.C., 1984).

Defence Modernisation, (Chinese People's Liberation Army Fighters' Press, Beijing, 1983).

Defence Electronics, January 1984.

Defense of Japan 1985, (Defense Agency of Japan, 1985), pp.83–88.

Delf, Robert. 'Cool Gusts Menace the Warm Moon of Liberalism', *FEER*, 26 December 1985, pp.85–6.

'Demobilised PLA Officers and Men "A Vital Force" in Rural Areas', *XH*, 25 July 1985, in *SWB*, 25 July 1985, FE/8012/BII/1–3.

'Deng in "Canton to Wield Axe" ', *SCMP*, 7 February 1982.

Deng Xiaoping. 'Comrade Deng Xiaoping Talks on Rectifying the Problem of Party Style', *HQ*, No.21, 1 November 1981, pp.2–8.

———. 'On Domestic Policy in CBS Interview', Beijing XH, 14 September 1986, in FBIS-CHI, 16 September 1986, B1–2.

———. 'Opening Speech to the Twelfth National Congress of the Chinese Communist Party', *HQ*, No.18, September 1982, pp.3–5.

'Deng Xiaoping Interviewed by Mike Wallace', Beijing XH, 6 September 1986, in FBIS-CHI, 8 September 1986, B2.

Deng Yingchao. 'Celebration and Memories', *RMRB*, 29 June 1981.

'Deng Yingchao, Others Meet Guangzhou PLA Cadres', Guangdong Provincial Service, 22 December 1985, in FBIS-CHI, 24 December 1985, K12.

Dibb, Paul. 'China's Strategic Situation and Defence Priorities in the 1980s', *The Australian Journal of Chinese Affairs*, No.5, October 1980, p.104.

———. *The Soviet Union: Incomplete Superpower*, (International Institute for Stategic Studies, London, 1986).

Dick, C.J. 'Soviet Operational Manoeuvre Groups, A Closer Look'. *International Defence Review*, 6/1983, pp.769–76.

'Differing Views on Kampuchea', Vol.XXXIV, No.2, *Problems of Communism*, March-April 1985, pp.138–40.

'Division Leaders Resolve Autos for Profits; Instructor Murdered', *Ming Pao*, 6 December 1985.

Domes, Jurgen. 'New Policies in the Communes; Notes on Rural Societal Structures in China, 1976–1981', *Journal of Asian Studies*, Vol.XII, No.2, pp.253–67.

Donnel, J.C. 'Vietnam 1979: Year of Calamity', *Asian Survey*, Vol.XX, No.1, January 1980, pp.19–32.

Dzirkals, Lilita I. *Lightning War in Manchuria: Soviet Military Analysis of the 1945 Far East Campaign*, (The RAND paper series, Santa Monica, 1976).

Economist, The, London, 12 December 1985, p.5.

Fan Ping. 'An Identification of Inclinations and Objective Effects of "Bitter Love"', *Jiefang Wenyi* (Liberation Literature), No.6, June 1981, pp.71–77.

Far Eastern Economic Review, Hong Kong: 20 November 1980, pp.24–25; 8 March 1984, pp.12–13; 14 June 1984, pp.46–47; 28 June 1984, pp.10–22; 4 April 1985, pp.17–18; 12 December 1985, p.25; 4 April 1986, pp.17–18; 24 April 1986, p.14; 27 May 1986, p.32; 7 August 1986, pp.22–23; 18 December 1986, p.24; 6 August 1987, pp.12–13.

Feng Jinqu. 'The Electrification of Railways on the Yunnan-Guizhou Plateau', *Tiedao Zhishi*, (hereafter *TDZS*), No.1, January 1984, pp.2–3.

———. 'The Electrification of the Chengdu-Chongqing Line', *TDZS*, No.2, March 1985, pp.4–5.

———. 'The Electrification of the Middle Section of the Longhai Line', *TDZS*, No.5, November 1985, pp.8–9.

Fieldhouse, R.W. *Nuclear Battlefields: Global Links in the Arms Race*, (Ballinger Publishing Company, Cambridge, Massachusetts, 1985).

———. 'Chinese Nuclear Weapons: An Overview', *World Armaments and Disarmament: SIPRI Yearbook 1986*, (Oxford University Press, Oxford and New York, 1986), pp.97–113.

Financial Review, 12 September 1986.

'Finback-A Revealed', *International Defence Review*, Vol.17, No.12/1984, p.1789.

Foley, S.R. 'Strategic Factors in the Pacific', *US Naval Institute Proceedings*, Vol.III/8/989, August 1985, pp.34–43.

Foreign Broadcast Information Service, Daily Report-China: 23 January 1978, E4, 11 September 1979, K6; 28 March 1980, S1–2, 2 September 1980, L10–22; 19 January 1981, K5 and K11; 11 August 1981, W4; 11 February 1983, K18; 22 April 1983, K7; 26 May 1983, K4 and 19 September 1983, K19–20; 6 June 1984, K3; and 18 September 1984, K6; 12 August 1985, K3, K5–7; 12 August 1985, K4–7; 19 August 1985, K9; 22 August 1985, K1; 26 August 1985, W2; 1 October 1985, K10–12, K14, and 2 October 1985, K4.

2 January 1986, W5; 6 January 1986, K23; 10 January 1986, K15–16; 16 January 1986, K7; 24 January 1986, K10–11; 25 January 1986, V1; 31 January 1986, K1–13; 2 February 1986, K13–15; 5 February 1986, K13–15; 10 February 1986, K15–17; 18 February 1986, K2–3; 19 February 1986, K19; 20 February 1986, W3; 4 March 1986, K12–13, K21; 1 April 1986, K24; 22 April 1986, K8–15; 24 April 1986, K9; 1 May 1986, W7; 6 May 1986, K7; 15 May 1986, K12–13; 20 May 1986; K10; 5 June 1986, W2; 10 June 1986, K12, W1; 13 June 1986, K16, 24 June 1986, W1; 17 July 1986, K29; 25 July 1986, K2–3; 29 July 1986, K5–6; 31 July 1986, K37; 6 August 1986, K9–10; 7 August 1986, K20; 15 August 1986, K13–16; 25 August 1986, K10–11; 8 September 1986, B2; 14 September 1986, B1–2, 15 October 1986, C2; 27 October 1986, K14; 3 November 1986, V1; 5 November 1986, B1; 10 November, 1986, B1; 2 February 1987, K19–20; 5 February 1987, K29; 12 February 1987, K21; 17 February 1987, R1; 20 February 1987, K39, 02–3; 25 March 1987, K28; 3 April 1987, G1; 21 April 1987, K23, K28; 11 May 1987, K13; 15 May 1987, S4; 18 May 1987, K23; 26 May 1987, K13–16, K19; 27 May 1987, K1; 29 May 1987, 02, K14; 1 June 1987, K24; 3 June 1987, K24–26; 5 June 1987, K9; 10 June 1987, K8; 11 June 1987, K13; 12 June 1987, K14.

Foreign Report, (The Economist Publications, London): 25 July 1985, p.5; 22 August 1985, pp.7–8; 12 December 1985, p.5; 6 March 1986, p.6.

Foss, Christopher F. 'China and UK Join Forces in New MICV Project', *JDW*, 11 January 1986, p.5.

———. 'China Releases Light Armoured Vehicle Details', *JDW*, 15 December 1984, pp.1062–1063.

Fu Zhong. 'Mao Zedong Military Science Is Forever the Chinese People's Treasure — In Celebration of both the Founding Anniversary of the CCP and the 54th Founding Anniversary of the PLA', *HQ*, No.15, 1 August 1981, pp.2–10.

'Full-Time Militia Cadres Aging, Youth Needed', in JPRS, *China Report*, No.77144, 12 January 1981, p.21.

'Further Reportage on Sino–Soviet Consultations', Hong Kong AFP, 14 October 1986, in FBIS-CHI, 15 October 1986, C1–2.

'Further Strengthen Militia and Reserve Work Around the Central Task of National Economic Construction', *Anhui Ribao*, 27 March 1986, p.4, in FBIS-CHI, 14 April 1986, 01.

Gai Yumin. 'People's Armed Forces Departments Reorganised', *Xinhua Ribao*, 2 May 1986.

Gauder, Terry J. 'Norinco's Range of Towed Artillery', *JDW*, 15 December 1984, pp.1008–1009.

Gansu Provincial Service, 26 April 1985, in *SWB*, 2 May 1985, FE/7940/BII/12–13.

Gao Yan. 'The Growth of Chinese Railways, 1949–1983, Part 1', *Ming Pao Monthly*, No.3, 1986, p.45.

Glaser, Bonnie S. and Garrett, Banning N. 'Chinese Perspectives on the Strategic Defence Initiative', *Problems of Communism*, Vol.XXXV, No.2, March–April 1986, p.42.

Goblat, Josef and Fern, Reginald. 'Arms Control Agreements', in *SIPRI Yearbook 1986*, p.578.

Godwin, Paul H.B. 'Mao Zedong Revised: Deterrence and Defence in the 1980s', in P.H.B. Godwin (ed), *The Chinese Defence Establishment* (Westview Press, Boulder, 1983), pp.21–39.

Godwin, Paul H.B. 'Towards a New Strategy?', in Segal and Tow (eds), *Chinese Defence Policy*, p.48.

Gold, Thomas B. ' "Just in Time!": China Battles Spiritual Pollution on the Eve of 1984', *Asian Survey*, Vol.XXIV, No.9, September 1984, pp.947–974.

Goldrick, J. and Jones, P. 'The Far Eastern Navies', *US Naval Institute Proceedings*, March 1986, pp.64–69.

Goldstein, Carl. 'KMT Power Grows Out of a Holstered Gun', *FEER*, 8 May 1986, pp.25–6.

'Gorbachev 28 July Speech in Vladivostok', Moscow Television Service, 28 July 1986, in FBIS, Daily Report, Soviet Union, 29 July 1986, R1–20.

'Grasp the Construction of Professionalism and Strengthen the Might of the Nation and the Army', *JFJB*, 18 September 1986.

Grazebrook, A.W. 'No.3. Big Naval Expansion Programs', *Pacific Defence Reporter*, Vol.XIII, Nos.6/7, December 1986/January 1987.

Greer, W. and Bartholomew, J. *Psychological Aspects of Mine Warfare*, (Professional Paper 365, October 1982, Centre for Naval Analyses, USA).

Guang Hua. 'The Way That Deng Xiaoping Rectifies the Army', *Kuang Chiao Ching*, 16 September 1985, p.16.

'Guangdong People's Armed Forces Committee Discusses Militia

Building', in JPRS, *China Report*, No.74875, 7 January 1980, pp.80–2.

'Guangdong Prepares Transfer of Armed Forces', Guangdong Provincial Service, 14 April 1986, in FBIS-CHI, 21 April 1986, P1.

'Guangzhou Military Region Educates Cadres', Beijing XH, 29 November 2985, in FBIS-CHI, 3 December 1985, p.1.

'Guangzhou PLA Solves Problems in Party Conduct', *Ming Pao*, 3 December 1985, p.5, in FBIS-CHI, 4 December 1985, W2–3.

'Guangzhou Rectifies Leadership of Armies and Divisions', *Ming Pao*, 23 July 1985, in SWB, 29 July 1985, FE/8015/BII/1.

Guo Zhongyi. 'An Investigation into the "Appropriate Position" of Political Work', *JFJB*, 13 November 1980.

Hahn, B. 'Hai Fang', *US Naval Institute Proceedings*, March 1986, pp.114–20.

———. 'Maritime Dangers in the South China Sea', *Pacific Defence Reporter*, May 1985, p.13.

———. 'PRC Policy in Maritime Asia', *Journal of Defence and Diplomacy* (Defence and Diplomacy Inc., McLean, Virginia), Vol.4, No.6, June 1986), pp.19–21.

Hai Yuan and Chen Hongwu. 'The New Formula to Grab Sea Control', *JFJB*, 20 July 1984.

Hall, Eric. 'An Army that "Wears Its Enemy Down"', *South China Morning Post*, Hong Kong, 1 March 1984.

Han Huaizhi. 'To Underline the Characteristics of Modern Warfare and to Raise the Warfighting Capabilities of Units under Nuclear Conditions', *JFJB*, 8 November 1983.

Hangkong Zhishi (Aviation Knowledge; Beijing), June 1983.

Hanoi Home Service, in *SWB*, 15 May 1985, FE/7951/A3.

Hartmann, G. *Weapons That Wait* (Naval Institute Press, Annapolis, 1979).

Hasenbohler, Robert C. 'The Swiss Militia Army', in Zurcher and Harries-Jenkins (eds), *Supplementary Military Forces*, pp.239–258.

'Having Communes Train Militia Leaders Works Out Well', in JPRS, *China Report*, No.76072, 18 July 1980, p.71.

He Zhengwen. 'The Basic Law For Building Defence Modernisation in Our Nation', *RMRB*, 8 June 1984.

'Heilongjiang Begins 1980 Conscription', in *SWB*, 31 October 1980, Fe/6563/BII/16.

'Heilongjiang Carries Out Transfer of Armed Forces', Heilongjiang Provincial Service, 23 April 1986, in FBIS/CHI, 1 May 1986, S1.

Hill, J.R. *Maritime Strategy for Medium Powers* (Croom Helm, London and Sydney, 1986).

Hinge, A. and Lee, N. 'Naval Developments in the Asia-Pacific Region', (Strategic and Defence Studies Centre, Australian National University); paper presented to the Asian Studies Association of Australia Biennial Conference, May 1986.

Hoffmann, R. 'Offensive Mine Warfare: A Forgotten Strategy?', *US Naval Institute Proceedings* (Naval Review), 103/891, May 1977, p.152.

Hollingworth, Clare. 'Massive Streamlining and Reorganization of the Armed Forces', *Pacific Defence Reporter*, Vol.XIII, Nos.6/7, December 1986/January 1987, pp.44–46.

Hongqi (Red Flag), Beijing, No.5, 1983.

Hsin Wan Pao, Hong Kong, 26 October 1986.

'Hu Qili Stresses Ideological, Political Work', Beijing XH, 18 January 1986, in FBIS-CHI, 21 January 1986, K3.

Hu Yaobang. 'Fully Initiating the New Situation in the Construction of Socialist Modernisation', *HQ*, No.18, September 1982, pp.6–30.

'Hu Yaobang on Work Style', Beijing XH, 10 January 1986, in FBIS-CHI, 10 January 1986, K2–3.

'Hu Yaobang, Xi Zhongxun and Hu Qiaomu Encouraging Workers in the Film Industry', *RMRB*, 30 December 1981.

Huang Huamin and Xiao Xianshe, 'A Summary Report of Major Views Expressed in the Conference on "Strategic Changes to the Guiding Thoughts for Our Army Building"', JFJB, 20 December 1986.

Huang Kecheng. 'On Assessing Chairman Mao and Attitude towards Mao Zedong Thought', *RMRB*, 11 April 1981.

Huang Zhenxia. *Mao's Generals* (Research Institute of Contemporary History, Hong Kong, 1968).

'Hunan: Mao Zhiyong Stresses the Need for Militia and Reserve Work', Hunan Provincial Service, 13 January 1986, in SWB, FE/8166/BII/10.

International Defence Review, Vol.19, No.6/1986 (Interavia SA, Cointrin-Geneva), pp.718–719.

'Interview with Zhu Qizhen, Vice Minister of Foreign Affairs of the

People's Republic of China', *Journal of Northeast Asian Studies*, Vol.III, No.2, 1984, pp.75–76.

'It is Necessary to Boost the Building of Spiritual Civilization', *HQ*, No.20, 16 October 1985, p.2, in FBIS-CHI, 12 November 1985, K3.

Jacobs, Gordon. 'Bringing China's Navy Up To Date', *JDW*, 25 January 1986, pp.113–114.

———. 'China's Auxiliary Ships', *JDW*, 8 March 1986, pp.435–437.

———. 'China's Destroyers', *JDW*, 23 February 1985, pp.322–324.

———. 'China's Frigate Classes', *JDW*, 5 January 1985, pp.28–32.

———. 'China's Submarine Force', *JDW*, 9 February 1985, pp.220–224.

———. 'China's Tank Armies', *JDW*, 1 February 1986, pp.159–161.

———. 'China's Type-59 and -69 MBTs', *JDW*, 27 July 1985, pp.171–174.

———. 'How China Monitors Pacific Missile Tests', *JDW*, 28 December 1985, pp.1416–1417.

Jacobsen, Carl G. 'Soviet Military Expenditure and the Soviet Defence Burden', *World Armaments and Disarmament: SIPRI Yearbook, 1986*, pp.263–74.

Jane's All the World's Aircraft 1983–84 (Jane's Publishing Company, London).

Jane's Defence Weekly, (Jane's Publishing Company, London): 3 March 1984, p.307; 24 March 1984, p.436; 11 August 1984, pp.84, 178–179; 3 November 1984, p.784; 8 December 1984, pp.1008, 1016; 15 December 1984, pp.1062–1063; 22 December 1984, pp.1099–1100; 5 January 1985, pp.28–32; 12 January 1985, p.51; 15 January 1985, p.1132; 9 February 1985, pp.220–224; 23 February 1985, pp.322–324; 13 April 1985, p.620; 27 April 1985, p.703; 15 June 1985, p.1132; 13 July 1985, p.72; 27 July 1985, pp.171–174; 10 August 1985, p.278; 28 September 1985, p.679; 12 October 1985, p.771; 7 December 1985, p.1218; 14 December 1985, pp.1307–1312, 1317; 21 December 1985, p.1367; 28 December 1985, p.1417; 11 January 1986, p.5; 25 January 1986, pp.113–114; 1 February 1986, p.161; 8 February 1986, pp.188, 205, 207; 15 February 1986, p.233; 22 February 1986, p.311; 4 March 1986, p.426; 8 March 1986, p.436; 22 March 1986, p.529; 10 May 1986, pp.848–851; 22 May 1986, p.529.

Jane's Fighting Ships 1984–85 (Jane's Publishing Company Ltd., London), pp.94–7.

Janowitz, Morris. *The US Forces and the Zero Draft* (Adelphi Paper No.94, IISS, London, 1973).

Jencks, Harlan W. 'China's Punitive War on Vietnam: A Military Assessment', *Asian Survey*, Vol.XIX, No.8, August 1979, pp.801–815.

——. *From Muskets to Missiles: Politics and Professionalism in the Chinese Army, 1945–1981* (Westview Press, Boulder, 1982).

——. 'Ground Forces', in G. Segal and W.T. Tow (eds), *China's Defence Policy*, pp.53–57.

——. ' "People's War under Modern Conditions": Wishful Thinking, National Suicide, or Effective Deterrent?', *China Quarterly*, No.98, June 1984, p.305–319.

Jetro China News Letter, No.60, January–February 1986.

Jiang Chenglu. 'The Building of Double-tracks for the Haerbin–Manzhouli Line', *Tiedao Zhishi*, No.1, January 1985, pp.4–5.

'Multiple Tracks being Constructed on the Haerbin–Suifen Line', *TDZS*, No.1. January 1986, pp.2–3.

Jiang Qinhong. 'The Attacker Avoids Shortcomings and Develops Strengths during Successive Penetrations', *JFJB*, 2 September 1983.

Jiang Wuyu and Wu Weirui. 'To Widen the Horizon of Defensive War', *JFJB*, 11 May 1984.

'Jiangsu's Achievements in Paying for Military Training Praised', XH, 25 December 1985, in *SWB*, FE/8145/BII/4.

'Jiangsu Leaders Discuss PLA "Support the left" Campaign', in *SWB*, 31 January 1980, FE/6333/BII/15.

'Jiangsu Militia Engage in Commodity Production', Jiangsu Provincial Service, 3 March 1985, in *SWB*, FE/7893/BII/12.

Jiefangjun Bao (Liberation Army Daily): 12 May 1982, 9 January 1983, 17 March 1983, 20 May 1983, 2 June 1983, 17 June 1983, 16 July 1983, 23 August 1983, 14 September 1983, 25 November 1983; 8 January 1984, 10 January 1984, 6 April 1984, 9 May 1984, 23 May 1984, 15 June 1984, 20 July 1984, 29 July 1984, 20 October 1984, 26 October 1984, 20 November 1984, 25 November 1984; 8 September 1986; 12 January 1987, 19 May 1987.

Jiefangjun Huabao (Liberation Army Pictorial): No.7, 1982, pp.1, 28–31; No.8, 1982, pp.30–33; No.9, 1982, pp.18–19; No.11,

1983, p.42; No.1, 1984, pp.2–5; No.2, 1984, pp.10–11; No.4, 1984, pp.2–5, 12, 16–19.

'Jilin First Secretary Wang Enmao at City Defence Symposium', in FBIS-CHI, 28 March 1980, S1–2.

Jin Ximin. 'The Future Battlefield under High Pressure', *JFJB*, 31 December 1983.

Jing Bao, No.2, Hong Kong, 5 February 1986.

Joffe, Ellis. and Segal, Gerald. 'The PLA under Modern Conditions', *Survival*, Vol.XXVII, No.4, July/August 1985, pp.146–157.

Johnson, Chalmers. 'Lin Piao's Army and Its Role in Chinese Society', *Current Scene*, Vol.IV, No.13, 1 July 1966, pp.1–10.

Joint Publications Research Service, *China Report* (Joint Publications Research Service, Arlington, Virginia): 7 January 1980, p.81; 7 July 1980, p.29; 17 March 1983, pp.103–107; 21 November 1984, p.66.

Jun Yan. 'Discussing Active Defence from Ancient to Modern Times', *JFJB*, 7 January 1983.

———. 'To Insist on Extensive Guerrilla Warfare', *JFJB*, 1 April 1983.

———. 'Objective Reality Is the Basis to Determine Strategic Guidelines', *JFJB*, 14 January 1983.

Kefner, John. 'The Dragon and the Bear: Asian Perception of a Sino–Soviet War', *America*, 24 September, pp.162–4.

———. 'Will the Soviets Attack China?' *America*, 15 May 1976, pp.421–23.

LAD Commentator. 'Actively Take Part in Party Rectification with a High Degree of Consciousness', *JFJB*, 28 November 1983.

———. 'The Emphasis Should be on Conducting Collective Investigation Well', *RMRB*, 24 May 1984.

———. 'To Learn from the Ideology of People's War and to Continue with the Strengthening of Militia Building', *JFJB*, 28 July 1983.

———. 'To Make Contribution to Building Strong Reserve Forces', *JFFB*, 8 January 1984.

Lee, Mary. 'Two Way Street for Arms', *FEER*, 12 December 1985, p.25.

Lee Ngok. 'Dimensions of China's Defence Policy from the 1980s and Beyond', *ASAA Review*, Vol.9, No.2, November 1985, pp.133–41.

————. *The Chinese People's Liberation Army 1980–82: Modernisaiton, Strategy and Politics* (Canberra Papers on Strategy and Defence No.28, Australian Natonal University, 1983).

————. 'The Militia in People's War under Modern Conditions, 1979–1983', in C.K. Leung and S.S.K. Chin (eds), *China in Readjustment* (Centre of Asian Studies, University of Hong Kong, 1983), pp.339–55.

Lee, Ngok and Hinge, A. 'Naval Developments in Southeast Asia', *Naval Forces*, Vol.VII, No.1, 1986, pp.33–4.

Lee, Ngok and Hinge, A. 'The US Bases in the Philippines (Comment)', *Naval Forces*, Vol.VII, No.3, 1986, pp.8–10.

Lehman, John, 'The 600-ship Navy', *The Maritime Strategy* (Supplement, US Naval Institute Proceedings), January 1986, p.33.

Leung, C.K. and Comtois, Claude. 'Transport Reorientation towards the Eighties', in C.K. Leung and S.S.K. Chin (eds), *China in Readjustment*, p.216–33.

Li Jian. 'Reliance on Present Equipment Can Overcome Tank Groups', *JFJB*, 27 March 1981.

Li Jianghe. 'The Multi-layer Three-dimensional Battlefield', *JFJB*, 23 April 1984.

Li Jing. 'Functions of Naval Aviation and Development of Weapons and Equipment', *Hangkong Zhishi*, Beijing, June 1983.

————. 'The Function of the Naval Air Force and the Development of Its Weapons and Equipment', *JFJB*, 2 June 1983.

Li Qianyuan. 'A preliminary Analysis of the Characteristics of Limited War in the Future', *JFJB*, 19 December 1986.

Li Wei. 'He Comes from the Battlefields — An Interview with He Qizong, Deputy Chief of Staff of the PLA', Zhongguo Xinwen She, 28 January 1986, in FBIS-CHI, 5 February 1986, K13–14.

Li Yuezhi. 'Liu Jingsong, Newly Appointed Commander of Shengyang Military Region', *Liaowang*, Hong Kong Edition, 13 January 1986, p.31, in FBIS-CHI, 23 January 1986, S3–4.

'Liaoning Holds Meeting on Army Transfer Work', Liaoning Provincial Service, 8 May 1986, in FBIS-CHI, 14 May 1986, S2.

Liaoning Ribao, 16 April 1984.

Liaowang, No.30, 28 July 1986.

Liaowang, Hong Kong, Overseas Edition, No.8, 24 February 1986, 20; No.23, 8 June 1987.

'Liaowang on International Disarmement Situation', in FBIS-CHI, 18 September 1986, A5.

'"Liberation Army Daily" New Year's Editorial', in JPRS, *China Report*, No.75841, 9 June 1980, pp.86–88.

'"Liberation Army Daily" on Elimination of Feudal Influence in the PLA', in *SWB*, 25 November 1980, FE/6584/BII/1–2.

Liu Dizhong. 'Beefed-Up Militia Aims to Improve Defence Strategy', *China Daily*, Beijing, 29 January 1985.

Liu Guoguang (ed). *A Study on Strategic Problems of China's Economic Development* (Shanghai People's Press, Shanghai, 1984).

Liu Yong and Qinhong. 'Outlook on Battlefields, at River Mouths', *JFJB*, 16 November 1984.

Luckow, U. 'Victory Over Ignorance and Fear: The US Minelaying Attack on North Vietnam', *Naval War College Review*, Vol.XXXV, 1/289, January–February 1982, p.24.

Luttwak, Edward N. *The Political Uses of Sea Power* (Johns Hopkins University Press, 1974).

MacCruther, Kenneth R. 'The Role of Perception in Naval Diplomacy', *Naval War College Review*, September–October 1974, p.4.

Manichi Shimbun, 21 March 1981.

Mao Tse-tung. *Basic Tactics* (Praeger Publishers, New York, 1966).

———. 'On Protracted War', *Selected Military Writings of Mao Zedong* (Foreign Languages Press, Peking, 1966), pp.187–267.

———. *Selected Works of Mao Tse-tung*, Vol.I-IV (Foreign Languages Press, 1967).

McCauley, B. 'Operation Endsweep', *US Naval Institute Proceedings*, Vol.100/3/853, March 1974, pp.19–25.

'Measures to Ease Return of Soldiers to Civilian Jobs', XH, 10 March 1985, in *SWB*, 14 March 1985, FE/7899/BII/10.

Mediansky, F.A. and Court, D. *The Soviet Union in Southeast Asia* (Canberra Papers on Strategy and Defence, No.29, Strategic and Defence Studies Centre, Australian National University, 1984).

Memorandum of the Ministry of Foreign Affairs of the SRV on China's War of Escalation and Aggravation of the Tension Along the Vietnam-China Border (Hanoi), 4 July 1984.

Meyer, Stephen M. *Soviet Theatre Nuclear Force, Part II: Capabilities and Implications* (Adelphi Paper No.188, IISS, London 1983).

'Militia Training Should Achieve the Integration of the Responsibility System and Ideological Education', *Xinhua Ribao*, 9 May 1983.

Mills, William de B. 'Leadership Change in China's Provinces', *Problems of Communism*, Vol.XXXIV, May–June 1985, pp.35–7.

Ming Pao (Hong Kong): 11 February 1982; 14 June 1983; 29 November 1983; 30 January 1984; 29 April 1986; 3 June 1986; 5 June 1986; 11 June 1986; 20 June 1986; 21 June 1986; 28 July 1986; 24 August 1986; 15 June 1987.

Muller, David G. 'A Chinese Blockade of Taiwan', *US Naval Institute Proceedings*, Vol.110/9/979, September 1984, pp.54–5.

———. *China As A Maritime Power* (Westview Press, Boulder, 1983).

Munro, Neil. 'Keeping Watch on the Amur and the Sea of Okhotsk', *Pacific Defence Reporter*, October 1986, p.18.

Munson, K., 'China's Aero Industry Serves More Credit', *JDW*, 14 December 1985, pp.1315–1317.

———. 'Fishbed, Finback and the Chinese Future', *JDW*, 21 December 1985, pp.1367–1369.

Myers, James T. 'China — The "Germs" of Modernisation', *Asian Survey*, Vol.XXV, No.10, October 1985, pp.981–97.

Nair, K.K. *ASEAN–Indochina Relations Since 1975: The Politics of Accommodation* (Canberra Papers on Strategy and Defene, No.30, Strategic and Defence Studies Centre, Australian National University, Canbeera, 1984).

'Nanjing PLA Region Improves Grass-roots Work', *Jiefang Ribao*, 7 November 1985, p.1, in FBIS-CHI, 15 November 1985, K15.

Nanning, Guangxi Regional Service, 2 March 1985, in *SWB*, 6 March 1985, FE/7982/BII/8.

'National Forum of Advanced Cadres of County People's Armed Forces Departments', XH, 5 March 1986, in *SWB*, 10 March 1986, FE/8203/BII/5.

Nations, Richard. 'A Mild Chill in Moscow', *FEER*, 11 July 1985, pp.10–11.

———. 'Joining the League', *FEER*, 14 April 1984, p.14.

———. 'Moscow's New Tack', *FEER*, 14 August 1986, pp.33–4.

'Navsea Mine Familiarizer', *Naval Mine Engineering Facility* (Yorktown, Virginia, 1977), p.22.

Nelsen, Harvey W. *The Chinese Military System* (Westview Press, Boulder, 1977).

'New Atmosophere Seen for Sino–Soviet Normalization', Hong Kong AFP, 16 October 1986, in FBIS-CHI, 16 October 1986, C1–2.

'New Senior Military Officers of the Military Regions', *Kuang Chiao Ching*, Hong Kong, 16 July 1985, in *SWB*, 20 July 1985, FE/8008/BII/4.

New York Times, 4 January 1980.

Ningxia Ribao, 27 June 1982, in *SWB*, 9 July 1982, FE/7873/BII/4.

Ningxia Ribao, 27 June 1983; 28 June 1983.

'NPC Discusses Draft Law on Military Service', XH, 22 May 1984, in *SWB*, 23 May 1984, FE/7650/CI/1.

O'Connell, D.P. *The Influence of Law on Sea Power* (Naval Institute Press, Annapolis, 1975).

Odom, E. William. 'Soviet Force Posture: Dilemmas and Directions', *Problems of Communism*, Vol.XXXIV, July–August 1985, pp.1–14.

Office of Liberation Army Daily, 'An Article Which Has Serious Errors', *Jiefang Ribao*, 28 September 1982.

Office of the Statistical Planning Bureau, Railway Ministry, 'The Great Achievement of Railway Building in the Sixth Five-Year Plan Period', *TDZS*, No.2, March 1986, pp.2–3.

'Official PRC Statistics: 1977–1978', *The China Business Review*, July–August 1979, p.45.

Oksenberg, Michel and Liberthal, Kenneth. 'Forecasting China's Future', *The National Interest*, No.5, Fall 1986, p.23.

'On Perfecting the System of Combining the Militia with Reserve Service', XH, 8 December 1985, in *SWB*, 13 December 1985, FE/8133/BII/10–11.

'Ordnance Cadre Training Unit', JPRS, *China Report*, No.76910, 1 December 1980, p.90.

Oudennaren, John Van. *Deterrence War-fighting and Soviet Military Doctrine* (Adelphi Paper No.210, IISS, London, Summer 1986).

'Our Army's Various Reforms Have Achieved Fruitful Results', *JFJB*, 24 December 1986.

'Our Combined Army Corps of the Ground Forces Showing Their Strength', *JFJB*, 13 September 1986.

'Party Committee Members' of the General Logistics Department Correcting Learning Style during Party Rectification', *RMRB*, 5 January 1984.

'Party Rectification in the Army Must Insist on High Standards and High Quality', *RMRB*, 21 August 1984.

'Party Style Rectification Emerges with New Atmosphere in the Party Committee of a Certain Unit in Beijing', *RMRB*, 19 July 1983.

'Peking Radio on the "Three Supports, Two Militaries"', in *SWB*, 7 February 1980, FE/6339/BII/9.

'PLA Conference on Mass Work', in *SWB* 3 August 1979, FE/6184/BII/7–8.

'PLA to Resettle 830 000 Ex-servicemen in 1986', Beijing Zhongguo Xinwenshe, 15 January 1986, in FBIS-CHI, 17 January 1986, K7.

'PLA's He Qizong Discusses Reduction Work', Beijing International Service, 30 January 1986, in FBIS-CHI, 31 January 1986, K1.

'PLA Unit "Agrees to Return Some People's University Building"', in *SWB*, 18 October 1979, FE/6284/BII/3.

Pollack, Jonathan D. 'China's Changing Perceptions of East Asian Security and Development', *ORBIS*, Winter 1986, pp.779–80.

'Possibility of Enemy Nuclear Attack Must be Considered', in JPRS, *China Report*, No.75825, 4 June 1980, pp.97–9.

'PRC Announces US Naval Visit to Qingdao', Beijing XH, 9 October 1986, in FBIS-CHI, 10 October 1986, B1.

Preston, A. 'The PLA Navy's Underwater Deterrent', in *JDW*, 28 April 1984, pp.659–660.

'"Problems Emerge among Army Officers": Circular Issues', *Ming Pao*, 23 July 1985, in *SWB*, 25 July 1985, FE/8012/BII/2–3.

Pye, Lucian W. *Asian Power and Politics: the Cultural Dimensions of Authority*, (Harvard University Press, Cambridge, Massachusetts, 1985).

Qi Yaokun. 'The Guangzhou-Maoming Line', *TDZS*, No.2, March 1984, pp.14–15.

Qi Zhengjun. 'To Be the "Designer" of the Future Battlefield', *JFJB*, 22 July 1983.

'Qin Jiwei Emphasises that Party Rectification Must Have the Strength to Conduct Simultaneous Rectification and Change', *RMRB*, 9 January 1984.

'Raising the Standards of Specialism Amongst Militia Work Cadres', *Dazhong Ribao* (The Masses Daily), 27 November 1982.

'Reform Militia Work and Lighten the Peasants' Burden', *Liaowang*, No.43, 28 October 1985, p.7.

'Reform in Tactical Training in Joint Operational Setting in a Motorised Division Achieve Outstanding Results', *JFJB*, 8 September 1986.

'Regulations on Militia Work', *Issues and Studies*, Vol.XVI, No.2, February 1980, pp.79–95.

Renmin Ribao (People's Daily; Beijing): 27 April 1981; 24 December 1981; 13 June 1983; 8 June 1984; 21 September 1984; 16 February 1985; 6 July 1985; 18 July 1985; 17 April 1986; 28 July 1986; 2 June 1987.

'Report on Communique', Beijing XH, 14 April 1986, in FBIS-CHI, 15 April 1986, C2.

'Reserve Division Established in Capital', XH, 1 February 1985, in *Ming Pao*, 2 February 1985.

Resolutions on CCP History (Foreign Languages Press, Beijing, 1981).

Richelson, Jeffrey. 'Monitoring the Soviet Military', *Arms Control Today*, Vol.16, No.7, October 1986, pp.14–16.

'Rogachev Leaves for Home', Beijing XH, 15 October 1986, in FBIS-CHI, 15 October 1986, C4.

Rogers, Paul. *Guide to Nuclear Weapons 1984–85* (University of Bradford School of Peace Studies, 1986).

Sabrosky, Alan N. 'Defence with Fewer Men? The American Experience', in Gwyn Harries-Jenkins (ed), *Armed Forces and the Welfare Societies: Challenges in the 1980s* (International Institute for Strategic Studies, Macmillan Press, London, 1982).

Sandus, Alan J.K. 'Mongolia in 1984', *Asian Survey*, Vol.XXV, No.1, January 1985, pp.122–130.

Sandschneider, Eberhard. 'Political Succession in the People's Republic of China', *Asian Survey*, Vol.XXV, No.6, June 1985, pp.638–658.

'Science, Technology and Industry for National Defence Should Strive to Serve the National Economy (editorial)', *JFJB*, 23 August 1983.

Segal, Gerald. 'China and Arms Control', *The World Today*, Vol.41, Nos.8–9, August/September 1985, pp.165–6.

————. 'Nuclear Forces', in Segal and Tow (eds), *Chinese Defence Policy*, pp.107–8.

————. *The Great Power Triangle* (Macmillan, London, 1982).

Segal, G. and Tow, W.T. (eds). *Chinese Defence Policy*, (Macmillan, London, 1984).

'Shandong: Liang Buting Speaks on Armed Forces Transfer', Shandong Provincial Service, 23 May 1986, in FBIS-CHI, 29 May 1986, pp.2–3.

Shang Mingang. 'The Perspective of City Defence Should be expanded to the Air', *JFJB*, 20 January 1984.

Shanxi Ribao, 30 January 1986, p.1, in FBIS-CHI, 13 February 1986, R1.

'Shift of Hebei Armed Forces Departments Progresses', Hebei Provincial Service, 3 April 1986, in FBIS-CHI, 18 April 1986, R2.

'Sichuan PLA Leaders Explain Change in Administration of Local Armed Forces', in *SWB*, FE/8044/BII/7.

Simon, Denis Fred. 'The Challenge of Modernizing Industrial Technology in China', *Asian Survey*, Vol.XXVI, No.4, April 1986.

'Smooth Development in Army Restructuring and Reduction-in-Strength', *RMRB*, 18 July 1985.

'Solving Problems of "Three Supports, Two Militaries"', in *SWB*, 7 February 1980, FE/6339/BII/9.

Song Shilun. 'Mao Zedong's Military Thinking is the Guide to Our Army's Victories', *HQ*, No.16, 16 August 1981, pp.5–15.

South China Morning Post, Hong Kong: 3 August 1983; 1 March 1984; 16 November 1984.

Soviet Military Power 1985 (US Government Printing Office, Washington D.C., 1985).

Special Commentator. 'To Do Well in Two Preparations and to Grasp Two Sets of Skills', *JFJB*, 11 March 1984.

Special *LAD* Commentator. 'Strive to Raise Our Army's Coordinated Fighting Capabilities', *JFJB*, 8 April 1984.

————. 'To Do Well in Two Kinds of Preparations and to Grasp Two Sets of Skills', *JFJB*, 14 March 1984.

'Speech by Wei Guoqing at PLA Political Conference', in SWB, 15 May 1980, FE6420/BII/5–6.

Staff Correspondent, 'The First Step Taken in the Seventh 5-Year

Plan', in Beijing *Liaowang*, No.2, 13 January 1986, pp.6–7, in FBIS-CHI, 31 January 1986, K13.

'Stand up against Intercessional Trend', *JFJB*, 20 January 1986, in FBIS-CHI, 4 February 1986, K4–5.

'State Council Praises Hubei Automobile Production', FBIS-CHI, 10 January 1986, in FBIS-CHI, 3 March 1986, K3.

'Strive Hard to Build the Artillery in the Militia', *JFJB*, 14 September 1983, p.3.

'Strive to Achieve Modernization in National Defense — in Celebration of the 20th Anniversary of the Founding of the People's Republic of China', in FBIS-CHI, 18 October 1979, L15.

'Strive to Raise Our Army's Fighting Capabilities under Modern Warfare Conditions (editorial)', *JFJB*, 8 January 1984.

Su Yu. 'The Great Victory of Chairman Mao's Guideline on Warfare', *RMRB*, 6 August 1977.

Summary of World Broadcasts: Part 3 — Far East, British Broadcasting Corporation: 2 February 1984, FE/7556/BII/4; 23 May 1984, FE/7650/C1/1; 23 June 1984, FE7677/BII/5; 28 June 1984, FE/7684/BII/3; 3 July 1984, FE/7685/BII/11; 4 July 1984, FE/7687/BII/1; 5 July 1984, FE/7687/BII/1; 10 July 1984, FE/7691/BII/7; 25 July 1984, FE/7704/BII/5; 27 July 1984, FE/7706/BII/1–2; 28 July 1984, FE/7707/BII/5–6; 31 July 1984, FE/7709/BII/9–12; 3 August 1984, FE/7712/BII/2–3, 6–8; 8 August 1984, FE/7716/BII/7–8; 18 October 1984, FE/7777/BII/2; 1 November 1984, FE/7789/BII/3; 12 December 1984, FE/7826/BII/10; 14 December 1984, FE/7826/BII/10; 18 December 1984, FE/7829/BII/5–6; 1 March 1985, FE/7888/BII/10; 14 March 1985, FE/7899/BII/10; 8 July 1985, FE/7997/BII/1; 9 July 1985, FE/7998/BII/1; 11 July 1985, FE/8000/BII/1; 10 August 1985, FE/8026/BII/7; 31 August 1985, FE/8044/BII/7; 26 October 1985, FE/8092/BII/11; 13 December 1985, FE/8133/BII/10–11; 1 April 1986, FE/8221/A3/3; 26 April 1986, FE/8168/BII/1; 29 April 1986, FE/8245/BII/1.

Sunday Morning Post, Hong Kong 12 April 1987.

Sutton, D. Boyd et al., 'New Directions in Conventional Defence?', *Survival*, Vol.XXVI, No.2, March/April 1984, pp.50–70.

Suvorov, Viktor. 'Strategic Command and Control, the Soviet Approach', *International Defense Review*, 12/1984, pp.1818–20.

'Suzhou Military District Organize the Militia', *Xinhua Ribao*, 18 April 1984.

Swanson, Bruce. 'Naval Forces', in Segal and Tow (eds), *Chinese Defence Policy*, pp.88–97.

Sweetman, Bill. 'Air Forces', in Segal and Tow (eds), *Chinese Defence Policy*, pp.71–84.

Ta Kung Pao, Hong Kong: 3 November 1983; 21 November 1983; 21 December 1984; 25 July 1985; 27 July 1985; 25 August 1985; 15 February; 1986.

Tass News Agency, Moscow, 10 July 1986.

Taylor, J.D. 'Mining: A Well Reasoned and Circumspect Defence', *US Naval Institute Proceedings*, Vol.103/11/897, November 1977, p.42.

Thayer, Carlyle A. 'Regularization of Military Bureaucratic Regimes: From Symbiosis to Coalition — The Case of Vietnam', paper prepared for the Asian Studies Association of Australia's Sixth Biennial Conference, Sydney, May 1986.

'The Armed Militia Doing Good Work in Enforcing Specialist Contract', *Dazhong Ribao*, 19 October 1981.

The Australian, 7 August 1986.

'The Cam Ranh Syndrome', *ASEAN Forecast*, June 1984, p.100.

'The Capital Established a Reserve Division', *Ming Pao*, 2 February 1985.

'The Central Military Commission Sends out the First Batch of Liaison Groups for Party Rectification', *RMRB*, 21 February 1984.

'The Central Military Commission's Resolution Concerning the Army's Political Work in the New Era', *JFJB*, 26 February 1987, pp.1–2.

'The Completion of Adjustment and Reform Work for Nationwide Militia Organisations', *JFJB*, 17 March 1983, p.1.

'The Constitution of the Chinese Communist Party', *HQ*, No.18, September 1982, pp.31–3.

'The Current Phase of Chinese Communist Militia Work'. *Issues and Studies* (Taiwan), Vol.XV, No.6, June 1979, pp.81–97.

'The Establishment of the Central Advisory Committee Is An Innovation in Chinese Communist History,' *Wen Hui Pao*, 12 September 1982.

The Military Balance 1986–1987 (The International Institute for Strategic Studies, London, 1986).

The Pacific Defence Reporter 1987 Annual Reference Edition (Peter Isaacson Publications, Victoria), pp.92, 99 and 144.

The Police Chief (International Association of Chiefs of Police, Gaithersberg, Maryland, May 1985).

'The Sixth Plenum of the Eleventh Party Congress Is Convened in Beijing', *RMRB*, 30 June 1981.

Thompson, R. *Peace Is Not at Hand* (Chatto and Windus, London, 1974).

Tian Ming. 'All Regions Are Establishing Reserve Divisions in the Ground Force', *Ta Kung Pao*, 3 July 1984.

Tian Sheng. 'Some Thoughts on the Improvement of the System of Ideological-Political Work', *JFJB*, 3 November 1980.

Time (Time Australia, Sydney), 10 February 1986, p.43.

Ting Xun. 'How Do Military Specialists make Use of Railways', *Tiedao Zhishi*, No.2, March 1984, p.19.

'To Adapt to Strategic Changes and Do Well in War preparation', *JFJB*, 1 November 1986.

'To Do a Good Job in Reserve Service Training', *JFJB*, 29 July 1984.

'To Seriously and Thoroughly Enforce the Guiding Principle of Conducting Rectification and Changes Simultaneously', *RMRB*, 1 April 1984.

'To Solve New Problems According to New Situations', *Dazhong Ribao*, 9 September 1981.

'To Split Thoroughly with the Theory of Continuous Revolution under Dictatorship', *Wen Hui Pao*, 10 September 1982.

'To Strengthen Training under Nuclear Conditions and to Grasp Two sets of Skills', *JFJB*, 10 January 1984.

'To Take Care of the Overall Situation and to Actively Strive to Secure the Smooth Completion of Resettlement Work', *Zhongguo Fazhi Bao* (Chinese Legal System Daily), 8 March 1985.

'To Take the Lead in Extending Activities in Frank Discussions', *RMRB*, 9 March 1984.

Tow, William T. 'Science and Technology in China's Defense', *Problems of Communism*, Vol.XXXIV, July–August 1985, pp.15–31.

'Training Centres for Reservists on Rotation', *Liaoning Ribao*, 5 October 1984.

'Training Officers of Reserve Divisions', XH, 25 June 1984 in *SWB*, 28 June, FE/768/BII/3.

Treverton, Gregory. 'China's Nuclear Forces and the Stability of Soviet-American Deterrence', in Christopher Bertram (ed), *The Futures of Strategic Deterrence* (Macmillan, London, 1981), pp.40–43.

Tullberg, Rita. 'World Military Expenditure', *World Armaments and disarmament, SIPRI Yearbook 1986* (Oxford University Press, Oxford and New York, 1986), pp.209–30.

Union Research Institute, *Glossary of Chinese Political Phrases* (Union Press Ltd., Hong Kong, 1977).

'Units in the Second Phase of Party Rectification in Kunming MR Seriously Enforcing Party Style Education', *RMRB*, 17 April 1986.

US Joint Chiefs of Staff, *US Military Posture for FY 1978* (US Government Printing Office, Washington, D.C.), p.118, in R.W. Fieldhouse, 'Chinese Nuclears Weapons: An Overview,' *World Armaments and Disarmament: SIPRI Yearbook 1986*, pp.97–113.

'US Navy to Make Port Calls in Qingdao', Kyodo, 30 September 1986, in FBIS-CHI, 10 October 1986, B1.

US News and World Report, 29 June 1981, p.10.

'US Secretary of Defense Continues Visit', Beijing XH, 9 October 1986, in FBIS-CHI, 10 October 1986, B1.

'Using the Four Basic Principles as Weapons To Overcome Erroneous Ideological Influence', *RMRB*, 21 April 1981.

'USSR Declines Deng Gorbachev Meet', Tokyo Kyodo, 15 October 1986, in FBIS-CHI, 15 October 1986, C3.

'USSR Plans Complete Troop Withdrawal from MPR', Kyodo, 3 September 1986, in FBIS-CHI, 3 September 1986, C1.

Vertzberger, Yaacov. 'Afghanistan in China's Policy', *Problems of Communism*, Vol.XXXI, No.3, May–June, 1982, pp.1–23.

Viet Nam News Bulletin, No.3/81

Wagner, D. and Barlow, D. 'National Defence', *China, A Country Study* (US Government Printing Office, Washington D.C., 1981), in R.W. Fieldhouse, 'Chinese Nuclear Weapons: An Overview', *World Armaments and Disarmament: SIPRI Yearbook, 1986*, pp.93–117.

"Wang Binqian Address NPC on Financial Affairs', in FBIS-CHI, 2 September 1980, L10–22.

Wang Fuyi. 'Development Should be Borne in Mind when Giving Full Play to Superiority — My Views on Guerrilla Research', *JFJB*, 27 March 1981.

Wang Kefu. 'To Establish the "Shield" under Modern Conditions', *JFJB*, 3 April 1981.

Wang Jining and Huang Zhenchun. 'To Go Further on Liberating Thoughts and Eliminating the Ultra-Leftist Line', *JFJB*, 5 November 1980.

Wang Mingkui. 'The Important Trunk Line to the Northwestern Border — The Northern Xinjiang Line', *TDZS*, No.6, November 1985, p.6.

Wang, R.S. 'China's Evolving Strategic Doctrine', *Asian Survey*, Vol.XXIV, No.10, October 1984, pp.1040–1055.

Wang Zhaoguo. 'Issues Regarding the Improvement of Party Style in Central Organs', Beijing Domestic Service, 12 January 1986, in FBIS-CHI, 14 January 1986, K2.

Washington Post, 18 June 1981, p.34.

Watkins, James D. 'The Maritime Strategy', *The Maritime Strategy* (Supplement, US Naval Institute Proceedings), January 1986, pp.4–15.

Wei Guoqing. 'Director Wei Guoqing's Speech in the Eleventh Conference of Military Academies and Institutions', *JFJB*, 8 November 1980.

Wei Guoqing. 'The Power of Political Work Developed in the Period of Historial Transition', *RMRB*, 22 June 1981.

Wen Hui Pao, Hong Kong: 25 May 1980; 6 August 1981; 6 September 1982; 6 April 1984; 13 June 1984; 31 July 1984; 24 August 1984; 6 March 1985; 10 June 1986.

Werner, R.A. 'The Readiness of US Reserve Components', in Louis A. Zurcher and Gwyn Harries–Jenkins (eds), *Supplementary Military Forces: Reserves, Militias, Auxiliaries*, pp.69–90.

Whitson, William W. *The Chinese High Command* (Praeger Publishers, New York, 1973).

'Why Does the Reserve Officer System Develop Rapidly?', *JFJB*, 9 May 1984.

World Armaments and Disarmament: SIPRI Yearbook 1986, (Oxford University Press, Oxford and New York, 1986).

Wu Qunjian and Han Mei. 'The Important Way Linking the Southwest and Central South — the Hunan-Guizhou Line', *TDZS*, No.3, May 1985, pp.2–3.

Wu Xiangqing. 'An Exploratory Discussion of the Nuclear Breakthrough Point', *JFJB*, 11 February 1983.

Xiao Fengmei. 'The Building of City Development and Its Protection', *Baike Zhishi* (Encyclopaedic Knowledge), No.3, 1984, p.16.

Xiao Hua. 'Chairman Mao's Revolutionary Line was the Beacon that led to the Victory of the Long March', *HQ*, No.9, September 1977, pp.75–82.

———. 'To Enhance Party Spirit and Party Style', *HQ*, No.22, 16 November 1981, pp.5–11.

Xiao Ke. 'The Great Principles in Army Building', *HQ*, No.8, August 1979, pp.2–15.

Xin Yang and Wei Bing. 'What Is the Way to Understand Strategic Changes to the Guiding Thoughts on National Defence Construction?', *JFJB*, 5 September 1986, p.3.

Xinhua, 6 July 1984, in SWB, 11 July 1984, FE/7692/BII/7.

Xinhua, 1 August 1984, in *SWB*, 8 August 1984, FE/771/6/BII/7–8.

Xinhua, 26 March 1985, in SWB, 4 April 1985, FE/7917/BII/5.

Xinhua, 3 March 1986, in FBIS-CHI, 4 March 1986, K12.

Xinhua, 2 May 1986, in FBIS-CHI, 6 May 1986, K17.

Xinhua Monthly, November 1985, p.45.

Xinhua Ribao, 2 August 1983.

Xu Jingyao. 'Li Jijun on New Stage of PLA Modernization', XH, 23 August 1986, in FBIS-CHI, 25 August 1986, K10–11.

Xu Peng. 'To Do a Good Job in Two Combinations and to Strengthen Defence Capability', *JFJB*, 9 January 1983.

Xu Xiangqian. 'Strive to Achieve Modernization in National Defence', *HQ*, No.10, 2 October 1979, pp.28–33.

Yang Dezhi. 'A Strategic Decision on Strengthening the Building of Our Army in the New Period', *HQ*, No.15, 1 August 1985, pp.3–7, in FBIS-CHI, 8 August 1985, K3–4.

———. 'An Important Guideline in Constructing Our Army in the New Era', *JFJB*, 16 July 1983.

———. 'On the Completion of Army Restructuring in Two Years', *Ta Kung Pao*, Hong Kong, 29 July 1985.

———. 'To Make Military Theories Prosper in National Defence Construction', *JFJB*, 11 September 1986.

———. 'To Quicken the Pace and to Strive for the Construction of a Standardised and Revolutionary Army', *Sixiang Zhanxian* (Ideological Front), No.9, 1984, p.4.

————. 'Unswervingly Uphold Our Party's Absolute Leadership over the Army-In Commemoration of the CCP's 60th Founding Anniversary', *HQ*, No.13, 1 July 1981, pp.68–72.

Yang Shangkun. 'On Cuts in Militia Training', Zhengzhou, Henan Provincial Service, 20 October 1985, in BBC *Summary of World Broadcasts*, 26 October 1985, FE/8092/BII/11.

————. 'On Reforming Militia Work', Peking Home Service, 25 February 1985, in BBC *Summary of World Broadcasts*, 1 March 1985, FE/7888/BII/10.

————. 'On Restructuring the Army and Reduction-in-Strength', *RMRB*, 6 July 1985.

————. 'The Army Should March in the Vanguard of Rectifying Party Style', Beijing XH, 13 January 1986, in FBIS-CHI, 14 January 1986, K9–10.

————. 'Yang Shangkun Advises at Rectification Forum', Beijing Domestic Service, 21 January 1986, in FBIS-CHI, 24 January 1986, K9–10.

————. 'Yang Shangkun Discusses Cuts in PLA Forces', Xinhua, 7 July 1985, in BBC *Summary of World Broadcasts*, 9 July 1985, FE/7998/BII/1.

————. 'Yang Shangkun on Reforming Militia Work', Peking Home Service, 1 March 1985, in SWB, FE/7888/BII10.

————. 'Yang Shangkun on Restructuring the Army and Reduction-in-Strength', *RMRB*, 6 July 1985.

————. 'Yang Shangkun Says Failure to Eliminate Factionalism in Military Academies Affects Party Rectification', *Wen Hui Pao*, 10 November 1985, p.3, in FBIS-CHI, 12 November 1985, W1.

————. 'Yang Shangkun Speech at Conference of Cadres of Central Organs on 9 January', Beijing XH, 13 January 1986, in FBIS-CHI, 14 January 1986, K9–13.

————. 'Yang Shangkun Stresses that the Army Must Strengthen Education in Party Style in the Second Phase of Party Rectification', *RMRB*, 26 August 1985.

Ye Jianying. 'Speech at the Meeting Celebrating the 30th Anniversary of Founding of the People's Republic of China', *Beijing Review*, No.40, 5 October 1979, pp.7–32.

Yu Qiuli. 'Communist Members Must Consciously Strengthen Party Spirit When Conducting Reform', *HQ*, No.13, July 1985, pp.3–5.

Yu Qizhong. 'The Artery to Our Country's Northwestern Border — the Lanzhou–Xinjiang Line', *TDZS*, No.2, January 1986, pp.6–7.

'Yunnan Military District Helps Militiamen to Get Rich', Yunnan Provincial Service, 18 March 1985, in *SWB*, FE/7905/BII/12.

Zhan Jingwu. 'The Development of Positional Warfare', *JFJB*, 11 March 1983.

Zhang Aiping.'On Reform Problems Concerning Defence Technology and Industry', *JFFB*, 20 November 1984.

———. 'Several Problems Concerning Defence Modernisation', *HQ*, No.6, 1983, pp.21–24.

Zhang Chunting. 'Making the Leading Squad of the Chinese Army Younger in Average Age', *Liaowang*, Hong Kong Edition, No.2, 7 October 1985, pp.11–12, in FBIS-CHI, 6 December 1985, K5–6.

Zhang Hongxian and Chai Yuqiu. 'On the Coordination of Resolute Defence and Guerrilla Warfare', *JFJB*, 10 April 1981.

Zhang Taiheng. 'Ascertaining the Campaign Objective Is the Primary Issue in the Study of Campaign Concepts', *JFJB*, 19 September 1986.

———. 'Firm Guiding Principles and Flexible Tactics', *JFJB*, 27 May 1983.

Zhao Falin. 'The Status of the Air Campaign Grows Ever Mightier', *JFJB*, 25 November 1983.

Zhao Yiya. 'Communism Is the Core of Socialist Spiritual Civilisation', *Jiefang Ribao* (Liberation Daily, Shanghai), 28 August 1982, pp.1–2.

Zhejiang Ribao, 25 April 1986, p.1, in FBIS-CHI, 7 May 1986, p.5.

Zho Wenyuan and Li Zhenxing. 'Double-track Construction Work for the Hengyang-Guangzhou section of the Beijing–Guangzhou Line', *TDZS*, No.5, September 1985.

Zhongguo Fazhi Bao, 8 March 1985.

Zhou Yushu. 'Military training should Adapt to Strategic Changes', *JFJB*, 5 December 1986.

Zhu Hongjun. 'To Gain Vigour from Mobility', *JFJB*, 11 March 1983.

Zhu Songchun. 'Chinese Scholars Discuss Strategy for the Development of National Defense', Hong Kong *Liaowang* Overseas Edition, No.29, 21 July 1986, pp.6–8, in FBIS-CHI, 25 July 1986, K3.

Appendix 1

Chinas use of foreign military technology and equipment: representative examples

Category	USSR	US	France	UK	Other
Technology transfer and/or production under licence.	Most ships, aircraft and Ground Force equipment of 1950s vintage.	H3 PTG;[1] Mk 46 torpedo;[2] AMC jeep;[3] artillery shells;[4] Bell helicopter.[3]	Z-9 Dauphin II helicopters[3] (assembly).	Spey turbofan engine; NVH-1 MICV[5]	(Japan) marine diesel engines;[3] (Austria) Steyr Daimler Puch trucks.[3]
Equipment purchase		S70-C helicopter;[6] Avionics for F8II;[7] Mk-15AA gun (Phalanx);[8] GE LM2500;[8] marine engine;[8] SIGINT facilities (presumed).[9]	Creusot-Loire 100mm naval gun mount;[3] Super Frelon helicopter;[10] ASW equipment for Super Frelons;[10] Alouette and Super Puma helicopters and, due in 1988, Gazelle anti-tank helicopters.[11] Matra Magic AAM (possible).[12]	Avionics for F-7;[13] avionics for A-5;[13] artillery fire control equipment; mortar location radar.	(FRG) Deutz V8 engine for H-1 APC;[14] (Israel) 105mm main tank gun;[15] (Italy) avionics for A-5 strike aircraft.[16]
Product improvement	MiG-19/F-6/A-5;[17] R-98F jet engine.[17] Tu-16/B-6 (possible);[18] F-8; PT-76/Type 63 tank; T-54A/Type 59/Type 69 tanks; STYX/HY-2/HY-4/ C-601 SSM/ASM;[19]				

China's use of foreign military technology and equipment: representative examples (cont'd)

Category	USSR	US	France	UK	Other
	SS-2 SIBLING/DF-1 strategic SSM.[20]				
Reverse engineering	MiG-21/F-7/F-7M;[21] SAGGER/HJ-73 ATGM; SA-7/HN-5 SAM (possible) B-6.[22] Type 80 SP 57mm AA gun system.[23]		Exocet/C-801 SSM (possible).[24]		

Notes

1 Designed by the US company H-3 Research and Development Group: see Goldrick and Jones, 'The Far Eastern Navies', p.65.
2 Negotiations have been under way since at least 1985, but up to late 1986 no agreement had been reached: see *FEER*, 4 April 1985, pp.17–18; and *FEER*, 18 December 1986, p.24.
3 *JDW*, 11 August 1984, p.179; and FBIS-CHI, 19 February 1986, K19.
4 Nayan Chanda, '"Superpower Triangle', *FEER*, 4 April 1985, pp.17–18; and *Time*, 10 February 1986, p.43.
5 In 1985 China's NORINCO and Vickers Defence Systems (UK) signed an agreement covering a market survey, which if successful, would be followed by co-production of this MICV: see *JDW*, 11 January 1986, p.5.
6 *CONMILIT*, No.95, October 1984, p.1100.
7 *Asian Aviation*, May 1986, p.42.
8 Goldrick and Jones, 'The Far Eastern Navies', p.65; and *Ta Kung Pao*, 15 February 1986, p.3, in FBIS-CHI, 20 February 1986, W3.
9 *US News and World Report*, 29 June 1981, p.10; *Washington Post*, 18 June 1981, p.34; *FEER*, 4 April 1985; p.18; and Bussert, 'China's C³ Efforts', pp.173 and 175.
10 *JDW*, 13 April 1985, p.620; *JDW*, 28 December 1985, p.1417; *JDW*, 25 January 1986, p.114; and *Ming Pao*, 5 June 1986, p.41.
11 AFP Hong Kong, 2 April 1987, in FBIS-CHI, 3 April 1987, G1.
12 *JDW*, 22 February 1986, p.311.
13 *Asian Aviation*, May 1986, p.42; and *Ta Kung Pao*, 15 February 1986, p.3.
14 *JDW*, 11 January 1986, p.5.
15 *The Economist*, 25 January 1986, p.24; and *JDW*, 1 February 1986, p.161.
16 *JDW*, 27 April 1985, p.703; BBC World Round Up, 4 November 1986; and *FEER*, 18 December 1986, p.24.
17 *JDW*, 14 December 1985, p.1317.
18 *JDW*, 22 May 1986, p.529.
19 *Foreign Report*, 25 July 1985, p.5; and *Ta Kung Pao*, 15 February 1986, p.3, in FBIS-CHI, 20 February 1986, W3.
20 *Handbook 1984*, pp.69–70.
21 *CONMILIT*, No.98, January 1985, p.67.
22 *Handbook 1984*, p.65; and *JDW*, 22 May 1986, p.529.
23 *JDW*, 10 May 1986, p.849.
24 Mary Lee suggests a French Exocet missile was transferred to China via Pakistan: 'Two Way Street for Arms', *FEER*, 12 December 1985, p.25. Other reports suggest Israel has assisted China in modern weapons development, including 'missiles' and guidance systems: see *JDW*, 11 August 1984, p.178; *Foreign Report*, 12 December 1985, p.5, and *Foreign Report*, 6 March 1986. Unaided reverse engineering seems unlikely.

Appendix 2

Combat and logistic support

GROUND FORCES

Combat Support

The main combat support capability not already addressed is engineer capability. The tasks of the PLA's Engineer Corps are similar to those of engineers in Western armies, including construction and clearance of obstacles, road building, mine warfare, bridging, camouflage and concealment.[1] In one respect the task of the engineers is simplified by the ability of PLA combat arms to construct strong, extensive defensive positions without specialist engineer support. In addition, the infantry is thoroughly trained in improvised water-crossing methods.[2] Combat engineer units are organic to most combat formations down to regiment level, while an engineer battalion with bridging resources is included in Army Troops.[3] Above army level are independent engineer regiments equipped with plant or bridging equipment. Since the formation of group armies, some of these previously independent engineer regiments may have been re-allocated to the new armies. Others may remain dedicated to tasks of strategic importance, such as maintaining the few highways into Xizang (Tibet), and ensuring emergency bridging over the Chang-jiang and other major rivers.

Engineer water-crossing resources include much equipment of Soviet design, some of World War II vintage. These are mainly bridging equipment, but include many varieties of small craft, from

377

collapsible assault boats to large motorised junks, rafts and ferries.[4] Bridges include light, medium and heavy types. Vehicle launched bridges are also believed to be held, for example the Soviet KMM type (class 15), and possibly the heavy capacity TMM (class 60).[5] In recent years the PLA has deployed a Chinese version of the excellent Soviet PMP floating bridge,[6] and a 'suspension pontoon bridge', which gives China 'a place among only five nations that can construct such bridges'.[7] While the details of the latter bridge are unclear, reports in 1984 reflected the development of a pontoon bridge of probable Chinese design and impressive characteristics. The PLA claimed that a bridging unit constructed such a bridge over the Changjiang (river) near Nanjing that was more than 1300m long. Construction time was less than an hour, and immediately on completion, a reinforced motorised division crossed it, including tank and artillery regiments.[8] The overall impression is that there has been a qualitative if not a quantitative improvement in the PLA's bridging capability.

In the field of mine warfare several developments have added to the engineers' capability. Most are related to the new concept of hasty minefields, and include delivery systems that deploy mines propelled by rockets or are dropped from aircraft.[9] In the field of mine countermeasures, the PLA has deployed a 'simple minefield breaching rocket',[10] and PLA journals frequently depict the development of demolition devices. In fact, media reports indicate a concentration on bridging and gap clearance. The production of an amphibious engineer reconnaissance vehicle reflects the PLA's focus on its gap-crossing capability.[11]

Logistic Support

Is a term that covers supply, transport, ordnance, recovery, repair and medical services. The stamina of the individual Chinese soldier and the simplicity of his needs help reduce demands on the PLA's logistic system. The ability to mobilise militia and civilian resources on a large scale has traditionally enabled the PLA to limit the size and scope of its own logistic services, in the expectation of always having a ready source of auxiliary assistance to turn to, particularly for transport and supplies. The practice of pre-positioning large stocks of supplies in likely areas of conflict was probably regarded as a legitimate alternative to developing more capable logistic support elements within the structure of manoeuvre formations.

It was probably not until the 1979 Sino–Vietnamese border

conflict that the PLA began to realise that the demands of modern warfare had outstripped the capacity of its traditional logistic resources. During that conflict weaknesses in the logistic system showed up, in particular the inability of the militia to adequately supply a large force outside its own localities. Reliance on the militia is believed to have actually slowed down the PLA's advance and limited the capacity of its supply lines.[12] The inability to deliver supplies to combat units was not, however, due solely to the militia. Lack of mobility, which has already been discussed, meant that the logistic system could not even keep up with the relatively slow advance of the infantry on an adequate scale. While apologists can point out that operations beyond China's borders pose greater logistic problems than those conducted within them, the vastness of the Chinese mainland, its inadequate transportation systems, and deficiencies in defence-related industries all restrict the degree of logistic support that the PLA can count on. Judging by the subsequent attention paid to training officers of the logistic services, their competence during the 1979 conflict was probably also considered to be inadequate.[13] Some observers believe that the PLA's inadequate procedures are as much to blame as a paucity of resources, maintaining that combat units are required to return to depots to collect their supplies, thus diverting scarce transport resources away from operational tasks. There is a division of opinion on this point, and it is instructive to note that the US Defence Intelligence Agency maintains that supply is by forward distribution, i.e. higher echelons are responsible for transporting supplies forward to lower echelons, as is the case in most Western armies.[14]

The formation of group armies, intended to operate with a higher degree of manoeuvrability than the PLA has attained previously, will place even more demands on the logistic system. The gradual increase in motorisation and mechanisation, and the introduction of technically more advanced equipment will inevitably require more POL, spare parts and specialised repair facilities in the field as well as better trained technical personnel. Logistic vehicles will need to be capable of keeping up with the mechanised forces they are meant to support. Tank and self-propelled artillery units, for example, have considerably greater cross-country ability than standard wheeled cargo vehicles. If their mobility is to be exploited to the full, logistic and repair vehicles with similar mobility will be needed to support them in the battle area.

There were indications during the Sino–Vietnamese conflict that the PLA's recovery and repair arrangements were inadequate. Shortages of technicians, spare parts and repair facilities may have contributed to this situation.[15] Since then efforts have been made to meet deficiencies in logistic support generally. Bulk refuelling tankers with multi-outlet dispensing systems have been introduced into a number of formations to facilitate rapid refuelling.[16] Their off-road capability, and thus their usefulness in tactical situations, however, is likely to be limited. An armoured 'transport vehicle' that will 'cooperate with tanks' has also been developed.[17] This is probably an armoured high mobility load carrier (HMLC) such as is used in some Western armies to carry first-line amuniton, POL etc. for highly mobile combat units. In addition, China is likely to seek co-operation from Western armies to develop land transport systems.[18] Computers are being used to assist in logistic planning,[19] although the application of ADP systems in this area seems to be piecemeal rather than widespread and systematic. Battlefield ambulances, including a version of the tracked type 63 APC, are beginning to appear in the PLA's inventory,[20] and numerous articles have been published in the *Jiefangjun Huabao* in recent years describing innovations in other aspects of providing medical services to forces in the field. The aim seems to be to improve medical facilities closest to the battle area, and thus increase the survival rate of casualties. The acquisition of S-70C (Sikorsky) helicoptors gives China the opportunity to utilise this civil version of the US Blackhawk armed helicopter[21] in military transport and casualty evacuation roles. The use of helicopters for resupply has been attempted before,[22] but the subsequent acquisition of technically advanced Western helicopters could enhance this capability, and would be particularly useful in difficult operational circumstances such as those in the Xizang and Sino–Vietnamese border areas. In recent years considerable attention has been paid to developing the military infrastructure in China's border areas. The upgrading of supply routes and logistic installations along the Sino–Vietnamese border was one of the first achievements to be reported.[23]

The PLA's recovery and repair system tends to concentrate major repair resources in fixed installations at military region level. While forward repair teams (FRT) are found at regiment level and above,[24] repair facilities at that level can generally only undertake minor repairs, and repair at the point of breakdown is often hampered by an insufficiency of mobile FRT.[25] Improvements to battalion and regimental repair capabilities seem, therefore, to be badly needed. One advance in this direction has been the introduction of the Type-653 armoured recovery vehicle (ARV). Based on the type 69-II tank chassis, this is a considerable improvement on the earlier, ill-equipped ARV which used a type-59 tank chassis. The Type-653, a multi-purpose vehicle which may be assigned to FRT or perhaps to the repair elements of tank units, can undertake major repairs in the field, such as a complete change of powerpack.[26]

In order to improve the quality of logistic officers, the training reforms introduced in 1986 not only provide for the establishment of a three-tiered schools system for command officers, but also for intermediate and advanced courses, of two and three years respectively, at specialised technical schools, which include logistic and engineer-related disciplines.[27]

The effectiveness of such measures on the PLA's combat and logistic support are hard to gauge. The Chinese themselves may have had difficulty in assessing progress. In 1982 they recognised that 'logistic work must be improved', to make it 'more streamlined, rational and efficient'.[28] A year later, an all-PLA forum held in November 1983, and attended by Yang Shangkun, Yang Dezhi and Yu Qiuli, acknowledged that the PLA's logistic elements had already 'developed into a logistic force (capable of) providing unified support to combined arms formations'.[29] Soon after this, however, concern about the ability of logistic units to exercise good financial and material management became apparent, which must have implications for logistic effectiveness in the field. On 13 December 1984, the Director of the General Logistics Department, Hong Xuezhi, warned logistic units not to stagnate because funds were tight, but to improve management practices and achieve better results.[30] In mid-1985 the reorganisation of military regions took place, necessitating changes in affiliation between logistic units and the formations they support. Although in September Yang Dezhi told the Central Military Council that this readjustment was progressing smoothly,[31] the formation of combined arms group armies was just gathering pace, and the CGS may have underestimated the time and effort it would take to make the adjustment. This seems to have been borne out three months later when Hong Xuezhi told an all-PLA conference on logistics that the supply control system must be reformed. A three-tier system of control must be established, covering strategic and operational aspects. Improvements were needed to ensure adequate provision of supplies, and medical and repair facilities in the combat zone. A computerised logistic information and management system was needed to improve logistic forecasting and planning.[32] This speech touches upon some fundamental aspects of logistic capabilities. It was followed in January 1986 by a statement from the PLA's

Depty Chief of Staff, He Qizong, to the effect that among the three
major tasks for the PLA in 1986, was the reform of the logistic
system.[33] Taken together, these suggest that the PLA's leadership is
no longer as sanguine as it was in 1983. The more the PLA develops
its combat capabilities, the more it must face up to the consequent
logistic problems.

The efficient maintenance of armies in the field requires a logistic
system based on flexibility, mobility and forward planning. We have
already seen that there are considerable limitations on the PLA's
logistic mobility. Flexibility and forward planning can only be promoted through reforms in logistic training. The process is complicated
by the PLA's traditional practice of producing a large proportion of
its own foodstuffs in unit farms. Not only does this divert a considerable number of personnel from their military tasks, but it has tended
to institutionalise a static logistic system unsuited to the new doctrines of rapid response and mobile warfare. In 1987 the PLA intensified efforts to expand agricultural production on fuel and other
consumables.[34] While this can be seen in the context of a general belt
tightening in the Chinese economy and as a response ('live frugally')
to the 'unhealthy tendencies' of bourgeois liberalisation, it also de-
tracts from the process of military modernisation.

The overall impression is that while engineer and other combat
support capabilities are being developed at a pace and scale commensurate with the PLA's requirements and budget, the logistic support system is lagging behind in development. It must be difficult, for
example, for PLA planning staff to have confidence in the logistic
services when units are operating away from their home bases without the massive support of local militia units. Thus current realities
in the logistic field probably bind the PLA much closer to Maoist
concept of People's War than its more progressive thinkers would
wish.

NAVY

Logistic and Auxiliary Support

The Navy has over 500 support ships and craft, including 38 fleet
support ships and three material support ships.[35] The vast majority
of these vessels are, however, unsuitable for open ocean operations.
They were acquired during the period when naval policy focused on
the defence of China's coastal waters, and the Logistics Department's
main tasks were the resupply of static installations and afloat support

in sheltered anchorages along the coast for submarines and torpedo and missile-armed small patrol boats. For some time the three Fuqing class ships were the only replenishment ships capable of providing underway refuelling, and have made an important contribution to logistic development. It was apparently one of this class that, in early 1987, conducted replenishment at sea to three ships simultaneously. This potentially hazardous operation was a 'first' for the PLA Navy.[36] These Fuqing class ships, together with a small number of other larger support and supply ships, including three Dajiang class submarine rescue ships, could probably only support one major task force per fleet in broad ocean area operations. In 1986, however, the construction of a new class of large fleet replenishment ship, the Binhai, was reported.[37]

Apart from inadequacies in ships and equipment, the Navy's Logistics Department has suffered from extensive problems in logistic management, ranging from failure to follow regulations to neglecting quality control. These have led to a serious waste of material and financial resources. The improvement of management practices is seen as a major task in the next few years.[38]

In recent years the Navy has become increasingly involved in supporting oceanographic research and the testing of missiles and satellite launch vehicles. The Navy operates several oceanographic survey ships such as the Xiang Yang Hong 5, apparently on behalf of the State Bureau of Oceanography, but which also, no doubt, contribute to naval operations in distant waters. The Xiang Yang Hong 5 also took part in the ICBM tests into the South Pacific during 1980, together with the two purpose-built space event support ships (SESS), the Yuan Wang 1 and 2, also operated by the Navy. These latter ships are specifically configured for missile telemetry collection. Of some 17 100 tonnes displacement, they are important assets for the PLA, providing distant ocean support for long-range missile events that China would otherwise be unable to monitor completely.[39]

In the future, the Navy will not only make determined efforts to improve the procedures and efficiency of its logistic services, but can also be expected to increase the number of larger supply and support ships capable of supporting extended operations of combatants at greater distance from China's shores.

AIR FORCE

Although in 1984 the commander of the Air Force, Wang Hai, acknowledged the gap in equipment and technology between China and developed countries, little has been openly revealed about the Air Force's standards of technical maintenance and logistics. Chinese-made jet engines, particularly those fitted to the F-7, were long assessed to have suffered from metallurgical problems, and thus were believed to require more frequent overhauls and replacement than their Soviet originals.[40] In terms of combat sustainability, this could pose serious problems, exacerbating the expected stock shortages the maintenance system would suffer during high intensity operations.[41]

The problems with metallurgy seem, however, to have been overcome. The previously low time between overhauls (TBO) — about 100 hours in the case of the Wopen 7A engine — is reported to have been considerably extended, and other engineering standards improved.[42] The Pakistan Air Force has remarked on the high standards of workmanship of the F-6 aircraft it has obtained from China. Manufacturing plants have virtually hand-built such aircraft.[43] Repair facilities supporting flying units, however, are believed to have limited capabilities, and the Chinese seem to have been sufficiently concerned about this situation that they formed a special committee under the China Aeronautics Society to examine aircraft maintenance and engineering.

During an interview in mid-1986, the chairman of this committee indicated that maintenance requirements and methods had not previously been thoroughly identified; there had been an over-dependance on periodic maintenance; technical checks on component servicability had been lacking; maintenance management and quality control were inadequate; and training was unsystematic. Measures to correct these problems were gradually being implemented, including the provision of mobile testing equipment for air frames, weapon systems, instruments and electronics, etc. A training system for maintenance personnel had also been established. The interview gave the impression, however, that the aircraft repair system was still a weak link in the Air Force's ability to conduct sustained operations.[44]

APPENDIX 2

1. XH, 27 July 1986, in *Ming Pao*, 28 July 1986, p.5.
2. *Handbook 1984*, pp.41–42 and 45.
3. *Ibid.*, pp.A–2 to A11.
4. *Ibid.*, pp.45–46.
5. *Ibid.* Accounts of various activities demonstrated by the En-

gineer Corps are contained in XH Domestic Service, 10 June 1986, in FBIS-CHI, 13 June 1986, K16 and *Liaowang*, No.30, 28 July 1986, in FBIS-CHI, 15 August 1986, K13–16.

6. Jencks, 'Ground Forces', in Segal and Tow (eds), *Chinese Defence Policy*, p.58.

7. XH, 27 July 1986, in *Ming Pao*, 28 July 1986, p.5.

8. *JFJHB*, No.2, 1984, pp.10–11.

9. Parachutes are used in aerial and in some rocket-delivered systems, and another system uses a fin-stabilised, rocket-propelled anti-tank mine: see N. Lee, *The Chinese People's Liberation Army 1980–82*, pp.9–10 and *CONMILIT*, No.90, May 1984, p.61.

10. Jencks, 'Ground Forces', p.64.

11. XH, 27 July 1986, in *Ming Pao*, 28 July 1986, p.5.

12. *AS*, August 1979, p.813, cited in N. Lee, *The Chinese People's Liberation Army 1980–82*, p.74.

13. *Handbook 1984*, p.12.

14. *Ibid.*, pp.12–13.

15. *Ibid.*, p.53.

16. One such formation is a mechanised combined arms group army: see *Wen Hui Pao*, 6 April 1984, p.3. Another unit was depicted in *JFJHB*, No.4, April 1984, p.12.

17. *RMRB*, 21 September 1984.

18. An agreement with Italy, signed in 1985, is reported to provide for such collaboration: *JDW*, 27 April 1985, p.703.

19. In 1984, for example, the logistic staff of a division in Nanjing Military Region used computers to calculate the division's supply and ammunition plans, completing the task 40 times faster than under the manual system: XH, 4 July 1984, in *SWB*, 10 July 1984, FE/7691/BII/7.

20. *Wen Hui Pao*, 6 April 1984, p.3 and *JDW*, 15 December 1984, pp.1062–3.

21. *CONMILIT*, No.95, October 1984, p.64.

22. *JFJHB*, No.7, July 1982, inside front cover, cited in Jencks, 'Ground Forces', pp.64–65.

23. *JFJB*, 5 June 1982, p.1 and *China Daily*, 6 March 1986, p.1.

24. *Handbook 1984*, p.53.

25. *Ibid.*

26. Fitted with dozer blade, crane and winch, the Type-653 can not only undertake repairs in the field, but can recover battlefield casualties, clear obstacles, and prepare firing posiitons: see *JDW*, 8 February 1986, p.207.

27. XH, 24 July 1984, in *SWB*, 27 July 1984, FE/7706/BII/1–2 and Zhongguo Xinwenshe, Hong Kong, 10 June 1986, in FBIS-CHI, 10 June 1986, K12.

28. HX, 18 November 1982, in FBIS 82–224, K2, cited in Jencks, 'Ground Forces', pp.61–62.

29. *Ta Kung Pao*, 21 November 1983.

30. XH, 13 December 1984, in *SWB*, 18 December 1984, FE/7829/BII/5–6.

31. Beijing Domestic Service, 28 September 1985, in FBIS-CHI, 2 October 1985, K4.

32. *Ming Pao*, 23 December 1985, p.5, in FBIS-CHI, 2 January 1986, W5.

33. NCNA, 28 January 1986, in FBIS-CHI, 5 February 1986, K13–15. Although the Director of the GLD, Hong Xuezhi, gave a slightly more optimistic account of progress in an interview published a few days later, he listed among future goals the establishment of a more efficient, systematized logistic service with greater mobility and rapid response capabilities to provide 'uninterrupted supplies' and to 'deal with emergencies': Zhongguo Xinwenshe, 7 February 1986, in FBIS-CHI, 10 February 1986, K15–17. In early 1987, however, Hong painted a more modest picture of future logistics developments. These centred on strengthening financial discipline; reducing expenditure and personnel levels; improving training; research and management practices; raising agricultural and side-line production; and improving the accommodation of minor units. See *JFJB*, 12 January 1987, p.1.

34. FBIS-CHI, 20 February 1987, 01.

35. *Handbook 1984*, p.56.

36. XH, Beijing, 29 May 1987, in FBIS-CHI, 1 June 1987, K24.

37. The strictly coastal defence policy, adopted from the Young School naval doctrine which the Soviets followed from the 1920's to the 1950's, was based on defensive rings formed by submarines, patrol boats, and shore-based aircrat to defend the coast against foreign incursion. The need for open ocean operations was not envisaged until the late 1970's, when the PLA Navy turned away from the Young School strategy in the face of the growing threat to China's maritime security posed by the strengthening of the Soviet Pacific Ocean fleet, and in response to China's increasing interest in developing its maritime economic resources. See D.G. Muller, *China as a Maritime Power*, pp.48–52. The Fuqing class AOR was an essential element of

this new policy. The new Binhai class (see A.W. Grazebrook, 'No.3 — Big Naval Expansion Programs', in *Pacific Defence Reporter*, Volume XIII, Nos6/7, December 1986/January 1987, p.39), when fully operational could provide the Navy with the ability to support more units in open ocean operations, especially if the Fuqing AORs remain in service.

38. From an account of a Logistics Department conference held in early 1986, reported in *Ming Pao*, 29 April 1986, in FBIS-CHI, 1 May 1986, W7.

39. Muller, 'China as a Martime Power', pp.198–199 and G. Jacobs, 'How China Monitors Pacific Missile Tests', *JDW*, 28 December 1985, pp.1416–1417.

40. *Handbook 1984*, p.66.

41. *Ibid.*

42. Munson, 'Fishbed, Finback and the Chinese Future', p.1367.

43. *Ibid.*

44. Zhongguo Tongxunshe, 23 July 1986, in FBIS-CHI, 25 July 1986, K2 and XH, 3 August 1986, in FBIS-CHI, 7 August 1986, K20.

Index

Active defence, 27–8, 118, 124, 133, 136, 139, 165, 171, 173, 267–8
Afghanistan, 123, 126, 132, 261
Air Force, 49–50, 56–63, 81–6, 262
  A-5, 10, 84
  A-5C, 10
  air defence, 82, 266
  B-5, -6, 84
  combined arms, 20, 81
  F-5, 82, 185
  F-6, 82, 84
  F-7, 56, 83–5
  F-8 avionic retrofits, 10, 37, 56, 83–4
  F-10, 84
  F-12, 84
  Frontal Aviation, 82
  H-5, 191
  J-7, 180, 191
  Long Range Aviation, 82
  mobility, 49–50
  Q-5, 180
  Taiwan capabilities, 183–5
  training, 85–6
Air Land Battle, 87, 152, 154–5, 163, 262
ASEAN,
  peace proposals, 122, 127–31
  principles of ZOPFAN, 177
  Vietnam, 188

Asia-Pacific region, 122, 131, 136, 175–80, 261, 264

Bai Hua, 232, 247–8
BAM Railway, 168
Batmonh, Jambyn, 127
Blitzkrieg, 152–5, 159, 166, 168–9, 173, 268

Cam Ranh Bay, 128, 187
Central Advisory Committee, 232
Chemical/biological warfare, 28, 55–6, 79, 155, 164, 166, 173, 268
Chen Xilian, 209, 226
Chen Yun, 270
Chi Haotian, 239–40, 258–9
Coalition Government of Democratic Kampuchea, 129
Combined arms and joint operations, 4, 12, 18, 20–9, 43, 51, 79, 81, 93, 155, 161, 164, 171, 175, 263, 265, 267–8
COMECON,
  membership, 129
Comprehensive Test Ban Treaty, 135
Cultural Revolution, 20, 65, 86, 103, 202, 209–11, 214, 218, 221, 224, 245, 247–9, 269, 271

Da Nag, 128

Defence budget, 6–12, 141, 145, 212, 263
Defence Modernisation,
  advanced world standards, 4, 40, 175, 266
  arms sales, 10
  arms transfer, 9–14
  military-industrial complex, 13–14
  military spending, 6–12, 89
  professionalism, 88, 258–9
  science and technology developments, 5–6, 10–14, 27, 34–8, 260–1, 266
  self-reliance, 9, 13, 261
  strategic outlook, new, 3–6, 39–40, 42–3, 175
  wartime mobilisation, 14–19
  weapons acquisition, 9, 12–14, 42–3
Demobilised soldiers, 11–12, 19, 102–6, 212, 249
Democratic tradition of PLA, 201
Deng Xiaoping,
  CMC Chairman, 139, 221, 224, 227
  'Correction of Party Style', 207–8
  defence modernisation, on, 4–5
  Dengism, 257, 271
  Deng's PLA, 257–8, 269–71
  distribution of cadres' age groups, 237
  in Guangzhou, 1982, 223
  joint warfare, on, 20
  military leadership 1980–87, 104, 209, 224–9, 234–5
  peacetime war preparation, 135–6
  reduction-in-strength, 31
  reshuffles in MRs in 1982 and 1985, 237–9
  response to peace initiatives, 130, 136
Deng Yingchao, 252
  rectification campaign, 208

Deterrence, 132
  by denial, 133, 149
  capabilities, 135, 149, 263
  minimum, 133, 149
Discipline Inspection Committee, 232, 244, 253
Disputed islands, South China Sea, 181–3

EEZ (exclusive economic zone), 181, 264
EFZ (exclusive fishing zone), 181
Eleventh Party Congress,
  Sixth Plenum, 139
Exercises,
  combined arms and joint services operation, 22–4
  CPX, 29, 33, 41
  FTX, 28–9, 33, 41–2, 44–5
  infantry units, 161
  'Iwo Jima', 80, 182, 264
  Motorised Division, Guangzhou, 44
  Ningxia militia, 114
  South China Sea, 79
  tactical field training, 44
  tactical nuclear, 54
  TEWT, 29, 41
  Zhangjiakou 1981, 21, 63

Falklands conflict, 61, 74
Five Principles of Coexistence, 122
Five-Year Plan,
  Seventh, 12, 89, 91–2, 97, 100, 117, 172
  Sixth, 12
Flexible Response, 149
Force structure,
  automation, 33–4
  command and control, 6, 18, 29–33
  communications, 34–6
  field armies, 25, 42, 81, 221, 227, 239–41, 262
  group armies, 25–6, 29, 42–5,

87, 139, 149, 262, 268
reduction-in-strength, 3, 8, 11–12, 25, 31–2, 46, 261
Reserve Forces, 3, 11, 14–19, 174, 267
single-arm, 20
survivability, 38–9
wartime mobilisation, 3, 14–19, 261, 265
Forward Defence, 153, 159–60
Forward Line of Troops, 56–7, 170, 262
Fu Zhong, 203–5

Gang of Four, 20, 139, 141, 204, 209–11, 217–18, 221, 225
General Logistics Department, 30–1, 236–7
General Political Department, 18, 30–1, 203–17, 236–7
General Staff Department, 18, 21, 30–1, 35, 67, 69, 81, 161, 235–6
Geng Biao, 224
Global war, 4–5, 42, 86, 121
Gorbachev,
Deng Xiaoping's response to, 130, 136
Vladivostok Speech, 124, 126–7, 130, 135, 261
Guo Zhongyi, 216

Haerbin, 97, 166, 172, 268
Hague Mine Warfare Convention, 1907, 195
Hainan Military District, 181, 190, 256
Han Huaizhi, 21, 32, 67, 161
He Qizong, 25, 236, 252, 270
Heilongjiang, 108, 157, 168
Hong Kong, 80, 183–4
Hong Xuezhi, 226, 258
Hu Changfa, 33
Hu Qiaomu, 247, 270
Hu Qili, 243–4
Hu Yaobang, 18, 110, 139, 223–4,

226, 230–1, 248, 269–70
Hua Guofeng, 6, 224, 226, 229
Huang Kecheng,
criticism of Mao Zedong, 141, 201–2, 227

IISS, 61
Independent foreign policy, 122, 133–5, 260
International Atomic Energy Agency, 135

Japan,
science and technology, 13
'unsinkable aircraft carrier', 176
Jiang Qing, 103

Kampuchean question, 122–3, 126–31, 187, 261
Kapitsa, Mikhail, 125
Khmer Rouge, 128–9
Kiangsi Soviet, 163
Korean War, 62, 93, 221, 226, 239, 259

Le Duan, 130
Li Desheng, 218, 221, 224, 235
Li Jian, 165–6, 172
Li Jijun, 171
Li Jiulong, 238–9, 241, 270
Li Lianghui, 63
Liao Hansheng, 210
Liberation Army Daily, 43, 61, 80, 85, 108, 144, 213, 215–16, 247–9
Limited wars, 5, 43, 86
Lin Biao, 140–1, 204, 209–11
Liu Huaqing, 69, 77, 264
Liu Jingsong, 238–9, 270
Local Force units, 11, 51, 97, 144, 159–60, 172, 267
'Luring the enemy in deep', 150, 163

Main Force units, 51, 59, 95, 97, 118, 144, 155, 159–60, 162,

165–6, 172–4, 267
Manchurian Campaign, 153, 155
Mao Zedong,
  Mao Zedong Thought, 205–6, 243
  Military Science, 201–6, 227
  People's War Concept, 103, 138–42
  Protracted War, 151
  reshuffles in MRS in 1974, 237
Mao Zhiyong, 109–10
Maritime power, 175–97, 264
  'blue water' capabilities, 175, 264–5
  chokepoints, 179
  clearance certificate, 185
  definition, 176
  mine blockade, 188–94, 264
  naval presence, 178–83
  quarantine, 184–6, 264
  sea denial, 179–80
Marxism-Leninism, 243–4, 256
McNamara, 162
Military leadership, 201–59, 269–71
  reshuffles, 209–14
Military regions,
  'defunct' MRs in 1985, 239–41
  Leftist influence, 217–24
  reorganisation, 89–90, 95–7, 159–60, 173–4, 267
Military Service Law, 14–17, 100, 103, 107, 117, 261
  conscription, 15–18, 100–2
Militia, 16–19, 40, 91, 102–18, 159, 265–6
  Chichihar Conference, 1983, 19
  economic construction, 108–13
  'Regulations on Militia Work', 113–14
  training, 108–13
  Urban Militia Conference, 114
Ministry of Defence, 30
Missiles, 64–8
  ABM, 132, 171
  DF-2, -3, 54–5, 64, 67
  DF-4, -5, 64, 67
  ICBM, 13, 35, 64–5, 67, 79, 134, 136, 175
  IRBM, 136, 155
  long range, 132
  LRINF, 54–5
  MIRV, 66, 132
  MRBM, 64, 136
  SLBM, 13, 65–6, 77, 86, 133–4, 146, 263
  SRINF, 168
  SS-20, 55, 124, 132, 134, 176

National Defence University, 26, 32
National People's Congress, Sixth, 14
NATO, 54, 149, 152–4, 159, 169, 177
  battle groups, 162
Navy, 31, 36, 49, 58, 60–2, 65, 86–7, 263–5
  air-to-air refuelling, 87, 263
  AS, 181
  ASW, 62, 69, 72–7, 87, 181, 186–7, 263–4
  coastal defence, 78
  combined arms operations, 20, 79
  DDG, 68, 70–1, 73, 79–80
  FFG, 70–1, 73
  FMPB, 181
  force development, 68–70
  HY-2 (CSSC-2), 180
  naval air force, 36–7, 74–5, 80, 264
  mini warfare and technology, 77–8, 193–4, 264
  mobility, 49
  ROMEO and WHISKEY class, 37, 68, 76, 179, 186, 190
  SSN/SSBN force, 65–7, 76–7, 177–9, 183
  training, 78–81
  'Two Surface Combatants and one Submarine', 197–8
  VSTOL Carriers, 73, 197
Nie Rongzhen, 235

Non-Proliferation Treaty, 135
Nuclear war and strikes, 4, 54–6, 131–4, 136, 142, 148–9, 161, 164
  battle conditions, 161, 173, 267
  breakthrough, 161–2, 267
  deterrence, 132
  first strike, 86, 124, 132
  intermediate nuclear forces, 134
  MAD, 133–4
  no-first-use, 131–2, 134, 149, 152–4, 165, 268
  nuclear free zones, 132
  nuclear 'shield', 164–5
  strategic forces, 64–8, 263
  theatre nuclear forces, 162, 268
  theatre/tactical nuclear weapons/ support, 53–5, 132–3, 159, 162, 166–7, 267
  theatre war, 153, 159, 267
  threshold, 149
  warheads, 132

Ogarkov, 158
Operational Manoeuvre Group, 154–5, 160–2, 164, 168–70, 172–3, 262, 267–8

Paracel Islands, 20, 182
Party Central Military Commission, 14–15, 35, 38, 42, 46–7, 159, 231
  Enlarged Conference, May-June 1985, 4
  December 1986, 251
Party Rectification, 245–9
  Anti-Bourgeois Liberalisation Campaign, 250–4
  Bai Hua, 247–8
  grass-roots level, 254–7
  Socialist Spiritual Civilisation, 242–3, 250–1
  Spiritual pollution, 247
  'Three Categories of People', 245
  Zhao Yiya, 248–9

Peng Dehuai, 141, 227
People's Armed Forces Department, 11, 16, 18, 100, 102–18, 252, 256, 265
People's Daily, 141, 212
People's War, 9, 124, 133, 136, 138, 141, 166, 266–8
  doctrine, definition of, 140
  impact of modernisation, on, 142
  Lin Biao, on, 140
People's War under Modern Conditions, 9, 118, 139–74, 226, 266–8
  active defence, 118, 139, 150, 152
  city, defence of, 147, 150
  combined operations, 148
  defence in depth, 139, 159
  doctrine, 144–7
  modernisation, 138–9, 144–7
  resolute defence, 150
  strategic defence, 139, 149–51
  strategy, 138–9, 148–9
  three-dimensional defence, 43, 139, 162–6

Qian Qichen, 125, 127, 130–1
Qian Xuesen, 46
Qin Qiwei, 238–40, 245, 255, 259

Railways,
  connectivity, 95–100
  freight performance, 92–4
Reserve Forces, 3, 11, 14–19, 40, 51, 59, 88–9, 91, 100–3, 110, 117–18, 174, 261–2, 265, 267
  mobilisation, 101–2
Resolution on CPC History, 204, 230
Rogachev, 127

Second Artillery, 64–8, 245
Second-strike capabilities, 67–8, 122, 131–2, 136, 146, 260, 263
Signals Intelligence, 36, 38–9, 171–2

Sihanouk, 129
Sino-American Relations,
  avionic retrofits, 10, 37, 123
  naval visit to Qingdao, 127, 260
  nuclear cooperation, 124
  SDI, 135
  SIGNIT facilities, 36, 171–2
  strategic implications, 177
Sino-Soviet Relations,
  Arkhipov's visit, 124–5
  border clashes, 155, 260
  confrontation, 86, 123, 153–72
  Gorbachev's Vladivostok Speech,
    126–7, 130, 135–6
  half-yearly talks, 125
  Indochina, 128
  normalisation, 129–30, 136, 264
  three obstacles, 123, 146
  'two-front' problem, 134, 136
Sino–Vietnamese Relations,
  border war 1979, 3, 7, 20–1, 26,
    34, 95, 103, 115, 188, 190, 226
  future conflicts, 147
  incursions, 32, 35, 37, 116–17,
    121, 266
  'second lesson', 129, 188–96
  Soviet bases, 126, 128
  troop withdrawal, 129–30
SIPRI, 54–5
Song Shilun, 202–3
Soviet strategy and doctrine, 152–8
  fire power, 167–9, 267
  group army, 163
  nuclear strikes, 162, 167, 267
  operational art,
    (KOPP), 154
    (LPZUs), 154
  Pacific fleet, 176–8, 180, 193–4
  strategic breakthrough, 118, 159,
    164, 166, 169–70, 267
  Tactical Aviation, 167
Spratley Islands, 62, 79, 80, 117,
  181–2
Stalin, 208
State Central Military Council, 30,
  38, 231

Strategic Arms Limitation Talks,
  128, 134
Strategic cover, 158
Strategic defence, 173–4
Strategic Defence Initiative, 135
Strategic Missile Force, 35, 67
Strategic outlook, new, 3–6, 39–40,
  42–3, 175, 266, 268
Strike,
  fire and troop, 165, 168–9
  first, 132
  pre-emptive, 133, 149
  second, 122, 131–2, 136, 149
  strategic, 158
Su Yu, 142, 151, 227

Taiwan,
  naval blockade, 183–7
  re-unification, 176
TEZ (total exclusive zone), 181
'Three Supports and two militaries',
  amnesty, 210–12
  military regions, in, 217, 229
  origin, 209
Theatre of Military Operations,
  153–4, 157–8
Theatre of War, 139, 149, 152, 165,
  169–70, 173
Tian Jisheng, 216
Transport and communication
  system, 117–18, 265
  railways, 91–100
  roads, 92–5
  waterways, 93–4
Tsedeubal, Y., 127
Twelfth Party Congress, 229, 257,
  269
  decline of the military, 235
  new constitution, 230–2
  new MR commanders, 239
  Party rectification, 242
  Second Plenum, 247

UNCLOS III, 181, 264
United States,
  bases in the Philippines, 176–7

Grenada, 43
Joint Chiefs of Staff, 35
mine blockade of SRV, 191–6
Pacific fleet, 176–8, 180, 195
'swing' strategy, 178

Wang Bingqian, 7
Wang Enmao, 114, 165–6, 172, 223, 241
Wang Hai, 33
Warfare,
  guerrilla, 19, 150–2, 163, 166, 170, 172–3, 267–8
  mobile, 150–1, 163, 170, 173, 267–8
  positional, 27, 118, 150–2, 166, 172–3, 267
Warfighting capabilities,
  air defence, 57–63
  air strikes, 62–3, 162–3
  air support, 56–7
  airborne, 62–4, 163
  amphibious, 60–2
  anti-air, 10, 166, 266
  anti-airborne, 10, 62, 163, 266
  anti-armour, 10
  anti-tank, 10, 166, 168, 267
  armour, 50–2
  ATGM, 50, 61, 63, 162, 168–9, 262
  combat and logistic support, 60, 77, 377–87
  coordinated operations, 28–9
  fire support, 52–6
  Main Battle Tank, 51–2, 166–8
  mobility, 48–50
  specialised operations, 60–4
  strategic nuclear forces, 10, 64–8
  tactical nuclear support, 53–6
  training, 28–9, 45–8
War preparation, 6, 12–14, 48, 89, 266
Wei Guoqing,
  political work, 202–4, 214–15, 227, 229, 235

Weinberger, 127, 260
Whitson, 221

Xiao Hua, 202, 207–8, 224, 229, 239
Xiao Ke, 143
Xingan Ranges, 155, 160, 166
Xisha (Paracel) Archipelago, 20, 41, 61, 179
Xu Huizi, 33, 236, 270
Xu Jiatun, 210
Xu Shiyou, 224, 227
Xu Xiangqian, 142, 235, 252

Yan'an Spirit, 113, 208, 245, 253
Yang Dezhi,
  CGS, 44, 223, 226, 235, 259
  future wars, on, 5–6
  Military Service Law, on, 14–15, 18, 21, 46–7
  People's War, 202
Yang Shangkun, 4–5, 11, 18, 21, 25, 31, 107–8, 235, 237, 258, 269–71
  Party rectification, 244–5, 249, 252–3
Ye Jianying, 20
  criticism of Mao Zedong, 202, 225, 227
You Taizhong, 241, 256
Yu Qiuli, 21, 235, 244, 250–2, 258

Zhang Aiping, 9–10, 226–7, 259
Zhang Chunqiao, 103, 214
Zhang Tingfa, 235
Zhang Zhen, 34
Zhao Nanqi, 236
Zhao Yiya, 248–9
Zhao Ziyang, 135, 139, 223, 237, 258, 270–1
Zhon Enlai, 210
Zhou Keyu, 236, 270
Zhou Wenyuan, 236, 270
Zhu Qizhen, 124